Anthropology, Colonial Policy and the Decline of French Empire in Africa

Anthropology, Colonial Policy and the Decline of French Empire in Africa

Douglas W. Leonard

BLOOMSBURY ACADEMIC
LONDON • NEW YORK • OXFORD • NEW DELHI • SYDNEY

BLOOMSBURY ACADEMIC
Bloomsbury Publishing Plc
50 Bedford Square, London, WC1B 3DP, UK
1385 Broadway, New York, NY 10018, USA
29 Earlsfort Terrace, Dublin 2, Ireland

BLOOMSBURY, BLOOMSBURY ACADEMIC and the Diana logo are trademarks of
Bloomsbury Publishing Plc

First published in Great Britain 2020
This paperback edition published in 2022

Copyright © Douglas W. Leonard, 2020

Douglas W. Leonard has asserted his right under the Copyright, Designs and Patents Act,
1988, to be identified as Author of this work.

Cover design: Tjaša Krivec
Cover image: Dahomey ships deck army illustration 1895 'the Earth
and her People' (© Beeldbewerking / Getty images)

All rights reserved. No part of this publication may be reproduced or transmitted
in any form or by any means, electronic or mechanical, including photocopying,
recording, or any information storage or retrieval system, without prior
permission in writing from the publishers.

Bloomsbury Publishing Plc does not have any control over, or responsibility for,
any third-party websites referred to or in this book. All internet addresses given
in this book were correct at the time of going to press. The author and publisher
regret any inconvenience caused if addresses have changed or sites have
ceased to exist, but can accept no responsibility for any such changes.

A catalogue record for this book is available from the British Library.

A catalog record for this book is available from the Library of Congress.

ISBN: HB: 978-1-7883-1520-3
PB: 978-1-3503-3732-9
ePDF: 978-1-7867-3619-2
eBook: 978-1-7867-2613-1

Typeset by Integra Software Services Pvt. Ltd.

To find out more about our authors and books visit www.bloomsbury.com
and sign up for our newsletters.

For Kathy, who does too much by any measure

Contents

Acknowledgments	viii
Introduction	1
1 Louis Faidherbe and the Construction of Intellectual Networks	9
2 Lyautey, Gallieni, and Early Efforts at Political Association Informed by Ethnology	27
3 Engaging Native Sources to Develop an Informed Colonial State	47
4 Escaping Durkheim: Marcel Mauss and the Structural Turn	79
5 Jacques Soustelle and the Ethnological State in Algeria	97
6 Colonial Inheritance: Pierre Bourdieu and the Struggle for the Future of French Social Theory	123
Conclusion	147
Notes	150
Bibliography	201
Index	231

Acknowledgments

As with any large work, it is not possible to thank everyone who contributed. I will thank some specific people below, knowing that I will inevitably miss someone. I can only say thank you to the many whose names do not specifically appear due to a lapse of memory on my part.

This book would not have come together without the contribution first of Alex Roland. He saw the potential in the work and helped me to frame my ideas in productive and useful ways. Bill Reddy was always available with sage advice on what it took to succeed in the academic world. Engseng Ho and Laurent Dubois offered superb advice that shaped this project in meaningful ways, particularly in my efforts to understand difficult anthropological theory or the strands that pulled the French colonial empire together. It is almost impossible for me to describe the debt I owe to Bruce Hall. Simultaneously mentor, colleague, and friend, Bruce's broad knowledge of the literature and history of Africa opened my eyes to a world of possibilities. I will never be able to reciprocate all that Bruce and his family have done for my family and me. I look forward to more collaboration in the years to come.

Coming after almost ten years of toil, this book would not exist without the figurative village of assistance. John Martin helped to shape my thought and writing at a time when I felt lost in the intellectual wilderness. Orin Starn introduced me to the fascinating world of anthropology and drove me to go beyond simple critiques of colonial scholarship. Jolie Olcott opened both her home and her wide range of contacts in the academic and publishing worlds, sharpening my research project at an early stage. Dick Kohn brought his unique set of governmental and historical expertise to bear for me in wonderful and inventive ways, including in his cogent and pointed criticism of very early versions of Chapter 1. Colleagues and mentors at the US Air Force Academy pushed me along in my research as well. To Dana Born, Mark Wells, John Abbatiello, John Plating, Derek Varble, and Larry Johnson, I therefore send a sincere thanks. Most important, I must thank Meg Martin, who gave me the time, space, and unflagging support that I needed to bring this to the finish line.

Ultimately, no historical research works without the assistance of the amazing professionals who help us find and make sense of sometimes obscure materials. I must thank Heidi Madden at Duke for her incomparable research support as well as the staff of the interlibrary loan office at Perkins library. In France I must thank the archivists and staff at the *Archives Nationales*, the *Muséum d'histoire naturelle*, and the *Société Historique de la Défense* (SHD) in Paris; the *Archives Nationales d'outre-mer* in Aix-en-Provence; and the *Institut Mémoire d'édition contemporaine* in Caen, who made research a smoother (and quicker) process than perhaps should be the case. In particular, André Rakoto at the SHD made my work in Paris easier and much more enjoyable. At Bloomsbury, I must thank Maddie Holder, Dan Hutchins, and Gopinath

Anbalagan for their phenomenal guidance and support. I would be remiss if I did not also thank Lester Crook, who first saw value in the publishing of my work.

At the same time, friends were crucial to my success. I could not have made it without the help, support, and laughs supplied by Jeannine Cole, Emily Margolis, Fahad Bishara, Julia Gaffield, Willeke Sandler, Samanthis Smalls, Wynne Beers, Daniel Bessner, Elizabeth Brake, Eric Brandom, Karlyn Forner, Vanessa Freije, Ketaki Pant, Erin Parish, Sean Parrish, and John Roche. Each knows what he or she has done to help me along.

Finally, I must thank my wonderful and ridiculously patient family. My daughters Cara and Katie simply could not wait until the day my book was done so that I could spend more time with them. Kathy's willingness to serve as a first-line copyeditor, despite my truculence, was amazing. Without their love and support, I could never have completed this work, which too often kept me away from them.

Introduction

Portrayals of an Africa frozen in time justified colonial conquest and rule, particularly after the 1830 invasion of Algiers ushered in a new era of colonial expansion for France. It was the nature of this colonial rule, though, that caused significant debate between those who advocated for a parallel "association" with local African social and political structures and those who pressed for a combined "assimilation" toward an ideal French social condition.[1] Association acknowledged difference as assimilation tried to eliminate it, but neither dealt with it effectively. Chinua Achebe described this contrast effectively in 1977: "If Europe, advancing in civilization, could cast a backward glance periodically at Africa trapped in primordial barbarity it could say with faith and feeling: There I go but for the grace of God." He continued, "Africa is to Europe as the picture is to Dorian Gray—a carrier on to whom the master unloads his physical and moral deformities so that he may go forward, erect and immaculate."[2] It fell to colonial scholars and functionaries to remedy this ugliness and to offer a solution that delivered a strong movement forward for all. They failed. French colonialism lacked any real consent of the governed and was thus an unsustainable political form. The basic "asymmetry" of the relationship doomed it to failure.[3]

These thinkers expanded the field of possible sources and introduced new concepts, but they continued to view native Africans as sources of information and only rarely as reasoning interlocutors and intelligent interpreters. Scholars laid analytical frames atop what Michel Foucault has described as a new mode of thought, one focused on "identity and difference" instead of the long-dominant search for "resemblance."[4] Seeking to improve and ultimately perfect French colonial rule in North and West Africa, French soldiers, scholars, and administrators engaged in complex conversations with thinkers from the metropolitan center, colonial power structures, and native intellectual communities on the nature of African colonies and subjects. Much as Helen Tilley has found in the British African colonies, French administrators across Africa found wide access through their positions, but also great restriction due to their narrowly defined roles in the uneven colonial power dynamic. Their native interlocutors in many cases used the interaction to stake claims to their own political positions.[5]

In this process lay the potential for productive intellectual engagement but also the seeds of political destruction. These conversations, conducted across time and space and involving a wide variety of texts and sources in translation, revealed the inherent contradictions of a larger project that required successful dialogue but delivered systems of exploitation. Conversely, these hybrid networks designed for political domination, instead, generated new descriptions of social construction that would long outlive their original purpose. Much as Charles Tilly has described in early modern Europe, attempts to shape or in any way "homogenize" populations that threatened the political or social essence of a subject people met with resistance of various types.[6] It was this intellectual resistance, sometimes delivered through an understanding of historical documents or concepts, that sustained French social and ethnological thinkers as they sought to understand colonial groups. It also offered an opening for non-Europeans to build an alternate intellectual space apart from the colonial state. Important critiques of race-based policy and science emerged in those spaces, within the colonial states themselves and from thinkers from a wide variety of backgrounds.[7]

Far from passive recipients of metropolitan thought, men and women in the colonies actively shaped metropolitan ideas on basic social structure and interaction as they emerged. In the French *science de l'homme*, intellectual innovation came not always from academics in stuffy rooms but instead from direct interaction and dialogue with the subjects of study themselves. These efforts ultimately fell under the rubric of "ethnology," a social science devoted to understanding distinctions between civilizations or races and employing historical, linguistic, and ethnographic tools of analysis.[8]

From General Louis Faidherbe (1818–1889) in the 1840s to politician Jacques Soustelle (1912–1990) and sociologist Pierre Bourdieu (1930–2002) in the 1950s and 1960s, a succession of soldiers, scholars, and administrators cultivated colonial sources to translate indigenous ideas for a metropolitan audience interested primarily in a more efficient form of colonial rule, in this case, the grafted associationist approach. It was this act of translation, though, that undermined the entire effort. French thinkers built their ethnological ideas through interaction with native sources, both living and written, but the simple act of selection artificially narrowed their view and doomed the colonial structures that followed. Building from a place of initial weakness due to limited language skills and local contacts, French explorers and administrators adopted local norms exulting Arabic language forms for diplomacy, trade, and religion.[9] Their insular approach, with head down toward the page instead of head up toward the sociopolitical events swirling through Africa and Europe in the nineteenth and twentieth centuries, caused them to grasp the wrong conclusions. These limitations were largely hidden from view at the time as these thinkers built intellectual networks wider than those employed by their predecessors, even confronting and countering theories proposed by social scientists such as Emile Durkheim (1858–1917).

By 1955, for instance, Soustelle adopted ethnological institutions and principles in an ultimately incomplete and failed effort to govern Algeria with an associationist eye while stamping out the nascent nationalist revolt. At the same time, in the work of Bourdieu and his associates, French Africanist ideas formed the core of a new, empirically grounded, and personally contingent alternative to the dominant structuralist, sociological, and anthropological perspective in France advocated by Claude Lévi-Strauss (1908–2009), among others.

James Clifford has framed this thought process in useful terms: "The ethnographic modernist searches for the universal in the local."[10] French Africanist scholars likewise spent significant time examining local histories, origin myths, and migration patterns in hopes of discerning distinct macro-civilizations. From there, they sought to design more effective political structures of rule while simultaneously building a better understanding of basic human social structures. Interestingly, the fourteenth-century North African theorist and polymath Ibn Khaldun (d. 1408) proved an important source and even indirect discussant with the ideas of Faidherbe, Marshal Hubert Lyautey (1854–1934), and French Africanist scholars Maurice Delafosse (1870–1926) and Paul Marty (1881–1936). It was in the collision of ideas along with these intellectual networks and conversations that the real outlines of association as a method of rule emerged, a political structure that by design instrumentalized information to harden further the apparatus of colonial rule.

European academics sought to build a social and political associationist state to link Africans to France across what anthropologist Arjun Appadurai has described as the rupture between past and present; modernity thus became an absolute, a singular achievement to which all others could only aspire.[11] French Africanist thinkers wanted to lessen the impact that an African transition to European-style modernity would have on "traditional" societies. In this sociopolitical project, French thinkers employed terms such as "evolution," "civilization," and "progress" as code for political dependence and justification for colonial rule. They did not seek to eliminate colonialism, a practice that they saw as helpful to Africans in numerous ways. Instead, they desired perfection of that system, building on centuries of European philosophy to arrive at a more refined, benevolent, and dialogic form of rule. This developmental approach never truly shed its assimilationist origins as colonial states continued to replace precolonial structures with new modes of rule and social investigation, creating what Edmund Burke has termed a "colonial archive" of social understanding.[12] In the end, these efforts failed due in large part to the unevenness of the transaction between the colonizer and the colonized. Instead, they substituted translation into the language of colonial rule and the use of ethnographic information as grist for the ever-turning mill of exploitation. More willing than many of their peers and predecessors to rely on African sources in building colonial policy, they nonetheless remained trapped in the colonial bind, unknowing or uncaring of the excesses they delivered.

In the words of Michel Foucault, "everyone knows that ethnology was born of colonization, but that does not mean it was an imperial science."[13] Indeed, colonial ethnology and the related refinements to the forms of political rule grew from a long tradition stretching back to early modern colonization of the Americas and the difficult debates of the European Enlightenment. From the Spanish Dominican Bartolomé de las Casas (1474–1566) to Montesquieu (1689–1755) and on to nineteenth-century theorists such as Alexis de Tocqueville (1805–1859), Henri de Saint-Simon (1760–1825), Herbert Spencer (1820–1903), and Auguste Comte (1798–1857), European conceptions of race, lineage, and difference built from limited interaction with non-European populations.[14] Tocqueville and his liberal colleagues, both British and French, advocated expansion and subjugation as a necessary part of the modern world and a vital driver of the national political prestige necessary for imperial competition. The resultant "enlightened" imperial structures would then govern their new subjects "naturally."[15] Colonial rule grew from political exigency; civilizing rhetoric masked inequalities of capability and status. All of that accumulated difference necessitated a grafted political rule that considered native structures as adapted to local circumstance, but only viewable through the limited ethnological lens offered by colonial personnel.

Historian C. A. Bayly has found in the British case that colonial agents worked with preexisting native informational structures in developing a localized understanding. In his words, "Colonial officials, missionaries, and businessmen were forced to register the voices of native informants in ideology and heed them in practice even if they despised and misrepresented them."[16] This study works from Bayly's example, and that of Emmanuelle Sibeud in the French case, in viewing colonial ethnology as growing from locally held ideas and preexisting networks but twisted to maximize colonial value and limit direct attribution to native Africans themselves. French colonial officials did not value African voices above those of other Europeans, but they were forced to make use of data provided by their subjects to describe and reform socioeconomic and political systems in Africa in particular. Understanding the process by which French colonial officials generated ethnological knowledge, and thus the technologies of rule, requires a move beyond the directives of metropolitan government or even colonial governors in African cities.[17] A true grasp of these complex interactions requires what Jonathan Wyrtzen has termed a "transactional" approach that avoids a specifically top-down or bottom-up approach.[18] Historians must consider the act of collection, translation, and interpretation in order to understand the roots of colonial policy.

Anchored in a dialogic understanding of epistemological agency, Gary Wilder provided a useful understanding of the French state as a political and social entity composed of coursing channels of communication that undergirded much colonial science in *The French Imperial Nation-State*.[19] The resultant "political rationality" provides a useful optic for understanding the reconceptualization of the colonial project as a justification of domination within a mutating rubric of civilization and republic. French reformers desired an idealized colonial space, one that incorporated both the universal human rights of early-twentieth-century republicanism and the more heavy-handed developmental approach of the modern, expansive imperial state.

Supported by networks of informants, colleagues, and collaborators, the French African sociopolitical apparatus relied heavily on dialogue. The networks supporting those exchanges were rarely neat. The structures of knowledge generation and exchange in French North and West Africa operated not as Foucault's microphysics of power but as sites for contestation and exchange. Such an understanding reveals the role of mid-level bureaucratic French scholars, in touch with but not privileging local sources as they built analytically informed policy. Tracing interpersonal connections and intellectual choices, however, poses a significant challenge. Each important thinker communicated with thousands of people in his or her lifetime. It is therefore important to isolate these experiences while remaining sensitive to their context, as Thomas Kuhn has suggested.[20]

Pursuit of a single idea, political association, offers a path through the seemingly infinite connections of any single human life. This approach offers a perspective that transcends national or racial divides, appearing in multiple times, places, and voices. Detailed examination of the lives of the core thinkers who built these ethnological concepts reveals that important ideas emerge from, as sociologist Bruno Latour has described, a small group of isolated people "so powerful and yet so small, so concentrated and so dilute."[21] Biography, then, offers a methodological window into the origins and effects of colonial ethnology. An understanding of the intertwining lives of these thinkers reveals their enormous political and academic impact as well as their scholarly limitations, collectively and individually. Their lives and experiences were as varied as science itself; generalization risks the loss of nuanced understanding of the causes and effects of these ideas.[22] As anthropologist Matei Candea has suggested with respect to Corsica, knowledge exists in the ties between people, places, and stories. The resultant "thick web of relations" stands as the most important object of study for any scholar hoping to describe the ways in which people understand themselves and each other.[23]

Such an approach also produces difficulties. Describing the appearance and function of these overlapping webs of connection remains problematic; indeed, this requirement has bedeviled most historians of colonial networks. Among the most commonly employed metaphors stand the wheel-spoke and the web.[24] The wheel and spoke model locates a significant point, a physical, ideological, or imaginary center around which the other individuals or ideas in the network revolve. Implicit in this idea is the notion of return, with the peripheral players moving between center and exterior regularly. These same players also move between exterior points; thus, the model is dynamic, featuring transit both linearly and centripetally. In the case of efforts by French colonial administrators, soldiers, and scholars to comprehend African social constructions, however, the wheel fails to convey the overlap and interconnection wrought by the colonial state. While it is dynamic, it is also two-dimensional and lacks possibility for growth. A wheel, whether composed of wood, rubber, or aluminum, leaves little room for change.

The web, on the other hand, offers an interesting alternative. It can grow almost infinitely; while it has a notional center, that location is not vital to the stability of the structure. Webs, in fact, are most often constructed from the outside to the inside. Ideas or people can move in an almost infinite number of possible directions, increasing the possibility of exchange and offering the explosive opportunities of rapid contact between elements on opposite ends. In the final analysis, though, this model also fails to describe colonial ethnology due to its lack of movement. The web itself rarely stirs (except by the vagaries of external wind), and most items that touch the structure are mired in place. Indeed, the French methods of knowledge production in French Africa, reliant on translation and interpretation, require a more organic description, one that considers human systems as living entities that move and mutate according to the unique logics of the participating individuals.

French poststructural theory provides the most appropriate depiction of these types of networks. Gilles Deleuze and Félix Guattari, in describing their approach to social and psychological examination as a series of seemingly isolated plateaus connected in almost imperceptible ways, used "rhizome," a term borrowed from botanical descriptions of root systems. Their application of the term, however, went far beyond the relatively static and hardened nature of tree roots. They wrote, "There are no points or positions in a rhizome, such as those found in a structure, tree, or root. There are only lines."[25] In the case of French African ethnology, soldiers and administrators moved along such lines, at times acting as moving nodes that then drew connections to other locations or people in the colonial superstructure. French African intellectual networks made use of what Deleuze and Guattari called "organizations of power" within the rhizome to further both the reach of their understanding and their places in the colonial structure. The ethnological systems thus moved of their own volition, driven not by "the supposed will of an artist or puppeteer" in the centers of power in Paris or Dakar, but rather by "a multiplicity of nerve fibers" both independent and interconnected.[26] Representations of human reality grew from the attempted overlaying of the French imperial state, via an associationist model, on scholarship and concepts present in Africa for centuries. French colonial officials did not control these systems; rather, they described the limited results that they understood or to which they had access in often flawed political and ethnological terms.

Much like Bayly's British colonial networks, the systems of intellectual exchange analyzed in this work lay on top of, beneath, and inside of extant African constructions. As Deleuze and Guattari explained, "A rhizome has no beginning or end; it is always in the middle, between things, interbeing, intermezzo … the rhizome is alliance, uniquely alliance."[27] French colonial scholars were firmly "in the middle" of the metropolitan-African relationship. In many cases, particularly for Delafosse and Marty, they served as the interpreters and translators of African history and social construction. They formed alliances with African thinkers and their written chronicles to convey instrumental truth back to the colonial power structure, as these men and women were intimately involved with governance from their positions as conquering soldiers, administrators, advisers, and governors. Unwitting, in many cases, of the real impact of their ideas, these writers, thinkers, and administrators generated networks that would ultimately undo the instruments of colonial rule while revolutionizing European continental social thought.

Unraveling this rhizome requires a biographical approach. This study will begin with an examination centered on Louis Faidherbe, a colonial officer for most of his career who served as one of the early governors of the French colony in Senegal and the subject of Chapter 1. Dedicated both to the associationist approach and to the somewhat limited form of anthropology then practiced in metropolitan France, Faidherbe engaged in an exploitative form of study that found little resonance in the academic community. He did, however, have enormous influence on colonial political thought as he passed on his academic methodology to Joseph Gallieni and Hubert Lyautey, future colonial soldiers and governors. The careers of Gallieni, and more importantly Lyautey, ranged from Algeria to Indochina, Madagascar, and ultimately Morocco in reforming the colonial system, events described in the second chapter. In the process, these "proconsuls" instituted a Faidherbe-style political association, one founded on ethnological examination geared toward a policy of "divide and rule" of native social groups. Most notably, these men employed (and exploited) African savants in French Soudan, Madagascar, Algeria, and Morocco in gaining the information necessary to widen these cracks in native social and political structures.

These high-ranking military men could only push the associationist approach so far. As the twentieth century progressed through its first decade, French colonial rule matured and required greater academic input to sustain the technologies of rule. Paul

Marty, a subordinate of Lyautey, spun the views passed on from Algeria and Morocco back into West Africa, where they met with the similar investigations of Maurice Delafosse, a process described in Chapter 3. More than any other people, these two men selected the political Africa most convenient to colonial rule. Employing vast networks of informants, they obscured those sources through their analysis, delivering a politically convenient view of kinship, race, and Islam as tools of control seemingly grounded in empirical research. Finally finding a foothold in the French academic community, though with limited engagement in the wider Anglophone conversation, Delafosse served as a prime correspondent of Marcel Mauss, preeminent sociologist, and teacher of a new a generation of ethnologists. Chapter 4 focuses on Mauss' engagement with the theoretical underpinnings of the ideas of his uncle and mentor Emile Durkheim. He broke from the Durkheim school by emphasizing fieldwork, even though he had little experience away from Paris. Mauss' relativism, informed by colonial ethnographic data, thus reshaped French social theory and pushed it in a new direction, away from the metropole and toward the colonies themselves. Hardly honoring native African sources, he extolled the power of colonial investigation as an important justification for colonial rule itself, generating intellectual and financial capital in a mutually reinforcing relationship with the teetering colonial state in the 1930s and 1940s.

Chapter 5 follows this sustainment to its logical political conclusion in the person of Jacques Soustelle, a Mauss student and the governor-general of Algeria in 1955–1956. Built on the ethnological principles espoused by Mauss and the political approach of Lyautey, Soustelle implemented a system of ethnological surveillance, believing that he could mitigate the causes of the nascent revolt through a resolutely internal study of the populace which, much to his later regret, largely ignored international trends and the more corrosive effects of his rule. Thus, he underestimated, and at times dismissed, the young, largely secular elites who had developed a sophisticated rhetoric that refused colonial cooperation in terms appropriated from nationalist, pan-Arab, and pan-Islamic movements. Ultimately frustrated with the lack of Algerian progress, Soustelle fell victim to temptation, permitting his forces to use torture and increased military force in a doomed effort to quell the rebellion. Into that breach stepped a young conscript named Pierre Bourdieu, the subject of Chapter 6, who was deeply contemptuous of his surroundings and became disenchanted with the contradictions of the colonial system. His new sociology stood in direct contrast to the structuralism of Claude Lévi-Strauss. Bourdieu's focus on contingency both in information collection and in human social development through the concept of habitus offered an important counterpoint to the long-standing insularity of the French colonial intellectual space. Only through reflexivity could sociologists truly probe their own biases; only through a similar self-examination could the French state realize its own culpability in the African condition.

Note on terminology, translation, and transcription

This is a work, at least in part, about translation. It is thus focused on works in translation as they influenced colonial policy making and the development of French ethnology and sociology as broader social sciences. The sources of that ethnology are important and called out frequently here, but not exhaustively. Instead, this study follows French thought through its representations in colonial ethnology and the resultant limitations, understanding that future work must further unspool the sources of knowledge among native African thinkers themselves.

At the same time, my own choices in translation from the French can be difficult in such a fraught subject. In the case of this study, I have chosen to employ the word "native" to mean those Africans (usually black sub-Saharans, but also at times including residents of Algeria, Tunisia, Morocco, or Madagascar) born locally and subject to colonial domination when the specific group described by the French colonial author remains unclear. The term "Africans," while perhaps preferable to "native" as lacking in pejorative colonial connotation, carried a different meaning in the French colonial world, as French colonial soldiers were collectively and colloquially known by that same moniker. Likewise, the word "Algerian," particularly in the nineteenth century, often denoted French soldiers in Algeria. Arab or Berber groups in Algeria were generally known as "Muslims," but that term failed to capture the full range of socioreligious constructions actually in use at the time. The terms "autochthon" and "indigenous" are far too weighted with meaning, as they overlook the swirls of migration across Africa, themselves so important for the ethnologists profiled in this study. "Local," while perhaps a useful descriptor in some ways, overlooks the important colonial distinctions, especially in Algeria, between French settlers, many of whom were born in Algeria by the late nineteenth century, and Arabs, Berbers, and Jews, to name the three largest non-French appellations. I have done my best to use "African" or more specific terms, such as "Kabyle" or "Peul," when the context makes it clear that the actors are in fact those people from Africa, not European settlers or soldiers.

The spelling and transliteration of literary Arabic words, proper names, and places follows the system used by the *International Journal of Middle East Studies*. I have avoided the use of diacritics to the greatest extent possible. I have left the original French transcriptions and accent marks, which differ at times from more recent usage, only when changing them would alter the flow of the phrase or change the spelling in the title of a published work. All translations from the French are mine unless otherwise indicated in the footnotes. Any errors that remain are my own.

1

Louis Faidherbe and the Construction of Intellectual Networks

L'honneur: tu l'emportas en tous lieux, Général
C'était ton bien sacré, c'était ton ideal,
Il te guidait comme une étoile
Et tu le gardas là, cet honneur pur et cher,
Ainsi qu tu l'avais gardé dans le desert
Sous ta rude tente de toile[1]

—Lille, October 25, 1896

With the erection of a new statue to a hero of France, poet Charles Manso stepped forward to honor the legendary figure. General Louis Léon César Faidherbe had died seven years before, but now stood resurrected in stone. His legacy, however, did not end with carved granite; rather, he stood as the progenitor of a network of colonial information transfer that began in Algeria and extended through Africa and beyond, as far as Indochina and Madagascar, across the vast majority of the French colonial world. His 1854–1865 governorship of Senegal, France's first sub-Saharan African colony, gained rather informally in the early nineteenth century, earned him a similar colonial statue in Dakar in the early twentieth century.[2] An early proponent of an associationist political structure, Faidherbe's influence also extended into science. In particular, Faidherbe engaged with ethnology and the shortlived discipline of physical-racial anthropology and ushered in an era of intellectually prominent colonial military officers.[3] These officers became part of a knowledge-oriented method of colonial governance. In so doing, they fostered an environment of increasing openness featuring opportunities for advancement not only in the military realm but also in academia and politics. By focusing on native contributions to ethnological and civilizational understanding, Faidherbe propagated the associationist emphasis on maintenance and respect of native structures. Implicit in this paradigm was some basic respect for native intellectual capabilities; more than simple savages, Faidherbe saw natives as intelligent interpreters and agents of their own social reality. They were thus worthy of dialogue with the French on this social state of affairs and the way forward in improving their condition. Nonetheless, he rarely credited their contributions as he continued to develop an exploitative colonial state, one that often looked across the French colonial structure and rarely acknowledged events outside its relatively narrow sphere.

Faidherbe did not exist apart from the colonial structure. He was very much a part of French efforts to classify and dominate racialized groups in Africa. From his earliest moments in Algeria, the young officer tried to apply the racial-determinist models of his anthropological peers. He saw his participation in anthropology as a crusade of sorts, an effort to "remedy the bad that compromises the future"[4] for Africans trapped in an undeveloped past. A former president of the prestigious *Société d'anthropologie de Paris*, Faidherbe pointed to the importance of this crusade for "courageous truth."[5] For his contemporaries, Faidherbe's work "was not confined to military labors" but found in the realms "of science, of letters, of philosophy … new ways to honor [his] nation."[6] From his position as the father of a network of information transfer, of circulation, Faidherbe stood astride the anthropological and military communities, exerting an influence in both "the nation and science."[7] He was not only a "military man and administrator who also found the time to interest himself in science" but an academic noted for his contributions to "historical, linguistic, geographical, and anthropological knowledge."[8] Anthropology, as practiced at the time, did not offer sufficient data to the colonial project in his mind. He thus devoted himself to ethnology, the comparative study of societies (often referred to as races) that employed ethnography as an important tool. This form of study avoided the physical measurements so important to the zoologists and anatomists, who dominated anthropology in the mid-nineteenth century.

The French colonial empire offered avenues for military and academic advancement that simply did not exist in Europe. France's previous effort at colonial expansion from the sixteenth to eighteenth centuries had ended in catastrophic failure. Defeated by the British in the Seven Years War, France lost all of its North American colonies, holding on to the islands of Guadeloupe, Martinique, and Saint-Domingue (Haiti) in the Caribbean as the sole talismans of lost preeminence and global rivalry. While the American Revolution offered a brief hope of the end of British overseas domination, in truth France spiraled downward into an inescapable cycle of debt and discontent, culminating in the chaos of the French Revolution after 1789. After losing Saint-Domingue to successive revolts in the early nineteenth century, the glory of French overseas civilization seemed past to many observers. Further expansion, inspired in part by the revolutionary fervor of the Napoleonic period, recommenced outside of Europe only in 1830 in Algeria as the dying Bourbon regime of Charles X tried to hold on to domestic legitimacy through foreign conquest, ultimately failing as it was replaced by Louis-Philippe's new monarchy. Imbued in many cases with utopian expectations of new societies in Africa, the soldiers involved in these conquests sought both to understand and to govern their new territory in Algeria, a campaign initiated in 1830 and contested especially from 1832 to 1847.

In seeking such ethnological knowledge, Faidherbe tapped into the existing networks of ethnographic knowledge already resident in Africa to develop his view of conditions on that continent. He thus grew these networks of organic intellectual life, linking them with each other and the metropole through a skilled manipulation of publication outlets, military and colonial communication channels, and scholarly societies. In the process, he hardened colonial political structures and enhanced his own academic reputation, sometimes at the expense of others working in the field. In the conduct of such a study, he looked for inspiration to the *bureaux arabes*, founded in 1844 by General Thomas-Robert Bugeaud in Algeria and the forerunner of French structures that culminated in what Martin Thomas has termed the "intelligence states" of the early twentieth century, an approach inherited by Hubert Lyautey in Morocco.[9] These military-led offices conducted ethnological investigations of the countryside and aided in communication with native groups at the grassroots level. Accused by some French settlers of Arabophilia, this cadre of native affairs officers, by and large, advocated for a form of "indirect rule" similar to the associationist ideas of Faidherbe. In conquests of West African states, Faidherbe and his subordinates pioneered the use of outposts employing skilled Arabic speakers, immersing in local political norms and communicating in the complex, hybridized exchange between Hausa, Peul, and other languages with Arabic.[10] By 1871, however, these officers had lost the battle in Algeria, overcome by civilian settlers and politicians who argued that the maintenance of preexisting "tribal" structures went against the egalitarian spirit of the French Revolution and disadvantaged settlers as a group. The institution nonetheless served as an example for Faidherbe of politically motivated social reform via military ethnological investigation and management.[11] Regardless of source, each contact added to the size of the Faidherbe's vast network of networks, creating connections across and below the surface of the colonial enterprise.

Education of a reformer

Louis Faidherbe grew up in an industrializing town in the north of France. His father served as a sergeant major in a revolutionary national guard regiment and later settled into life as a haberdasher.[12] Academically gifted, Faidherbe attended prestigious preparatory schools and ultimately earned a place at the center for "diffusing Cartesianism throughout French society," the *école polytechnique*.[13] The future soldier entered the school during a transitional period. In the forty years prior to Faidherbe's arrival, it had been the primary site for discussion of the utopian ideals of Henri Saint-Simon and his disciples, Prosper Enfantin and Auguste Comte. In 1826, Enfantin had written to a colleague on the importance of the *école* to the Saint-Simonian movement, referring to the school as the "channel by which these ideas [of positivism and industrial advancement] reproduce in society; it is the milk that we have sucked from our dear school that will nourish the generations to come."[14] While many of the proponents of these philosophical currents had moved on by Faidherbe's entrance in the summer of 1838, their influence was still strong in the military at large. In fact, Faidherbe would cross paths with several Saint-Simonians in Algeria in his early career.[15] While not imbued with the revolutionary sentiment of some of these theorists, Faidherbe did place great value in firsthand observation, a core idea in Comtean positivism. Faidherbe also imbibed the principles of liberal republicanism that he would try to spread to non-Frenchmen throughout his career.[16]

Faidherbe graduated in 1840 as one of twenty lieutenants to enter military engineering, one of the most demanding and sought-after fields of specialization.[17] In his assignment to colonial service, he followed in the tradition of preceding *polytechniciens*, who made use of the "versatility" of their academic training to develop and manipulate scholarly networks in the colonies. For example, prominent alumni founded the *Société archéologique de Constantine* and the *Société historique d'Alger*.[18] From his time in Algeria forward, Faidherbe participated in many of these organizations founded by fellow *école* graduates and military officers. Through this involvement, he encountered the long history of North Africa. At first a mystery to the young officer, the area would become central to Faidherbe's understanding of colonial rule as he gained contacts throughout the region.

Early colonial experience: Construction of an understanding

Following engineering training in France, Faidherbe moved on to his first military assignment in an Algeria still in the throes of violent resistance to French colonial rule, a rebellion led by Abd al-Qadir that would continue until 1847. The years 1844–1846 saw Faidherbe serving as part of a suppression campaign under the command of General Thomas-Robert Bugeaud. While he and his commander likely had very little direct contact, Faidherbe ultimately developed views similar to those of his military superior. Bugeaud was famed for his willingness to consider what would later become known as the "hearts and minds" of the Arabs, attempting to win them over even as he ordered mass executions of rebel bands and the burning of entire villages. He famously raced into the street, undressed and unshaven, to subdue and arrest a Maltese he saw mercilessly beating an Arab.[19] Likewise, Faidherbe, in letters to his mother, contrasted the "majesty," "gravity," and "intelligent bearing" of the Arabs he encountered with his understanding that Algeria required a "war of extermination," as "one dead Arab means two fewer Frenchmen assassinated."[20] Algeria thus presented Faidherbe with the impossible duality of the colonial situation. He could see both the humanist possibilities of a colonialism that considered native methods as useful and valuable in their own right and the terrible brutality required to "pacify" a hostile population.

Faidherbe's subsequent assignment to Guadeloupe pushed him further down the humanist, associationist path. During this period, Faidherbe may have met Victor Schoelcher, famed abolitionist and senator in the new French government; in any case, the officer developed a strong relationship with the crusading reformer, ultimately dedicating his last work (1889) to "Mister Schoelcher, Senator, ex-member of the Provisional Government of 1848 ... beloved teacher and old colleague."[21] Whether inspired by this relationship or by the poor conditions on the island, Faidherbe made a rapid transition from unremarkable officer to one with significant insight on native populations. Although listed as having no discernible linguistic skills in 1847, his evaluation of 1848 described his knowledge of languages, which he "studied voluntarily," indicating that he "knows a little Italian and Spanish." He also impressed his superior with his learning in "geology and natural history." This 1848 report also reflected the superior's perspective on Faidherbe's political views: "Inclined towards socialism ... can be easily impassioned by radical opinions—must be kept on the straight path by good advice."[22] The young captain, far from toeing the party line, had undergone a transformation seemingly overnight. He saw language as the gateway to a deeper understanding of native societies, insight that would enable better, more human colonial rule. His superiors had come to see him as a potential opponent of conservative colonial institutions.

Faidherbe's expansive mind grew beyond basic improvement and trendy theories of social reform. At some point in his early career, the young officer compiled an extensive notebook with translations of poetry into thirty-one languages and dialects, including Berber, Arabic, and Guadeloupian Créole.[23] These notebooks do not reflect fluency in all of these languages; however, they do show an increased interest in and familiarity with foreign societies. It seems unlikely that Faidherbe acquired this language skill in a single year; rather, his earlier work had probably not attracted the attention of his superiors, who focused more on his shortcomings. Maturing rapidly both professionally and intellectually, he developed a taste for new ideas on social composition and order even as he worked hard to expand his ear for languages, ideas he would combine later in his career, particularly in Senegal.

Upon his return to France, now speaking "a little Arabic," the young officer spent much of his time "in the study of languages."[24] After his recovery, he returned to the center—for him—of all things ethnological and political, Algeria. While there, he could apply both his newfound language skills and his broader perspective on colonial rule. His subsequent experience in Algeria, followed almost immediately by prominence in Senegal, allowed him to mold a number of individuals ready to follow his leadership. In the process he would reorient the production and sharing of colonial knowledge, encompassing groups both in the metropole and in Africa.

Algeria: Building local understanding

Faidherbe's return to Algeria in 1849 coincided with the explosion of a new revolt. This time the resistance came not from the traditionally demonized Arab tribes, but instead from the respected Berbers of the Kabylia region in the Aurès Mountains. The revolt would serve as the centerpiece of Faidherbe's tour in the colony, as he would spend much of his time fighting in the area.[25] French Algeria had also become intellectually vibrant, as the *Faculté de Lettres* in Algiers developed new colonial scholars in following the lead of General Bugeaud, who had founded the first Algerian society for arts and letters in 1847.[26] Now more senior and with considerable colonial experience, Faidherbe found himself a valued member of the French effort in an area that offered opportunity for academic study. In fact, he was given command of the construction of an outpost at Bou Saada in late 1849, earning praise from General Jean-Baptiste Philibert Vaillant, formerly Faidherbe's commandant at the *école polytechnique*, now inspector general of the army in Algeria, in an 1851 report. Vaillant cited Faidherbe for "true valor" for his role in combat operations where he had engaged in direct clashes with the rebellious Berbers despite his nominal role as a rear-echelon engineer.[27]

Now viewed as courageous and honorable in both bourgeois and military circles, Faidherbe escaped the marginal ratings he had received earlier in his career. He was living an "honorable life" according to the French bourgeois customs of the time. In the colonial milieu, that distinction became all the more important as a mark to set himself apart from both his subordinate soldiers and the supposedly primitive natives against whom he fought. He thus began to compile the "charisma" that would later enable him to reach great heights in the French colonial bureaucracy.[28] Now judged as a competent and perhaps even above-average soldier, Faidherbe was able to spend more time on native study. He could work harder to understand native social constructions because he had covered himself in what his contemporaries saw as heroic glory. Martial success gave him a buffer from close oversight; he was free to develop his intellectual capabilities and discover those of his subjects.

Faidherbe applied this freedom to work toward a better understanding of what was required to pacify the restive region. His experience had shown him both sides of the colonial method. He concluded that subjugation of rebellious natives required a combination of local ethnic and linguistic understanding, on the one hand, and the iron will to impose harsh sanctions, on the other. These opposing methods appeared in Faidherbe's correspondence much as they characterized the action in his first Algerian tour in the 1840s. In March of 1850, Faidherbe described Bou Saada as "rather debauched like all the towns of the desert" but presented a nearby valley in 1851 in very different terms: "I have not yet seen an area as beautiful and rich as this one, even in Europe ... one finds a beautiful village at each turn." Faidherbe was torn by these two seemingly contradictory approaches to colonialism: benevolent humanism and violent repression/destruction. Algerian villages like those depicted in Faidherbe's correspondence would at times fall victim to military necessity as they were burned and the residents executed in summary fashion by Algerian natives fighting for the French, known as *tirailleurs*.[29]

By promoting the employment of native troops, Faidherbe initiated a new era of French colonial warfare. Such tactics did not end in Algeria; indeed, he formed similar units in his time as governor of Senegal.[30] In the officer's mind, the use of violence must differ with location and circumstance; he believed that his combination of local knowledge and commitment to understand tempered the need for the destructive *razzia* raiding parties favored by many French officers in the conquest of the Sahara.[31] Instead, he understood the value of the show of force, employing small military parties to travel into the interior and speak to native leaders. He rejected the implicit assumptions of his peers in Algeria and the Sahara, who saw native groups as simple and unsophisticated obstacles to rapid conquest. Small expeditions, Faidherbe believed, would deliver native political allegiance to the French colonial state by displaying the humanity and knowledge of the colonial occupier. Expanding these contacts would also help Faidherbe to increase his store of local information. From this localized data, he could discover, exploit, and then resolve intranative political disputes in favor of expanded French mediation and control.

Local understanding grew not from abstract study, but from dialogue in the native language, a pursuit to which Faidherbe dedicated himself in Africa. Faidherbe worked hard on Arabic during this period, remarking to his mother that he "every day made new progress in Arab as I do not hear anything else spoken." At the same time, the young officer developed a rudimentary ethnographic method that involved basic observation. He infused this system of observation with value judgments based on the perceived developmental position of native groups. He spent time at a "Moorish café" near Bou Saada, observing the "savage" activities of the local tribesmen and their dancing girls.[32] He defined savagery, in this case, as the stunted moral development that enabled these nomads to consider women as dancing possessions and sexual objects.

Faidherbe's tenure in Algeria coincided with the first full French translations of Ibn Khaldun's universal history, the greatest exposition of medieval Arabic political philosophy and development that considered nomadism a necessary precursor to more developed and sedentary "civilization."[33] Faidherbe thus encountered Khaldunian thought directly: "Let us look at civilization, born in the fields and ending with the foundation of cities and trending strongly towards this end. As soon as the people of the country acquired this level of well-being and luxury ... they allowed themselves to adopt the sedentary lifestyle."[34] Rural life preceded urban life but could not withstand the allure of greater leisure, wealth, and prestige eventually offered by cities. The nomadic desert-dwellers possessed a war-like spirit; their bravery gave them the ability to conquer others. These "savage peoples," for all their martial strength, improved when they came into contact "with a more advanced civilization" and eventually abandoned the pastoral lifestyle. A sedentary existence remained far superior to its nomadic equivalent.[35] However, no achievement ensured permanent strength. The agricultural lifestyle over time created occupational social classes that eventually hardened into immutable castes unable to mix with each other.[36] Inevitably, these advanced urban centers crumbled with the onset of decay and excess. While it represented the height of human development, urban life could not last, as it also caused civilizations "to stop and to become corrupted." Societal change halted with the assumption of a life of luxury; in a cyclical fashion, the civilization "began to retrograde ... to fall into decrepitude" and returned to its natural state, ready to reinitiate the cycle.[37] Faidherbe saw himself as an important conduit in this Khaldunian cycle of intellectual advancement. In collaboration with like-minded native and French intellectuals engaged in the colonial project, he sought to associate with and develop African social and political groups while employing their focused intellectual sophistication. He thus turned to a variety of other groups to better understand African social structures. Faidherbe set a new standard for rule by ethnological investigation, one invariably turned inward on the local inhabitants and their seminal social texts and away from the lived violence of the colonial state and the turbulence of European-dominated world affairs.

Tribal affiliations and genealogies served as vital sources for this understanding, particularly if they displayed connections to groups in Algeria "of whom we have an intimate knowledge today."[38] Faidherbe's early articles on the interactions between Berbers, Arabs, and blacks served as continuing references for him; over time, he made marginal notes on many of them. In some of these scribblings, he credited the Arab writers Ibn Battuta, Ibn Khaldun, and Muhammad Bello with providing useful information on the chains of political leadership and academic learning that shaped social life in the Maghreb.[39] As early as 1855 he discussed his time spent in "researching geographical and historical ideas on Central Africa in the Arab authors of the middle ages in order to reconstitute the history of these countries."[40] He quoted from Ibn Khaldun in numerous instances, particularly regarding the Yemeni origins and movement of Arab tribes and the intermixing of the Hassanid Arabs and the Senhadja Berbers.[41]

Locally authored manuscripts served an important role as well, as they could assist in isolating and eliminating the bias of Christian and Muslim sources. Faidherbe saw value in the maintenance of knowledge "lost from view in Europe" but maintained in the "manuscript chronicles of the marabouts of the Adrar."[42] Direct examination of African societies, however, could supplement the strength of these documentary sources.

His time in Algeria saw the rise and at least the beginning of the fall of the *bureaux arabes*, offices and officers dedicated to understanding Algeria in ethnographic and geographic terms. These local native affairs offices, officially eliminated with the rise of civilian government in Algeria after 1870, persisted until the early twentieth century in outlying regions despite accusations of corruption. Officers of the *bureaux*, focused on direct observation and the outlining of "moral topography," in particular conducted detailed studies of the Sufi Islamic brotherhoods so central to later French scholarship.[43] Although the *bureaux* studies were somewhat limited in their scope and insight into religious institutions, they still proved valuable to Faidherbe. Conducted largely by untrained French soldiers, these writings offered Faidherbe important insight into the social and political landscape, key in his mind to the promotion of "controlled association." This concept depicted societies at different political stages deserving specifically tailored colonial measures.[44] Faidherbe's view grew in importance in the 1850s and 1860s in light of the accession of Napoleon III and the declaration of the Second Empire in 1851. The emperor's conception of an "Arab kingdom" in North Africa jibed closely with Faidherbe's ideas of association and lent credence to his calls for administration by local political structures.[45]

Convinced of the effectiveness of the intellectual interaction of military ethnologists and native savants but hoping to avoid the excesses of soldiers hungry for power away from the French Algerian center of military and political authority, Faidherbe instituted the *bureau* model in Senegal. He hired officers with language ability in the *Direction des Affaires Politiques* (DAP), an organization that conducted detailed ethnographic surveys of the local area with the assistance of Muslim scholars.[46] While Faidherbe did not model Senegal on Algeria politically, he viewed the North African space as a point of reference, important in understanding future colonial undertakings.

Faidherbe N'Diaye: Building an ethnological colony in Senegal

In 1852, on the heels of his early Algerian deployments, Faidherbe gained transfer to Senegal. He had written the minister of the marine and colonies, an acquaintance from Guadeloupe, to request the move. Senegal offered an opportunity to develop his anthropological acumen in a less restrictive environment while avoiding the prying eyes and increasingly long reach of the French colonial Algerian administration. Senegal offered what amounted to a blank slate in Faidherbe's mind, the perfect location to implement and test his ideas on colonial rule that respected and incorporated native institutions. He could do this in something of a vacuum, untainted by international affairs and turned inward on the colony and its people. The area, first frequented by Portuguese traders as early as the fifteenth century, had slowly come under French control by the early nineteenth century. Saint Louis, where the Senegal River emptied into the Atlantic Ocean, served as the primary base for French trading into the interior. However, few French administrators of the area had considered further conquest; it seemed enough to participate in and correspond with the existing local trade networks. Faidherbe, searching for a greater name for himself and expanded commercial territory and political control for France, saw the area as ripe for colonial growth. The region had not suffered the privations of the French conquest of Algeria in 1830; it was relatively unstained by colonial warfare, offering native populations still employing their own unique political and social forms.

Faidherbe's first Senegalese residency culminated in assignment as chief of engineers in Saint Louis. From this position of authority and drawing on his previous combat experience, Faidherbe participated in a number of expeditions into the interior, also concluding some rudimentary ethnological studies. At some point in this period, Faidherbe came to the attention of the Maurel family, a powerful Bordeaux trading clan that held a controlling interest in French Senegalese trade. Interested in a man willing to venture into the interior in search of developmental contacts, the Maurels saw Faidherbe as a potential ally. Following him into the interior, they reasoned, could yield significant new opportunities for economic growth and exploitation. Influenced by these business interests, the new minister of marine and colonies recommended Faidherbe for the governorship in 1854. In his note to the minister of war, the colonial director pointed to Faidherbe's "remarkable intelligence" and "special experience" in Algeria as important factors in his selection. Although Faidherbe was relatively junior, the minister of war, his old commandant and commander, Jean Vaillant, ultimately granted the request in August of 1854, making Faidherbe a major and the governor of the French colony.[47]

By all accounts, Faidherbe was quite pleased to find himself in Senegal, particularly in a position of such power. In a break from his predecessors, he fashioned himself as a native of sorts, going to ceremonies such as weddings or baptisms in local dress and earning a nickname employing a common local surname: "Faidherbe N'Diaye."[48] He also took a local wife, in the fashion of some colonial administrators, learning several languages from her, including Wolof. Diokounda Sidibé likely bore several children to Faidherbe and certainly served as a key player in the network of local informants the governor would develop to facilitate the growth and consolidation of French rule in the area.[49] At the same time, their relationship symbolized the power Faidherbe exercised over both the colony and his ethnographic informants, leaving his Senegalese subjects as virtual servants to his political and sexual power.[50]

Nevertheless, Faidherbe exploited these contacts to develop networks of like-minded intellectuals, both French and native, who contributed greatly to the success of his gubernatorial administration. He later listed the greatest accomplishments of his first five years as governor (1854–1859) as the creation of a government printing office (1855), the founding of the *Moniteur du Sénégal* (1856), the creation of a battalion of *tirailleurs sénégalais* (1857), and the organization of an interpreter corps (1857).[51] Not surprisingly, Faidherbe placed great weight on any measure that expanded the French power base and aided in administration. Successful governance required talented subordinates from all corners of colonial society, both native and French. These thinkers could grow in capability and stature through intellectual interaction both in the colonies and the metropole itself. Through these networks, Faidherbe thought to solidify the regime in Senegal while gaining an empire-wide dissemination of his ideas on colonial association.

He promoted the intellectual growth of his subordinates by pushing them to publish in the daily *Moniteur du Sénégal* or in the more prestigious *Revue Maritime et Coloniale*, published by the Ministry of the Navy and Colonies in Paris from 1861 to 1868. Most of the articles printed in this journal included ethnographic descriptions completed during military campaigns or voyages of exploration or diplomatic negotiation with native political elites.[52] Publication in the journal brought the Senegalese exploits of Faidherbe and his officers to the attention of French political leaders at the ministerial level in Paris and across the colonies as a whole. The African descriptions they provided in the journal, notionally mediated by ministry officials in Paris, thus gained official sanction. Faidherbe thereby grew his network beyond the bounds of the Senegalese colony, beyond even the African continent. He gained support for his form of investigation and rule through the tacit governmental support of his techniques conferred by official printing.

His efforts to grow a strong group of subordinates did not end there. He expressly included natives in his administration, giving them publication and educational opportunities as well. He planned to spread French in the Senegalese interior, hoping to supplant Arabic as the second language by creating a Francophonic elite. Arabic, by the 1850s, was the language of revolt, employed by the jihadist states then challenging his authority. Employing his knowledge of the Arabic language and the power of Arabic sources in Africa, the governor actively sought to minimize the language's reach and importance so as to enable colonial control. To that end, he published the *Moniteur du Sénégal* and the *Annuaire du Sénégal*, both focused on history and anthropology, entirely in French.[53] In order to make these publications successful, though, Faidherbe had to create an elite group of native administrators and scholars capable of publishing in French and appealing to a readership composed of other French-speaking colonial elites, both native and French. He necessarily turned to education as the first step.

While decrying "cruel and intolerant fanaticism," Faidherbe provided funds to Qur'anic schools in the hope of improving primary education for Muslims.[54] He thus undermined some Islamic elements that sought to reestablish a Caliphate and reject the French by offering official legitimization of Franco-Arabic combinations. At the same time, the Islamic model of education provided a point of entry to the African intellectual world. Islamic teachers were already in place and spread widely; their techniques and curricula needed only the impetus added by the inclusion of French perspectives on the modern world. Drawing on his previous experience, Faidherbe proposed a primary education structure that would "imitate that which is done in Algeria," a similar approach with combined Islamic education and European methods.[55] Faidherbe thought that graduates of these schools, imbued with the spirit and language of the modern European world, would then go on to serve as important interpreters of social reality and leaders of a new colonial order.

From this strong foundation, Faidherbe could pick and choose the members of his network. In that spirit he took over Saint Louis secondary education from a missionary order and created the *école des otages*, an effort to discourage anti-French revolts by holding sons of local chiefs in French territory as educational "hostages." Faidherbe said he hoped to "create some elite locals to aid us in our civilizational work and to ensure at the same time the recruitment of interpreters for the diverse languages of the country."[56] These new elites could serve two purposes in his mind: the furtherance of French occupation and colonization as well as the growth and dissemination of a body of ethnographic knowledge of the area that would feed back into the colonial effort. From this historical and ethnographic understanding, Faidherbe believed that French administrators could devise the proper program to increase French support of preexisting African institutions. The inclusion of this local detail would enable and deliver a more human and humane form of governance contrary to the violent excesses Faidherbe had seen in Algeria.

Faidherbe claimed immediate success in this venture, as his school boasted graduates or students from virtually all of the French-controlled areas of the Senegal River basin by 1859.[57] The school did more than teach; in Faidherbe's words, it transformed students "in terms of education, ideas, [and] tendencies," particularly those who had lived "without having developed a full understanding and feeling of affection for France."[58] Alumni would then serve as colonial functionaries. They were vital in countering the complaints of urban and detached French colonial administrators in Saint Louis, who lamented, "certain locals desired that the French authorities remain ignorant of things in the country." Such complaints rang hollow with Faidherbe, as these social interpreters were vital to associationist thought. Local schools aided in understanding and thereby manipulating the social and political structures found in Senegal. He reported that 103 students attended the school during his tenure, with 56 proving "useful" to the colony. Eleven became local chiefs, while nine served as interpreters, two died in French military uniform, and numerous others served on merchant vessels, in colonial government, or as local leaders.[59]

Faidherbe's African network included a number of native administrators who contributed to his governorship and his ethnological knowledge. In particular, Faidherbe relied on his corps of interpreters not only for their language skill but also for their diplomatic know-how and access to local intelligence. Faidherbe's chief translators worked closely with local officials on ethnological research and administration. Each had enormous Islamic credibility as local *tamsir* and *marabout* with experience in the Sahara, particularly Morocco and Algeria, in Arabia, and even in continental Europe.[60] These men played key roles in the development and maintenance of contacts between the French government and local religious and political leaders. They were so successful and well connected that they continued as government translators beyond Faidherbe into the tenure of his successor. African intellectual middlemen informed the expansion efforts of the governor and were critical to the efforts of Joseph Gallieni, a succeeding director of the DAP.[61]

Faidherbe's efforts to employ local notables for political association also included an academic component. Yaro Diao, among the first graduates of the *école des otages*, left his position as a chief to compile the first study of Wolof oral traditions for the *Moniteur du Sénégal*.[62] Descended from an old noble family, Diao worked initially from notes compiled from his father's oral sagas. He intended these notes purely as mnemonic devices, but ultimately recognized their importance as a general history of the Senegal River basin from 1200 to 1800. His work came to form the basis of twentieth-century academic work on Senegalese history; his studies appeared in numerous journals with the assistance and editing skill of acclaimed French ethnographer and folklorist Arnold van Gennep as well as French colonial academics and administrators Henri Gaden and Maurice Delafosse.[63] Unfortunately, Yaro Diao was something of an aberration; few of Faidherbe's subordinates gained real academic prominence and instead served as silent contributors to his efforts. Even as early as the 1850s, native African savants contributed to the generation of ethnological knowledge in West Africa in this limited way. From such information, Faidherbe began to piece together the history of the area, allowing him to see the swirling interconnections of peoples in local sociopolitical entities.

In dealing with this complexity, Faidherbe had long conceived of the Sahara as the key to African economic and social development as an ancient site of transport and exchange. The Sahel in particular hosted a remarkable mix of groups coded by the natives themselves as "white" and "black" according to a long-standing calculus of genealogy, Islamic heritage, and socioeconomic class.[64] Once in place in Senegal, Faidherbe saw the border between his new and old duty locations in Algeria and along the Sahel as offering an important view into the socioeconomic complexity of African societies.

To that end he wrote to the Paris geographical society in 1853, his first year in Senegal, to request the body's support to take "several steps in geography and ethnology," an interest he indicated as "one of the principal motivations that drove me to request assignment in Senegal." He took a particular interest in the "Moors" of the right bank of the Senegal river (then the northern edge of French advance in the area), describing them as an "Arab-Berber mixture." He requested help from the society in formulating a research agenda dedicated to understanding what he thought of as an odd cohabitation of "victors and vanquished" in the area, a reference to the centuries-old story of Arab conquerors from North Africa subjugating the Berbers, who then developed new positions as a clerical class. This view descended from a generation of French Algerian scholarship and the medieval analysis offered by Ibn Khaldun.[65]

Building on older Greek and Arabic philosophical works, Ibn Khaldun had written of Sahelian and sub-Saharan blacks as inhabitants of the equatorial zone in an overall scheme of racial and intellectual characteristics tied to latitude, as "living in savage isolation and devouring each other."[66] This isolation, which was also ironically present in the ethnological approach of Faidherbe and his successors, in part explained African primitivity; these peoples were far from the civilizing effects of Islam and the urban lifestyle of the littoral. They could hope to improve only through mixing with other groups. As an example, Ibn Khaldun pointed to the Arabs, originally "a race of looters and brigands" living a nomadic lifestyle and acting as an obstacle to the "progress of civilization." They advanced to a higher developmental level only by a total change in societal construction, as "the sedentary lifestyle is favorable to the progress of civilization."[67] Arab genealogists could make important claims to descent from early Islamic families, but they could not deny the importance of the infusion of non-Arab blood. Though lacking in nuance, this analysis proved influential for Faidherbe as he searched for originary sociopolitical structures.

This same 1854 issue of the geographical journal hosted Faidherbe's first scholarly contribution regarding the Moors, who he saw as an "errant and miserable" combination of Arabs and Berbers.[68] He portrayed the mix as unnatural in a linguistic sense and with respect to the Berber conversion to Islam, an event he painted as superficial and expedient. He did not stop with a basic analysis of these "white" groups. Over the next ten years, he spent much of his time in deciphering the results of black and white interaction. He paid particular attention to the migrations of "whites" and "blacks" in sub-Saharan Africa. Like many of the French savants who would follow, he attempted to understand the Peul (Fulbé) people, who seemed to sit astride the black/white divide. He attributed their presence in the West African Sahel to a long-ago migration from Egypt while also describing them as "more open to civilization."[69] The mixing of white and black civilizational groups, north and south, occurred for several reasons in Faidherbe's analysis: the caravan trade, which enabled movement between North and West Africa across the Sahara; the commerce in black slaves; and the repeated military conquests of the North African littoral, from the Phoenicians to the French.[70]

Far from a negative, Faidherbe viewed the product of these liaisons as useful, stating that the Moors could survive only with "an infusion of blood of a young and vigorous negress" as the "star of the Berbers and the Arabs" fell. These unions produced "moral and intellectual progress" as the blacks converted to Islam, maintaining "good native qualities" while rejecting the "inherent vices of Islamism."[71] This new social grouping would combine all of the best aspects of local groups, in the end delivering a people ready to accept and participate in the colonial project. In this model, the French could assist the process by battling the Tuareg and other "savage and ferocious hordes of the desert" who, in Faidherbe's mind, wanted only to convert and radicalize their southern neighbors.[72] Blacks in this case had not been tainted by radical Islam. Blacks, simple but full of potential, would revive decadent North and West African groups to a state more amenable to colonial interface.

Faidherbe believed that the social and intellectual elites who emerged from this racial mixture would lead Africans in a more benevolent French colonial structure. Islamism, which Faidherbe defined as juridical and political rule by Islam, was employed only by those without the imagination to seek a better form of governance. French-educated blacks offered him a way out of this conundrum as they worked closely with the French colonial administration. Islam, then, was not inherently wicked; indeed, Faidherbe saw much social and political value in adherents of Islam who were open to negotiation with other groups. He employed native informants, including military veterans, to gather information on West African history and society. Faidherbe gave a larger-than-average mention to one of these veterans, who he saw as a "very educated Muslim" because he had resisted the urge to join the West African jihadist cause in the 1850s and because he provided outstanding oral accounts of the histories he read and overheard.[73] Natives were capable of both understanding and relating complex histories; they could be counted on, assuming a basic level of education, to act as intelligent interpreters of social reality. Thus, they could eventually be expected to control their own political destinies. Islam, despite the presence of reactionary jihadist states, served as both a stabilizing force and a source of political and social information, particularly in understanding the history of West Africa and its relationship with the Arabs and Berbers of North Africa.

In a Saint Louis speech given on Bastille Day in 1860, Faidherbe acknowledged the differences between African groups, but did not favor one over the other. Instead, he recommended to his native audience that they model their views on those of the colonial subjects in the Congo, who had gone from "savage" to "administrator or magistrate" in twenty years of colonial rule. They should look not to the "Moors of the desert, an intelligent and energetic race" completely dissimilar to "us, who like peace and order, who are sedentary, productive, commercial traders liking prosperity, pleasure, and luxury, like you." Any failure to "listen to this counsel" would lead to "conditions of humiliating inferiority vis-à-vis the other black nations" that rejected the Arab-led resistance in Algeria.[74] Faidherbe believed that only a close association with French ways of life and governance would bring peace and prosperity to Senegalese political groups. He did not reject Islam as a force for civilization, but rather its extremist proponents.

In taking this position, Faidherbe placed himself as contrary to the more explicitly racialized concepts, cloaked as physical anthropology, advocated by scholars such as Paul Topinard, who believed that French problems in North Africa stemmed from a fundamental mistake. He felt the French needed to "appropriate the indigenous race of Algeria, the Berbers." In doing so, they had to remember to avoid "treating them like the Arab race."[75] This basic bifurcation, an effort to divide and conquer, treated the colonies as a Manichean space with "good" Berbers and "bad" Arabs. Berbers could assimilate quite easily to French political, legal, and social forms due to their perceived proximity to the extant French model. Arabs, on the other hand, had little to offer and a long way to go, perhaps inherently incapable of equality with the French.

Battling this simplistic view, Faidherbe made use of the significant Algerian journals and scientific societies resident in Algiers or other Algerian cities such as Constantine; prominent metropolitan historical publications offered little outlet for African information beyond brief exchanges in the minutes of meetings of anthropological societies. In the process, Faidherbe made use of the small but flourishing intra-African intellectual network, one that he would take great pains to expand. Following his final departure from Senegal in 1865, he spent much of his time on scholarly ethnology, ruminating on civilizational migrations, movements, and mixing.

Political association as springboard to metropolitan science

Even as he conducted ethnological investigations in Algeria and Senegal, Faidherbe remained a military officer. He took advantage, as did some of his military peers, of the fluidity of academic groups in Paris to gain entry despite his limited academic qualifications. After all, he had only an undergraduate engineering degree to his credit. Most importantly, he parlayed his field experience and significant history of publication to gain entrance to the most prestigious anthropological group in the world at the time, the *Société d'anthropologie de Paris*, founded by the prominent biologist, physician, and physical anthropologist Paul Broca in 1859. The organization and its founder were part of a larger European-wide effort to employ physical distinction as racial markers. According to this school of thought, scientists could classify the potential and capabilities of populations according to their perceived locations not only along a linear evolutionary system but also on a hierarchy of races.[76]

Broca specifically sought to distinguish the newly developed "anthropology" from its older predecessor, "ethnology." Broca pointed to the "primacy of the study of the physical characteristics of man" as vital to understanding "the human races." Ethnology, in his eyes, lacked "cohesion," as it was not "built on the solid base of anatomy, the most positive fundamental of natural history." Ethnology, while rigorous in its study of societal custom, remained subject to analysis "outside the scientific method, opening itself to the most venturesome speculation unless grounded in reality by the guiding hand of observation." Physical anthropologists rejected just the sort of examination advocated by Faidherbe as lacking in science. In Broca's discipline, only scientific measurements, such as cranial capacity or the length of the brow, could differentiate races.[77]

In joining this particular group, Faidherbe gained professional connections, credibility, and a larger publishing opportunity. The group had long-standing ties to the French overseas academic community, corresponding regularly with societies in Algeria by the 1860s.[78] Although his views on the importance of ethnography and sociocultural distinction did not jibe with the biological bases of the society's founders, Faidherbe saw the group could provide him with the academic legitimacy necessary for him to influence both intellectual and policy-making circles in the metropole and in the colonies. He adapted well enough to the society's message that within seven years of membership, Faidherbe had gained the society's presidency.[79]

By this time, now-General Faidherbe's network of contacts extended far outside Africa to the highest reaches of the French academic community. Indeed, Faidherbe's relationship with Broca and another of the founding members of the society, Armand de Quatrefages, ran sufficiently deep that they joined him in sponsoring a new candidate for society membership during Faidherbe's presidency.[80] He could count prominent scientists of the day as his close collaborators, delivering to him greater access to the most advanced anthropological theories of the day while also providing an outlet for him to spread his basic ideas on civilizational development. The anthropological society had ties not only to the academic community but also to colonial political support and funding tied to the French state's 1864 recognition of the group as an "establishment of public utility."[81] This web of contacts, interestingly, remained steadfastly focused on France and its colonies with only limited interaction with British, German, or American colleagues.

Much of Faidherbe's success stemmed from his association with Algeria, viewed generally by this time (as Faidherbe had seen it since the 1840s) as the central French colonial site for understanding the human condition. Many French Algerian scholars gained honorary inductions into other societies.[82] Faidherbe parlayed these associations, particularly his long-standing correspondence with the Paris geographical society, into publication opportunities. His study of the neolithic carvings in the Canary Islands stemmed from an initial report to the geographical society, gaining him the notoriety necessary to gain a place as correspondent of the prestigious *académie des inscriptions et belles-lettres* (part of the *Institut de France*, also home to the *académie française*) and the résumé to publish in the exclusive *Revue d'anthropologie*.[83] Faidherbe made great use of the professional connections he cultivated in Paris. He gained entrance to new avenues of publication while also locating more extensive sources of financial support for his research that did not rely on his position as a military officer. Enhanced funding enabled the now senior officer and scholar to develop new ethnological sources both within French academia and in native societies encountered while on more extensive and focused research trips. He could then expose that history to a greater audience, thereby revealing the past achievements of North African groups while displaying the possibility for future advancement.

Faidherbe's most prominent contribution to French anthropology was, with Paul Topinard, the *Instructions sur l'anthropologie de l'Algérie*, first published in 1874.[84] This document presented an interesting combination of the two modes of inquiry that Broca had previously characterized as oppositional. Faidherbe presented the ethnological or ethnographic view, while Topinard wrote as a physical anthropologist in search of more materials to measure. Continuing earlier conclusions, Faidherbe remarked in these instructions: "the Berber and the Arab are both white at birth."[85] The Arabs "will not rally" to the French "mode of civilization." The Berbers, on the other hand, displayed great similarity to the French, including "perhaps a community of origin."[86] Faidherbe argued that the Berbers originated in the tribes of Northern Europe, as witnessed by "the continuous line of stone markers that one finds from the shore of the Baltic all the way to Tunisia."[87] Faidherbe's model placed a past version of these native blond-haired and blue-eyed Algerians on par with the Franks, who shared these physical traits. Despite his efforts to establish some ethnographic distance, Faidherbe could not escape the Eurocentric and racist views so prevalent at the time. Arabs and Berbers were distinct groups for him; the violence of Arab resistance to the French colonial presence had convinced him that the nomadic Arabs were not ready for full political association without first mixing with the blacks or at least the Berbers.

Faidherbe's research agenda thus existed on the line between the relativist views that would emerge from French African ethnology in the twentieth century and the biological determinist views of many prominent physical anthropologists. He pressed for dialogue among French scholars-administrators, natives, and African oral and written sources to determine the historical origins of civilizational groups. His scholarship thus aimed to reform the system from the top-down and inside-out by offering a better-informed and consequently more effective form of rule. To gather this data, he turned to the ethnological networks he knew in North and West Africa. For instance, he employed "4 Moroccan informants" to describe the writing on the stone monuments of Demnat and Makech. Bowing to his desire for unadulterated truth and to a bit of ethnocentrism, he hedged his bets and "recognized the necessity to temper them with information gathered by a European." Thus, he also consulted reports provided by the French minister to Morocco, "who does research in geography and archaeology."[88] These records, once deciphered, offered a glimpse into little-known North African groups.

African residents and researchers remained important to Faidherbe's research long after his permanent return to France in the 1870s, providing the empirical basis for his social understanding. In his work retracing the writings of Herodotus in Libya, he consulted the definitive grammatical studies of Kabyle and Arab dialects in the area, produced by a soldier-scholar like himself, along with reports from explorers.[89] He did not settle for the explanations of those who had never been there. The ethnographic present, simultaneously primitive and reflective of the powerful influence of the past, revealed the potential for social and political linkage to the French colonial state. Such original work won Faidherbe some measure of academic acceptance in France perhaps in spite of his use of nonmetropolitan sources. Few other "amateur" scholars of the period held such a position.[90] He had risen to great heights in both colonial governance and metropolitan academia, thereby connecting the worlds even as he remained outside of them. A full resident of neither Parisian academic circles nor colonial policy making, Faidherbe could investigate and influence both from the margins, from their points of overlap.

Continuing connections and a forgotten legacy

Great success in the Franco-Prussian War of 1870–1871 gave Faidherbe additional space in which to work, earning him heroic acclaim, political office, and ultimately the prominent position of Grand Chancellor of the French Legion of Honor.[91] Although Faidherbe's health failed him, as he could no longer walk by 1876, he continued to study Africa vicariously through his connections. His position in the Legion of Honor permitted him to direct young colonial officers to visit him in his offices or at his home.[92] Through one of these visits in 1886, Faidherbe met young Henri Monteil, recently returned from Senegal. Faidherbe, in the imperious style of a man used to power and fully cognizant of the approach of death, told the officer that his recent journey up the Senegal River was the culmination of the general's work. Flush with the excitement of the "Scramble for Africa" among the great European powers of the late nineteenth century, Monteil enjoyed his time with Faidherbe and returned periodically to check in with the patriarch of French ethnology. The system of connections established by Faidherbe had already paid great dividends for the young explorer, who had worked with two native chiefs under the guidance of Joseph Gallieni, one a graduate of the *école des otages* and the other a former guide and translator for Faidherbe, while on expedition.[93]

Monteil did not stand alone in accepting the wisdom of the now-frail Faidherbe. Administrators and governors visited him on several occasions and made specific reference to his example in developing policies. Faidherbe's legacy of close collaboration with native intellectual and political elites set the standard for the French colonial service, both military and civilian, with an increasing willingness for open intellectual discourse among Europeans with their heads down and focused in the colonies. This was a rare achievement in the dark years surrounding the Dreyfus Affair. Gallieni, in fact, based much of his West African ethnological understanding on the work of Faidherbe, particularly the "origin and history of the population."[94] He first interacted with Faidherbe while still a lieutenant, working to develop the West African railroad Faidherbe had long labored to bring to fruition, a project Gallieni would advance through the use of a *corvée* system of forced labor.⁹⁵ Ultimately, Gallieni saw Faidherbe's efforts, both intellectual and military, as foundational. Gallieni felt that without Faidherbe's example, the French could not have expanded their rule over West Africa.⁹⁶

Faidherbe and his ideas linked North and West Africa and formed a bridge to Gallieni, Lyautey, and the leaders and theorists to follow. Parisian ethnology courses attended by Maurice Delafosse in the 1890s, for instance, relied heavily on Faidherbe's writing regarding civilizational groups in West Africa. Early-twentieth-century colonial Arabic scholar Ismael Hamet cited Faidherbe's 1859 work on Senegal for unearthing the "secrets of Central Africa" by initiating the acquisition of important documentary and oral evidence of group origins.⁹⁷ Hubert Lyautey, a direct disciple of Gallieni in Tonkin and Madagascar, applied the principles of local understanding to his time in Africa, from Algeria to Morocco.⁹⁸ Natives also connected French intellectuals and colonial functionaries in a common conversation and realm of experience. Descendants of Faidherbe's chief translators worked with French ethnologists and soldiers in Mauritania and along the Sahel, studying Sufi brotherhoods under funding from the Algerian and West African colonial governments.⁹⁹

Faidherbe stood alone in his time as a man thinking about informational networks in the colonial sphere. He placed himself in many camps, from native to metropolitan academic in an effort to influence the flow of information in, to, and from the colonies. In so doing, he founded a network of transfer reliant on men, and some women, with significant impact on the direction of France in the colonies and, in some cases, in the metropole. His recognition of the importance of Algeria established a center for these networks, the point from which his successors would emerge. While the *bureaux arabes* disappeared from Algeria, their essence remained in the successive Muslim policy organizations in West Africa manned by Joseph Gallieni, Maurice Delafosse, and Paul Marty, among others. Faidherbe's death on September 29, 1889, did not destroy the network he helped to create. Instead, the reach of ethnological knowledge grew only larger, flourishing among the subterranean connections encouraged by Faidherbe and now including native intellectuals as well as French scholars. Ethnological knowledge, informed by a hearty dose of racial paternalism, nevertheless grew increasingly from contact and dialogue with native idioms of race and distinction as French colonial domination continued in Africa. This growth was far from singular; instead, it was made up of individual entities connected by their personal research and networks. Social and political knowledge became a primary concern of these chaotic systems, ordered only by the possession, retention, and dissemination of information deemed local and often considered apart from the metropole.

2

Lyautey, Gallieni, and Early Efforts at Political Association Informed by Ethnology

During an 1881 assignment to Algeria, French captain Hubert Lyautey tried to learn more about daily Algerian life from conversation with locals while traveling into the interior. After returning from his detested job as an aide in the office of the commanding general of French forces in Algiers, he spent two hours each day at the café of a local notable. While there, young Lyautey learned the language and discussed Arabic scholarship, including the work of fourteenth-century philosopher Ibn Khaldun, with religious and political luminaries of Algiers.[1] His mind spinning from these interactions, he returned to his Algiers apartment and dressed "in the Arab manner, which is to say in shirt and burnous," spending the rest of the night "surrounded by my beloved books, my pencils, [and] my Arabic notebook," the primary tool for his regular language studies with the secretary of the local *bureau arabe*.[2] Desperate for field experience to combat the daily drudgery in Algiers, the young officer took part in desert expeditions and conducted anthropological and archaeological expeditions with local French academics.[3]

In the evening of one such trip, Lyautey heard the strains of music in the distance. Straying from his campsite, he found a wedding that he described as "rather poor and primitive, but what color!" Continuing his nighttime walk, he soon found himself in a village of non-Arab blacks, where he gained the assistance of a former *tirailleur* as his translator. His lack of scientific training did not stop him from offering his own take on social roles among the native population: "We never see anything like it among the Arabs, but among the good blacks, the women are something."[4] Even in his youth, Lyautey sought to understand social groups in a comparative frame, viewing the treatment of women as a key marker. The treatment of women, in his eyes, served as a marker of a society's political readiness for association. In some ways replaying the ideas of Louis Faidherbe, he believed that the "simple" blacks offered more opportunity for rapid advancement into European-style modernity. Arabs, on the other hand, had become set in their decrepit ways; it would take much more to move them from this stunted position.

At times a romantic,[5] the young Lyautey perceived a need for social reform in order to improve the political present and future for colonial subjects.[6] For Lyautey, colonization served as a site where "the population rushes to gain the shelter of our colors knowing we will liberate them and provide them with peace and protection."[7] Social examination could yield such a political state, one where political association replaced abject exploitation. These views proved enormously influential in France and set the foundation for the next generation of colonial scholars, some of whom worked for Lyautey, to continue his efforts to examine so as to conduct political rule of African peoples.

Once described by his superior during assignments to Indochina and Madagascar, General Joseph Gallieni, as "the perfect colonial officer," Lyautey constantly pressed for the study of subject populations in order to develop better social and political measures of rule.[8] Such policies would deliver Africa and Africans into a locally adapted form of social and industrial modernity that would be more productive economically and intellectually for both the French colonial governments and the African populations themselves. Such study could not occur in the confines of an office in this view; it required constant movement and examination of the populations in their environment. Lyautey often repeated Gallieni's dictate of "right man in the right place" and emulated his reliance on an "organization on the march," avoiding the nefarious influences of the "killer bureaucracy" in Algiers and Paris.[9]

By the time of Lyautey's entrance into full-time colonial service in 1894, the French colonial system spread across the globe, from Indochina, where conquest began in earnest in the 1880s, to French Polynesia, the Indian Ocean Seychelles, and across the African continent to Senegal. Governed by the French Third Republic, a democracy dominated by legislative in-fighting and the regular collapse of coalition governments, colonial leaders understandably grew tired of bureaucratic inertia in the metropole. Carrying on the tradition of Faidherbe, colonial soldier-scholars turned inward on their colonies, largely ignoring European events while courting scholarly recognition. Lyautey joined Gallieni and their peers in colonial leadership in battling against governance dictated from the center, a method expected to play out according to some universally applicable checklist or playbook. A close examination of Lyautey's correspondence indicates that he remained, throughout his career, an intellectual interested in ethnological examination conducted in full consideration of the surrounding environment; theory could follow from work done in the field.[10]

Scientific investigation, a category into which Lyautey placed ethnology, gave the officer, particularly in his role as resident general in Morocco, more tools by which to work with subject populations in a political association. This ethnological partnership, particularly as he installed it in Morocco from 1912, was "above all intellectual, that of the spirit and that of the heart. I believe that it is the true means by which to safeguard the cooperative regime of France and the Muslim nation of Morocco."[11] Generated in a period of significant internal unrest and violence in the Moroccan Rif, Lyautey's hopes centered on the idea that understanding came from collaborative scientific study. Over time such effort would restore "the order, the security and the unity of the Sharifian empire" while also leading to "economic development and social progress to an extent the old Morocco never knew."[12] Lyautey, despite his calls for relativism, thus built an ethnocentric political structure. As Paul Rabinow has pointed out, Lyautey believed that a European-style "technical modernity" would restore Morocco's luster while retaining its local institutions. When applied, however, this approach did not include infrastructure improvements in "Muslim" areas of Moroccan cities, districts that became islands void of French influence.[13] Scientific modernization operated in a number of different ways across locales, a direction that, while certainly descended at least in part from unequal relations of power, also reflected Lyautey's basic insistence on protectorate rule as a collaborative process. Indeed, the complex and symbiotic nature of precolonial Moroccan society meant that efforts to divide and rule via an associationist grafting of colonial political structures were doomed to failure as rural groups resisted the centralization of authority.[14] This basic miscomprehension contributed significantly to Lyautey's failure to pacify rebellions across the protectorate over the course of his tenure. He was a product of his times and a myopic colonial view.

As a successor to Faidherbe and Gallieni, Lyautey became France's foremost colonial soldier and expert on political rule of foreign populations while making the first real efforts at an instrumentalized ethnology in the form of political association. Gallieni, a disciple of Faidherbe in West Africa, had conducted important and successful campaigns of conquest both in the French Soudan (modern-day Mali) in the 1880s and Indochina in the 1890s; it was during this last assignment that Major Lyautey encountered then-colonel Gallieni, the most important figure in his military and ethnological development. Lyautey said of his conversations with Gallieni: "I drink in his Soudanese stories and his vast and supple notions of organization and administration," tales that made Lyautey see the "joy of action that destroys the bitterness of stagnant garrisons in the suburbs."[15] Gallieni's depiction of the French African and Asian colonies rang true for Lyautey. He agreed with his mentor that only through an administration that adapted and changed according to local requirements could the French effectively govern their colonial subjects. Gallieni, at once soldier and ethnologist, stood as the embodiment of this technique for Lyautey.

Lyautey thus tried, throughout his colonial service (1894–1925), to use his experiences as the foundation of a wide-ranging network bent on understanding all the complexities of conquest, colonial rule, and native social structure. He proposed strategic alternatives to the brutal and costly methods of colonial expansion employed in the first half of the nineteenth century in Africa, at the same time rallying against the "anti-militarism" in a fin-de-siècle France rocked by the divisions of the Dreyfus Affair. The young officer did so first by developing techniques that reconceived the military as a force for peace, echoing many of the notions of Faidherbe in an environment that also fostered the growth of a powerful pro-colonial lobby in Paris.[16] Taking his cue from Faidherbe's call to respect local political and social structures, Lyautey advocated for "associating without absorbing, guiding without administering, moving towards progress without altering."[17] This model of governance required Lyautey and his subordinates to work in harmony with native intellectuals, who he saw as the inheritors of the postcolonial state following France's departure. Unable to grasp fully the great diversity of Moroccan society, his colonial service ended in the horrific fighting in the Rif that sought to stamp out any potential for ethno-political resistance.

Origins of a colonial mind

Born on November 17, 1854, in eastern France, Louis-Hubert-Gonzalve Lyautey did not spring from a humble peasant family. Rather, his mother's family claimed descent through twenty-two generations from Saint Louis and Louis XIV had ennobled his father's ancestors.[18] Both families had significant traditions of military service, as Lyautey's maternal grandfather graduated from the *école spéciale militaire* at Saint Cyr and his paternal grandfather served under Napoleon I in Russia and commanded an artillery corps under General Thomas-Robert Bugeaud in Algeria.[19] His father, a military engineer in Lorraine, wished for his son to follow in his footsteps by attending the *école polytechnique* and entering the military.[20]

Drawing on his noble and military background, Lyautey eventually fashioned himself into a provincial intellectual. He gained access to some of France's best secondary and university schools, in the process coming into contact with social reform movements swirling around ideas of religious-moral regeneration, workers' rights, and toleration of difference. He emerged from these experiences as a military man with very clear ideas about the future of France. The young officer wished for a homeland not led by relatively mindless bureaucratic automatons. Rather, he envisioned a future where France and its colonies existed as a politically homogenous group led by a benevolent intellectual class intent on ensuring the continued moral, economic, and intellectual development of all its subjects. He thus picked up the bits of Saint-Simonian and positivist thought left by Faidherbe and parlayed them into a new rationale for colonial ethnological investigation: the need to understand difference so as to fashion a better form of rule.

In some ways reflecting the colonial military and social space he would later dominate, Lyautey grew up in the borderlands. Hard on the line between the German states to the east and the French state to the west, Lorraine and its sister province Alsace often provided the fodder for conflicts between political and ethno-linguistic groups. With the devastating defeat of France in the Franco-Prussian War of 1870–1871, parts of Alsace and Lorraine passed under the control of the ascendant German state. While spared the transition to a new German citizenship, Lyautey the teenager surely felt the repercussions in the area torn by war and the subsequent campaign of French guerrillas resisting the Prussian invaders.

In 1872, Lyautey left Lorraine to attend a year of preparatory school in Paris. While not happy as a boarding student, Lyautey fell under the spell of a brilliant teacher at the school. Recognizing the student's potential for study and leadership, the priest pushed him not to France's leading school for the preparation of engineers and government functionaries, the *école polytechnique*, but instead to the military academy at Saint-Cyr.[21] The military institution, second only to the *école polytechnique* in terms of prestige as a preparation for service in the army, better fit the intelligent young student not quite willing to accede to the bourgeois standards of his Parisian peers. Perhaps most importantly, Lyautey's time at the school introduced him to Captain Count Albert de Mun, a crusader for "social regeneration" in France and member of the *Cercles Catholiques d'ouvriers*. The young officer significantly influenced Lyautey's views on appropriate social and political forms.[22]

Following his graduation from Saint-Cyr in 1875, Lyautey entered staff college in France, an unhappy time for a man ready for reform and adventure. He lamented his plight, remarking that the soldier's life did not agree with him and declaring his existence based on "protest against all that is the object of my profession."[23] In an effort to reinvigorate his perspective and perhaps to discover ground for reform following the drudgery of military education, Lyautey and fellow de Mun collaborator Prosper Keller traveled to Algeria as tourists in 1878.[24] Their fires stoked by conversations with de Mun just prior to departure, Lyautey and Keller met with workers' organizations in Tlemcen and sought such opportunities throughout their travels.[25] In an effort to understand the groups he purported to reform, Lyautey conducted ethnographic studies and began to learn Arabic, both written and spoken.[26] He sought individuals among the working classes who could converse with him about social life, about the prospect for the remaking of Algerian society along Western lines on an Arab-Islamic foundation. Natives capable of understanding and explaining their own social organization were those best poised, in the young officer's opinion, to act as the vanguard of social reform, the new intellectual elite.

In his explorations, Lyautey delighted in the "swarming" crowds in Constantine who emitted "an odor that was *sui generis*." He discovered a taste for Arab clothing on his visit to a Moorish bathhouse and exulted in the experience of "the city of Jugurtha" and its "teeming and colored" casbah alleyways.[27] He felt the residue of what he believed was a great Arab-Berber civilization of the past conveyed via archaeology. Algiers possessed architecture "but little style," left as a place "civilization has gone past."[28] He felt the city had lost most of its character, blending with French fashion and style and in the process losing its Arab character. For Lyautey, history served as an important tool in understanding natives and the difficulty that would come in building an appropriate political form. Lyautey believed detailed study would reveal this lost history and thus present an opportunity to dissect and rectify the social problems retarding North African development.

Two years after his tourist visit, Lyautey returned to Algeria as a staff officer from 1880 to 1882. Still focused on studying the local populations, he impressed his superiors with his "love of study" and his willingness to learn Arabic, all in an effort to "perfect himself."[29] The renewed Algerian experience pushed him to consider several different paths for this refashioning: the emulation of famed French explorers such as Lieutenant Colonel Paul Flatters, lost in the Sahara; conversion to "the intellectual life of the *bureaux arabes*"; or even a journey into Tunisia to "create something completely new."[30] The young officer ultimately chose the path of the *bureaux*, spending significant time at those offices in his last year in Algeria. This informal apprenticeship brought him into contact with native political and intellectual elites, perfect for a young officer hoping to better understand the social and political world of Algeria.

"The *bureau arabe* [in Orléansville] gave me *carte blanche* and I made use of it: I spent three hours a day there … I listen and I watch, ensconced in a corner of the captain's office, not opening my mouth but opening my eyes and ears to absorb this process," recalled Lyautey. From his vantage point he could interact with local Muslim leaders there for a myriad of administrative purposes, becoming "the friend of all the caïds [native Algerian political leaders] within ten leagues." He made use of the interpreter, "increasing my Arab vocabulary each day," also accomplished by spending many hours in the local café.[31] Such *bureaux* stood as a "marvelous instrument of conquest and administration," founded in Algeria to better conduct the "incessant and ill-defined conquest of barbarism by civilization."[32] Lyautey thus fully appreciated the unequal power relations resident in the concept of the *bureaux*. He adopted a paternalist attitude similar to that of Faidherbe, studying the natives so as to develop a colonial policy that could improve their lot. Lyautey would not return to Algeria until 1903, but the memories of the local *bureaux* and the intricacies of North African life remained with him throughout his career, acting as both example and foil.[33] His career, though, would allow him to push his influence beyond the colonies and back to the metropolitan center.

During subsequent assignments in France, particularly around Paris, the young staff officer rapidly gained notoriety for his professional publications and "careful method."[34] He parlayed this attention into entry to the suburban Saint-Germain-en-Laye chapter of a social reform group founded on the teachings of Frédéric Le Play (d. 1882), who advocated social reform based on careful positivist study.[35] Lyautey had developed a reputation as one of the leading intellectuals of the French army by this time, even visiting numerous salons in Paris.[36] Through contact with this Le Playist group, Lyautey gained contacts that enabled him to pursue even greater efforts for metropolitan social reform. In particular, he met Viscount Eugène Melchior de Vogüé, author, intellectual, and member of the *Académie française* since 1888. Famed for his writings on the Orient and a prominent member of the powerful pro-colonial *comité de l'Afrique française*, de Vogüé encouraged Lyautey to make use of his intellectual connections outside of France to encourage reform. He provided introductions for Lyautey at many of the major journals of the day, using his influence to let the soldier write anonymously so as not to sacrifice his career through direct critique of the conservative opinions of some senior officers.[37] Deeply impressed by his time in Algeria, Lyautey found a like-minded individual in de Vogüé, a former resident of Constantinople. The young officer drew on the "echo" of his intellectual mentor's writings for inspiration.[38] Those same echoes then reverberated through Lyautey's tours in Indochina and Madagascar.

Associationist proving-grounds: Indochina and Madagascar

In letters from Indochina, Lyautey made clear that the intellectual currents in France remained important to him. "Do not forget me," he wrote to de Vogüé in 1895, "as I am very far away and also far from the movement of ideas among which I so passionately lived these last years; I do not want to lose all contact."[39] While still fascinated by the social reform pursued by his metropolitan intellectual partners, Lyautey dedicated himself to a new endeavor, one that could sound the death knell on his military career: an assignment in the colonies. Despite the best efforts of officers such as Faidherbe and Gallieni, colonial service remained the least sought-after assignment in the French military. Distance from the metropole, in the view of some military officers, meant distance from the political sponsorship that could bring elevations of both rank and social status. The action, it seemed, was in Europe in the aftermath of the Franco-Prussian War. The Third Republic, ostensibly committed to support of the growing colonial empire, focused its military attention on the eastern border and the possibility of another conflict with the powerful German state. For the moment,

French strategic thought focused on the defensive. Colonial service, while exotic, lacked in the direct prestige of the preparation for renewed continental warfare, as it focused on small-unit, offensive measures at the expense of the large-scale defense expected by many planners.⁴⁰

Indochina recalled Algeria for Lyautey. France's largest Asian colony was very much like the Algerian Kabylia, in Lyautey's opinion, particularly in terms of the topographical features and the population, composed primarily of a "good aboriginal race, [the] Thô."⁴¹ Indochina thus offered an important example of a colony that appeared backward. However, it contained, as did all other colonies in Lyautey's mind, distinctive intellectual classes capable of political association following the installation of systematic colonial ethnological study and influence. Lyautey saw real possibilities both in Asia and Africa for what the governor-general of Indochina termed the "protectorate," shorthand for political association with an eye toward progressive political independence.⁴² The protectorate method, Lyautey reasoned, had succeeded in Tunisia while Algeria remained in a "vegetative" state. "A new colony must have a proconsul who can put down the metropole," he realized, "and that the parliamentary regime will not take well."⁴³ Lyautey's vision thus placed colonial administration outside the hands of meddling Parisian politicians and indicated the necessity of an internal viewpoint focused on the local over the international. In Indochina and elsewhere in the empire, a failure to grant some autonomy to French colonial government risked the reinstallation of the Algerian bind, where the interference of the metropole had precluded sufficient ethnological study of the population and led to the establishment of a directly governed colony.

Most importantly, an Indochinese campaign introduced Lyautey to Joseph Simon Gallieni (1849–1916) in the summer of 1895, a period during which Lyautey learned many of the fundamentals passed on from Faidherbe in West Africa.⁴⁴ Famous in France after his escape from captivity in West Africa in 1881, Gallieni spent much of his early career following in the footsteps of Faidherbe.⁴⁵ The rising colonial officer gained command of all French forces in the West African Soudan in 1886, in part through the intervention on his behalf by Faidherbe, still influential despite his failing health.⁴⁶ Contemporaries found the officer quite similar to his famed mentor: "His traits brought to mind those of General Faidherbe, or at least those captured in engravings and portraits of Faidherbe, who himself never fit the classical type of general of his time."⁴⁷ Like his illustrious predecessor, he quickly discovered the utility of ethnographic study, engaging in detailed examinations of local groups near Dakar as early as 1877. Gallieni's Saint-Cyr classmate Louis-Parfait Monteil lauded his ability, even when leaving on an 1878 campaign, to use "his free time and all the hours of rest to increase his understanding of all things."⁴⁸ He ascribed his need to collect documents from his campaigns and commands to the importance of subsequent review, discussion, and debate. He learned this lesson from Faidherbe, who had taken such an approach "when he created our Senegalese colony."⁴⁹

Experience in the French Soudan convinced Gallieni of the importance of continual learning. He employed a "network of secret agents" to understand and control public opinion among groups along the Niger bend,⁵⁰ and put special trust in his interpreters and clerks to gather valuable information on local alliances and ethnic divisions while on campaign. In the final 1886 campaign against a West African Islamic caliphate, Gallieni gave special credit to his senior clerk and interpreters for their care of valuable documents, crediting them for the "favorable results of my mission."[51] The commander similarly instructed his officers on campaign to conduct detailed ethnographic studies of surrounding groups in hopes of understanding their social, cultural, and linguistic links, connections and disputes he could then manipulate to France's advantage.[52] Optimum local study and rule occurred in tandem with, rather than in spite of, local elites and those knowledgeable of African social forms. Only through their assistance could the French hope both to understand and to advance native interests as described in French voices and in the uniquely French intellectual and political idiom.

Climbing rapidly through the ranks, Gallieni had brought these ideas and methods with him to Indochina, striving to duplicate the "penetration" of civilization he had helped to achieve in Africa by permitting the "slow and progressive action of principles."[53] The success of both men ultimately drove them to accept additional assignment to Madagascar in 1897.[54] As these colonial thinkers moved to another area that appeared to them ripe for conquest and enhanced political rule, French society suffered through the drama of the Dreyfus Affair. This conflict, which sprang from largely fabricated accusations of espionage against a French army captain, Alfred Dreyfus, saw people divided into ideological camps that hardened along views on religious toleration, military reform, civil rights, and the role of intellectuals. During the height of this struggle in 1899–1900, as Dreyfus suffered through repeated trials and incarcerations, Lyautey and Gallieni returned to Paris to drum up financial and political support for the final conquest of Madagascar. As military officers, they did their best to remain strictly neutral in the political machinations in the capital, as Gallieni indicated: "I climb into the car of my commander, the Minister of Colonies, and I ask him for his orders." Lyautey added, "I know only one commander, General Gallieni, under whose orders I serve," expressly removing himself from the Dreyfusard battles except to proclaim himself opposed to basic anti-Semitism.[55] Staying above the fray, the colonial officers spent much of their time visiting academic societies, universities, pro-colonial lobby groups, and even city chambers of commerce.[56] The voyage to France put them in contact with other reform-minded thinkers, including those with ties to the nascent pro-colonial movement in the legislature. Thinking pragmatically, Gallieni and Lyautey sought the financial support that came with political sponsorship.

While their mission was first one of fundraising, they also strove to raise the profile of French colonial efforts and their potential to build a new form of political rule. These powerful colonial thinkers stressed the importance of local understanding, of research on the ground, to the pro-colonial lobby in Paris. In pushing this agenda, Gallieni and Lyautey visited a group of Le Play disciples, emphasizing to the assemblage the important role of colonial soldiers in generating knowledge about foreign peoples, particularly in learning local customs and languages. Lyautey described himself and similar "agents of civilization in close contact with the population" as in the best position to enhance the social and political state of foreign societies.[57] The model of colonialism promulgated by Lyautey and Gallieni, involving detailed study of subject groups so as to develop close political cooperation, thus coincided with the rise of metropolitan associationist theories and a more powerful pro-colonial lobby.[58] Gallieni and Lyautey influenced policymakers, intellectuals, and political interest groups in the metropole through their compelling discussion of the benefits of study by soldier-scholars. In their eyes, native study not only enhanced colonial political rule; it added to the growing literature on non-European social structures.

Gallieni and Lyautey applied this sociopolitical approach in Madagascar. The senior officer labeled this technique the "progressive method" or "oil spot," in which his formations moved against forces of resistance only with the help of locals in translation, guide services, and the collection of ethnographic information.[59] The detailed understanding of the local area offered by the natives ideally permitted Gallieni to apply military force only as needed, slowly spreading across the countryside like a creeping oil stain on a hard surface. After this initial conquest and close study, Gallieni expected to apply the *politique des races* that called for the administration of native elements by others of the same social group to the greatest extent possible.[60] Conquest and pacification thus reintroduced an important aspect of Faidherbe's method: dialogue with the natives. Gallieni, however, lacked detailed knowledge of the area of conquest. He came armed with two primary weapons: overwhelming military force and a belief in social evolution.[61] In his mind, natives would spring to the French colors once they realized that France stood at the height of political development. While Gallieni stressed the importance of local information gathering, he saw the information, in large part, as instrumental. Lyautey would later refine that doctrine, respecting native societies, insofar as he could do so in a model of colonial domination, for their unique contributions to the world.

Both Gallieni and Lyautey realized that the information gathering so important to these processes must not occur in an office. In Gallieni's eyes colonial commanders would achieve "physical and intellectual development of the conquered race [and] social improvement" not through static study and interviews, but via yearly tours of the colony, discussing and assessing the results of development efforts with all concerned.[62] He made some efforts to improve the quality of this discussion by generating a new class of Malagasy (native of Madagascar) intellectuals. He founded the *Académie malgache*, consisting of both French and Malagasy scientists, in 1902 to conduct historical, ethnological, linguistic, and sociological studies of local populations. He charged the new organization to understand "the mentality of the populations and the evolution of their social state."[63] Intellectual cooperation made sense in his mind both for the stability of colonial rule and for the sociopolitical development of the colony. It was these ideas of study, cooperation, and targeted sociopolitical development and rule that formed the core of Lyautey's colonial politics from that time forward even as his career progressed.

With the completion of his time in Madagascar and his Gallieni-inspired education in 1903, Lyautey moved on to a new assignment, recommended by Gallieni for promotion to brigadier general and an assignment on the volatile borderlands of Algeria and Morocco. Through the remainder of his career, Lyautey remained mindful of Gallieni's advice to "give to these people, in effect, a political organization appropriate to their political and social state."[64] Reassignment offered him an opportunity to apply these lessons on his own, infused with his own brand of study, reform, and association.

Building the associationist state: Command in Algeria and Morocco

Lyautey assumed command of the French army subdivision at Aïn Sefra, in Algeria along the border with Morocco, during a turbulent period for both European states and their colonies. Conflict in the Balkans threatened to spill over into European war as Russia sided with Serbia in disputes with Austria-Hungary and other regional states. Germany, Britain, and France engaged in a naval arms race as each developed newer and better vessels geared for combat. This growing rivalry passed overseas as well, as Germany remained jealous of the profitable colonies controlled by France and Great Britain in Africa. While the Germans exercised some control over areas in southwest and eastern Africa, they could not match Algeria, Egypt, Senegal, or Kenya.

Morocco, the most appealing African state not yet under European control, offered a tantalizing option. It stood across the Mediterranean from Gibraltar and could aid in future German efforts to dominate or at least choke Mediterranean trade routes from the Atlantic. Conquest and control of the large and prosperous urban population of Morocco offered a counterpoint to the British hold in Egypt and the prospect of greater international prestige while threatening France's North and West African empire. By 1904, only a year after Lyautey's arrival in Algeria, the British had agreed to exclusive French access to Morocco as a "zone of influence." Disputed by the Germans, the agreement led to a series of conflicts between the European powers. International attention remained riveted on the area for the next five years as Germany, France, and Britain nearly engaged in military combat in 1906 and 1911, each time averting outright warfare as the French maintained some political control in exchange for territorial concessions to the Germans elsewhere.[65]

In this charged atmosphere Lyautey quickly drew the ire of metropolitan colonial politicians. Worried over the potential international repercussions of any French missteps on the border, political leaders demanded restraint from military forces in the area. Lyautey's first concern, however, was not for international political intrigue; he had little desire to serve as a "French tri-color pennant" that did little more than sway with the winds of distant metropolitan policy decisions, a chip in the grand bargains going on across the continent.[66] In concluding an early report on this "border region," Lyautey stated, "due to our progressive contact, to our political actions and our military operations, the rebellious elements were reduced to a minimum in this region that forms the *glacis* of our Algerian territories."[67] The Moroccan border stood out as a place for change, the forward edge of Lyautey's plan to develop a new political form in the colonies. He wanted to protect the French Algerian territory by halting what he saw as socially and economically destructive raids across the border by Moroccan tribes. As France gained its zone of influence in Morocco in 1904, Lyautey launched a raid of his own across the border into that state to strike rebellious tribes, hoping to deter future attacks. The action, which Lyautey thought had been conducted with restraint, drew criticism from metropolitan officials.

Forced to defend himself against Parisian political critics, particularly the socialist Jean Jaurès, Lyautey cited the "pacific and civilizing character" of the force, in his mind "certainly the first military column to act thusly." His policy, he explained, was "deference in principle" to the requirements of the Moroccan administrative organ, the Makhzen.[68] The newly minted brigadier general felt colonialism would not work without the right of commanders to operate on their own, to make decisions with the local knowledge that could only come from residence and study in the area in question. To his superiors, Lyautey acted without consideration of the wider conflict engulfing much of Europe in some fashion. In his mind, the actions were not rash, but the product of a dialogue with the Moroccan government and the peaceful influence of the French along the border. In fact, he relied on a long line of French studies of Morocco that found little political complexity and obscured historical nuances in favor of generalization.[69] Lyautey thus set out to create a modern state informed by a more focused study.

Shielded by Algerian Governor-General Charles Jonnart, for the most part, from further direct interference from Paris, Lyautey set his sights on a proper study of the Algerian border regions, an area that previously held little scholarly interest for the French. He lobbied for a new *bureau arabe* in Aïn Sefra served by two officers, an interpreter, and numerous local soldiers to provide "political and administrative service" for French soldiers and natives alike.[70] Lyautey argued that any effort to bring peace, prosperity, and progress to the region must include a more complete understanding of local affairs, particularly the movements and motivations of what French officials referred to as "tribes." He and his team of geographers and ethnographers thus developed maps showing French descriptions of tribal, racial, or ethnic divisions in the area. The information present in these maps did not emerge from academic study in Algiers; rather, he and his staff gathered it through direct contact with native elites themselves.

Following the methods prescribed by Gallieni and Faidherbe, Lyautey set out on an expedition to meet with tribal leaders in 1905, accompanied by a young *bureau arabe* officer from Géryville. *Bureaux* officers could assist Lyautey, he believed, in understanding the class structure of Arab tribes who he coded with racial language as the "most feudal" or "most warlike." He found most disturbing the continued practice among some border tribes of black slavery, an institution that he characterized as rendering the servants "subject to caste like the janissaries of the sultan."[71] Even their dress seemed to him straight from the "middle ages," as they wore long robes with gold decoration while on horseback. As the first French general to visit the tribe in seven years, Lyautey found the going difficult as he fought their "racial pride."[72] It appears that Lyautey saw this intransigence emanating from several directions. First, long periods without contact with the West had hardened the resolve of the Ouled Sidi Cheikh group to resist French political and social control in spite of its salutary effects. As he had discovered in Indochina and Madagascar, it took long periods of intense conflict for two distant sociopolitical groups to understand each other. Conversation between groups would result, from his experience, in a better understanding of native society for both the participants and the French colonial officials. Such mutual comprehension would then force the natives to conclude that their political future lay in close association with France.

Also standing in the way of communication for Lyautey was Islam. While he viewed Islamic education and science as sophisticated and in general a good influence, Lyautey also perceived the corresponding social structure as mired in place and resistant to change. Religion, he feared, impeded scientific and administrative access to the basic structures of society. Lyautey considered Arab-Islamic groups on the borderlands isolated "in time, in space … enveloped in the same shroud, defying life, movement and thought."[73] Trapped in the way of life practiced by the medieval Arab invaders of North Africa, the Sidi Cheikh seemed to Lyautey to refuse the helpful influence of contemporary Europe. Islam, once a progressive force, ceased to act in that way in the isolated desert, instead becoming "immutable … petrified in its implacable dream."[74] Only the jarring arrival of the French military, he mused, had the potential to push these people out of their cage in the deep past. Until the French found a way to force societies to move through time again, he thought, they had no chance to change things for the better.

Lyautey's reified vision of Islam as a cultural essence did not permit him to grasp either the potential influence of other Islamic groups or the importance of nomadic lineages in North and West African history. As Paul Marty and Maurice Delafosse would later find, African Islam existed in multiple forms. While Lyautey had spent significant time in conversation with native elites, he had not truly absorbed the importance of religious scholars in virtually all French African societies. Islam played host to vibrant intellectual communities concerned about matters from science to jurisprudence. North Africa alone had seen the exchange of intellectual currents from Morocco and Algeria across to the Arabian Peninsula and back, a process that in truth had been harmed and limited most by the colonial incursion itself. Although he was a lay reader of Ibn Khaldun, he paid little attention to the historical examples laid out by the scholar. Lyautey failed to consider Ibn Khaldun's conclusions on the adaptation of societies to their physical environment, particularly in political form, as a necessary antidote to urban decay and excess.[75]

Indeed, Ibn Khaldun saw sprawling imperial space as both the height of civilization and a necessary prerequisite for grand construction. He wrote, "To found a capital or construct a large city, there absolutely must be an [absolute] sovereign and an empire to provide the order," particularly as such an urban center would allow this "civilization" to drive the arts, literature, and science to "approach perfection."[76] He advised his readers that true development and advancement required the "loss of independence" by a people as they "allowed themselves to be directed by an authority outside of themselves. Divine law does not produce this effect, because its coercive power resides in our hearts."[77] Only a state could provide such structure. Much as French colonial thinkers and administrators argued, though, it was the power of state "sovereignty" that offered an intervening force, enabling rulers to protect their people while also controlling their output. Such sovereignty relied on "the sword and the quill" as the "two instruments deployed by the sovereign in the conduct of government."[78]

It was just this spirit that informed Lyautey's approach to colonial governance as he conquered with the "sword" and studied and recorded with the "quill." To accomplish change through scientific examination, Lyautey required control of both a colonial population and a military force. Geopolitical events, as mentioned above, gave him this chance. Lyautey (now a general of division) began the relatively slow conquest of Morocco in 1907, moving from his base along the border to occupy the Moroccan area of Oudja (near Marrakech), which he and his superiors believed was a base of raiding activity. Reassigned in 1908 to command the military region around Oran in Algeria, Lyautey had nonetheless earned the support of political leaders in Paris through the efforts of both the Algerian governor-general Jonnart and the powerful Eugène Etienne. The Agadir crisis of 1911, prompted by the arrival of a German warship in the Moroccan port city of that name and the deployment of a British force in reaction, brought the European conflict over the area to a head. French diplomats helped to resolve the crisis by passing control over some Central African territory to the Germans in exchange for total rights to "protect" Morocco from further international manipulation. In 1912, the French signed a new treaty with the Moroccan sultan, recognizing the need for a French protectorate modeled on that in place in Tunisia since 1881 and maintaining the Sharifian (implying descent of the Sultan from the Prophet Muhammad) government as titular head enjoying the support of the French resident general.

Lyautey, reassigned to command a French army corps in the French homeland in 1909, emerged as an obvious choice to lead the new combined state. The Franco-Moroccan administration required a new approach to colonial governance. In this new method, Lyautey paid homage to the Sultan even as he dictated and controlled political, military, and educational policy. As resident general from 1912 to 1925, the officer had his desired opportunity to experiment with change in a contained social, political, economic, and military environment. Indeed, Abdellah Hammoudi has described the enormous power of the Arabic translation of "Resident-General," a term that implied an omniscient, omnipresent leader who not only gazed down on his subjects from a position of authority but also inhabited their political, economic, social, and intellectual lives.[79] Much like Faidherbe in Senegal, Lyautey realized that Morocco was a complex skein of disparate cultural and social threads and conceived of himself as the person employing such referential power to combine them into a unified Franco-Moroccan fabric.

Blessed with a long history of centralization and a powerful state, Morocco lent itself to a simpler "social reconstruction" than the French had experienced in Algeria, Lyautey believed. Very few metropolitan French people lived in the area; it was far from a settler colony. Governance, thus, stood as a radically different task from that faced in Algeria. He argued for a protectorate based on "association, the collaboration of two races." Such a system protected "all the things that make up the soul of these people, their traditions, their customs, their beliefs, their hierarchy, their religion," an approach particularly important in light of what he perceived as the inextricably linked threads of Islamic religious, political, and legal practice.[80] He intended to maintain parallel political systems, reinstalling the Sultan (briefly displaced in the confusion surrounding the 1911 events) in 1912 with a promise to "bring him the pacification of his empire, the development of his resources and the progress of his institutions with the most complete respect for his beliefs and his religion."[81] Lyautey and his staff intended to convey this respect in the form of close study and cooperation with native populations.

Lyautey spent the bulk of time between 1912 and 1925 in Morocco, departing annually to argue for budget appropriations in Paris or on rare occasions for medical treatment. Most importantly, though, he left Morocco in December of 1916 for a short-lived appointment as the position of Minister of War as the First World War raged. When in Morocco, his only real interaction with the war had been to send off several of his subordinates as senior officers as well as a steady stream of native Moroccan soldiers. His failure to gain recognition for Moroccan soldiers for the highest French military honor, the *croix de guerre*, forced him to warn his superiors of the "disillusionment" their disavowal by metropolitan officials would spread in the protectorate.[82] Lyautey remained adamant about the need for close cooperation and dialogue with natives for the rest of his time in Morocco; during that time, though, resentment against the regime only grew.

Back in Morocco in 1917 after his abortive stint in metropolitan leadership, Lyautey found that reuniting Morocco would prove a difficult task. The resident general addressed this problem by implementation of the policy of the *grands caïds*, or reliance on native political chiefs to lead pacification and governance efforts at the local level. Lyautey saw these political chiefs, some of them intellectuals in their own right, as the best class to govern the more modern Morocco he was fighting to create. Many of these leaders were from the Moroccan aristocracy, a reinforcement of the existing social order that he viewed as productive.[83] Lyautey's emphasis on these noble, urban elites at the expense of the common, rural population cemented in his promulgation of "useful" and "useless" Morocco, a fundamental misunderstanding of sociopolitical structures that drove much of the unrest in the mountainous areas of the Rif for the entirety of his rule.[84] No amount of study could correct such myopia. Nonetheless, the French leader tried.

He and his staff, in an effort to control and to understand the social complexities of Morocco, examined extant Sharifian legal and political records while also consulting with the political elites themselves. He felt that only a detailed documentary and ethnographic study enabled colonial officials to bypass the "incoherent" approach that had long ago ruined Algeria, "sabotaged by an absurd native policy."[85] Development of this coherent native policy required a full consideration of Moroccan history. His administration embarked on a wide-ranging study to catalog all Moroccan groups, including both Berber and Arab, in order to adapt forms of political rule.[86] Regrettably for his administration, this historical and ethnological study fell short.

Most importantly, he failed to appreciate the complexities of the current Moroccan political system and their historical origins. Lyautey's associationist policy propped up those individuals who appeared to him legitimate heirs to power. He never considered the possibility that his choices for leaders reflected the echoes of French racial policies comparing Berber to Arab or the manipulations of Moroccan natives themselves looking for an increase in power under the paternalistic French administration. This failure to comprehend the sometimes dependent, sometimes dominant status of the Moroccan bureaucracy as part of the French colonial effort contributed significantly to Lyautey's failures later in his Moroccan tenure, revealed particularly by his inability to control the revolt of Abd al-Krim in the inhospitable Rif.[87] Indeed, in this misalignment of perception and reality lay the seeds of Lyautey's ultimate failure and that of the French colonial state. Initially ignoring the Rif rebellion as a minor regional dispute, Lyautey missed the transregional links of some rebels and instead applied heavier forms of political surveillance, a technique that would fail catastrophically again for Soustelle in Algeria of 1955.[88] These heavy-handed methods only stoked the flames of discontent even as some Moroccans gained insight on political alternatives. Ethnology could not deliver political legitimacy, regardless of its depth or breadth. Nonetheless, the general felt he could solve Morocco's problems through the conduct of a series of academic studies on Moroccan social life and continued the approach throughout his tenure even as the scope and scale of rebellion grew.

Conducted by native and Frenchman alike, Lyautey believed these studies could of themselves help to pacify the country. The general, since his time at Aïn Sefra, had periodically led campaigns into the Moroccan countryside to protect French citizen. In one such instance in 1903 near Casablanca, Lyautey received letters in both Arabic and French from rebel leaders seeking peace. Lyautey interpreted these gestures as natives expressing their admiration for the general's facility and interest in the Arabic language and Moroccan culture. In his mind, these leaders saw the possibilities afforded by closer cooperation with the French, via the policy of the *grands caïds*, and in working with a general willing to consider their particular social and political conditions. He does not appear to have considered, either then or in his later efforts to edit his correspondence and shape his image in the 1920s and 1930s,[89] the possibility that these leaders might have been manipulating his not insubstantial ego and belief in the power of learning. Indeed, he felt that knowledge could cure nearly all ills. Lyautey reported a 1915 conversation with a northern rebel leader, who, overcome by "an irresistible curiosity," requested safe passage to see the Casablanca Exposition. Presumably seeing the power of French knowledge and arms, Lyautey characterized the rebel leader's realization in dismissive terms as "he could do no better than to submit."[90] Scientific and ethnographic knowledge offered Lyautey power in the colonial context, however, only when its legitimacy stood beyond reproach. Scientific legitimacy and trustworthiness were vital to establishing his credibility as a colonial leader knowledgeable of and interested in his subjects. He tried to attain this level of legitimacy through one primary method: widespread and highly publicized ethnographic study in tandem with natives.

For the new resident general, political and social stability and progress came with detailed study in the location of interest. He ordered his experienced subordinates to conduct surveys of Morocco, moving "in automobile, without escort, from Rabat to Fez, from Casablanca to Marrakech," voyages he expected to enable them to "tell what they think of the state of the country and its inhabitants."[91] Implicit in these directions was the requirement to learn from the local populace, to converse with natives fluent in the language of their own social and cultural constructions. Such information could also come from cooperation with the colonial neighbors to the south in French West Africa, or *Afrique occidentale française* (AOF), formed as a unified colonial political entity in 1903. Since the combat of Faidherbe against the Islamic state of el-Hajj Umar Tal in the 1850s, governors in West Africa had dealt with local insurgencies in Senegal, Mauritania, and Côte d'Ivoire, to name a few.[92] Drawing on the understanding of "black" African-Islamic writing compiled by French Africanist scholars in West Africa, Lyautey's staff sought to develop more insightful ethnological institutions and policy dealing with native practices.

Lyautey turned to several prominent AOF Islamic and educational scholars to aid him in developing a systematic approach to understanding Moroccan social constructions. Paul Marty, former director of the native affairs bureau on the AOF staff in Dakar, moved to Morocco in 1921 to work for Lyautey in Islamic education and Muslim policy. Georges Hardy, former director of education in AOF, led the directorate of public education in Morocco, an effort that also incorporated heavy ethnological study. Hardy, long a collaborator of Marty, Maurice Delafosse, and other scholar-administrators in West Africa, brought the idea of administration by ethnological examination to Morocco. Hired at the end of 1919, Hardy carried an educational background focused on history and geography. He applied the principles of those disciplines to education, searching for "authentic" Moroccans frozen in time, an effort that privileged local Arabic sources sometimes at the expense of *evolué* natives capable of speaking, reading, and writing French.[93] Enfranchised francophonic Africans had enjoyed French legal and political rights in the so-called "Four Communes" of Senegal since the nineteenth century. In Algeria, where early French experiences had convinced administrators that Islam was ingrained, French-speaking elites gained French citizenship only if they renounced the political and legal institutions of Islam. French ethnological administrators such as Hardy or Delafosse distrusted, in general, these groups for what the French scholars believed were efforts to gain French favor through a superficial assumption of French norms.

Hardy presented his idealized vision of "traditional" societies in North and West Africa as *sui generis*, each requiring specifically tailored political or racial policies.[94] According to this approach, French scholars had to conduct ethnography with care, avoiding the pitfall of "fixing, crystallizing customs without the color of adaptation." Instead, Hardy advised colonial administrators to "take the continuing process of evolution into account."[95] In other words, Hardy had little use for a basic synchronic approach to ethnography. Change over time was at least as important as the social norms analysts could discern from a contemporary observation. For Hardy, only comparative analysis across time offered a chance to dissect societies.

In line with the concepts outlined by the French Africanist scholars of West Africa, comparison yielded a relatively sophisticated conceptual scheme for Hardy. Ethnology in his view produced a "sense of collective psychology," perhaps better referred to as "psycho-geography."[96] Hardy thus presented his case for the depiction of native peoples in collective terms. Scholars could distinguish, and thus better develop policy for, these groups through an appreciation for their unique modes of collective thought tied to their geographic location. A full grasp of their physical and social landscape in his view could come only from reading and hearing histories of the era as conveyed and interpreted by native savants themselves, with the additional analytical tools afforded by Western sociology and psychology.

As Lyautey had seen early in his career, information on social groups and the impetus to effect change came not from the top, but from those in daily contact. He saw consular personnel and other French functionaries, even settlers, as "the best source of information and the best catalyst for action."[97] With that said, Lyautey recognized the need for a deliberate information-gathering process. He had long recommended soldiers for such tasks. To that end he developed a new *service de renseignements*, run by the native affairs bureau of his staff, an organization he described as "a political service made up of intelligence officers and native people."[98] Drawn from the colonial service, Lyautey expected these French officers to exercise some Arabic-language ability and a willingness to serve in remote locations among native social and political groups.[99] He hoped for officers modeled after the service's first director, Colonel Henri Berriau, who Lyautey regarded as having not only knowledge of literary Arabic but also "the affective comprehension of the race." Lyautey hoped that this deep level of mutual understanding, which his language implied extended to the emotional realm, enabled these French officials to interact with natives on the same plane as if "they came from the same race." In his mind, all officers working with and among natives needed "the most modern, most practical, most audacious sense of the evolution that these people can accomplish,"[100] information best attained by ethnological and historical studies conducted in conjunction with the population.

While never as widespread as the original *bureaux arabes*, Lyautey employed 194 such officers in 1913. By the time of his 1925 exit from Morocco, Lyautey had convinced Parisian officials to increase the service to 273 officers. The officers came from wildly varied backgrounds, some like him from aristocratic families. Only one native Muslim North African commanded an office—Saïd Gueman in 1925 in Kebab.[101] Regardless of background, Lyautey expected these experts in native affairs to expand their knowledge by any possible means, from manuscript study to conversations with native elites.

In the style of most Western military administrations, Lyautey and his staff also worked to issue, to a certain extent, this native understanding to the officers charged with that day-to-day interaction. By controlling the tone and range of French officer knowledge on Moroccan society Lyautey ensured their efforts stayed in line, avoiding the problems that had befallen the *bureaux arabes* in Algeria. The program for officer education initiated by Hardy under Lyautey's watchful eye focused first on language ability. Responding to calls for more study of groups viewed by his subordinate commanders as not subject to "Arab civilization," Lyautey created an institute of Arabic and Berber language study in Rabat and a Berber studies center at Meknes in 1915. The resident general chartered the Berber studies center to focus on the reeducation of soldiers with experience in Algeria, including study of "a collection of works relating to Berber questions."[102] By 1921, the Arab-Berber school hosted courses and conferences for native affairs officers, including material from studies generated by the Berber studies institute.[103]

Conferences intended to explore these categories revolved, not surprisingly, around the social base for an improved political structure. At a 1921 instructional course, native officials from the *Direction des affaires chérifiennes*, the bureaucratic arm of the Sultan's government embedded in the French protectorate political structure, and French officials from the service of antiquities, arts, and historic monuments delivered a lecture on preservation of archaeological artifacts. The lecturers instructed native affairs officers in the importance of conservation even as the war of conquest continued, working together to avoid any repeat of the destruction in Algeria and Tunisia. The officials portrayed Moroccan cities as the beautiful "frame of Arab life" that reached back to the sixteenth century when "the degree of civilization was basically the same in France as in Morocco." Hewing to Lyautey's doctrine, the instructors described North

Africans who fell behind "the march of progress" as they failed to grasp the importance of new technologies, remaining tied to "tradition." Lyautey's staff thus directed the new French officials "to protect" as well as "a bit paradoxically, to civilize them [Moroccans]." Officials engaged in the *service de renseignements* and deeply concerned with native affairs were critical, lectured the bureaucrats, in maintaining the "long chain that links the country across the ages ... the poetry of the past."[104] Lyautey's subordinates thus passed on his vision of a glorious Moroccan past, one that remained beneath the veneer of underdevelopment and poverty. In the resident general's view, French officials could improve Morocco politically by embracing these basic fundamentals and molding new political, economic, and social structures to fit atop them.

During his tenure in Morocco, Lyautey also created political organs to promote more direct intellectual transfer between the French colonial and native Moroccan structures. The Native Policy Council (*conseil de politique indigène*, or CPI), created in 1921 to give equal voice to both the native affairs bureau and the Moroccan Sultanate, included Marty as secretary.[105] Marty's long colonial career included significant experience in developing native contacts, particularly along the Sahel. Over time, he had grown these networks to gain ethnological knowledge on social divisions and the reach of Islamic scholarship in West Africa. Marty thus brought important techniques on developing close relationships with Islamic elites, a vital skill in the process of governance that Lyautey proposed.

Georges Hardy, also a member of the council in his role as director of Public Education, contributed an additional ethnological perspective. His bureau ultimately included the *Institut des hautes etudes Marocaines* (IHEM), a scholarly research organization, and the *école des hautes études musulmanes* (EHEM), focused on the creation of a new educational track for professional Moroccans.[106] Both of these structures served as proof of the French right and need to govern as the keepers of knowledge.[107] However, education offered more than political justification or an instrument to generate the core of colonial functionaries. Departing from the original and more instrumental ideas of Faidherbe, the resident general proposed the equal involvement of both natives and Frenchmen in developing a new ethnological and historical understanding of the area and its people. Lyautey often attended conferences, lectures, and courses at IHEM and EHEM, making it clear that research drove policy decisions. Lyautey's scholarly organizations put together a journal, *Les archives berbères*, which offered publication opportunities for both native Moroccan and French scholars to go along with numerous conferences on languages, ethnography, and folklore.[108]

At one such CPI conference in 1921, Lyautey spelled out the importance of links between past and present for modern study of Morocco. He remarked, "We found here the crumbling vestiges of an admirable civilization, a great past ... Do not forget we are in the country of Ibn Khaldun, who arrived in Fez at the age of 20."[109] The resident general thus reminded his charges that Morocco, and Arabic intellectuals more generally, had much to contribute to the world, particularly through the remarkable insights of their intellectual class. In close cooperation with this group, Lyautey thought, the French stood a chance of understanding of local events. They could accomplish this, in his view, not through paternalism but rather through mutual admiration and association.

Lyautey's charge, however, overlooked the actual practice of his colonial administration, as William Hoisington has demonstrated. Despite Lyautey's calls for indirect rule and political administration by native Moroccan officials, the day-to-day operations of the protectorate functioned only at the behest of French officials themselves. Despite years of educational reform and bureaucratic expansion, decision making in the end lay only with French officials. The French presence, resented by Moroccans since the early twentieth century, prior to the protectorate, never provided avenues for political advancement for educated native leaders. Consequently, these elites, the only real hope for a continued French hold, disliked and worked actively against the French state in greater numbers, culminating in the Rif rebellion.[110] The employment of academic study and education did nothing but blind the administration to the sociopolitical reality in Morocco. Collaboration and association were not possible at scale regardless of the number of interviews conducted or books read.

Nonetheless, France's resident general operated from a basic assumption: Morocco and France would function better collaboratively. For example, he introduced French as the basic language of Moroccan schools, in the process bypassing Arabic in hopes of executing political ideas through a common European idiom. Rather than use the shared language to better understand Moroccan social and political norms, though, many of Lyautey's subordinates, particularly civilian administrators in the cities, instead saw French language as a mark of distinction, further solidifying the division between the superior French and lowly native Moroccan.[111] He expected, perhaps naively, that his subordinates shared the same passion to preserve, to respect, and to assist Moroccan society. He honestly believed that social knowledge would stoke the fires of reform and improved political rule that burned, in his view, in all intellectual classes.

He reminded his subordinates that Franco-Moroccan cooperation held the key: "The secret is the offered hand, not the condescending hand but the loyal man-to-man handshake made to understand one another."[112] This handshake, conducted in particular through the IHEM, could occur both in person and through a careful translation and analysis of archaeological and documentary evidence of the past. The work of Delafosse, Marty, and colleagues such as Ismael Hamet was vital, in Lyautey's depiction, to understanding the documentary links between past, present, and future.[113] Lyautey pushed this agenda at all levels of his administration; even the newest members of the interpreter corps in this period cited "Arab authors" in their ethnological-historical studies of the local countryside.[114] Attracting even French metropolitan academics,[115] Franco-Moroccan conferences featured presentations by native intellectuals.

In saluting the work of native scholars on education in 1922, Lyautey commented on the importance of close intellectual collaboration in Morocco, an effort that "had never before been achieved in such a skilled and even fashion." These exchanges were vital in his opinion to the advancement of the French cause, important enough to necessitate a mandated "purely native" group of presentations at each gathering of the IHEM.[116] Lyautey's program failed as the revolt of Abd al-Krim in the Rif grew worse in the 1920s. His inability to contain the revolt led the minister of war to send Marshal Philippe Pétain, the great French hero of the First World War, to intervene. Stripped of his all-encompassing powers, Lyautey left Morocco in 1925 for retirement in France, brought down by a revolt that he could neither defeat nor understand.

Continuing influence: Association through study

Lyautey's death from kidney disease in 1934 did not end his influence. He had maintained strong intellectual links between North and West Africa, working from the example of Faidherbe and Gallieni through his own experiences along the Mediterranean and in the Sahara, finding common ground in developing a strong, local understanding of social creation, composition, and tailored political rule. Maurice Delafosse, though he preceded Lyautey in death by eight years, also contributed to these networks. Like the renowned colonial general, he saw native institutions as entities that "needed protection and preservation," linked to a more glorious past that, with the proper intervention, could work in tight cooperation with France in an associationist structure. Delafosse was inspired by Lyautey's willingness to "administer the country in accordance with its institutions."[117] Later cited by Charles de Gaulle as a "man among men" working tirelessly on a "human project," Lyautey was initially buried in Rabat in October 1935, where he had been "profoundly respectful of the ancestral traditions of the Muslim religion held and practiced by the inhabitants of the Maghreb, beside whom he wanted to rest, in this earth he so loved."[118] Lyautey's attempt at an ethnologically informed associationist state had failed. In failing, it had provided Moroccans with political alternatives revealed in the inadequacies of pseudoscientific, artificial rule. Further scholars would take up the mantle of a rule informed by such study, in the process exacerbating the problems in what they attempted to solve: political inequality.

3

Engaging Native Sources to Develop an Informed Colonial State

Colonialism bred violence.

> They then ripped the skin from his back, which they held in front of his eyes; then his buttocks, then his anus. Following that, they pulled out one of his eyes that was then presented to the other, unhappy eye. Finally, they removed his sexual organs, which they inserted into his mouth. M. Rubino, still breathing, was then cut into pieces.[1]

Paul Marty offered this clinical description of the massacre of a French train conductor in 1910 as evidence of the savagery of some of the inhabitants of the forested region of northern Côte d'Ivoire, paying little attention to the conditions that caused such anger. Marty and his French Africanist colleague Maurice Delafosse worked hard to unearth and explain such deviations from European social norms. They hoped to uncover fundamental social and political structures so as to understand and employ natives in colonial governance, but only so far. Final authority must remain in the hands of French administrators, who could employ native Africans as sources and as occasionally intelligent contributors, but on French terms and often in something of a vacuum, removed from the reality of day-to-day colonial life.

In the process they tapped into preexisting networks of ethnological scholarship in and on West Africa. Both men served on the staff of the French colonial political federation, *l'Afrique occidentale française* (AOF), as advisers on Muslim affairs before and during the First World War. Their ethnologies of French West Africa ultimately shaped the official, political depiction of Islam and African societies while also informing the more theoretical sociological studies emerging from the French metropolitan center. It was their work that set the terms of discussion on political association and a new social science that embraced individual variance over immutable and linear rules of development and evolution.

Unlike their predecessors Louis Faidherbe, Joseph Gallieni, and Hubert Lyautey, Marty and Delafosse brought highly developed language skills and an ability to work in direct concert with both local French officials and native informants in developing their conclusions. These scholars made use of long-standing West African traditions of letter-writing as a form of political negotiation dealing with everything from border disputes to religious dogma. In translating and republishing these letters, French thinkers credited their thoughts without considering the possibility that the correspondence differed fundamentally from what had come before. In this typical anthropological bind, they failed to see that they altered the social system by their very presence as observers and translators.[2]

Instead, contact with these networks, turned to colonial purposes, permitted Marty and especially Delafosse to insert what they regarded as the native voice into discussions of development and political association occurring both in the colonies and in France. In this way they participated in the early moments of what James Scott has labeled the "socio-technical" and "middling modernist" effort to reform society via "technical procedures."[3] Shaped by colonial circumstances, these scholars believed in a more human form of colonial rule informed by the words and methods of the natives themselves. Hardly reformers, these thinkers nonetheless elevated the voices of carefully chosen native elites, valuing in particular the ideas found in referential manuscripts from the area. In so doing, they changed the conversations occurring in the colonies and the metropolitan center on the appropriate nature of colonial rule and on the method for achieving deep social understanding. Their analyses were largely internal, looking inward toward the colonies and rarely considering wider international trends or events. Reliant on native sources, they fit them into a narrow ethnological prism informed by their choices in translation and interpretation.

Penning the bulk of their analyses between 1912 and 1921, these French Africanist scholars observed a West African sociopolitical transition caused, at least in part, by the First World War. As France and the Entente worked to contain the German-Austrian-Ottoman alliance, they paid particular attention to the possibility of an anti-European Muslim solidarity. Consequently, French authorities, including Minister of War Gallieni, publically recognized that West Africans had "so generously [given] their blood for the safety of the wider nation."[4] Benefiting from this renewed government emphasis on Muslim support, Marty and Delafosse enjoyed significant monetary and investigative support from the colonial administration and the military during the period.[5] At the same time, these colonials constructed and credited links with other French academics, soldiers, administrators, and even missionaries.[6] Regardless of local connections, their colonial policy efforts centered on one important theme: the necessity of the French retention of power at virtually any cost. Marty's plaudits for AOF governor-general William Ponty's *politique des races* focused on the policy's modernity as a "derivative of the national principle that triumphs today among the armies of civilization," a concept that "proclaimed the equal human value of all peoples and their right to exist."[7] Marty saw this approach as optimum for the maintenance of French control but with an informed approach to native life, thereby facilitating both respect of native social and political structures and a closer working relationship between those entities and the French colonial state. Delafosse added to this platform a deliberate "program of study" that included anthropological, genealogical, ethnographic, and linguistic examinations of native populations.[8] In short, Delafosse and Marty struggled against the "assimilationist" view of colonial governance, voiced most powerfully in the First World War era by Blaise Diagne, a native African who represented the Senegalese four communes in the French legislature.

The communes, composed of the oldest French West African holdings of Saint Louis, Dakar, Gorée, and Rufisque, enjoyed status as a French department. Commune residents thus also enjoyed French political franchise. These populations, as evidenced by Diagne's presence in the French legislature, were citizens integrated into the French polity, unlike their Muslim peers in Algeria, who could gain full citizenship only through a renunciation of their rights to Islamic legal review. The success of these four polities, established as trading outposts by the French in the seventeenth century, served as important evidence for the validity of the assimilationist doctrine in the French colonial debate. For associationist French administrators, conversely, Diagne and his peers "ignored" the long civilizational history of Africans who had followed a developmental "path in a different direction." Efforts to move entirely to French-language instruction and governance, Marty and Delafosse scolded, employed assimilationist tenets that were either "false" or "premature," sometimes falling victim to the temptation to "tyrannically install our values in place of native customs."[9] Marty and Delafosse countered these political opponents by cultivating support in Parisian policy circles, achieved through both lobbying of French colonial parties and the publication and dissemination of their writings.

Far from drowned out by the power of metropolitan sociology, these academics actively shaped discussions of native structure and the processes by which it was created. In the words of Raymond Betts, "practice seemed to be preceding theory."[10] Important concepts came from dialogue with networks of natives in Africa. The dialogue with African intellectual elites occurred in both textual and oral forms with an emphasis on the textual. This choice of intellectual elites over a more common understanding limited the perspective of French Africanist scholars and caused them to focus on class, kinship, and Islam as key descriptive categories. These interpretations came to form an important component of French colonial rule, as both French colonial and native African exploited those connections to his advantage while creating a mutual unintelligibility.[11] The French tightened political control through the manipulation of African alliances and rivalries discerned through ethnological examination even as African elites solidified their political and social positions in the unequal power distribution of the colonial world by, in part, appropriating colonial language. At times missing real potential insights into political consequences offered by seminal scholars such as Ibn Khaldun, the resultant publications, methodologies, and concepts proved enormously influential in both metropolitan sociological and colonial policy circles. Employing methods advocated, but only partially achieved, by Faidherbe and Lyautey,[12] Delafosse and Marty provided the empirical and political core that would fuel the ethnological theories of Marcel Mauss into the 1930s and the machine of Algerian governance run by Jacques Soustelle in the 1950s.

The efforts of Marty and Delafosse, along with their colleagues Octave Houdas and Ismael Hamet, offer an important window on to the flowering of the intellectual rhizome under consideration here. French Africanists proposed a cultivation of native intellectuals, the "priestly and scientific flower of the population."[13] From this flowering, they expected to harvest leaders prepared to engage in a long-term collaboration with France as economic and intellectual partners. The growth and operation of this rhizomatic network demands close attention. It is thus important to turn away from a chronological study of scholarly lives and focus instead on the conversations informing and surrounding their work and the impact of those transfers. As the principal translators of the small but important trove of Arabic-language documents emerging from West Africa and reaching as far back as the fifteenth century, they acted as gatekeepers to native-generated knowledge on Africa.[14] Their demonstrations of the power of African learning influenced their peers in the colonies and the metropole to privilege information originating not in France but in the field, but always at the expense of native African writers and thinkers.

Class and the construction of networks

In building access to a wide array of sources, both Delafosse and Marty relied on long experience in Algeria, Morocco, Tunisia, and West Africa. Renowned for his language skills, Marty earned degrees in Arabic, history, and secondary education, expertise that set him apart from many of his colleagues and enabled him to delve deeply into the intellectual heritage and potential of Africa.[15] The young interpreter quickly earned recognition for his "perfect knowledge of the language" that included "idioms and customs of the region," even prompting a 1909 assessment as "a perfect observer who deeply understands the native mentality."[16] This evaluation, written during Marty's time in Morocco (1908–1912), found him seconded to Lyautey's Oran division. Lyautey praised Marty's "tact and great enthusiasm for work," as the junior officer pursued a deeper knowledge of local history.[17] Marty, now seen as "in the first rank of Arabic-speaking authorities,"[18] saw his military superior as "the great organizer, the genius leader who kept a finger on the path to the future."[19] Raised and educated in Algeria, Marty understood the necessity for an associationist approach built on local networks.

Delafosse's early academic and colonial career also revolved around colonial social study. Delafosse's teacher at the *école des langues orientales* beginning in 1890, Octave Houdas, served as his most important influence in this direction. He passed to his pupil the need to assemble a large "corpus" of native sources before reaching any conclusions; in particular, he emphasized the importance of textual recordings as central to any analysis of native civilization.[20] Such an emphasis required Marty, Delafosse, and their peers to privilege local elites in order to gain access to these sources. This required them to select specific intermediaries. In that quest they naturally focused on those willing to express both an interest and an agreement with colonial ideals of good governance. In short, French Africanists sought an intellectual class. They found such a group by weighing education, lifestyle, and relative social position.[21]

Finding such a class required further examination. Delafosse, who governed with an ethnographic eye during his tenure as *commandant de cercle* in Korhogo, Côte d'Ivoire in 1904–1905, issued explicit instructions to subordinates to find people with experience, particularly "old men."[22] Unconventional sources such as missionaries offered another access point. As teachers, these local inhabitants could assist in "penetrating the native mind" with notebooks of oral histories side-by-side with linguistic primers.[23] Marty also adopted this technique in his compendia, placing copies of native letters and documents side-by-side with French translation and commentary.

Searching for fellow intellectuals, Marty brought renewed energy to updating so-called *fiches de renseignements* (information cards) on Islamic leaders via communication with the French *commandants de cercle*, who provided raw data on prominent Islamic leaders. Each *fiche* contained basic biographical information: habitation, occupation, political disposition (e.g., "to be surveilled"), level of education, students, and any additional notes.[24] Many of these colonial administrators, perhaps current on Marty's latest publications, worked hard to provide information on Islamic education and the expansion of Sufi brotherhoods in the area.[25] Though abstracted from the day-to-day violence of the colonial overlordship, Marty and his peers actively participated in the knowledge enterprise that allowed such exploitation to continue.

French Africanists located these accounts via direct interaction with native intellectuals. These elites provided access to sophisticated oral histories. Delafosse recognized the importance of these troubadours to modern scholarship: "It is thanks to these traditional griots that we have some insight into the ancient stories of numerous native states."[26] Much like current scholars, Delafosse worried over the accuracy of such accounts. However, he found some satisfaction in a triangulation of sources: "As there are in general multiple *griots* dealing with the same task simultaneously it is possible, in consulting them one at a time, to cross-check and arrive at, if not certainty, at least a satisfactory approximation [of the true story]."[27] A comparative analysis of the oral accounts provided by multiple speakers aided Delafosse in this act of reconstruction by finding commonalities between stories.

Local elites offered decoding of this complicated combination of sources, particularly relating to history, genealogy, and Islam. Delafosse cultivated ties with the Senegalese Shaykh Musa Kamara, who provided him with strong insight into Islamic religious practices and history and offered a glimpse of early drafts of his Soudanese history.[28] Kamara was an accomplished scholar in his own right, focusing on Peul tradition with strong insights into the rise of Islam in West Africa.[29] Paul Marty maintained a similar association with many native scholars, including their work on genealogy of Sufi brotherhoods in annexes to his work in an implicit endorsement of their religious and political positions. In a telling example of such *quid pro quo* reproduced by Marty as exemplary, a native *shaykh* wrote to the AOF governor-general to request "your help and your surveillance" as well as "precise information" on nomadic raiders attacking his people. He offered his political allegiance and information on the local area in the language of the French civilizing mission, calling the French colonial administration the sole entity "who can improve this critical and primitive state."[30] The *shaykh* in this instance called on a French colonial tradition of suppression or control of Saharan Tuareg groups, who they perceived as destructive raiders of peaceful Sahelian sedentary communities. More than passive recipients of colonial largesse or even partners in an even dialogue, they participated in a larger discussion on the nature of African civilization while staking their own political claims.

These techniques of correspondence gave some native African elites, at the expense of their rivals, opportunities to gain a voice in the formulation of colonial policy via the scholarly representations of sociopolitical forms and particularly of Islam. Even the minimal or sometimes implicit respect given to these ethnographic correspondents by colonial ethnologists gave African natives credibility. In the process, these elites gained some measure of relief from the forms of direct colonial intervention proposed by other theorists. The ethnological approach of Marty and Delafosse thus informed the humanist reform impulse in the AOF and countered assimilationist ideas.[31] The search for the socially literate, often found at the top of religious and political communities, consumed Delafosse and Marty.

In this context knowledge led to power. Prominent Islamic scholars gained high positions in nearly all of the West African societies in part due to their connections to the wider world of Islamic scholarship, an interesting contrast with their French ethnological correspondents, who seemed blissfully ignorant of wider world affairs. These connections, in existence since as early as the tenth century, became particularly important between 1300 and 1550 as a surge of Islamic writing from outside the region entered local libraries.[32] West African intellectuals struggled both to connect themselves to this long line of Islamic learning and to show they had something to contribute to the larger discussion. In a vivid passage, late-eighteenth-century Arabic-language scholar al-Bartili cast those who "ignored science" as akin to "a blind beast" or even "a camel unable to see before it." In short, such limited thinkers simply "attributed information from a predecessor to a successor."[33] Each scholar had to create his own unique place while remaining mindful of the contributions of the surrounding community. It was precisely this technique that Marty and Delafosse pursued and, to a certain extent, emulated.

Native African elites, more than just intellectuals with similar views of the world, acted as brokers with access to manuscripts and oral histories. In one such instance, prominent West African Islamic scholar Shaykh Bay al-Kunti exchanged access to manuscripts for time with a French explorer's wide-ranging collection of genealogies. "The view of my manuscripts visibly piqued the curiosity" of the cleric, recalled the explorer, as "he extended an impatient hand, wanting to see with his own eyes the genealogies of *sharifs* that I possessed." With the examination complete, the *shaykh* "opened the centers of learning and before long my baggage grew with [the addition of] interesting manuscripts."[34] Shaykh Bay was no colonial stooge. He expected and received French gifts in exchange for his loyalty. In return, he offered support of the French military and political presence as a necessary evil brought on by power imbalances.[35] He acted as an independent entity physically removed from colonial power centers and manipulating the colonial state as best he could from a position of military impotence. Sahelian intellectuals shaped discussions with French scholars regarding lineage, working hard to maintain or overturn existing social structures so as to benefit themselves. They could manage such an exchange through the provision of those genealogies and histories that supported their political and ideological goals.[36]

Intellectual alliances then grew into political alliances, aiding the colonial state in its quest to develop and nurture sympathetic African political and social elites so as to make rule and ultimately development much easier. At the same time, this technique offered intellectual access to a new realm of knowledge and thus a new era of relative political stability achieved by the conversion of prominent native thinkers to the French cause. Most famously, Marty cultivated a strong relationship with Saad Buh (1850–1917), a prominent Sufi leader in West Africa, gaining from him significant insight into the composition of religious orders through family genealogies and correspondence.[37]

From these items, Marty located additional political and familial connections and rivalries ripe for political exploitation, in the process exposing colonial channels of communication for potential use by savvy local Islamic leaders.38

The Sahel in the early twentieth century stood exposed to such an intervention. The area had been in turmoil since the rise of the jihadist state of el-Hajj Umar Tal (d. 1868) in the 1850s. This powerful new Islamic movement worked to eject both the French and any remaining animist groups from the Saharan fringes of the Soudan and Mauritania.39 Saad Buh's father Muhammad Fadil, a prominent Sufi mystic and political leader, had initially aligned himself and his Sufi brotherhood with Umar, but eventually withdrew his support and retreated to the desert. The jihadist movement split populations along the Sahel into opposing camps, reigniting old debates between Tuareg, Arab, and black African groups.40 As Umar and his descendants suffered defeats at the hands of the French, led most notably by Faidherbe and Gallieni, in the second half of the nineteenth century, Saad Buh's brother Ma' al-Ainin rose as a new leader of the Islamic resistance movement to what he saw as the infidel colonial state. By 1909, still predating Marty's tenure in West Africa but reflective of the technique of "divide and rule," the native affairs office worked with Saad Buh to control the restive population. He was in a unique position to act in this capacity as a long-time correspondent, French ally, and leader of a powerful Sufi order that generally refused to support jihad.

Saad Buh's letter to his rebellious brother, then moving in the Mauritanian-Moroccan hinterlands, advised him to lay down his arms in the face of a vastly superior foe, a doctrine of nonviolence that had been the centerpiece of his father's political beliefs. In calling for an end to the jihad, the cleric depicted France as the carrier of stability to West Africa, an area torn by internecine warfare: "From the moment of my arrival in the Sahel, I found the entire Soudan region occupied by governments of powerful kings, tyrants, chiefs, savants. Since then France has constantly conquered them." The French were powerful militarily. Instead of resistance, Saad Buh advised that native scholars should focus on study and scholarship to develop a program of Islamic education, improving the lives of all people in the area.41 Such a message appealed to Marty and his colleagues for its call to nonviolence, the goal since Faidherbe's alignment with chiefs in the move into Cayor and other Senegalese territories in the 1850s. French scholars looked to their Islamic counterparts to extol the virtues of French civilization, as men such as Saad Buh, particularly in the early twentieth century, had significant authority and influence over other thinkers and religious leaders without strong connections to the colonial state.42

It took deep understanding of local societies to gain such access and influence. French Africanists believed this understanding came not from a single source but from an analysis that took the time to "compare written documents with oral traditions and to take everything possible from this comparison."43 While these French scholars stressed the importance of textual sources, they did not dismiss oral discussion. In an environment of few written documents, stories and legends sometimes offered the only chance to see history through native African eyes. These sources were authentically African, never before translated into European languages, completely devoid of "foreign influence," and representing in many cases, in Delafosse's expression, "a veritable emanation from the negro mind."44 Pre-Islamic history in particular appeared, for Marty, only after a close examination of literature, art, numismatics, and ethnographical data.⁴⁵ Ismael Hamet, a translator in the employ of the French colonial government in Algeria and AOF, found that "the culture of Arab letters climbed to a level of significant distinction" as chronicles and genealogies slowly replaced and recorded oral traditions. The lack of early texts made those that did survive all the more important. However, he advised that French scholars must not overlook the importance of oral transmission "from age to age, from generation to generation" of important historical facts. Hamet wondered, "Is there not, in these truly human documents, more scientific veracity than in the most authentic and carefully decoded parchment?"⁴⁶ Indeed, in the difficult environmental conditions of the Sahara and Sahel written information was precious, as a Marty informant commented: "I had old books belonging to my ancestors; the termites ate them. I have only those I copied myself."⁴⁷ Nonetheless, written records permitted immediate and long-lasting insight without personal inflection. Such sources would prove politically and scientifically invaluable. The translation of those documents into French gave colonial scholars great authority over African knowledge and the ability to shape wider views of African capabilities. History was an intellectual battleground.

French scholars of the Sahel thus took great interest in the content of native African libraries as a window on to a "center of active literature … important for the complete understanding of its [AOF] history."⁴⁸ Examining the libraries of Islamic scholars with "predominant" influence revealed the growth of an intellectual civilization "even in the middle of the Sahara."⁴⁹ Paul Marty found libraries and related university histories could generate a "sketch of the political and Muslim history [that] is indispensable for relating the past to the present and explaining one by the other."⁵⁰ Such documents could provide remarkable insight into the lineage of ideas in Africa. Consequently, AOF governors-general, guided at least in part by French Africanist scholars, sanctioned numerous expeditions to gain raw ethnographic data, including documents, in the early twentieth century. As early as 1903, AOF and Algerian governors collaborated closely on ethnographic examinations along the shared border between the colonial zones.⁵¹ All such expeditions necessarily focused on utility to the colonial enterprise, particularly the relationships between West African Sufi brotherhoods and the colonial state. One of these missions, from 1908 to 1909 and 1911 to 1912, netted 812 inscriptions and 223 manuscripts totaling more than 4,000 pages under the sponsorship of both colonial governors and academic institutions in the metropole.⁵² Another, smaller trip to the Timbuktu area in 1911–1913 found numerous obscure manuscripts and fragments that later became critical in the efforts of French Africanists to piece together the history of population movements in the area.⁵³ The empirical information gained by these expeditions served as fodder for the analyses of academics and scholarly colonial officials such as Marty and Delafosse.⁵⁴ Their choices in translation and representation were thus crucial to the flawed understanding of African society that informed colonial policy-making.

Prominent among these manuscripts stood the *Tarikh es-Soudan* (TS), long referenced by locals as the most important and comprehensive history of the Sahel into the sixteenth century. Indeed, many native African scholars sought access to the document themselves so as to better understand the area's history.⁵⁵ French scholars described the work as a "history of the blacks" with a detailed examination of the powerful and geographically extensive Songhay state and its successors. In translating and analyzing such an old text, French Africanists had to chase leads, matching partial fragments to form one large, complete manuscript that could be seen as definitive.[56]

Octave Houdas, Delafosse's mentor, led the translation effort of the TS. Developed from an examination of three separate manuscripts,[57] Houdas' version of the work focused on the apparent racial conflict between the more sophisticated and warlike "whites" from North Africa and the pure, underdeveloped blacks. The work appealed to the French scholars as it approached the Songhay Empire and the rest of the Sahel through critical intellectual eyes, paying homage to rulers who cultivated academic and literary development in the area.[58] It was the descendants of this esteemed intellectual class that interested Delafosse and his peers as key interlocutors and potential leaders.

At the same time, the manuscript offered easy-to-understand categories of local people. Houdas' introduction focused on the "feudal" nature of pre-Moroccan society in West Africa, where local notables "destroyed the governmental unity of the country." It took the Moroccans to generate a "protectorate" to allow for the continuation of local social structures with undue political unrest.[59] Such categories depended on local idioms, local social construction, and most importantly local histories and chains of knowledge. The long influence of Islam had driven an increasing focus on genealogy as an expression of difference, of class, of political form, even of race. These categories easily fit preconceived French notions of African society, making this writing a particularly fruitful source for translation and analysis.

Native Islamic elites placed significant weight on genealogy; it only made sense for French Africanists to follow their example and employ their modes of communication and analysis. The TS was an important example of this style of scholarship, as it fit squarely into a long tradition of Islamic writing that stretched across Africa and back to the Near East. In considering the TS, Delafosse, Houdas, and their peers had to reconstruct its place in the genealogy of African learning, in the process uncovering its importance and legitimacy as a source.

In French translation, the African author of the TS described the fall of the great Songhay dynasty to Moroccan invasion after 1591; by 1603, the Moroccan state in Timbuktu had fallen into a state of "decadence."[60] The author described the decline of the invading Moroccan empire as it slipped into excess, sacrificing purity as it became increasingly urban. Succeeding Moroccan dynasties, while claiming great power in the region, in truth led the area only further into disrepair and diminished the important intellectual world of Timbuktu while despoiling its place as a center of Islamic learning. Such description made great sense to French Africanist scholars seeking to understand so as to better link to black Africa and the Sahel.

Delafosse and Marty placed great stock in the historical depictions advanced by the author of the TS. In understanding the Arab-Berber-Black interaction along the Sahel in Mauritania, Senegal, French Soudan, and Niger, Marty made extensive use of the TS, in particular the stories relating the origins of Arab tribes and the progress of Islam across the Sahara.[61] From this early-modern chronicle, Houdas, Hamet, Delafosse, and Marty could begin to make sense of the convoluted relationship among civilizational groups in AOF.

The translation of the TS proved so important that French scholars sought similar documents to aid them in unraveling the region's convoluted history. French Africanists thus set their sights on a document rumored since the earliest days of European conquest. Explorers had told of an all-encompassing Arabic document on the history of the area, one that could serve as "the fundamental base of all historical documentation of the countries of the Niger delta."[62] Delafosse and Houdas set out to make the work, known to French Africanists as the *tarikh el-fettach* (TF), available in both French and Arabic in 1912 following its recovery by French explorers.[63] Despite questionable authorship, Houdas and Delafosse saw the chronicle as an important view into the intellectual capacity of people along the Sahel from the sixteenth to nineteenth centuries, as "blacks of Soninké origin" employed Songhay histories and Arabic script in a unique telling of local events.[64] The work, French scholars believed, offered outstanding insight into the origins of African groups and the genesis of moral laws. These laws, far from a structural given, were generated and manipulated by the people themselves, not imposed from outside.[65]

The mysterious author offered the work as a vital history of West African peoples. When approached by the king to write the history, the author at first declined. He ultimately undertook the work in part because "there is nothing anywhere else on most of these princes and there is no work dealing with those who took the title of king."[66] In this telling, Africans were as curious, if not more so, as the Europeans when it came to their origins. This curiosity, though, also complicated ethnological analysis. Ultimately, the history added confusion to the effort by French Africanists to understand West African societal origins. The author delved into pre-Islamic history to describe the originary "Kayamaga" and other Berber groups as deriving from non-Negro stock. The author proposed a migration of Himyarian soldiers from Yemen to the Sahel, where they intermarried with local women in the ancient capital of Gâo on the Niger and then spread southward, eventually participating in the conversion of the region to Islam.[67]

Exploration of these stories required Delafosse and his peers to employ more sophisticated, interdisciplinary techniques. To decode this history, he turned to archaeology, reading the Arabic sources closely to lead him to new sites. Medieval Arab geographical and travel accounts, when combined with TF and TS, provided insight on the locations of ancient Malian capital cities and even old Jewish settlements. Archaeological ruins revealed ancient settlements at sites indicated in medieval chronicles. Delafosse further discovered that many of these settlements carried local symbols indicating origins outside the region, including the "wells of Beni-Israël" and the town of Yani or Niani.[68] Written accounts thus gained greater credence through a separate but overlapping series of archaeological excavations.

Historian P. F. de Moraes Farias, however, has discovered numerous West African sources that highlight the holes in Delafosse's historico-archaeological methodology, however groundbreaking it may have been at the time. The privilege Delafosse accorded to written sources skewed his vision of West African history and left some deficiencies in his efforts to build an appropriate comprehension of overlapping political structures. Although Octave Houdas considered grave inscriptions and epigraphs as sources in that history, Delafosse dismissed them as ahistorical and of little real value, instead preferring the textual accounts from the TS and TF.[69] In the process, however, Delafosse lost sight of the specific late-sixteenth- and early-seventeenth-century moment in which the authors produced the texts. Moraes Farias has pointed out that the Timbuktu chroniclers so valued by Delafosse took little note of the centuries of epigraphy that surrounded them, instead attending to local political concerns. They wrote in order to negotiate a new status for the former Songhay ruling classes overcome by the Moroccan invasion of the late sixteenth century, thereby ignoring or overlooking the contributions of other African groups to political and social events in the area.[70] In his fervor to examine the written words of what he viewed as true African intellectuals, Delafosse generated a developmental portrait that privileged the claims of Timbuktu elites at the expense of a more complete and composite depiction of local events, an example of the power of African elites in negotiation with French colonial ethnologists, even across the centuries. Such a limited approach was in line with the general limitations of Delafosse's brand of ethnology and colonial governance, one built on the local and the internal.

This is not to say, though, that Delafosse considered only seventeenth-century chronicles in his work. Rather, he considered accounts from a variety of sources that proved, in at least some measure, the ability of African groups, both "black" and "white," to achieve great things. In just such an effort, Delafosse collected a series of stories relating to the area of Futa Toro located along the Sahel in Senegal, an area where "whites" and "blacks" frequently came into contact. Locally produced oral sagas, as opposed to the more traditional efforts to link West African Islamic lineages back through North Africa to the original Arabic conquerors or Yemeni immigrants, extolled black virtue. Delafosse's source, an African intellectual from the area, converted oral accounts into written documents and attributed them to an "ingenious savant": "I was disgusted by the religion of the whites and I came among the blacks to instruct myself in their religion and abandon the doctrine of those who hardly believe at all."[71] All history in West Africa was not dominated by notions of Arab invasion and the arrival of Islam as the key moments in history. Blacks extolled their own virtues in song, legend, and text and passed these on to French scholars in deliberate efforts to inject this view into the colonial project with an eye toward a more sympathetic and forgiving government. Hamet reflected, "Not only does the introduction of Arabic literature in the Sahara reach far back, this literature was wonderfully cultivated there, with success, by the Soudanese and Berber natives."[72] While many of these chronicles reported origins in Yemen or among the original Islamic conquest of North Africa by 'Uqba in the seventh century, some African authors remained skeptical, a critical marker for Delafosse and his peers in determining the legitimacy of historical accounts.

For example, in examining a fragmentary history of the Peul (Fulbé) people of West Africa written by Sultan Muhammad Bello, Delafosse praised the ruler for his "prudent conclusion." He found that the "author did not have great faith in the tradition he reported and for which he had searched, without much success, to clarify."[73] In other words, French Africanists expected critical analysis in legitimate local African academic writings. Historians who applied their desired critical eye and evidentiary requirements to local accounts gained significantly in credibility. The existence of critical local histories proved to French Africanists that West Africans, when held apart from their North African neighbors, were themselves capable of high literary and intellectual civilization and a self-critical analysis of origin myths. Because most of these analyses occurred in Arabic using Islamic techniques imported from the Middle East, French Africanists ascribed the sophisticated arguments, at least in part, to the influence of that tradition. French scholars then had to isolate and interact with the appropriate intellectual class, one viewed apart from racialized categories of difference.

One such West African group, the Sahelian Kunta people, had sophisticated written and oral histories of their prophetic lineage. These accounts, particularly when further substantiated by Ibn Khaldun or other medieval travelers and geographers, provided French Africanists with an opportunity to delve more deeply into links and discontinuities across the Sahara. Through a cross-examination of these origin myths, French Africanists hoped to grasp more fully the results of civilizational meetings along the desert edge. Paul Marty strove to find and to dissect these oral and written sources in what he called "historical reconstruction." Kunta elites, who Marty described, at times employing their language, as "white," "Moor," or "Arab," offered a voice similar to that of French Africanists, a link that appealed to the French scholars as they searched for a more definitive ethnological "truth" of African history. Marty appropriated local idioms that approximated European notions of race, dividing "true moors" from their "former slaves." The "Sahel Moor," in this depiction, was quite different from those originating in the "black states." These views, stemming from works such as the *Kitab et-Taraif* of Shaykh Sidi Muhammad (d. 1826), grew at least in part from contact with the libraries and ideas of local elites.[74] In searching for all angles of this "truth," French Africanists explored genealogies and local categories in ever-greater depth, relying in large part on their perceptions of locally generated idioms.

Kinship and the role of race

Delafosse made his first foray into the academic publishing world by tracing the non-African origins of groups, trying to explain the differentiation and sophistication of some West African societies, in particular the Peul through their ties to Hadrami Arabs in Somalia.[75] Although not cognizant of the implications at the time, Delafosse had entered one of the most sophisticated debates among native West African intellectuals. The Peul had long seemed outsiders to the area; their language and appearance simply did not fit with those of their neighbors. Peul intellectuals, anxious to depict their society as more developed and thus more capable of assuming leadership over neighboring groups, pointed to their status as white outsiders linked either to long-ago migrations of pre-Islamic Arabs from Yemen or to the original Muslim conquerors of North Africa. Conversing in this African language of race and origins gave Delafosse and Marty credibility to expand their networks of contacts in the region.[76]

In unraveling these myths, Delafosse and Marty focused on what they determined through conversations with locals as the most credible oral and written sources. Correspondence with Ismael Hamet and local elites such as Cheikh Sid Mohammed ben Cheikh Ahmed Ben Suleimane revealed key genealogists and their most important sources, from locally produced regional histories to the work of Ibn Khaldun. Indeed,

Ibn Khaldun had described a world in which "each tribe has its own group and family spirit," one that was both reinforced by and productive of the nomadic lifestyle. In the medieval thinker's analysis, "of all the connections that can unite a people, those of blood are the most intimate and the most forceful."[77] For the Europeans, following such links could provide final answers to larger debates on the effects of Arab invasions on local populations, for example.[78] Fear of the loss of what Timothy Cleaveland has termed "social or ethnic identity" drove many Arab or Berber authors to claim such descent, claims that rapidly gained powerful backing in the work of Marty and Delafosse.[79] Residents of colonial Mauritania such as Muhammad ibn Ahmad Yura ad-Daymani generated treatises claiming descent from the Beni Hassan Arab invaders, a touchstone of local African genealogical creativity.[80] Building from such emphasis, Delafosse could report traditions of "children of the sky" moving from the Yemeni coast or the Sinai to Africa, thereby reinforcing the social and political power linked to ancient and foreign origins.

Comparison of multiple texts offered a potential pathway to a sort of triangulated truth. Such a process, though, carried the risk of privileging locally reported concepts of social and political status.[81] As a result, Paul Marty considered such genealogies with caution, compiling massive numbers in the appendices of his writings to counterbalance one another, putting special credence on those coming from his closest native correspondents, particularly Shaykh Saad Buh. Delafosse noted the significant discrepancies between Arab and West African accounts, finding that adherence to Islam fundamentally changed the emphasis of descent claims. He found black African groups who, rather than follow the animist "wish to conserve and enhance the memory of divine ancestors," focused on links to early adherents to Islam through Arab bloodlines.[82]

Recent scholarship has focused on these genealogies as important for a number of reasons. To a certain extent, they became matters of "convenience," giving an easy linguistic link to pre-Islamic Arabian tribes. North African social groups, in many cases, appeared to graft names from ancient epics of invasion and conquest, using these stories to fill historical gaps and claim a more impressive lineage. This refashioning may have begun in the Western Sahara as early as the fifteenth century, when elites began to claim ties to Almoravid conquerors. But the spread of medieval Arabic literature in the eighteenth and nineteenth centuries provided a simple means to depict contemporary social turmoil as the product of a long-running process. African intellectuals accomplished this new self-description by writing local histories as continuations of famous texts, thereby legitimating the position of present elites. These rulers could claim status as the product of a long history of "arabization," where Berber elites struggled to maintain prominence as they fell under the control of Arab invaders. Claims of descent both constructed and legitimized later hierarchies and made the distribution of social roles seem an historical inevitability. Ties to Islamic conquerors and holy men strengthened political or ideological claims made by later rulers.[83]

At the same time, African slavery offered an important means by which to diversify, maintain, and even enhance the position of a kinship group. Kinship was far more than simply a notion of relatedness; in fact, it encompassed relationships between even the disparate political, religious, and economic groups involved in African slavery. Genealogical renderings of these groups, then, denoted more than descent. Proclamations of kinship tied elites to the management of economic and political structures that came with leadership of West African social groupings.[84]

Eighteenth- and nineteenth-century writers of these genealogies and chronicles, largely Muslim, thus fit themselves into a much longer line of intellectuals and complex social structures. By claiming ties to early works and thinkers, they spoke to a local Islamic audience while claiming a level of knowledge and truthfulness on par with their illustrious predecessors, avoiding any break in the chain of knowledge. Warrior-nobles could link themselves to the powerful Hassan Arab conquerors; clerical groups could gain moral authority, political prominence, and "charismatic capital" from links to sophisticated intellectual movements and religious commentators.[85] Along these lines Paul Marty noted, "The success of a Moor, of necessity a Sharif, is always assured in the land of the blacks." Claims to Arab-Islamic descent, generally recorded as oral histories but on occasion (as in the case of the Kunta) in written documents, served as the currency of social interaction.[86] By the twentieth century, Saad Buh, Shaykh Sidiyya, and other prominent West African religious intellectuals, still mindful of these links, also reproduced genealogies for a new, Western audience seeking an obvious ruling class. This connection to Western scholars provided an additional outlet through which leaders could proclaim their lines of descent. Through genealogical reproduction, the kinship group grew in power and credibility as its claims became more widespread and gained the legitimacy that came with reproduction in multiple circles. Native West African elites saw the power of genealogical Islam as a marker of their level of sophistication and worked to exploit connections with Westerners so as to claim the political and religious legitimacy that came with well-developed Islamic genealogies.[87] With this prominence came risk, however, as French scholars could manipulate the divisions introduced by kinship diagrams to their political advantage.

In searching for the best form of political association, Delafosse and Marty realized the need to engage this long genealogy. The success of the colonial state might depend on successful exploitation of those lineages. The French scholars settled on these kinship ties, or what they called the "extended family," as the most important and fundamental manifestation of African social order. Indeed, Marty's research indicated that even the Islamic conversion of prominent animist African lineages "had no influence … on their social life"; instead, kinship and descent formed the bedrock of African societies.[88] French Africanists concluded that African Muslims fixated on genealogy and descent as means by which to access political power, not to satisfy religious requirements. Genealogy was an African, not a Muslim, need.

However, the French scholars took the analysis deeper, determining that the need for genealogical connection drew, at an unconscious level, from a "primordial" need to remain connected to the "extended family."[89] Delafosse remarked that this extended family provided the "social element on which native society is based" while also acting as the only solid political structure. From his interactions with both animist and Sufi Islamic leaders, and the work of Marty on the latter, Delafosse concluded that African societies formed around a patriarchal system of political rule. Leaders of Sufi brotherhoods, sometimes in possession of both spiritual and temporal power, in his mind, capitalized on the prestige that came with claims to long Islamic descent.

Political chiefs who could tout not only a political position but also long links of kinship with prominent families, he thought, enjoyed far greater prestige and likely a larger swath of authority.[90]

In the typical Eurocentric view, Delafosse and Marty saw these links as reminiscent of the European Middle Ages when commoners at times took the name of and claimed kinship with local lords. Social, political, and religious power, they thought, came from these relationships; any French efforts to investigate or manipulate these connections had to take the family unit as the starting point.[91] The extended family represented both the "base and the term of social and political evolution" of native groups. Delafosse harangued his superiors that reform would occur only after understanding this inherently "patriarchal" form; developmental efforts would succeed only after the implementation of a deliberate program of reform centered on kinship.[92] The family, however, could not form the basis for a colonial state; for that, administrators had to consider groups of interconnected families as unitary civilizations. Delafosse proposed that French West African policy focus on collectivities, not individuals, as the basis for social and political organization.[93] A properly categorized and recognized collectivity must necessarily include kinship units as its basic social and political components. From this scientific description, Marty and Delafosse thought, the French colonial state could prepare and implement progressive policy. Such implementation, though, required a detailed understanding of social structure beyond the family group. They had to think about clans or tribes, avoiding transregional political complexity.

Political and social entities had undergone relatively rapid change in the preceding centuries, at least in part from climatic shifts. Historian James Webb has described the region's shifting frontiers of ethnicity and climate. Sahelian residents endured both "rapid ecological change" and successive Arab invasions that forced groups into contact beginning in earnest in the fourteenth century. With this movement came new groups, pastoralists who self-identified as "white" to set themselves apart from their "black" neighbors to the south. Pastoral nomads in many cases became "warrior" groups, in contrast to tributary sedentary groups employed as farmers or religious scholars fleeing the growing desiccation of the area.[94]

Similar processes played out, in Delafosse's description, across sub-Saharan Africa as environment shaped social development, an idea in line with the theories of Ibn Khaldun. Delafosse observed the shifting of social roles as pastoralists gained power in an area altered by a lack of rainfall. Côte d'Ivoire, on the other hand, suffered in some areas from too much vegetation. While similar to the Sahel as a site of civilizational crossing, the forest belt hosted bands mired in relative isolation. As for Ibn Khaldun, environment and social organization were intertwined. Building on ideas proposed by Greek and Roman theorists in antiquity, the great medieval scholar had found societal divisions and identities came first from climate, as color "came from the combination of the air with excessive heat," particularly near the equator, even as people of more northern climes "all had white skin because of the mixture of the air with extreme cold." Such interactions could also cause emotional changes, from the "gaiety" of warmer areas to the "sadness" of those in colder zones.[95] Arabs, for example, were "a fact of nature," whose appearance in "the course of human civilization" was environmentally predetermined. Lifestyles and social structures emerged from human interactions with the surrounding area. Life was proscribed. Arabs and Berbers remained most pure when in a more basic nomadic form because of the "poverty and privations" they suffered from "barren and hostile regions."[96] Transition occurred only with increased contact between groups, risking purity but infusing new ideas and driving people toward a sedentary lifestyle.

Delafosse engaged Ibn Khaldun on this idea of "common origins," as societies in West African locales had "evolved" into an "infinite variety" of new forms. Social and political groupings ranged from "savage" bands in the forests to the highly developed clerical and warrior lineages in the Sahel. These forms owed their differences to the effects of "geographic milieu on social and material activity" more than any other factor.[97] Intent on understanding the distinctions between even the sub-groups that made up these geographically determined "races," Delafosse looked to the past for an answer. He saw West Africa as subject to a swirling series of influences that moved on trade and migration routes, especially those from Egypt that "seemed to have influenced the civilization of most of the Negroes of West Africa."[98] The Saharan edge, then, served as an important site of civilizational contact, where North and East African "whites" encountered sub-Saharan "blacks."

Ibn Khaldun again offered a point of departure, a forum for discussion. Operating primarily through an historical lens, the fifteenth-century thinker tried to work by "applying general principles" that generated "rules that provided both philosophy and an understanding of the nature of beings." In his view, sedentary life must follow nomadism. The transition was inevitable, particularly as empires built cities and monuments to their political and social power. From these cities came contact with other peoples and the growth of art, architecture, and larger economic structures. For example, the growth of Tunis owed much to "the proximity of Europe" and the resultant contact that brought "many … practices that significantly augmented previously existing arts in the city."[99] Such transitions generated paradoxes as contact settled uneasily across the area. As empires grew a sedentary lifestyle, desert Berbers in the "poor class" lived as subsistence farmers while the "high class" continued a nomadic lifestyle, employing camels to move and fight with "lance in hand."[100] Berbers and Arabs existed in a tight but complex embrace, full of contradiction.

Delafosse and Marty also found these groups living side-by-side, on occasion intermixing, a state of affairs that proved baffling. However, with this confusion came opportunity. Delafosse and Marty saw the Sahel as host to a mix of "two great peoples, where two civilizations and two races interpenetrated and partially based themselves on each other."[101] The region operated as a crossing, producing not only new racial groups but also innovative intellectual products that reflected trans-African thought. Delafosse remarked that "most cities of the Sahel bring to mind Morocco or Algeria as much as the true black Africa; some are more Moroccan or Algerian than Negro."[102] Unbraiding the complex twisting of these groups required even deeper analysis. The process was not always positive, particularly with respect to its impact on the French ability to shape political forms to local needs.

Islamic Arab invasions had retarded the development of Berber groups, who could have had a salutary effect on black societies. Paul Marty lamented the Arab invasions as "altogether regrettable," as they caused the destruction of "Berber civilization, practical and progressive," and replaced it with Arab practices "derived from inveterate nomadism, incompatible with all serious evolution."[103] Ibn Khaldun had portrayed the Berbers as the original peoples of the area, who since "the oldest days" had "populated the plains, the mountains, the plateaus, the coastal regions, the countryside, and the cities." This originary strength was punctured "in the year 443 [1051–2]" when "Arabs entered Ifrikiya [modern-day Libya]," led by a warrior remembered as Ibn Yahya.[104] Building on this idea, French scholars described waves of Arab-Yemeni[105] invasion across the Sahara into the Sahel that had altered social structures and had given birth to new class divisions in the area. Warrior elites had then forced Berber groups into service as Islamic intellectual vassals. The French arrival in Africa halted this process, creating "centrifugal forces" that he expected, in time, to tear apart the political "confederation" of Arab and Berber.[106] These divisions could prove useful to French political requirements but did not fully satisfy French needs for social description.

Searching for another mechanism, Delafosse had in 1902 proposed linguistic and ethnic distinction as key to understanding social and political order among West African groups. During his survey of Ivorian border areas, he discovered that groups tended to cluster as linguistic units. Language served as the basic building block of nationality, ethnicity, and political allegiance, he proposed.[107] Ethnography could provide a more complete description of the distinctions between linguistic groups. For example, Delafosse described the linguistically defined "Northern Mandé" as a unitary Soudanese civilizational group. These "intelligent" people, he thought, were capable of close association with Western civilization, capable even of modeling themselves on the Western example. While "fanatical" Muslims, they were sufficiently flexible so as to make expedient political choices. Ultimately, these groups were "naturally attracted to progress [offered] exterior to their civilization."[108] Moreover, any belief in a total alteration of the complex African growth of nomadic and sedentary groups into a homogenized French product was, in Marty's words, "a beautiful utopia" beyond the grasp of the colonial state.[109] Developing a coherent political and social strategy to deal with this variety would require a deeper understanding of categories for use by the political state.

Marty tried to understand these important distinctions in the Soudan. He struggled to distinguish between the "local ethnic element" and "a caste of fishermen and watermen … who with time will end up as a veritable ethnic unity."[110] In his mind, caste structures were transitory, existing only as a stop on the way to well-defined, European-style ethnic divisions. In trying to describe a Songhay village, he alternately considered race as a "conglomeration" of "people with the same name" and as a cluster of former slaves from various areas that came together. After "losing memory of their origins," these peoples formed "a social class in truth, but one with people not far from being considered a race."[111] Marty thus proved himself unable to reconcile the complex interrelationship between socioeconomic status, genealogy and descent, and physical appearance. He attempted to link all such differences to European race, a concept not sufficiently diverse to describe local reality.

Delafosse, on the other hand, was more willing to see caste as a basic social form. He saw tripartite West African social divisions, with a ruling class, a large group of professionals or artisans, and slaves composing the three basic elements. The ruling class generally came from "a nobility composed of all those who can establish their genealogy and show that they have the right, since some ancient period, to carry the name of an honored clan." The professional, caste-bound group in the middle position of the hierarchy could claim descent from others of similar occupation; in this way, they assured their social position through historical recollection. Below these professionals lay slaves and former slaves, "those who do not know their background."[112] Genealogical memory proved an important distinguishing factor between groups in this model. Ultimately, Delafosse advocated for an understanding of race as foundational in 1924. "There is nothing but race," he wrote, each type sharing a unique mentality shaped primarily by environmental factors.[113] Embracing local complexity, Delafosse adapted his language late in his career to generate impact in French metropolitan and high-level colonial thought.

Delafosse could contrast these views, built from field observations, to the teachings of armchair anthropologists at the *Muséum d'histoire naturelle*.[114] Museum anthropologists depicted Africa as shaped by the movement of the "Hamitic [African descendants of Noah's son Ham] and Semitic [Near Eastern descendants of Noah's son Shem] groups." The migration of Arab-Semitic people into North Africa, a movement advanced by many French physical anthropologists who saw races as separate subspecies, became the motor of historical change in this model. For those who ascribed to this theory, "few Arabs" remained in the area, as the Berbers represented the predominant racial group with an overlaid Arab civilization: "the Arabs succeeded the Greco-Latins, and that is it."[115] Delafosse evaluated this approach as overly simplistic when compared with the great variety of African "civilizations" he had seen in person. True sociopolitical understanding necessitated further examination. This work required a deeper study of Islam, the confusing but seemingly pervasive force that the French had to co-opt in order to rule humanely but effectively.

Adapting to Islam

Islam could prove a useful force for the French colonial state. If understood and employed properly, the great politico-religious construct provided a means by which French Africanists could overcome their difficulties in understanding kinship and employing European racial concepts. In Marty's analysis, Africans, from "warriors" to "serfs and slaves," fled restrictive political and social rule in search of "another, more welcoming collectivity." Islam, French Africanists thought, had become entrenched in some communities in the sixteenth century by grafting on to the preexisting feudal order.[116] Islam was therefore a medieval entity. However, it had successfully placed itself atop existing African structures in a manner similar to the associationist state desired by the French Africanists. The establishment of a coherent Islamic policy would, in the eyes of Delafosse, help France to move past the significant distinctions between Islamic groups. Black Muslims, in contrast to animists, possessed a "mind opened by a more developed education and extended contacts with peoples of other regions." He concluded that those populations, however small, "have been the best collaborators with our native policy in West Africa."[117] French Islamic policy, according to this theory, had to consider the religious and social variations occurring across Africa. There could be no unitary Islamic policy; each branch of Islam, often based on a specific Sufi affiliation, deserved consideration for its unique merits. Such a varied view of Islam matched well with the French political approach in West Africa of distributing power by governing from the center but administering locally in order to adapt to local custom.[118] Islam would be key to the continued success of this method.

Delafosse recognized that "France has nothing more to fear from Muslims than non-Muslims in West Africa," owing at least in part to what he and his peers characterized as the largely superficial Islamic conversion of many black Africans. French policy, he concluded, should therefore rest on a "strict neutrality" when considering African religion.[119] In contrast, Marty saw Islam as one moment in the development of West African society. West Africa had entered this "Islamic stage of evolution" due to the guiding hand of "the preceding generation" of French colonial leaders in Senegal.[120] "Islamic renewal" pushed West African societies to the next stage of development both intellectually and politically, although it remained important for French officials to shape this process along pro-colonial lines. Sufi brotherhoods, so important in North Africa and growing in strength along the Sahel, could serve as "more than a religious banner." Instead, they could act as the basis of a "national principle."[121]

Thinking pragmatically, Marty saw these new national entities as useful structures for colonial control. The emergence of political forms based on a "French" Islam enabled close control by colonial officials. West African blacks lacked the "aggressive spirit" found in long-time Islamic converts elsewhere in Africa; he echoed Delafosse in concluding that the "Islamic danger" did not exist among these groups.[122] Marty thus took a more instrumental approach to the power of Islamic brotherhoods in West Africa. He disagreed with Delafosse's condemnation of colonial support of opposing Islamic orders as "deplorable." In contrast, Marty saw little harm in "religious rivalries" that augmented "racial animosities."[123] Clearly echoing the "divide and rule" ideas of Gallieni and Lyautey, Marty saw Islam as useful for colonial control. French policy beginning in this period moved along these lines as French administrators, intent on development, focused on support to clerical Islamic groups over those with less progressive, warrior-based leadership.[124]

Marty advocated fostering Islamic savants able to appeal to both Islamic and non-Islamic intellectual elites. Religious leaders, particularly those teachers who fit in the category of "intelligent and educated marabout [Islamic notable who also held some informal political authority]," exerted significant authority over all people in Côte d'Ivoire, including the "fetishists of the region."[125] While a long-standing French Algerian sentiment depicted Islam as a force working against the French presence, Marty perceived some individuals within the seemingly monolithic structure as interested in close cooperation. He praised the loyalist views of Shaykh Saad Buh and, in particular, Shaykh Sidiyya. Of the latter he remarked, "He permitted two people, two civilizations and religions to know one another and to consider themselves. He took a giant step ... towards the evolution our presence in Mauritania can offer to the Saharans."[126] Marty believed that Islamic leaders willing to view France as a useful, if not benevolent, force in the area could augment French political control while also enhancing the ability of natives to take command of their own political and social destinies. Islam, when considered in terms of its most liberal and pro-French elements, offered the means both to understand and to elevate African civilizations. Finding these elements required the cooperation of administrators and native Africans alike.

Information provided by AOF administrators, while not always completely accurate, did help Marty understand the active networks of religious and social knowledge production in West Africa, greatly aiding in his efforts to correspond with important Muslim scholars and leaders. These studies traced the connections of Islamic teachers to their affiliated Sufi order and even to their initial instructor, while also providing a demographic breakdown of the next generation of students.[127] Networks could yield information vital to the day-to-day maintenance of French colonial authority while also providing a means to access oral and manuscript histories of the local peoples. Marty could then use these sources to inform his larger analyses of Islam as both progressive and retarding force, particularly in education. In so doing, he missed any opportunity to consider the power of external, transregional connections outside of the West African sphere.

In the early twentieth century, Marty gathered information on the increasingly powerful Mauritanian Sufi leader Shaykh Hamallah bin Ahmed. He described him as an important mystic distrusted by some other Sufi leaders, but hardly dangerous. However, as Marty's tenure came to an end and ethnographic collection slowed, ill-informed French administrators saw Hamallah as a powerful anticolonial leader, a new version of their old adversary, Ma' al-Ainin. They exiled Hamallah and launched heavy military campaigns against his followers in the Sahel. French colonial administrators, lacking in ethnographic information and still unclear as to the relationship of the religious practices of the unconventional Sufi brotherhood to "traditional" Islam, ultimately targeted Hamallists as an anticolonial movement.[128] Marty, on the one hand, certainly saw Islam as a potential threat to be contained but did his best to gather sufficient information so as to inform colonial policy. On the other hand, his successors, at times lacking that critical ethnographic eye, tried to keep the colonial peace through the rapid suppression of any possible agitator, in the process alienating those they wished to govern.

In spite of some of his protestations, Marty struggled to place reformist Sufi orders, particularly along the Sahel. The Murid order of rural Senegal offered a particular challenge to his views. While Marty described the group as an aberrant threat to be contained, recent scholarship has found that it emerged from the interplay between its founder, Amadu Bamba, and the multifaceted world of colonial conquest, economic privation, and Sufi mysticism. Renouncing temporal power, Bamba led a group of devoted followers in creating a state within the French Senegalese colony devoted to brotherhood and learning. In the process the group gained significant control over West African trading networks and a measure of independence through a long process of give-and-take with colonial administrators and local populations.[129] Overlooking the salutary effects of Senegalese control of their own political and intellectual lives in an associationist political model, Marty depicted this Sufi order as disruptive of social norms and what he viewed as the traditional native values of work, allegiance, and the family.[130] However, the obvious differences between the Murid Sufi order, on the one hand, and more secular, animist chiefs, on the other, presented an opportunity for development. The rise of the Muridiyya, Marty thought, showed that the "Islamic religious wave" of jihadist states had slowed, leaving African societies fragmented in a number of different, localized variants.[131]

Fragmentation offered political and investigative opportunity for these French African scholars. Marty's views fit with those of most Western scholars of the early twentieth century in depicting the arrival of Islam in sub-Saharan Africa as occurring via movement from Libya, Algeria, and Morocco. These paths converged along the Sahel, offering varied approaches to Islamic learning and worship that contributed to the unique strains of the religion practiced in Niger, for example.[132] In colonial Upper Dahomey (modern-day Benin), Marty described Islam not as indigenous but as introduced like a sickness spread from neighbors in Niger,[133] much in contrast with the Peul of the Middle Niger basin, whose Islamic roots reached back, in his analysis, to the thirteenth century. The Peul maintained intellectual contact with thinkers in Arabia, at times perhaps hosting "white" proselytizing holy men.[134] Despite these long-standing ties to the larger world of Islam, Peul intellectuals had left little written scholarship of their own.

Marty concluded from this widespread lack of sub-Saharan black Arabic scholarship that black Islam in its most sophisticated form stood on a relatively static bedrock of local religion; innovation occurred not from within, but from without. Sahelian Islam, he thought, remained purely superficial; it survived and grew only via outside contact. The correlation between numbers of intellectuals and socioeconomic success, Marty theorized, perhaps explained the slow Islamic growth (when compared to the rest of the region) in Côte d'Ivoire. The French soldier-scholar depicted Ivorians as having little interest in the flow of people and ideas from North Africa and the Middle East, important sources for Islamic learning.[135] He felt some West Africans had not really accepted Islam in full social, intellectual, and even economic terms. Marty described the persistence of Sufi brotherhoods in West Africa, particularly the Tijaniyya and Qadiriyya, as dependent on North Africans: "They [black Africans] in general maintain epistolary relations with the Moorish shaykhs who taught and consecrated them and send them gifts from time to time."[136] While Marty thought French administrators needed to contain violent or anticolonial forms of Islam such as splinters of these brotherhoods, the African variant of Islam did not in truth threaten the colonial state.

Delafosse perceived the relative positions of Islam and animism a bit differently than did his colleague. In general, movement eastward along the Senegal and Niger rivers yielded fewer and fewer Muslims; many of those who had converted, Delafosse speculated, had done so only superficially, absorbing "Islamic civilization" without the religion. In the new colony of Haut-Sénégal-Niger, Delafosse reported roughly 1.1 million Muslims against 3.7 million animists. He identified only 600,000 of those Muslims as black Africans, with the rest identified as Arabs or Berbers.[137] Such statistics convinced Delafosse to press for more consideration of animism as an important religious and social source for native African communities. Many of these natives, he thought, operated under "a very deep attachment to their native soil." In Delafosse's opinion, a religion tied to the land seemed perfectly suited to this belief system: "Molded to his mentality and according to his desires," native animism stood "adapted to the milieu in which he [the native] lives; it suits him and is enough for him." This flexible form of religion permitted social and political development. Delafosse pointed out that even as Islamic states rose to great heights and crumbled, animist states such as the Mossi Empire persevered.[138] Islam was thus best as a developmental vehicle, not as a statement of political organization.

Along these lines, Ismael Hamet wrote, "The true principles of Islam have a civilizing value that accommodates the most deprived areas, that brings back the most barbarous humans."[139] For students of French West Africa, these "true principles" boiled down to those that helped to maintain the peace and enhanced cooperation with the colonial power and search for knowledge. Traditional Islam, despite its long history of animosity with the Christian West, provided a way to improve native thought patterns and learning techniques. For Paul Marty, "Islam constitutes certain progress in the primitive mentality of blacks … some of these blacks have actually already evolved."[140] Islam, when cosmopolitan and dedicated to the pursuit and spread of education and learning across the population, catalyzed native intellectual development. French Africanists agreed that Islam was, in the final analysis, most useful to colonial rule and the future civilizational advancement of West Africa when diluted by local animism and French scientific-educational inputs.

Ironically given his determinedly isolated approach to ethnological analysis, Delafosse imagined that societies in North and West Africa grew only through exposure to external forces. He compared Africans with children suffering from a "neglected" education but not lacking in intellectual capacity. In his mind, they needed teachers, not disdain. "For having entered the school of humanity late, they are no less dignified in taking up their place."[141] French colonial states, in Delafosse's mind, needed to investigate the intellectual condition of natives so as to present them with a tailored educational program. Islamic growth in the early twentieth century stemmed from the religion's allure as a source of renewal. Black Africans desired literacy and the apparent higher standard of living that came with Islamic identity. Not only did they become Muslim, but also they sent their children to develop Arabic literacy with Islamic marabouts.[142] French administrators, moreover, had to remain neutral in this growth of Arabic learning. Marty concluded that madrasas met with failure in black Africa, where Islam had not sufficiently "evolved." Only with the full spread of Islam into all corners of daily life would a society build an "entente cordiale between religion and science, between the faith of the sons of the Prophet and French civilization."[143] French Africanists thus theorized that the introduction of Islam into traditionally black areas would increase the emphasis on Arabic language learning, a useful fact in building a political-intellectual class ready to lead under French stewardship. High-level converts, Delafosse theorized, adopted Islam from a desire to "differentiate themselves from peasants." Through study of Islamic learning and theology, these converts claimed, according to Delafosse, "at least the appearance of scientific superiority," an important marker of intellectual, and thus political, preeminence.[144] A complete examination of the roots of Islamic adherence thus provided French scholars with significant insight into what they perceived as class distinctions and their social consequences.

Although not the "gleaming" center of learning depicted in legend, Marty thought Timbuktu served as a salutary example in this regard, as the "intellectual and moral" level of the city's residents far outstripped "that of other Soudanese," even if that progress was minor in comparison with that found in Europe or even Algiers.[145] Delafosse agreed with Marty's finding that Islamic learning represented the key to native attainment of hitherto unseen levels of education, particularly when exposed to the more refined and cosmopolitan ways of urban centers.[146] Literacy, intellectual growth, and political intelligence could only emerge from a tripartite exchange between the people, their religious and intellectual elite, and colonial officials.

Education stood as the key to this process. Direct access to pedagogy, in Marty's words, presented an opportunity not to create new Frenchmen but instead to strive for "the adaptation of future men to new conditions ... and the continuous evolution of the world."[147] Africa needed new leaders, "young men of good Muslim comportment and sufficiently knowing European civilization so as to enable them to contribute to the moral evolution of their country towards its new destiny."[148] Without question, these populations were ready for advancement; they lacked only a catalyst to push them to link to European structures.

In that willingness Marty saw opportunity. France would attract the loyalty of the upper classes of each African society who "desired progress."[149] In hopes of just such a movement, the French had set up combined Franco-Islamic schools known as *médersas* (madrasas) in North and West Africa, particularly near the Sahara, and staffed them with native intellectual elites and French teachers. Saharan intellectuals, for Marty and his colleagues, would contribute to the education of sub-Saharan blacks as they offered a certain "moral ascendancy" and "superiority of method" over their peers to the south. Black Africans, he thought, required further exposure to a distilled version of Islam, one imbued with the modern, rational views of secularized France to contain any possibility of anticolonial dissent.[150]

At the same time, the importance of Islamic learning provided insight into the values of the societies in question. Hamet commented that a rare manuscript became a "relic" in the hands of a family who zealously guarded the prestige that came from such a rare gem.[151] Houdas recognized the remarkable fluency of much of the West African writing, "sometimes more developed" than that found in North Africa. "The Soudanese seem to have better understood the task of biography and, as long as the sources do not lead them astray, they do not hesitate to speak with a certain grandiosity."[152] Delafosse made more significant strides in this regard, working with the director of primary education in AOF to promote publication by native scholars in the AOF scientific and educational bulletins.[153] Never privileging the views of his ethnographic informants in policy discussions, Delafosse nonetheless brought his filtered and translated notions of their ideas to wider conversations on the appropriate forms of scientific investigation and colonial governance.

Ethnological mobility, political influence, and theoretical impact

Shaping colonial policy required sway both in the colonies and in Paris. Delafosse, in writing about a fictional character named "Broussard," described these challenges in autobiographical fashion. The protagonist, having spent fifteen years in AOF in a life not unlike that of Delafosse, found "his name known in West Africa and at the same time not completely unknown in Paris," a depiction that fit the Africanist scholar as well.[154] Delafosse, Marty, Houdas, and Hamet developed important networks and reputations as thinkers and political theorists. As Islamic scholars in the Sahel and Sahara built up large libraries to develop their knowledge of religion and the world and to demonstrate intellectual sophistication, so too did Delafosse, Marty, Hamet, and others collect Arabic language works in an effort to gain a larger voice in policy circles. They could claim to speak in African terms, employing locally important expressions of social and political reality.

In their minds, French governors should model themselves on traditional African methods of rule, where intellectuals were trusted advisers. This view came, at least in part, from African chronicles. These native works described the political and social importance of such knowledge acquisition for Islamic elites: "Nacer Eddine did nothing without having consulted the savants and without their assent. He showed them much consideration, honored them and held them in particular esteem."[155] Much like their intellectual forebears, African thinkers made use of their environment to reshape their political destiny, using the language of science to construct connections and ideas that allowed them to build communities below and beyond French activity. Building those rhizomatic networks required years or even generations of effort and the adaptation of language employed by French Africanist scholars.

French Africanist language also evolved over time and through experience. With significant linguistic expertise and the support of metropolitan academics and powerful colonial officials, Delafosse earned his first position as a deputy regional administrator in Côte d'Ivoire in 1894. Working in the areas of Baoulé and Toumodi, Delafosse continued his research into 1895, establishing close ties with French academics who could give him access to networks of local African informants and their manuscripts across the Niger River region.[156] Throughout this time, Delafosse cultivated local ethnographic sources in developing his understanding of the area, finding significant time to conduct research in Côte d'Ivoire under the sponsorship of both Parisian academics and colonial administrators.[157] By 1901 the minister of colonies called on him to investigate the Côte d'Ivoire border areas, an area he had "brilliantly served since 1894." His presence was particularly important, the governor continued, in light of his knowledge of "the ethnographic character, the values and the language" of the local populations.[158] In 1902, the future AOF governor-general François Clozel, in publishing his then-definitive ethnographic work on Côte d'Ivoire, found Delafosse the greatest of Africanist scholars. The young social scientist showed Clozel "all that African ethnography and linguistics can hope to be."[159] Following in the footsteps of Octave Houdas, Delafosse disseminated his ethnological work across the AOF bureaucracy, as early-twentieth-century ministers and governors pressed their subordinates to consider scholarly works in local policy-making.[160]

Policy prominence brought metropolitan opportunity to French Africanists as well. When compiling his extensive geographic and ethnographic study of the border region in 1903, Delafosse traveled to Paris to work in the geographic service at the ministry of the colonies, an ideal location to ensure his ideas received attention. While never published as an academic study, these reports found their way into the hands of ministry officials who valued them sufficiently to give Delafosse a number of extensions to enhance the quality of his work.[161]

While Delafosse enjoyed this early prominence, Marty toiled in relative obscurity. However, his 1912 assignment as director of the Muslim Affairs bureau on the AOF staff in Dakar suddenly brought him to the fore. The AOF governor-general remarked in 1914 that "since his arrival in AOF [Marty] has not ceased to move and learn. He wrote very interesting travel reports from his particular point of view. His studies ... on Muslim traditions were widely commented on."[162] A later AOF governor-general may have purchased as many as 167 copies of Marty's *L'Islam au Sénégal* to teach new administrators the wide variance of religious beliefs across the region.[163] He gained academic credibility in metropolitan France as well, receiving academic prizes from the Collège de France, the Ministry of Public Instruction, and the Geographical Society of Paris.[164] Working closely with Delafosse, who had moved to AOF in 1915 as a special adviser to the recently appointed Governor-General Clozel, Marty influenced colonial policy from the ground up. They found some success during the two-year reign of Clozel, as their influence contributed a new political policy favoring association via chiefly lineages instead of the imposition of direct rule.[165] Renowned for his "erudition in the study of Islamic questions," Marty's publications gained the attention of AOF governors-general for the "important documentation" he offered to the leadership who noted their "importance and value" for local governance.[166] Indeed, Marty's publications continued to provide the primary description of native groups in contact with French colonists well into the twentieth century, influencing native and French analysts alike.[167]

Marty admired efforts of scholar-administrator-soldiers to understand native perspectives, particularly when they informed a political policy that he thought was to be "envied" for its liberal approach to native affairs.[168] Marty found AOF circulars of 1909 and 1911 particularly revealing of this approach: "Absolute and equal respect for all peoples, our subjects, their religious faith, their religious liberty and their customs and traditions as they are not at all contrary to the principles of our civilization."[169] Publishing these ideas in newspapers allowed French Africanists to disseminate their ideas while also gaining the political and fiscal sponsorship of powerful colonial ministers and lobbyists. For example, Delafosse pressed his argument in an influential colonial newspaper, *La Dépêche coloniale et maritime*, with a circulation of approximately eight thousand by 1913. He advocated for a colonial program based on "helping them [West African groups] to regain lost time." With Western assistance these groups would have the chance to "evolve towards a more finished state."[170] Delafosse, by then an important figure in political and academic discussions in both the metropole and the colonies, sought to counter persistent assimilationist thought through a public discussion of his findings. Each social group, in his view, had its own version of structure, as "civilization is multiple and no human civilization is of itself superior to others ... civilization is the manner by which men live in society."[171] The ideal colonial structure respected African political and social structures while giving them the support needed to regain their international footing. Only France could provide this assistance. The ideas seemed clear. They needed only to expand the audience.

The French found such an audience in fellow administrators and, in Delafosse's case, metropolitan students. He had lived in Paris from 1905 to 1910, teaching at the *école coloniale* and the *école des langues orientales*. The scholar thus enjoyed significant notoriety in Parisian academic circles, attracting the attention and assistance of prominent academics, in particular Arnold van Gennep and Marcel Mauss. Georges Hardy considered himself a disciple of Delafosse, agreeing in full with the need for "a simple entente, a simple alliance" with native groups. Hardy modeled his colonial policies and instruction on Delafosse's desire for "true progress, progress in depth, solid and durable progress."[172] He took this approach with him to a later position as director of the *école coloniale*, the training ground for administrators and Delafosse's former teaching post, where he could pass it on to future generations. Fellow graduate and Delafosse disciple Henri Labouret, graduate of the *école coloniale* and prominent administrator, academic, and theorist beginning in the 1930s, found that assimilation had failed at least since Colbert's 1674 directives to colonists to "instruct them [the peoples of Canada] in the maxims of our religion and our values."[173] European ideas on the appropriate form of colonial rule stretched back centuries and went beyond the political into the intellectual.

More than purely French phenomena, conversations on colonial ethnology took place on occasion in a multinational environment. Delafosse in particular worked closely with Lord Frederick Lugard, the influential former governor of British Nigeria and perhaps the most famous proponent of "indirect rule." Lugard, sometimes openly critical of European colonial policies, viewed ethnological inquiry as crucial to knowing and ruling subjects better.[174] Holding many of these same views, Delafosse saw the British statesman as both kindred spirit and example, as he and his form of colonial governance revealed that "the best method, to ensure the material and moral well-being of the population and its social progress, is to permit its [an African civilization] development along its own racial path."[175] The two men worked together in the years preceding Delafosse's death to form the International Institute of African Languages and Cultures at the University of London.[176] Much like the journals founded by Delafosse and his successors in AOF, Lugard's organization intended to foster "a closer association of scientific knowledge and research with practical affairs." This "connecting link between science and life" must necessarily include "brochures or texts written or dictated by Africans."[177] Delafosse and Lugard thus hardened the links between Africa and metropolitan academic and political centers. The views of Delafosse and Marty, including those of their close native collaborators, now appeared in international academic circles and propagated via newspapers, journals, and monographs.

Delafosse, Marty, and their peers founded a variety of journals dedicated to reformist principles, working in both France and Africa with French and native authors.[178] In 1929, Labouret teamed up with Hardy to run the journal *Outre-Mer* with a decidedly associationist slant, banking on the prestige a connection to Delafosse brought across the French and British colonial systems.[179] Working from Delafosse's earlier efforts to publish native ideas in French translation, Hardy and Labouret pointed out the "absolute necessity" of properly schooled administrators ready to deal with the "educated native" who was "devoted" to the French cause. Natives, they wrote, operated not only as ethnological sources but also as scholars in their own right, building on the work of trailblazing French scholars. To that end, the journal editors offered a prize for native authors writing in French in 1930.[180] These native writers had long been a part of colonial publication, stretching back to the efforts of Faidherbe in the mid-nineteenth century.

Following the cataclysm of deployment and return of the First World War, native scholars sponsored by Delafosse and his peers gained a foothold in colonial ethnological circles. Many of them first appeared as simply "courtiers" of French scholars such as Labouret or Delafosse.[181] However, several of them rose to prominence in later years, in particular Mamby Sidibé and Amadou Hampaté Bâ. Sidibé gained a scholarly reputation in French ethnological circles from publication in *Outre-Mer* and Hardy's *Bulletin de l'Enseignement de l'Afrique occidentale française*, building and participating in networks of scholarly and political exchange that contributed to the political order after the Second World War and into the postcolonial period. Perhaps most importantly, Sidibé founded a Niamey (Niger) branch of the *Institut français d'Afrique noire* (IFAN) in 1946. IFAN, which initially intended to offer a native perspective to French ethnological research and policy-making, ultimately created a core of intellectual elites who occupied high-level positions in government and academia in the new postcolonial states.[182] Sidibé and a few others also published in the most prestigious AOF journal, the *Bulletin du comité des études historiques et scientifiques de l'Afrique occidentale française*. Generated by a committee that originally included both Marty and Delafosse, the journal proclaimed itself the purveyor of the most scientific ethnological analysis and collection in the region.[183] These journals provided a means by which native Africans could position themselves both within and without the colonial state, appropriating colonial language for decidedly local requirements.

In this way, Africans generated what François Manchuelle has called "cultural nationalism" for West Africa, an idea echoed by James McDougall in the Algerian case.[184] For instance, a 1938 author using the pseudonym "Bou Haqq" considered the progress of civilization along the Sahel, the meeting point between "white" and "black." The Tuareg, formerly masters of the area, had fallen back into "decadence," living as though they were "feudal lords of another age."[185] The author, clearly well acquainted with colonial language of domination and racial distinction, turned it on local groups in an early form of political positioning, setting the stage for sociopolitical conflicts to come as the colonial state declined. Native Africans could not change or remove the system overnight. Instead, they devised local solutions to long-standing problems of colonial governance. They would stand ready to deploy these newly adapted idioms by the mid-twentieth century, most notably in Algeria as the French stubbornly clung to control. French scientific ethnological publication had given shape and voice to these concepts. Though inadvertent, these influences were hardly the last for French Africanist scholars.

Indeed, the connections they had generated had significant impact on French metropolitan social science as well. Delafosse recognized the potential for colonial connections to Parisian academia even before his time as an influential administrator. His alter ego "Broussard" discovered that presentations on native life at the Sorbonne sparked interest, but they were "insufficient and too vague" for someone hoping to understand life outside Europe. Scholars and eager students alike, the colonial functionary advised, would find the best information by asking someone who had been there and had seen native African societies in action.[186] Some metropolitan social scientists, having grown tired of armchair theoretical models, looked to Delafosse as the bridge between abstraction and empiricism: he stood as both a "man of action" and a "man of study."[187]

In addition to his colonial service and teaching requirements, Delafosse helped to form professional societies, including his cofounding of the new Parisian society of ethnography in 1920. Brought into close contact with Lucien Lévy-Bruhl, Arnold Van Gennep, Marcel Mauss, and other prominent sociologists in the metropole, Delafosse gained a reputation as the most important source for insight into questions on societal structures among "primitive" groups.[188] Lévy-Bruhl, when working with Mauss to develop the *Institut d'Ethnologie* (IE) at the Sorbonne in the early 1920s, consulted Delafosse first not only for his ethnological experience but also for his ability to destroy bureaucratic obstacles.[189] Mauss himself teamed with Delafosse in the Paris teaching community until the latter's death, and counseled student Alfred Métraux that Delafosse's language courses were "perfectly sufficient" as credit toward a degree at the IE, negating any need for further study.[190] Delafosse's views informed a more nuanced depiction of native groups. Rather than primitive sketches of European life in a previous era, they described alternate forms of social structure, worthy of study in their own right and helpful in determining the weaknesses in absolute models propagated by Emile Durkheim, Arthur Radcliffe-Brown, and other functionalist theorists of the early twentieth century.

Although not as well-connected as Delafosse in Parisian academic circles, Marty still felt himself part of the conversation regarding "primitive societies." In his work on Côte d'Ivoire, Marty viewed some of the inhabitants of the forest belt as exemplifying "what the Durkheim school calls the 'prelogical' mentality."[191] His statement, while a misguided description of Lévy-Bruhl's work as representative of Durkheim and his followers, nonetheless demonstrated his engagement with metropolitan social theory. Colonial scholars such as Marty were both aware of and interacting with metropolitan scholarship on African societies. French Africanists saw abstract Parisian social theory as limited while also neglecting the potential utility of new British, German, or American ideas. Consequently, these colonial scholars engaged largely with French work while trying to correct some of what they perceived as misinterpretations and generalizations. Without the means to do much of the research themselves in the early twentieth century, metropolitan sociologists began a slow turn to African scholars to lead the way. In this relationship, French Africanists provided empirical and at times theoretical support to publication and education in France proper. It fell to Delafosse to lead this movement.

Delafosse had written previously that efforts to define civilization or society outside of the "actual state of culture" implied a basic comparison of all collectivities to "the Civilization, ours."[192] Delafosse thus continued to find reconciliation of the profoundly Eurocentric views of the colonial civilizing mission and his basic notions of important, localized African culture and society quite difficult. He had long tried to remove himself from this bind by conducting detailed on-site observation and analysis that he hoped would deliver a holistic view of African civilization in its own right, not warped by any ideological prism.

Such a study was possible for Delafosse only in regions with a relatively unitary social structure. He thought he had found such an area in Haut-Sénégal-Niger during the first decade of the twentieth century. The Senegal and Niger river basins hosted populations organized around the same "guiding principles of customary law" as well as "organization of the family," "conception of justice," and "social state." He could thus demonstrate and explain "the characteristic principles of the native civilization" of the area.[193] The scholar examined the population through a three-part lens: the first focused on "anthropology (the body)," the second considered "ethnography (values)," and the third looked at "linguistics (dialects)." He thus acknowledged that physical differences, "the body," existed between groups, at least in the form of tattooing or other locally initiated physical changes. In determining a group's "values," he tried to discern the structure and mechanics of social organization. Delafosse ultimately found that "ethnic divisions" created a "social group, composed principally of a combination of extended families having a unique origin."[194] Social groups, in his view, distinguished themselves not by belief systems or physical characteristics, but by linguistic variance.

Delafosse wrote, "One of the best means to arrive at an understanding of the institutions of a human collectivity consists in collecting and analyzing the terms used by that collectivity to express the concepts related to these [social] institutions."[195] Local idioms, Delafosse theorized, offered insight into the very structure of the society they sought to explain. This approach considered natives as, at least subconsciously, intelligent interpreters of their own social reality. Linguistic analysis, he believed, must occur in the host language; he held that interpretation that followed on translation risked losing the nuances of a word's meaning found only in a full social context.[196] Delafosse thus considered the linguistic "stage of evolution" a classification that "did not necessarily indicate a shared heritage between these groups [societies sharing a similar language]."[197] In other words, Delafosse did not define a civilization by language. In his experience, several groups in West Africa shared a language similar to Peul, but they came in radically different migratory waves and from different origins in Africa or the Middle East. Societies at the same stage of social evolution, regardless of origins, might at the moment of ethnological examination overlap, thus giving the appearance of ancient kinship. He concluded that civilizations moved through some sort of absolute succession; there was a commonality between the "stages" reached by each group. For instance, he described "Negro-African languages" in three basic categories or stages, finding an "evolution of linguistic phenomena and a parallel evolution in the state of civilization" as languages changed to meet the material requirements of European societies resident at the apex of human development.[198] Delafosse's views deeply influenced Marcel Mauss and later thinkers as they struggled to deal with new structural concepts that seemed to remove the possibility of true human agency. Only with specificity could scholars gain real insight. Religion and race offered useful concepts for such examination.

The study of African religion, be it animism or Islam, yielded important gains in colonial administration and in science for these ethnologists. Scholars thought that religion offered a window into the fundamental composition of social groups, a prospect advanced most prominently by Marcel Mauss and his colleagues at the *école pratique des hautes études* in the first decades of the twentieth century. Moreover, Delafosse saw religion as a universal, timeless force always acting to "adapt and superimpose itself" on preexisting rituals and beliefs. Similar processes of adaptation unfolded, he wrote, "in all ages and in all human societies."[199]

Marty saw socioeconomic divisions rooted in racial distinctions that reached back centuries, as opposed to the intellectual self-selection proposed by Delafosse. For example, he wrote that Mauritanian groups with "Semitic blood" managed, by the passing down of an "uninterrupted tradition of [Islamic] faith and Arab culture, to conserve an Islam very close to that of the Orient." He proposed that racial groups generated by distinct historical, social, and political contexts employed different forms of social life.[200] In Marty's mind, African religion and social construction were both reflexive and intertwined; it was difficult, if not impossible, to extract one from the other. Religion expressed social structure, but was not at the base of human organization. Instead, he described religion as an important but still derivative form of larger societal structures.[201] Marty concluded that African civilization was not as simple as some previous writers had depicted; it took more than a brief examination of religion to get at the essence of West African societies.

Marty and Delafosse thus dismissed, perhaps inadvertently, the socioreligious theories of several prominent British social anthropologists as overly simplistic explanations of a more complex African social reality. By the late nineteenth and early twentieth centuries, social evolutionary theorists working from the ideas of Herbert Spencer had pointed to "aboriginal" populations in Africa and Australia as simple precursors of European modernity, locked in an older stage of a unilinear developmental path. This viewpoint, advanced most powerfully by British anthropologist Sir James Frazer, depicted all religion as descending from African "totemism" or "fetishism." Simply put, "totemic" theory held that Africans worshipped items or animals for religious meaning and as a means of proving kinship, thereby ensuring reproduction occurred only with those outside the kinship group with those of another totemic "tribe." Delafosse decried these efforts to describe local social structure as fundamentally religious and founded on "totemism" as badly misplaced. He cited Mauss in condemning the poor science involved in ethnological analyses that employed "a very large number of absurd and generalized uses of the word 'totem.'"[202] "This institution [totemic-clan names] appears to be," wrote Delafosse, "of an historic and social nature and does not carry any other significance, definitively, than as the memory of ancient feudal nobility."[203] Local study and circumstance revealed great variety in social forms and processes. Metropolitan scientists would have to take further steps to define the terms of engagement.

Conclusion

These two most prominent French scholars of West Africa lived relatively short lives, as Delafosse passed away in 1926 and Marty in 1938, both at the age of fifty-five.[204] Delafosse and Marty participated in a movement to humanize French colonial rule even as they struggled to understand and employ Islam as a tool of governance following the First World War. They operated in a time of tumult but remained characteristically, for French colonial scholars, ignorant of the effects of global conflict. The true contributions of Delafosse and Marty, though, were not in their ethnographies, studies that viewed African ideas through a largely translated European lens. Their colonial ideas adhered in many ways to presuppositions that placed black Africans at the bottom of a civilizational hierarchy, in some cases freezing them in time on a developmental spectrum.[205] Rather, their emphasis on knowledge gained at the source, in the colonies themselves, ultimately aided future generations of native Africans in their efforts to describe the worth of their civilization outside the dictates of the colonial state.

However, Delafosse, Marty, and their peers remained trapped in the colonial bind, conducting studies for the purposes of increasing European political domination. In doing so, however, they overlooked some of the more important of Ibn Khaldun's theories. Specifically, they lost sight of the fact that "foreign domination" served only to "extinguish the spirit" of subservient groups, in the process forcing the "retreat of civilization." Indeed, Ibn Khaldun had cautioned that "the system of government" had two options. The first proposed that rulers place "the interests of the public" before the needs of any sovereign. The second, more pernicious, placed the "interests of the sovereign" first in order to "consolidate his authority and grant him the force to dominate everyone else; the public good is nothing more than a secondary concern." Little more than lay readers of his work, Delafosse and Marty failed to understand their own role in enabling this domination. For Ibn Khaldun, the state, based on the centralization of power and force, threatened the public good if oriented incorrectly.[206]

Though failed as political theorists, Delafosse and Marty succeeded, at times inadvertently, in giving voice back to native African subjects. In the words of Léopold Sédar Senghor, later president of independent Senegal, Delafosse "not only affirmed the civilization values of black Africa, but proved them." Delafosse enabled an important "cultural dialogue" between France and Africa that proved enormously influential in academic and policy circles in the forty years following his death.[207] This dialogue informed metropolitan social theorists as they tried to understand human social composition. Moving beyond basic Durkheimian notions of ideal types and primitive representations of the European present, Marcel Mauss and his students focused on information gathered in the field from intelligent natives themselves, drawing on the vast repository of knowledge, however mediated, resident in the works of Marty and Delafosse. The metropolitan engagement of Mauss and his peers with African-generated ethnology, and its subsequent radiation back to the colonies for political implementation through a new generation of students, pushed this colonial rhizome ever further, changing form even as it grew.

4

Escaping Durkheim: Marcel Mauss and the Structural Turn

Dedicated to "combining the elements of scientific inquiry," Emile Durkheim and the founding members of the prestigious *Année Sociologique* (AS) journal vowed to study history in tandem with sociology if only to tap into the facts provided by examination of the past. The discipline provided them with a window to an earlier time of simpler social structure. Building on the foundation laid by Auguste Comte, Durkheim and his followers, including his nephew Marcel Mauss, formed the most powerful block of social scientists in France by the end of the nineteenth century. They rejected what they viewed as the overly simplistic notions of the physical anthropologists.[1] As the AS group stated in the journal's first issue, "Facts have no significance ... except when they are grouped in laws and types."[2] Durkheim and his disciples thus set out to understand the composition and activity of social groups; individual variation played little part.

Marcel Mauss, correspondent and professional colleague of Maurice Delafosse in Paris, was initially firmly in his uncle's camp with respect to the power of group analysis. Much more than Durkheim, though, he understood the implications of French colonial holdings and the debates raging over the proper political, economic, and social structures for governance. In his quest for a better sociology and a better ethnology, he both employed and undermined the French colonial state. Not avowedly political, Mauss nonetheless adopted the more relativist positions held by the associationist camp of Delafosse and Marty.[3] To that he added a powerful layer of metropolitan theory. In the process, he expanded and altered the range of possibilities available to colonial administrators and ethnological theorists. In Mauss's view, too many French social scientists operated with a flawed "sociological and prehistoric romanticism,"[4] which considered the European model as the baseline and overlooked the more local and individual origins of societal difference. Mauss constructed a new metropolitan French ethnological sociology based on knowledge generated in the colonies. In the process he spawned a new generation of social scientists grounded in empirical investigation and dedicated to firsthand observation of the colonies themselves.[5] By pressing for the use of on-site observation as part of university education, Mauss took advantage of a French academic establishment slowly reforming to permit views from outside the mainstream, with universities altering the staging of courses and the choices of degree concentrations apart from governmental dictates.[6] His concepts then radiated back to the colonies via fieldworkers and later political leaders.[7] Engaged in conversations with scholars from around the world, Mauss' emphasis on colonial information broadened his source base while exposing him to the internalized limitations of the ethnological approach of Maurice Delafosse and his colleagues. He did not heed the warnings of Georges Balandier and other late contemporaries of the powerful theoretical problems wrought by the "colonial situation" as it introduced compromises in the scientific method and cast doubt on any resulting conclusions.[8] Colonial science was beset by contradictions overlooked by Mauss in his search for an empirical basis for larger studies.

Although clearly not a colonial scholar, Mauss accepted the inputs of colleagues operating in Africa in formulating sophisticated theories of social structure and the sociological method. Pragmatically, Mauss and his colleagues at the *Institut d'ethnologie* (IE) in Paris employed the language of colonialism to gain state sponsorship of on-the-ground research. Hardly ardent colonial ideologues, Mauss and his colleagues nonetheless valued the colonies as sources of information, finding Africa and other non-Western locales sites of important insight into the basic social forms that evaded their investigations.

In chasing these social forms, Mauss reimagined the sociological and ethnological enterprise as part of a larger process of colonial information generation and theoretical explanation, again reducing the potential impact of broader international scholarly networks. Drawing on a wide range of sources from questionnaires to manuscripts,[9] Mauss and his students hoped to discern basic commonalities, ultimately leading to broad concepts such as the universality of the ritual of gift-giving.[10] These universal expressions, each of which he considered a "total social phenomenon," would combine the religious, legal, moral, familial, economic, and political forms of any society in one structure. The scholar's views both sustained and fed off descriptions of European exceptionalism, particularly those of the French Third Republic, which justified colonial domination of African and Asian peoples, as well as the teaching and research world emerging to support this new political and ideological plan.[11]

Such a bold research agenda demanded expansion of the ethnological rhizome. Mauss marshaled this growth with great skill. He cultivated contacts, disciples, and colleagues across the world. His British and American colleagues looked to Mauss as a central figure of the emerging anthropological discipline. He maintained ties to nearly all of them, from cultural relativist Franz Boas in the United States to pioneering fieldworker Bronislaw Malinowski in the United Kingdom.[12] At the same time, he trained the next generation of thinkers, driving them to understand society at its source, in the field. His teaching, characterized by Claude Lévi-Strauss as "highly esoteric," nonetheless exerted an enormous influence.[13] Future Algerian governor-general Jacques Soustelle found him "almost magically informed of everything, possessed of great flashes of insight." Other students praised the "man without preconceptions" who had "no dogmatism in him" and always placed "freedom and respect for others" ahead of other requirements.[14] The sociologist "ignored conventional contexts and never ceased to insist on the necessity in field ethnography of an insatiable curiosity across all domains," which he argued could result in an "encyclopedic" knowledge of a society and its artifacts.[15] For Mauss, the most important moment for social study occurred when people understood and took control of their social destinies. He wrote, "It is by considering the whole entity that we could perceive ... the fleeting moment ... when people become emotionally aware of themselves and of their situation vis-à-vis others. In this concrete observation of social life lies the means to uncover new facts."[16] Mauss thus found that social analysis fundamentally required an understanding of subjects, regardless of their status as European or non-Western, as intelligent interpreters and actors in their own social dramas, able to comprehend their own conditions. In the African field lay such possibilities.

Turning sociology toward ethnographic empiricism

Emerging on the social scientific and colonial scenes at the ideal moment, Mauss found himself at the center of the most important discussions in France. His willingness to bring sociology to the colonies and the colonies to sociology set him apart. His global connections enabled him to bring social knowledge together in ways never before possible in France or its colonies. It was this expansion, these connections, which enabled his ultimate theoretical successes.

Indeed, Mauss entered French academia at a moment of great transition, particularly in the social sciences. As the Third Republic struggled to establish a viable, long-term political structure for France, the population tried to come to terms with the humiliating defeat at the hands of Prussian invaders in the conflict of 1870–1871. Public and academic discussion, stoked by reformer politicians such as Jules Ferry in the 1880s, focused on the need for social renewal by means of a detailed sociological investigation and examination in the metropole. The searing effects of the Dreyfus affair beginning in the 1890s made this need even more urgent, as French society split over the proper involvement of religion and race in social and political organization.[17]

Several new sociological camps emerged in an effort to take advantage of the new opening provided by republican ideology. Republican thinkers in this period sought to legitimate imperial expansion by encoding their conclusions with what Pierre Bourdieu has described as the "symbolic efficacy" of the "absolute, universal, and eternal" truths promised by the French university and research establishment.[18] Durkheim emerged as the most powerful of these new sociologists, in the process developing his own school of like-minded thinkers, the aforementioned AS team. Establishing prominence for his new discipline required Durkheim simultaneously to widen his field of view to incorporate exciting new minds in linguistics, philosophy, and economics and to demarcate his science from others. His personal brilliance, recognized across the French academy, helped to push his work and that of his collaborators beyond that of historians, who when compared to him seemed to write only dense studies without obvious applicability to the modern world.[19]

Such distinction seems to have come from a natural inclination in both Durkheim and Mauss. Raised in strict Jewish households in Lorraine, the two men grew up with ancestors from both sides of the Franco-German border. In later life, Mauss remarked that this strict Jewish upbringing caused both he and his uncle to rebel against that lifestyle, instead dedicating themselves to science and rationality.[20] Acting as what historian Venita Datta has called "state intellectuals," Durkheim and Mauss entered a mainstream society that saw itself as increasingly secular.[21] The uncle's position at the University of Bordeaux, while perhaps on the margins of the rising French intellectual state, nonetheless offered access to further positions such as his 1902 appointment as a teaching professor at the Sorbonne. The resultant state-based funding and the opportunity for greater research allowed for the formation of the AS team in 1896 and for young scholars such as Mauss to build an ever-more ambitious agenda.[22] In the words of Bourdieu, Mauss faced few risks: his "position as glorious assistant saved him from the ridicule usually evoked by theoretical professions of faith of the crudest kind," helping him remain immune to many of the polemical attacks launched on his superior.[23] He could experiment with new theories and views, particularly in consultation with his good friend, historian, and AS colleague Henri Hubert.[24] "We were not a simple school of blind disciples around a master, a philosopher," he explained.[25] Instead, he pointed to the "superior certitude" the "descriptive sciences," such as ethnography, provided when compared with the "theoretical sciences," such as metaphysical philosophy. He thought that no single method, speculative or not, could adequately explain social phenomena. Rather, such exploration required ethnographic, historical, linguistic, and archaeological investigations capped by a more informed sociological analysis of the whole.[26]

Mauss and Durkheim wrote of this progression: "It is to ethnography and history that one must turn to trace the lines of civilization, to reattach diverse civilizations to their fundamental origins."[27] In this model, understanding civilizational groups required first the efforts of ethnography and history. From there, sociology could consider both the "most elementary" and the "most advanced" aspects of each society in formulating a unified theory. Sociology and ethnography needed each other; only from the combination of the sciences could analysts propose anything approaching the truth of social organization. While theoretically sound, this multidisciplinary approach failed to consider conditions in the colonies in their full context, particularly the compromised manner of information collection in an environment of unequal political, social, and legal rights.[28] Instead, Mauss focused on the potential for a massive growth of rich material for sociological and ethnological description.

In an effort to reach a wider empirical base, Mauss expanded the reach of the AS group. To that end, he induced Durkheim to work closely with Delafosse as early as 1911. Together, the men formed the *Institut français d'anthropologie*. Through this association and its successors, metropolitan and colonial ethnographers and linguists collaborated closely in developing a shared vision of the origins of social structures and their functions.[29] Ethnological conclusions were possible for Mauss only with the assistance of a "corps of ethnographers, whether professional or amateur, who can observe on site, with their eyes, who can furnish documents and assemble the material for collections." These fieldworkers were on the frontlines to conduct an "intensive ethnography." This examination consisted of "deep study of a tribe, a study as complete and quick as possible without omitting anything" and could conclude within "three or four years."[30]

Ambitious and hungry, by the late nineteenth century, Mauss stood as an *agrégé* ranked on a level commensurate with the more renowned philosophy graduates of the *école normale*.[31] Enrolled at the *Ecole pratique des hautes études* (EPHE) in Paris since 1895, Mauss spent time with fellow students and future social scientists Hubert and van Gennep. Ultimately, most interested in the social aspects of the newly formed section on "religious science," Mauss accepted a position teaching "religions of uncivilized peoples" in 1901.[32] The EPHE, at this time an upstart and unconventional institution in the conservative world of Parisian academia, added courses of study such as religious science, while the Sorbonne or other universities refused to change. Consequently, Mauss, a man from the edges of mainstream French society and operating against academic convention, employed the EPHE as a center of correspondence. From Paris he exchanged letters and served in academic societies with contacts in the colonies, particularly Africa, and in France to inform his ethnological studies.[33] These sources, both peers such as Delafosse and lower-level functionaries who served as information gatherers, shaped his understanding of foreign societies as unique in their own right. Each society developed implicit rules that governed interaction, but those forms appeared to the observer only after an in-depth examination.

During this period, no political movement could give as cosmopolitan a view of extra-French developments as socialism. Academics joined left-wing groups in part to retain a voice in political affairs, as they found themselves increasingly pushed to the side by political parties focused on the divisions of the Dreyfus Affair.[34] Mauss collaborated with the famed philosopher Lucien Lévy-Bruhl and other AS colleagues on socialist causes. Many of these academics published in the communist-leaning daily *l'Humanité*.[35] A fellow philosophy *agregé*, Lévy-Bruhl taught history and modern philosophy at the Sorbonne.[36] Most importantly, he provided Mauss a window on the colonies through his writings on the "primitive mind" and his connections with prominent French African intellectuals and administrators who he had met during previous travels in West Africa. Lévy-Bruhl's notion that "with very few exceptions, primitive peoples have no history" provided an easy strawman for Mauss to knock down.[37]

Lévy-Bruhl's conclusions echoed those of many metropolitan theorists of the era, who found that native groups had little to contribute to civilization, representing either an earlier stage of human evolution or simply standing as a breed apart. Mauss and other unconventional scholars challenged this reading of non-European thought processes as tainted with belief in the cultural superiority of European language and religion. Despite this basic disagreement, Lévy-Bruhl did provide Mauss access to a large network of colonial soldiers and administrators engaging in research "in place." He had a close relationship with a lieutenant governor of Niger and later governor-general of *Afrique occidentale française*, who encouraged research by metropolitan scholars to eliminate a perceived "lacuna" in metropolitan understanding of "our [French West African] races, so curious, so diverse."[38] Mauss saw the value of such associations and worked hard to find avenues to access African information. However, such links required the generation of new structures purpose-built to allow such examination on a wide scale.

Compromising with the colonial state: Institutionalizing ethnography

In order to ensure the long-term survival of ethnographically informed sociology, Mauss sought French state support and funding. He succeeded. However, that success brought with it a compromise, one that tied ethnography to the needs of the colonial state even as it sought deeper intellectual understanding of Africa and Africans. The process began relatively innocently, through Mauss's web of academic contacts both in the metropole and abroad. It grew from there to a large and well-funded enterprise devoted to colonial investigation in pursuit of the elusive total social fact but in fact generating more invasive forms of colonial control.

Mauss's views on the subject became even more important in the wake of the First World War. Highly decorated for his actions, Mauss returned home a changed man, as did most other veterans of the conflict.[39] Many of his colleagues died on the front lines and Durkheim passed away in November 1917. Mauss then took up Durkheim's mantle as the leader of French sociology: "I defended sociology everywhere and compromised from time to time on its behalf."[40] Many of Durkheim's closest disciples, who remained wedded to Comtean positivist progress, found themselves as anachronisms in an era torn by cataclysmic conflict and infused with pessimism. Consequently, no immediate analytical alternatives to the AS school emerged in postwar France. In fact, only two schools of scholarship remained open to sociologists: the colonial-international ethnological research institute of Mauss and academic sociology focused on metropolitan France. The latter found its center in Paris at the *école normale* and became the new standard in French social science. Many scholars with views outside this mainstream, unable to find jobs at universities or research institutes, fled abroad to the Soviet Union, the United States, or Germany. Perhaps employing the not-insubstantial residual influence of his uncle, Mauss fought this tide ably, establishing himself as a leading sociological voice in France while pressing the benefits of ethnology via his international and colonial connections.[41]

Arnold van Gennep, Mauss' prickly classmate at EPHE and ethnographic veteran of Algeria, aided his colleague in these moves. Beginning in 1901, van Gennep applied his wide-ranging intellect to ethnographic study,[42] developing questionnaires for use by colonial functionaries and advocating for the institutionalization of the science in France and the colonies.[43] Information collection, so critical to van Gennep for "knowing the needs and tendencies of the governed and administered," had to take place in the field. Seeing themselves as kindred spirits, Mauss and van Gennep worked together in the first decade of the twentieth century to insert ethnography into university curricula, hoping to correct the "lamentable situation" in which the discipline found itself in France. Their collaboration culminated in Mauss' 1913 article on the state of French ethnography.[44] In that article, Mauss complained of the poor state of the discipline in France, finding strong examples only in the work of Faidherbe and several other colonial officers and administrators since 1830.[45] This article called for a new method of social understanding, a crusade that resulted in the creation of the *Institut d'Ethnologie* (IE) at the Sorbonne in 1925. Mauss' recommendation for the improvement of French social investigation rested on a simple requirement: respect for native knowledge. Van Gennep's experiences and input certainly informed Mauss' perspective, as the former had spent time in Tlemcen cafés, observing what he saw as the rapid disintegration of native Algerian society due to French influence.[46] Mauss' fervor to rebuild sociology as an empirical science drove him to ever-greater collaboration with the colonial state as both cure and cover for administrative problems.

He joined forces with Lévy-Bruhl, Delafosse, and anthropologist Paul Rivet to institutionalize this ethnological approach. In 1920, this union formed the *société française d'ethnographie* from the remnants of various ethnographic and folklore associations. Dedicated to assembling colonial ethnology as fuel for the emerging generation of French social scientists, the men initiated a new era in education. "A new horizon appeared before our eyes," recalled Jacques Soustelle, among the first students of the new IE. "We young researchers discovered a whole new world and our teachers gave us the keys."[47] Beyond a simple professional society, the social scientists had to create the IE structure, which when properly funded would allow for full-scale investigation and data-gathering. Gaining sponsorship required assumption of colonial rhetoric. "When a colony includes populations of an inferior civilization, or very different from ours," wrote Lévy-Bruhl, "good ethnologists can be equally as necessary as good engineers, good foresters or good doctors."[48] The French state thus needed this investigation to ensure its long-term success in the colonies.

Mauss, leveraging his international reputation and position as Durkheim's intellectual heir, successfully lobbied the director of Higher Education and the rector of the University of Paris to assist him in convincing the minister of public instruction to create the IE. Couched in the language of colonial governance and reform and modeled on the work of Delafosse and his peers, Mauss called for the institute to "organize, encourage and accelerate ethnographic study in France and in particular in the French colonies." He argued that the resultant studies of "inferior races, peoples, civilizations" were critical enablers of a colonial administration able to provide "our tutelage" in helping colonial subjects to "prosper." Mauss concluded that ethnological examination would refine colonial methods and aid decision-makers in their efforts to "definitively and practically assess colonial policy." Finally, he convinced academic and colonial officials that ethnology was most important as the "sole means of providing for the education, the march towards civilization of these peoples."[49] Mauss's proposed fieldwork thus gained political credibility and legitimacy through direct association with the civilizing mission. Colonial ethnology in Mauss's conception would reveal native societies and thus inform policy adapted to those forms. Intent on the advance of his research agenda, Mauss remained ignorant to the lived experience of colonialism, finding it a useful vehicle for study without considering the political and social violence it wrought. Colonial connections were useful for academic legitimacy.

As proof of their positive colonial intentions, Mauss and his affiliates needed only to point to their long history of collaboration with Africanist scholars. Beyond Delafosse, Mauss and the AS team had worked with Edmond Doutté, a sociologist and Islamologist of North Africa, beginning as early as 1913. Mauss enjoyed Doutté's "sociological and ethnographic sense" and his desire "to be useful to civilization, to the progress of his region, to his friends the Berbers and Arabs." He even concluded that Doutté's views on religion in Morocco "formed the base on which the actions of the republic rested during the protectorate." Mauss thus credited the scholar for the success of the colonial mission in North Africa: "it is Doutté who founded the tradition to which Marshal Lyautey adhered."[50] Lyautey's administration in Algeria and Morocco appeared in French ethnological literature as taking a progressive view of Islam, a religion helpful in the ultimate goal of enhancing native intellectual capabilities through its position as a conduit to a dynamic civilizational past. French colonial governments, in this model, had to cultivate native intellectual elites as the leaders of local political structures supported by a largely separate French colonial state. Delafosse offered an important avenue to explore these policy and academic angles further.

The Africanist scholar had been important to Mauss's ethnological thinking since the years preceding the First World War. While he recognized the brilliance of Delafosse's wide-ranging ethnographic depiction of African societies as distinct, important, and complex in *Haut-Sénégal-Niger* in particular, he lamented that French Africanists had not yet provided an equally exhaustive study of other groups on the continent.[51] The very brilliance of the few extant studies pointed Mauss to the need for a more systematic approach according to the principles pioneered by Delafosse and Marty. Mauss and his colleagues could then apply these data to more general conclusions on the universal forms of human interaction.[52] Mauss suspected numerous colonial administrators were capable of insights equally important to the development of ethnology and sociology. Mauss and Lévy-Bruhl thus called on Delafosse not only to develop such sources himself—he was largely absent from the colonies after 1919—but to push other administrators to conduct similar investigations throughout Africa.[53]

Delafosse then activated networks of interested colonial reformers and savants to conduct such research. For example, in 1921, Henri Labouret, a young French army captain then in Upper Volta, filled out an ethnographic questionnaire on the local population generated by Mauss, Delafosse, and Lévy-Bruhl. In his reply, he requested Mauss respond to ethnographic and sociological questions he would submit "from time to time in the course of my research."[54] Mauss, now an important figure in international ethnology, served as a personal waypoint for the transfer of analysis. Both ends of the African-Parisian ethnological exchange benefited from the reciprocity implied by this communication. Mauss collected ethnographic data and astute ethnological analysis when available from colonial scholar-administrators such as Delafosse. In return, his French African correspondents enhanced their metropolitan academic connections. The resultant networks of ethnological knowledge served as a sort of clearinghouse, a "center for receipt and dissemination" of ethnology generated outside France.[55] Though anchored firmly in the conclusions of French thinkers at the expense of native Africans, this approach nonetheless brought credibility. The strength of this seeming diversity would protect the IE via the patronage of colonial leaders and a firm place in French academia above the line of any potential budget cuts. Connection to the colonies and to colonial thinkers gave the institute more permanence and less risk.

At the same time, colonial knowledge had to reduce intellectual risk. Mauss and his colleagues had to take adequate steps to secure valuable source material and local colonial information. In no position to criticize the ethnographic work of French Africanists due to his lack of time outside of Europe, Mauss identified himself as lacking in "the competence of missionaries or colonials" in dealing with native matters. Mauss thus acknowledged the importance of scholarly networks. He never did any true ethnological fieldwork, but did, on one occasion, travel to the "field" outside France. He saw his own brief 1930 foray into Morocco as "a bit of ethnography, but as an amateur, entirely at my cost and for my own education."[56] He left it to the next generation of scholars, trained in Paris but with significant field experience, to bridge this divide, linking up with powerful networks of ethnological knowledge already resident in the colonies and yielding a more informed sociological product. Mauss thus failed to understand the real limitations of colonial African information gathering, one filtered through translations and dependent on colonial interaction with African elites providing the material for analysis. These connections were valuable but came without real intellectual self-examination or caveat.

Delafosse enhanced these two-way connections by tapping both metropolitan and colonial academics to serve on the boards of scholarly ethnographic and ethnological societies and to publish in journals. These associations ultimately linked the "laboratories" of African field ethnology with language and colonial schools in the metropole, thus providing a point of entry for colonial savants or administrators to an increasingly receptive sociological community searching for an identity in the wake of Durkheim's death.[57] Together the groups, which Lévy-Bruhl characterized as "concerned with the same questions," advanced "ethnological science and put the results of that science at the service of our native policy when it is requested."[58] Working closely with professors from the Sorbonne, the *Collège de France*, the *Muséum national d'histoire naturelle*, the EPHE, the *école coloniale*, and the *école des langues orientales*, Mauss and his colleagues positioned the IE to train students from all of those schools to conduct ethnological fieldwork in support of both academic and colonial requirements.[59] The limited and mediated views of this approach then radiated widely, ensuring the survival of the methodological flaws.

Through liaison with these governors, the IE sent investigations across the globe, adding to the storehouse of social knowledge and providing colonial governments with studies of "native races" and "social facts" intended to further their understanding of Berber political structures in Algeria, for instance.[60] Despite the power of information generated in the colonies, explained Mauss's mentor and fellow IE board member Louis Finot, colonial governments needed to be "stimulated by pleas coming from Paris and bearing the official stamp." Only through a combination of local knowledge and metropolitan political pressure could academics develop a broad base for ethnological research, from there moving into publication, Finot advised.[61] In other words, the organization would have neither political nor academic impact without an administrative and organizational foundation beneath the colonial surface. Reform of both science and the form of colonial governance required a sort of deal with the devil, working with the colonial state so as to influence it.

Mauss and his colleagues recognized that funding stood as the most important variable in the long-term survival of institutional ethnology. They exploited connections in the French metropolitan and colonial governments to establish a financial base for ethnographic study. Soustelle recalled that they "managed to extract from the clutches of government officials and the pockets of private patrons the funds needed to send young researchers, fresh out of the Sorbonne, to their first assignment in the field."[62] Much of this money came from French governmental agencies, such as the anthropological establishments of the *Muséum* and most importantly the *Conseil National de Recherche Scientifique* (CNRS), an organization that included Mauss, Rivet, and Soustelle on its advisory board at different times.[63]

Mauss, Delafosse, and the other IE founders placed heavy emphasis on support from these agencies. Reaching out to their colonial correspondents, the board members cajoled additional funding from the International Institute of African Languages and Cultures founded by Delafosse and Lugard and managed by Henri Labouret in the 1930s.[64] The IE most prolifically exploited connections to the American Rockefeller Foundation for grants beginning in 1926. Employing his status as esteemed colleague to Arthur Radcliffe-Brown, Boas, and other celebrated anthropologists of the era, Mauss toured research institutes in the United States and United Kingdom and garnered financial sponsorship for research in Africa, including more than 400,000 francs for Marcel Griaule's paradigm-shifting Dakar-Djibouti mission of 1931–1933 and 150–200,000 francs for a later Griaule mission to West Africa. This money helped the IE and French government proclaim "a Centre of Ethnological Studies" in French African territories.[65] The IE also sent research teams to Indochina, the Pacific island colonies, and the Americas.

Mauss and the IE sent these fieldworkers to conduct their examinations with an array of ethnographic guides. With these guides, he hoped to standardize the collection of ethnographic information, making it more useful for subsequent ethnological and then sociological analysis. Based in part on the earlier anthropometric directives by Louis Faidherbe and Paul Topinard in Algeria, the new materials also included a detailed ethnographic questionnaire developed by Mauss, a guide on the conservation of art, and an additional linguistic form.[66] Mauss's lessons to prospective fieldworkers included three primary focus areas. First, he expected them to understand "social morphology," or basic social representations, including demography, human geography, and the use of technology. He also stressed "general phenomena," such as language, reaction to natural occurrences, international interaction, and "collective ethnology," or the society's own depictions of itself relative to other civilizational groups. Finally, he pushed his students to understand the "physiology" of a society, including their day-to-day techniques and technology of esthetics, economy, law, religion, and science.[67]

Griaule's Dakar-Djibouti expedition of 1931–1933 was a notable example of the scale of these ethnological efforts. A student of Mauss, Griaule possessed expertise in African languages and archaeology and had led a previous expedition to Abyssinia (Ethiopia).[68] His trans-African expedition demonstrated the potential of ethnographic fieldwork. Funded by twenty-three different French government organizations and the American Rockefeller Foundation, Griaule and his group collected, by their reckoning, 3,500 ethnographic objects, 6,000 photographs, and 200 specimens while retaining notes in more than 30 languages.[69] Griaule followed Mauss's teachings closely as he directed his team to use "extensive" examinations to collect a wide range of objects, a process that Alice Conklin has called "parasitic ethnography" in recognition of its reliance on taking rather than studying in context.[70] In any case, Griaule's teams reported the selection of important items for "intensive" examination, considering them not as detached artifacts but in a detailed ethnographic context. From this level of description, Griaule formulated numerous conclusions as to the nature of social construction in the area while also providing data to inform metropolitan theory,[71] a progression close to Mauss's ideal model for social analysis. Discussions with natives permitted Griaule to describe the cosmology of groups such as the West African Dogon, providing an important addition to the studies of Delafosse and Marty on native religion.

This brilliant interwar cohort of Mauss's students at the IE also included Germaine Tillion, part of a new wave of prominent French female scholars. She initiated her studies in "people known as 'non-civilized'" in 1930. Mauss acted as her thesis supervisor from 1934 to 1940, strongly suggesting to her that she conduct fieldwork in Algeria.[72] He saw her as a "serious and conscientious" student who would ultimately produce "the best application of exhaustive research methods on an organized society."[73] Women such as Tillion had the potential, in the eyes of male metropolitan scientists, to access a heretofore largely untapped ethnographic resource: native women. Unlike Faidherbe or Delafosse, who had both married native women in Africa, Tillion could interact with African women without the hindrance of long-running European perceptions of gender inequities. From this perspective, Mauss and his peers thought, female scientists would deliver unmatched insights particularly into home life.

During her time observing the remote Berber groups living in the Aurès Mountains, Tillion wrote regularly to Mauss for counsel and to provide progress reports. In 1937 Tillion confirmed, "We [Tillion and colleague Thérèse Rivière] are adhering to the directives that we received from you; we have studied the rest of the Aurès and have found that the choice of the Oueld Abderrahmane to study was the best."[74] During their time with this Chaouïa Berber group, the students gathered numerous ethnological sources, including descriptions of what the French portrayed as "prehistory"; an ethnographic study of 300 notables with further analysis of their family names and affiliations; objects for display in the museum; and a collection of songs and origin myths.[75] Working from the example set by Delafosse and Marty, Tillion, Mauss, and others then used this ethnographic data in an effort to describe the complex relationship between Islam, genealogy, and kinship in Africa. Although certainly never complete or fully understood, they began to attach ethnographic collections to sociohistorical context.

Mauss's influence on ethnological method extended beyond that practiced by his students. Claude Lévi-Strauss, the most celebrated French anthropologist of the twentieth century, never took a class with Mauss. However, even he felt the direct impact of the man he saw as the "master" of ethnography and ethnology.[76] The two initiated correspondence in 1931, when Lévi-Strauss sought to interview Mauss regarding his military background. Their association continued through the 1930s. Mauss, with the assistance of Soustelle and Rivet, helped Lévi-Strauss gather 40,000 francs to continue his Brazilian research in 1936. The young scholar later claimed that his ethnological conclusions, based on research conducted "on the ground," agreed with those proposed by Mauss.[77]

Owing in part to his long relationship with Delafosse and Doutté, Mauss understood the value of ethnological knowledge generated in the colonies, employing it in his own understanding of race and civilization. As he wrote to Arthur Radcliffe-Brown in 1924, "The good old comparative method, improved, has me as its defender. But it must be agreed that this typology of civilizations instead of societies is beginning to take shape. I hesitate to subordinate us to historians, but we must take it into account."[78] A basic sociological comparison of civilizational groups did not suffice for Mauss in this new order. He believed that he and his peers required a fully informed depiction of native societies to understand the past, present, and future of social groups in totality. His teams would struggle, unfortunately, to place these data in the necessary context that followed the tainted circumstances of collection and analysis.

The search for the total social fact

Relative comparison remained the hallmark of Mauss's methodology throughout his sociological and ethnological career. While he agreed with Durkheim that the study of "primitive societies" was essential, he found non-Western groups important to sociology not because they were evolutionary predecessors to Western society but because they were complex and distinct forms opened by colonial rule to a detached, cross-sectional scan. The truth of social organization, in this view, appeared only after extensive observation followed by comparative ethnological and sociological analysis. Mauss harbored positivist thoughts of the value of scientific examination descended from those of Delafosse and pushed those concepts to his students in understanding the world as a whole.

Mauss saw that observation was vital in understanding societies; he believed that fieldwork provided the only reliable data for informed conclusions on the origins of social behavior. However, that positivism did not jibe with social evolutionary theories. Mauss rejected the position of many of his illustrious predecessors who studied "primitive" societies for the light they could shed on the European present and past. As Lévi-Strauss recalled, "He once told this writer it is easier to study the digestive process in the oyster than in man; but this does not mean that the higher vertebrates were formerly shell-fishes."[79] Mauss felt that evolutionary social scientists committed one grave error: they discerned a direct developmental link between societies that were in reality quite different. At the same time, he eschewed disciplinary dogmatism in favor of an interdisciplinary view of subject societies that included history and geography molded together under the umbrella of sociology. Such a "comparative method" avoided some of the pitfalls of Durkheimian and Comtean sociology, as it was "less pretentious but simpler and more nuanced."[80] Mauss felt this relativism enabled him to see societies through a wider lens; focused and synchronic investigation risked losing perspective.

An obsession with pure observation tended too far toward positivism and its now-rejected call for universal progress through the worship of objective science. Mauss remarked that adherents of Comtean positivism ended up "observing nothing but coincidence." Instead, he argued that ethnographers must perceive each society in its present state. This analytical and methodological approach would, in his view, permit scientists to combine a "positive policy" with a "complete and concrete sociology." Scientific examination gave Mauss some hope for alleviating colonial problems: "If it [science] does not yield practical solutions, it will at least provide a sense of the rational action [to pursue]."[81] Mauss's view of colonial ethnology presupposed a deep understanding of native societies built not from abstract theorization but from experience on the ground among and in conversation with the natives themselves. Only after detailed ethnological analysis, he claimed, could sociologists develop theories to describe the foundational realities of interpersonal interaction.

African society, long viewed by many Europeans as among the most primitive in the world, seemed enormously complex to Mauss. Influenced by the detailed studies of Delafosse and his peers, Mauss saw the French Soudan as "composed of amalgamated peoples since the twelfth century." Attempting to break down societies by linguistic or topographical barriers presented significant problems for Mauss, as some societies had links via language or land that stretched back to the "origins" of the groups themselves.[82] To answer these problems, he advised social scientists to turn to the natives themselves as intelligent interpreters of social reality. Like Delafosse and Marty, Mauss proposed to unearth the foundation of "social cohesion" among these peoples by a deep analysis of their oral traditions and histories that contained "the precepts and ideas" and ultimately the "perception that the tribe held of itself."[83] Acknowledging native intelligence stood as the first step in this method. Next, social scientists had to rely on the historical and sociological accounts of intellectuals like themselves, preferably those in writing, to discern the origins of structures and tendencies. It was here that Mauss and his colleagues placed great value in the derivative analyses of African civilizations written by Delafosse, Marty, and others. Africanist studies, when considered as a coherent group, had the potential to deliver an encyclopedic knowledge of a society; from that level of information, skilled analysts, such as Mauss, hoped to discern fundamental structures that shaped social life. It was here that Mauss's conclusions carried the greatest risk, as colonial analysis with an eye toward the improvement of political rule did not offer the distance and impartiality he so needed.

Mauss expected that although morals and belief systems varied by people and location, they generally found expression in a similar manner. Mauss thus applauded the utility of proverb collections assembled by scholars such as Delafosse; these sources contained great insight into native intellectual capabilities and structures.[84] Mauss's ethnologists had a much larger obligation than observation. Indeed, he expected social analysts to "reattach the institutional and structural to the *mentalité* and the reverse."[85] Natives themselves assisted Mauss in assembling his conclusions on social life through their verbal descriptions of conventions and norms. A collected recording of these individual commentaries, he thought, amounted to a description of *mentalité*. People, he thought, acted according to implicit guidelines governing their interactions. *Mentalité* stood in for social structure to an outside observer. It was of course difficult to penetrate this relationship; all native discussions did not reflect structure, and he also saw that these conversations acted every day to alter or at least to obscure the very forms for which he searched so longingly.

Mauss proposed to escape this bind by a retreat along the temporal developmental scale. Like his Africanist brethren, he saw that the possibility for civilizational advancement lay not in assimilation but in recognition of parallel development and the return to an originary state from which an accelerated path of progress could begin anew. From this "protohistory," he proposed that sociologists develop an understanding of "total social phenomena" that linked religious, juridical, moral, political, familial, and economic structures into one belief.[86] Lévi-Strauss described the resultant "total social fact" as "three-dimensional" and capable of making "the properly sociological dimension coincide with its multiple synchronic aspects; with the historical or diachronic dimension; and finally, with the physio-psychological dimension. Only in individuals could these three dimensions fuse."[87] In other words, Lévi-Strauss interpreted Mauss's key tool, the total social fact, as composed of several elements. Sociology, at the top of the pyramid, considered all dimensions of any social structure as it existed at multiple, frozen snapshots in time. However, analysis also had to consider changes in the edifice produced over time. Mauss hoped that a sociologist could follow these changes back in time, thereby giving insight into basic forms before later individuals changed the outward conventions. Comprehending social reality thus required Mauss to appreciate contingency, of the role of individuals as actors in social life. Variability, however, did not rule out the possibility of structure. Human beings still interacted within a larger social construct; Mauss theorized that some forms of that interaction were common across all societies.

Mauss saw some ideas, most famously his notion of gift exchange, as fundamental in all human societies and anchored in human performance of social belief. In a sweeping intellectual examination that encompassed groups from Australia to Africa and North America, Mauss concluded that all human groups, regardless of the level of development, based much of their interaction on the exchange of gifts, whether for reproduction, sustenance, or civility. He concluded that the existence of such "universals," or beliefs held in common by all members of the species, revealed that all human sociocultural groupings were constantly developing, led by individuals who progressively became cognizant of "themselves and their situation vis-à-vis others."[88] Individuals, then, held the key to understanding the fundamental principles that guided societies.

In his mind, these principles derived from the interactions of "men and groups of men." The sociologist pointed to one central fact of sociological study: "It is the feelings of men in spirit, in flesh and blood that are acting and have always acted everywhere." Societies in earlier stages of development modeled the complicated process that created modern Europe in a long-running "social evolution."[89] This evolution, though, was not unilinear, as described by Spencer or Durkheim; non-European civilizations did not exist purely as echoes of a distant Western past for Mauss. Basing his conclusions at least in part on French Africanist scholarship, Mauss portrayed civilizations as moving along repeatable and similar paths of development and decay. These cycles overlapped and influenced each other, and all groups passed through certain marked stages at different times (e.g., nomadism, sedentarism, feudalism). This system of mutual influence and interference, however, did not mean to Mauss that civilizational groups were necessarily inferior or subordinate. Rather, his ethnology informed by history acted as a window for him to see "the first form of collective representation that has since become the foundation of individual understanding."[90] In short, Mauss argued that individual variations emerged as new manifestations of a primordial social moment. Mauss discerned complicated cycles of development in each society's historical arc. From these cycles, he sought commonalities and overlaps between the specific arcs. Time was relative and important to Mauss in discerning the distance and mutation of current social practice from its original and fundamental forms.

Recognizing this complex reality, Mauss proposed that social scientists had to avoid easy conclusions based on simplified assumptions. For example, he participated in ongoing discussions in the ethnological community on the evolution of belief systems. Religion, as a seemingly universal social structure, was an easy target for oversimplification. Following the lead of van Gennep and Delafosse, Mauss rejected simple explanations of the religious practices of native African and Australian groups that Durkheim, Radcliffe-Brown, and other prominent social theorists of the time saw as the most primitive on earth. Foremost among these oversimplifications, in Mauss's mind, stood the idea of totemism, a theory whose advocates proposed that modern religious and marriage practices descended from ancient associations with representative animals.[91] For example, a group that named itself the "crocodile" tribe held that animal in high esteem and its members were forbidden from harming any crocodile they came across. At the same time, the society enforced a ban on marriage of crocodile men to crocodile women; they would instead have to find mates in another tribe, perhaps one associated with another stereotypical African animal, such as the monkey or the zebra.

Totemic theory resulted not from a strong combination of empirical investigation and theoretical development, in Mauss's view, but from a series of mistaken assumptions and flawed conclusions. Here Mauss escaped, however briefly, from the colonial bind and its corrupt bargain with basic theories of racial superiority. He characterized totemism as descended from an "immense misunderstanding between two civilizations, the African and the European; it has as its foundation only a blind obedience to colonial usage."[92] Each Maussian civilization existed on its own terms and according to the needs of its individual component parts. In Mauss's opinion, social structures, however similar in appearance from the outside, were in fact products of different historical processes and intended to fulfill a different purpose. Structure, classification, and progress rested largely with each civilizational group. "Over the course of human progress in the genealogy of societies, the form of each [civilization] has varied," Mauss wrote; when taken together this variety appeared as a "kaleidoscope" of ever-evolving structures. "This mixture," he continued, "particular to a given society at a given moment, gives it ... a unique appearance."[93] Mauss argued that belief in the spiritual power of all things, and some material objects above others, did not link social construction across all societies. It was not a reflection of a linear evolution.

In these refutations of European depictions of totemism, Mauss relied heavily on Delafosse's descriptions of African religious life. "Animism," the term preferred by Delafosse to describe pre-Islamic West African religions, respected the power of all living things. European analysts spent too much time, in Mauss's view, trying to link African religious expression to the European present. He suggested instead that different societies at different times conceived of the relationship between the natural, the supernatural, and the human in radically divergent ways. Attempts to extend the religious beliefs of one group to the past of another rested on faulty assumptions. For Mauss, the West did not stand at the top of a unilinear process of evolution. As it had for Delafosse and Marty, African political, economic, and social progress remained possible, but only when considered in full relative terms.

Although they both admired Comte's emphasis on empirical investigation, Mauss followed Durkheim in rejecting Comte's expectation of universal progress that, in his mind, presupposed that all human societies developed along the same course. Mauss wrote, "If there is not *a human civilization*, there were and always will be diverse civilizations that dominate and contain the collective life of each people."[94] Working from the evidence gathered by scholars on the ground in Africa, Mauss perceived civilization occurring in myriad forms and existing at multiple developmental phases; each deserved separate and independent investigation in an effort to find commonalities that could assist both in understanding the "total social fact" and in finding a specific, tailored form of intellectual and moral progress. Total social facts, when viewed as living ideas shaped by the generating civilization, revealed change over time and the fundamental mechanism by which social groups structured their interactions.

Mauss concluded that sociologists employing his methods would be able to discern the "chronological and geographical linkage of societies," a process that did not follow a "unilinear development." Instead, societies and civilizations were multiple. Mauss wrote, "Numerous are the evolutions never achieved, numerous are the disappeared phenomena, numerous are the fusions that have occurred." He believed ethnology did not make all societies equal; it simply compared their particular social structures and mentalities.[95] It was this mind-set, born in the colonies, which shaped the associationist paradigm in Africa. Mauss succeeded in theorizing the debate over colonial governance in terms understandable by the intelligentsia.

Conclusion: Knowledge radiation in France and beyond

Rapidly losing influence during and after the Second World War, Mauss fell into poverty and obscurity, finally passing away on February 11, 1950. His funeral drew few mourners.[96] Nonetheless, his influence on the colonial African discussion was secure. Studies of Africa in the AS had increased in the early twentieth century as Delafosse and his peers increased their metropolitan contacts. The resultant ethnological networks paid particular attention to the internal development of African civilizations while also admitting that external influences, most importantly Islam, had played, and would continue to play, a significant role in African affairs.[97] Saharan Africa thus became, for Mauss, a realm of "international transmission and circulation," where scientists discerned continuity and change as well as a unique "historical morphology."[98] It fell to others to take the study of this morphology further.

Marcel Griaule in many ways took over his mentor's role. He taught at EPHE and the successor to the *école coloniale*, the *école de la France d'outre-mer*, even chairing Delafosse's International Institute of African Languages and Cultures.[99] Griaule, with Labouret and other peers, stood in the vanguard of a new generation of scholars and colonial officials questioning the very basis of the colonial order. Colonial policy, they thought, should focus not on exploitation, but on respect and association. In their view, Europeans must create "an inventory of spiritual riches in a community of thought and action with the blacks themselves." Assimilation stood as the "unacknowledged child of racism" that denied the importance and vitality of African civilizations.[100]

Africa stood as not only subject but also producer of ethnological knowledge for this generation. In the same vein as Faidherbe, Delafosse, and Marty, Mauss included Africans (through the mediation of French Africanist scholars) in the process of understanding Africa itself. No ethnographer, he thought, could penetrate the mysteries of a society without dialogue with the members of the community. African employees in French schools and museums in Dakar had contributed to the collection and understanding of ethnological data by Mauss and his peers, even as others came to France to attend courses at the IE and elsewhere.[101] Most importantly, French universities in the 1930s hosted African intellectuals who shaped the next fifty years of African political and social thought. Léopold Sédar Senghor, later a founder of the postcolonial Senegalese state, participated in the *négritude* movement (with Aimé Césaire, among others) while a student at IE and the Sorbonne in 1933–1934. Inspired by the teachings of Mauss and Griaule, Senghor saw immense value in literature, art, and oral traditions as refutation of simplistic views of "Hamitic" and "Semitic" binaries in African history. Any close examination of "Negro-African civilization," in Senghor's view, led ineluctably to an understanding of "the power and the complexity of black thought," the foundational premise of ethnological humanism.[102] Thus, ideas regarding African civilization as interpreted by French Africanists radiated back to Africa via their close interactions with metropolitan scholars.

Following Mauss, the next generation of ethnologists grasped the thread of his civilizational ideas and took them in several directions. Claude Lévi-Strauss, by the 1950s France's most influential ethnological scholar, refined Mauss's "total social fact" by an examination of American (non-European) mythology. He found inspiration in the work of Durkheim and Mauss on antonyms such as the "sacred or profane, pure or impure, friend or enemy, favorable or unfavorable," oppositions that, in Lévi-Strauss's rendering, formed the basis for all human interaction.[103] In a quest similar to that pursued by Mauss, Lévi-Strauss sought immutable structures; in his mind, he found them in these binaries. Breaking with his intellectual mentor, he saw "the progress of scientific knowledge could only have been and can only ever be constituted out of processes of connecting and recutting of patterns ... inside a totality that is closed and complementary to itself."[104] Unlike Mauss, who saw civilizations as in constant flux due to the interactions of the internal and the external, Lévi-Strauss conceived of systems of belief as shut off to external input; they worked from preexisting materials periodically reshaped and recast by *bricoleurs* using a finite store of materials. Universal beliefs were not only possible but also common for Lévi-Strauss.

Mauss's search for empirical evidence to support social conclusions influenced other thinkers as well. Pierre Bourdieu found great worth in these ideas, particularly as he found himself between French worlds, much like Mauss's experience as a French Jew in the late nineteenth century. Resident in Algeria during enormous upheaval, Bourdieu saw social structure not as universal but as localized, contingent, and defined only by repeated observation and investigation rather than theoretical divination. Descended from a similar intellectual tradition, Bourdieu ultimately voiced a powerful counter to Lévi-Strauss's structural viewpoint through his concept of habitus, an idea that took Mauss's perception of individuals as important social actors and expanded it to include a compilation of cultural and symbolic capital and the accrual of historical and social background.[105] Most importantly, he turned ethnology in on itself, pressing for a reflexive approach that considered the ethnologist as social actor. Bourdieu thus stands as the most important intellectual inheritor of Mauss's ideas among African ethnologists, as he incorporated both an emphasis on locally generated information and a notion of the distinctiveness of civilizations.

The development of Bourdieu's approach owed much to the war raging between France and Algerian separatists in the mid-1950s, a conflict that increased in intensity during the governor-generalship of Jacques Soustelle, Mauss's former student. Interested in a policy of association or "integration," Soustelle's political leadership focused on ethnological examination of the populace so as to better understand their discontent. Although ultimately unsuccessful, Soustelle's policies grew not only from his education with Mauss but also from a long legacy of Africanist scholarship that considered certain African sources as valuable and saw African civilizations as unique, important, and worthy of development in a colonial context.

5

Jacques Soustelle and the Ethnological State in Algeria

French ethnologist Germaine Tillion (1907–2008) described the sometimes symbiotic, sometimes parasitic relationship between the French colonial state and the Algerian natives it ruled as an "equilibrium of soil, fauna, flora and men." Grafted onto an idealized, composite Algerian society since the mid-nineteenth century, Tillion suggested that the French system at first lived side-by-side with Algerians to the benefit of each group. However, the industrial growth of France and the rest of the "civilized" world left native Algerians, a group she depicted as "Canadian birches," subjugated by the invasive but more powerful "mushroom" of the French colonial state.[1] It was this type of convoluted metaphor and analysis that powered the ethnological state of Jacques Soustelle during his 1955 tenure as governor-general of Algeria. Never fully comfortable with Algerian political reality, Soustelle retreated into ethnology while unleashing military efforts to stamp out revolt, in the process missing the real origins of conflict and widening the violence. He thus stood as a true academic disciple of Marcel Mauss and his peers at the *Institut d'Ethnologie* (IE) in Paris, employing the ideas of many of these "intermediary" figures in the development of colonial policy and in the growth of French ethnology as a discipline.[2]

Soustelle took over colonial Algeria mere months after the eruption of violent unrest in the Aurès Mountains on November 1, 1954, an effort led by the nascent *Front de Libération Nationale* (FLN). His tenure as governor-general brought the ethnological rhizome first expanded by Louis Faidherbe in the 1840s full circle, back to its origins in France's oldest African colony. Soustelle recognized the need to find a "practical solution" to the problems of governance in the colonies, particularly Algeria. He tried to gain such insights via conversations with "young Africans such as Léopold Senghor," as they taught him of the inefficiencies of the colonial system.[3] Exposed to some of the best African minds in the French colonial empire, Soustelle concluded that native Africans provided invaluable insight into the colonial condition and an important avenue by which to study social structure. These ethnological networks gave him administrative and political access into what he thought were the root causes of native Algerian discontent, unrest that seemed to emerge from the rural, uneducated poor. He and his team of fellow social scientists thus set out on a "strategy of contact" in rural areas, hoping to connect with natives, particularly women, as sources of ethnographic information.[4] Detailed ethnological studies of the plight of the Algerian peasantry offered long-term prospects for success. However, under the harsh spotlight cast by wartime conditions, science failed to comprehend the very real disenchantment felt by the politically astute members of the revolutionary movements both in Algeria and abroad. Relying on simplistic conceptions of the interrelationship of time, history, and Islam, Soustelle failed in interpreting the language and source of revolt. Searching for particularity that would allow him to understand and rule more efficiently, Soustelle ultimately worked from generalities that failed to recognize what his contemporary Georges Balandier saw as the varied contact between the local and a larger "global society."[5]

Indeed, Soustelle's policies did not account for the sophistication of the separatist camp that had concluded before his arrival that further peaceful negotiation with France was futile.[6] The governor-general believed that Islam offered some help in this regard, as Soustelle and his staff saw it as a generally progressive institution "trying to evolve, to adapt itself to the modern world."[7] In fact, as James McDougall has shown, Islam instead served as a unifying force for people struggling to develop a new nationalist discourse.[8] Hardly aiding French colonial rule, Islamic leaders instead undermined the colonial state's ethnological politics and thus fed into mid-century fears of transnational, communist-style movements outside of colonial control.[9] Connecting native Algerians and scientifically inclined colonial Frenchmen, Soustelle's new government built political institutions based on ethnological examination and analysis, in the process missing the very causes of unrest.

Committed to stamping out the revolt by addressing its social causes, Soustelle and his staff refused to treat with active rebels, specifically prohibiting his personnel from discussing the rebellion with the population, causing some of those administrators to later call his actions "treasonous."[10] Lacking a full range of sources, the ethnological conclusions of his government thus stemmed from two primary types of informants. Despite the emphasis of the colonial state, the peasantry offered little, as they lived in daily fear of FLN reprisals and had limited information on rebel activities and desires. His other primary informants, Western-educated, *evolué* politicians, had nothing to lose by supporting the French government, as they stood to have little status in a future state governed by the remnants of the FLN, an organization that had already begun to target people labeled as French collaborators.[11]

Soustelle's rule in Algeria, however brief, ultimately appears as conflicted as his policies. He was first an anachronism, applying ethnological techniques refined by Maurice Delafosse and Paul Marty in West Africa thirty-five years before. As one of his problematic Arab-Algerian interlocutors, Ferhat Abbas, recalled, Soustelle was perhaps the right man for the job; he simply arrived a half century too late.[12] Soustelle overlooked the fluidity of the African postwar moment, assuming that African societies had not changed in the intervening decades, a myopia that certainly contributed to the ultimate failure of his policies.[13] His ideas of "ethnological governance"[14] hardly began with him. In fact, he often drew upon the examples of Faidherbe in 1850s and Senegal and Bugeaud's Algerian *bureaux arabes* of the 1840s. Perhaps most important stood Lyautey's *politique de la tasse du thé*, an idealized, urbane, and dialogical approach to native contact conducted over a shared tea service. Like his forebears, Soustelle missed the international and the transregional as he focused on the local and the ethnographic.

This dated approach simply did not conform to colonial and metropolitan reality. Senior officials in France sought to make colonial policy more efficient. A new model of colonialism, known as "trusteeship," emerged to return some "efficiency" to European colonial relationships. Cognizant of their inability to fulfill the social and economic needs of their colonial subjects, some French leaders proposed a federal model with an eye toward near-term independence, in the process remaking the colonies with a new political and economic structure focused on "efficiency, science, progress, and welfare." Metropolitan and colonial officials alike held that their native subjects were not yet able to govern themselves; the problem lay in the inability of the home governments to meet their increasingly well-articulated social and economic demands. A more scientific approach, theorists held, made it possible to cover all angles. It would generate a federalized, "rehumanized" government adapted to local conditions.[15] Economic and political change was now an important policy goal for metropolitan politicians looking to rid themselves of the expense of the colonies without international loss of face. Colonial development offered a way out by giving colonial populations tools with brief instructions on how to use them. Even this approach, with its low likelihood of success in convincing a subjugated population to cooperate with failing colonial governments, did not appeal to Soustelle, who pushed for ever closer political linkages. He failed to see that the colonial intervention was itself the problem.

Soustelle instead advocated the French follow a policy of association with deep ties to metropolitan France. Algerian social and political structures could change, but in Soustelle's mind, this transition would occur only after a long period of "integration" with France. He defined this concept in a June 1955 broadcast on Radio Algiers as "neither subversion nor stagnation but evolution within the framework of the French republic and its justice, its humanity." He indicated his policies would respect the "ethnic, linguistic [and] religious" elements of native life in transforming Algeria into a "true French province in the administrative, economic, social, and political domains."[16] Walking a fine line between the historically ambiguous policies of assimilation and association, Soustelle advocated a future Algeria that was politically integrated into France while retaining its "traditional" character. Doomed to failure, his new policies pushed a warped sort of republican universality that pushed Muslims away from the colonial state rather than bringing them closer by demanding a specific form of French political and legal status.[17] He rejected calls for an independent Algeria, as in his mind the civilization was not yet progressing sufficiently to warrant separation from France. For Soustelle, the great gap between France and Algeria required a long-term political and social recombination of the two. Either not cognizant of or in denial over the political and socioeconomic negotiation and concessions required in what Balandier termed the "technical" phase of international relations after the war, Soustelle proposed a reinvigoration of the basic French civilizing mission.[18]

His tenure as governor-general revealed in stark relief the problems in this scientifically paternal approach to government. He did not consider the swirl of international forces that drew Algeria together with Egypt, Indochina, and Indonesia in a potent mixture of nationalism and decolonization. He did not consider the larger impact of violence against his revolutionary opponents. His FLN opponents, however, did not overlook the importance of the international arena, basing their strategy from the beginning of the conflict on a sophisticated mixture of Arab-Islamic nationality, the independent rights of citizens as recognized by the international community, and calls for social equality that resonated in the postwar world.[19] At the same time, European metropolitan governments after the Second World War became increasingly reluctant to engage in costly campaigns to put down rebellions, particularly with American Marshall Plan dollars riding on their willingness to grant citizenship and wage equality to a wider base. The delicate balance between these international forces, on the one hand, and the complex interrelationship of Algerian domestic sociopolitical groups, on the other, doomed Soustelle's government from the start.

His approach, informed by decades of French ethnological work in Africa, is perhaps best described as social engineering, in this case an effort to transform fundamentally the way of life in Algerian populations. In this regard, Soustelle's efforts at social transformation are best understood through a comparison with what James Scott has termed a "high modernist ideology." Scott has described four elements that characterized "modernist" social engineering: an "administrative ordering of nature and society," the adherence to a "high-modernist ideology" that included enormous state "self-confidence" in the power of technical prowess, the presence of an authoritarian state with unilateral ability to conduct social experiments, and a "prostrate civil society" unable to halt those reforms.[20]

Scott's model is useful in thinking about Soustelle's time in Algeria, and in considering the French colonial approach by the 1950s. Secular Algerian nationalists had created a state-in-exile in Egypt and Tunisia, an endeavor that incorporated notionally nonpolitical Islamic intellectuals as well. Certainly not powerful, Algerian civil society was also not entirely "prostrate," in spite of the privations spurred by the guerrilla campaign launched by radical separatists. While Soustelle believed in the power of science to reform Algeria, he did not intentionally discard the past altogether, a key component of Scott's criteria. He considered history as an important factor in civilizational development, rather than viewing all non-Europeans as in possession of an irrelevant premodern "tradition." Without question, Soustelle was a "modernist" reformer, but one who descended from a very specific French colonial lineage that viewed local histories as vital in comprehending the possibility for economic and social change.[21] Ethnology, in this model, relied on an appreciation of historical context.

Activating the ethnological rhizome

Echoing Delafosse, Soustelle described his deep interest in studying the world outside France: "as far back as I can trace my memories, I always had a passionate desire to learn about distant countries and, especially, distant peoples." His career as an ethnologist sated this thirst while also providing "an appealing element of sport and adventure."[22] Soustelle emerged as one of France's leading colonial thinkers due to his long interaction with the French ethnological rhizome and, most importantly, the associationist theories of Marcel Mauss. Finding success in these networks, Soustelle realized that the colonial project itself, which he saw as similar to his wartime pursuit of intelligence in the name of Free France, depended on information gleaned from what he and his staff portrayed as intellectual elites. He came to Africa because of war; he remained interested in Africa and Algeria for their ethnological and developmental possibilities. Unfortunately for the Algerian population, that interest did not translate to great administrative or political skill.

Born in Montpellier, France on February 3, 1912, Soustelle enjoyed enormous academic success in school in Lyon and Paris, in the process meeting his future wife, Georgette, a fellow scholar who also trained as an ethnologist and traveled with Jacques to Mexico and Algeria in later years.[23] A 1929 graduate of the elite *école normale supérieure* (ENS), the young scholar earned an assistantship under Paul Rivet, the director of the ethnographic museum at the Trocadero, and served on the team, building displays of African villages and Asian temples for Lyautey's Colonial Exposition of 1931.[24] Soustelle thus saw firsthand the view of the colonies held by distinguished colonial officers, in the process coming under the influence of Rivet and the growing interwar Parisian ethnological world.

Soustelle's most important influence in this period, not surprisingly, was Mauss, then a professor at the *école pratique des hautes études* (EPHE) and the *Collège de France*. Introduced to the great thinker by an ENS professor, Soustelle found himself awed by his new mentor's powerful intellect: "No one who had the privilege of knowing Marcel Mauss will hesitate to agree that he was one of the greatest minds of our times."[25]

In Mauss he found an outstanding teacher, one who "profoundly influenced an entire generation of researchers. By a curious paradox, it was this man who never did field work (he was the last and greatest of the armchair anthropologists) who inspired us to go out and follow trails in every corner of the world and who armed us with rules and advice."[26] Soustelle combined this teaching with the ideas of other intellectuals, such as Lucien Lévy-Bruhl, in developing his own unique approach.[27] Soustelle sought to examine each society in its own right, on its own terms, informed by local conditions. No two were alike. The young ethnologist took this approach forward in his studies, applying to work in the field as part of the first generation of IE graduates.

Already celebrated for his numerous academic achievements, Soustelle conducted fieldwork in Mexico in the early 1930s and completed his doctoral thesis on the Otomi-Pame Indians of Mexico in 1937. His initial arrival in Mexico made him realize his own perspective as a European who "measures civilization by the height of the houses and the lower level of temperatures" and searches for the "dances of men brandishing lances and bones."[28] He could see in himself a tendency toward the misguided Durkheimian assumption of non-European "primitivity" as a necessary evolutionary stage on the path toward modernity. He thus reinserted context into the social equation in a method that omitted "neither somatic anthropology, nor ethnography, nor history" in assembling a composite picture.[29] Soustelle followed Mauss in advocating for a combined approach to societal analysis. No social science could fully describe reality; science instead promised an approximation of "truth" through the composite use of multiple techniques.

Mexico offered numerous examples of variation induced by contextual differences. Even after a relatively short exposure to this variety, Soustelle grew disgusted with ethnographies unable to adequately describe societies of a "pure race." At this early stage in his work, Soustelle posited that individual groups, particularly those who had retained vestiges of precolonial, pre-Western society, were "not homogenous."[30] It was the responsibility of European ethnology, he believed, to discern older structures so as to dissect the present. French ethnologists, he hoped, would then use this knowledge to shape the native path to a more modern form. Scientists, he cautioned, must appreciate each society or civilization for its own worth. Mexican civilizations, far from primitive precursors to European societies, were in fact important and old in their own right, as demonstrated by their long links with other groups spread across the globe. For example, Lacandon native musical instruments showed significant similarity to those employed by some North African groups, in Soustelle's mind reflecting a long history of cultural contact introduced by the trade in "black slaves." After recognizing these connections, Soustelle's idealized social scientist would then "introduce a bit of order into the chaos of languages and tribes" in Central America by categorizing the distinctions and overlaps of each group with the others.[31]

Upon his return from Mexico in 1937, Soustelle took up a place as assistant director of the Trocadero while teaching at the *école coloniale*, earning a chair in American antiquities at the *Collège de France* in 1938.[32] At the age of twenty-six Soustelle thus found himself in the highest echelons of the French academy and in position to interact with people from all corners of the French colonial system, as Mauss had intended.

Following on to the example set by the IE, the Trocadero, and its successor, the *Musée de l'Homme* (MH), provided important sponsorship to French ethnologists in interwar France. In 1942 Soustelle recalled the MH as a "veritable palace of the social sciences" devoted to "studying the life of exotic peoples [and] pulling up from the soil the accounts of lost civilizations." French science, particularly the ethnology practiced by those affiliated with IE and MH, was on the leading edge of the French colonial effort. This undertaking, dedicated to the development of "universal ideas," acted in Soustelle's mind as "a challenge to racism, to the degrading doctrines of slavery and exploitation, to the new barbarism that already threatened the world."[33] He felt that museums and their employees must conserve, protect, and exalt the "intellectual riches" of native societies while pushing for a "new humanism." This effort, he thought, enabled colonial subjects to "know themselves and gain an understanding of their civilization."[34] Soustelle thus proposed French science as the vanguard of a new approach to colonial development, one that allowed colonial subjects to see the glory of their locally created civilizations by looking in the reflection provided by museum preservation, thereby restoring to them their humanity.

Mexican experience showed Soustelle that knowledge constituted the "riches of civilization" and that intellectuals acted as the "carriers" of that tradition. He admonished ethnologists and colonial administrators to treat locally generated ideas as "precious stones" appropriate for display "so that they can be seen by all."[35] Europeans and native groups alike could then view and consider these jewels in fashioning a new and better society. In his view this knowledge permitted Europeans to understand their global neighbors; from that comprehension would grow a mutual appreciation. Knowledge of non-European groups came from intimate contact in their native areas. Soustelle later remarked that a civilization that "has never pleaded its own case" could only "be unjustly belittled" by those with no intimate knowledge.[36] The ethnologist ultimately felt that all people were in some way civilized and engaged in combat with other groups and with nature. Natives could contribute both to the pure scientific understanding of their structures and to their own political and moral development through a dissection of social structure, one mediated by French ethnologists prepared to analyze and interpret events and rituals.[37] From this analysis, he expected to deliver a tailored approach to political, social, moral, and economic development in full consideration of the unique history and intellectual capabilities of each civilization. It is here that Soustelle fell into the Maussian trap, failing to see the real and daily damage done by the act of viewing, by the weight of colonialism itself. He remained committed to a rudimentary humanism.

The academic idealism Soustelle displayed in the interwar years abated somewhat with the explosion of the Second World War in 1939. Soustelle worked in a variety of capacities, typically in intelligence, during that conflict. He joined de Gaulle's Free French in 1940, ultimately serving as the minister of information in 1942.[38] In this capacity, he became a prominent advocate of the Free French language of liberty, desiring above all else to release France and its colonies from Nazi and Vichy captivity. Indeed, the notion of an escape from tyranny infused much of his ethnological work from that point forward, describing his postwar goal as the restoration of humanity to colonial subjects. Like those under the thumb of fascism, Soustelle felt that Europeans must liberate Africans and Asians from their desperate economic and political situations. He saw ethnology as a key instrument in preserving and protecting these societies, restoring to them some measure of their precolonial existence. While humanist in conception, Soustelle's efforts to "preserve" native societies instead froze those groups in time, in the process denying the very vitality he exalted. Even in retrospect, Soustelle proudly trumpeted his "fundamentally rational" perspective on Algeria that drew on "the historical, ethnic, religious, and economic reality" of the colony, assuming in the process the existence of some unitary "Muslim personality" that the French must respect and maintain. In his mind, he was adhering to the wishes of Algerians themselves, who wanted him to treat Algerian "culture" as a "precious stone."[39] Such a synchronic approach caused him to misunderstand Islam as representative and fixed rather than as a medium for nationalist and anticolonial thought.

In ethnology the young leader found a framework through which to expand his intellectual and political contacts. Throughout the Second World War, Soustelle leaned on the connections and techniques that grew from his time at the IE and MH in Paris. The ethnological community, specifically centered on the MH, had served as an active site of resistance to the Nazi occupation; several members were incarcerated or killed by the Gestapo. Germaine Tillion, for instance, was forced into a labor camp at Ravensbruck following accusations of her participation in the French underground movements. "I was part of this small, fervent team, [and] I am still part of it despite distance and war," Soustelle remarked in 1942, "and there is nothing in my life of which I am more proud except for having responded yes to the call of General de Gaulle."[40] As the later director of the new *Direction générale des services spéciaux*, an umbrella espionage organization consolidating French intelligence efforts in Africa and Europe, Soustelle continued to build networks of informants in Africa and around the world. Although not a field intelligence specialist himself, Soustelle employed and worked with chains of French, American, British, and native African operatives from Morocco and Algeria to the Congo.[41]

Work in Africa inspired two important conclusions derived at least in part from the findings of previous French ethnologists. In the first place, networks composed of non-European local inhabitants were enormously important to understanding the social terrain both in wartime and in customary colonial rule. Local informants had acquitted themselves well in both circumstances, demonstrating their centrality in any effort to decipher local structures. In the second, Africa played host to an enormous range of complex societies with a strong intellectual capacity in their own right. In Soustelle's mind, Africa represented more than a weak partner in a one-sided assimilationist campaign. Africans could and should contribute to their own future in tandem with a benevolent, understanding France. He never questioned the place of France as a civilizing force. While he lamented the erosion of native social structures, he ultimately concluded that French developmental assistance was vital to the future of Africa.

Following the war, Soustelle participated as an elected deputy in the constitutional debates to determine the future of the provisional government and its successor, the Fourth Republic. As former intelligence chief, minister of information, and minister of colonies (from October 1945 to January 1946), Soustelle's word on colonial matters carried credibility. In a debate on March 23, 1946, Soustelle agreed with native African delegates who saw colonial issues as "a problem of civilization, a problem of institutions, [and] a political problem." He argued that French administrators and politicians needed to understand the rich history of Africa to prepare for a long, shared future. He pronounced that the political way ahead lay neither in "assimilating Africans to metropolitans, nor in metropolitans to Africans, but in blending two cultures and two peoples." In the future, Soustelle proposed, Africa would "transcend the antinomy of colonizing people and colonized people" with an eye to a later "flowering of a new people and a new civilization" growing from the roots of its predecessors.[42] Now more than ever, Soustelle blurred the line between assimilation and association. Because he valued native intellectual contributions, Soustelle saw them as important to the future of France, although not necessarily as equal partners. Soustelle, at least implicitly, conceived of France as the dominant player in any colonial partnership.

Soustelle proposed to recast the French future through fusion with the vibrant societies of Africa. Through close cooperation with African ethnological networks, Soustelle hoped to develop a new form of colonialism, one that began with political association but inexorably led to the export of a new French federal state to Africa and around the world. He did not account for the remarkable diversity of non-European intellectuals in Africa, nor did he consider the marginalized position of French-speaking African thinkers in the postwar context, the increasing sophistication of anticolonial arguments, or the irreversible effects of colonial legal regimes and political violence. He lived and worked in a charged postwar French political world, where he was cast first as part of a discredited right-wing party in the late 1940s and early 1950s and then as a member of a failing left-wing coalition. Despite promises to the contrary, de Gaulle's transitional government and the succeeding Fourth Republic succeeded only in kicking the colonial can down to the road, failing to provide for the political rights of colonial citizens and setting the stage for decolonization and ultimate independence in Africa. Soustelle was part of that problem, existing in an idealized intellectual world in which social science could cure all ills.

Operating a colonial government through ethnological examination

After almost a decade in postwar governments, Soustelle appeared to be just another politician. However, the explosion of war in Algeria in 1954 brought his name back to the lips of metropolitan politicians willing to overlook his right-leaning Gaullist allegiances. The French Premier, Pierre Mendès-France, and Minister of the Interior François Mitterrand hoped that he brought instant credibility due to his wartime association with Africa, his attendance at the 1944 Brazzaville conference, his brief tenure as minister of the colonies, and his participation in the postwar constituent assembly. When appointed governor-general, Soustelle proposed to quell the violent unrest in Algeria by understanding the sources of that discontent. In order to discern the causes of unrest, he enlisted the assistance of a number of prominent French ethnologists of Africa to unravel the complex interrelationship between religion, law, and social interaction in France's oldest colony. Several of the most prominent, including Vincent Monteil and Paul Schoen, had served in the *affaires indigènes* bureau initiated by Lyautey.[43] Their subsequent efforts at reform fell woefully short as they struggled to understand the reality of Algerian resistance and discontent.

French colonial policy in the immediate postwar era had grown from de Gaulle's comments at the 1944 Brazzaville conference. Although uttered largely to gain the political support of native AOF and AEF delegates, de Gaulle's promises of "moral and material" profit for Africans working closely with France framed the efforts of future colonial administrators. Soustelle, in particular, took on de Gaulle's pledge to work with the colonies "for their own development and the progress of their population, to integrate them into the French community with their personalities, their interests, their aspirations, [and] their future."[44] De Gaulle's new vision of a French union gave Soustelle a political end-state that jibed with the civilizational relativism advocated by Mauss. When approached by Mendès-France and Mitterrand (a socialist government) to take over the post of governor-general in Algeria in early 1955,[45] Soustelle accepted with the understanding that he was acting in accordance with the wishes of de Gaulle, then in self-imposed exile.

Political and social conditions in Africa in 1955 were a far cry from those in 1945; the colonial world analyzed by Delafosse and Marty in the 1910s and 1920s was a distant memory. Soustelle was curiously unaware, from a review of the policies, writings, and speeches of his governor-generalship, of many of the internationally circulating ideas of nationalism and anticolonialism. European colonies had become increasingly interconnected by transnational efforts at collaboration as they tried to "modernize," in the process providing a means by which ideas could move rapidly around the world, even to previously disenfranchised peoples. Women played a particularly important role in these discourses, causing Soustelle and his cabinet to give particular attention to them even as conservative French Algerian settler groups used their status as a rallying cry for reform and conflict with the FLN.[46] At the same time, labor movements grew stronger in public discourse in West Africa, where strikers used colonial terms of "liberty" and "equality" to demand pay and enfranchisement equal to their metropolitan peers. They rejected European relativism, in the process casting doubt on ethnological efforts to peg pay to an imagined African "way of life." Metropolitan politicians in France realized the enormous social and economic costs of continuing the developmental mission as before, setting their empires on a path toward eventual self-government even as Soustelle advocated the anachronistic notion of "integration" of Algeria and France.[47]

Algerians also tapped into these postwar international currents. Messali Hadj, the leader of the separatist, though peaceful, *Etoile Nord-Africain* since the 1920s, was rapidly supplanted by more radical separatists who concluded that only violence would deliver full political rights and, ultimately, citizenship. Drawing on the centrist nationalist messages espoused by Hadj and Abbas, the long-standing historical-nationalist rhetoric of powerful religious leaders and scholars, the *'ulama*, and a superior organization, the new FLN proposed to "channel the immense waves that stir up patriotic enthusiasm of the nation."[48] Soustelle had somehow missed the large-scale change in African context. Europeans were weakened by war as Africans, including Algerians, emerged from the conflict with a stronger will for political independence. Africans themselves were no longer willing to accept a relationship based on unequal power. African politicians asserted their rights to control their own destinies and, ultimately, their own form of government even if achieved through violent means. The French government in Paris, which focused on reducing expenditure and rebuilding the metropole in both economic and social terms, offered little support to Soustelle's ethnological efforts in Algeria.

Given this turmoil, it is not surprising that the appointment of Soustelle caused uproar in both metropolitan and Algerian *pied noir* (French settler) political circles. It seemed a strange marriage of center-right ideologue with left-wing government for most observers. At the same time, French Algerian settlers feared the actual implementation of de Gaulle's promised Brazzaville policies, altering the legislative structure in Algeria and giving greater voice to the almost 8 million native Algerians while diminishing the position of the nearly 1 million Frenchmen in the department. French settler fears had been stoked by the November 1, 1954, onset of the FLN war, building on the traumatic French defeat at the hands of Vietnamese separatists at Dien Bien Phu.

Into this complex political mess flew Soustelle on February 15, 1955, leaving a French snowstorm for what he later described as an equally chilly reception in Algiers.[49] His appointment proved too much for the Mendès-France government. It fell a few days later due in large part to the growing discontent of many metropolitan politicians with the left-leaning administration of the colonies. Edgar Faure formed a new regime and, in August, reaffirmed Soustelle's place in Algeria for six additional months even as he remained suspicious of socialist-inspired efforts at colonial reform.[50]

Tied to socialism through his association with Paul Rivet and the MH team, Soustelle appeared a mass of contradictions to his opponents and supporters alike. For his part, Soustelle intended to use his governor-generalship as a platform from which to inform the average Frenchman of conditions in the colony. As he later recalled, part of his approach on taking office was "penetrating the stupefaction of the metropolitan who has never been to North Africa," a powerful statement that echoed the ideas of many right-wing French settlers who saw themselves as underrepresented and unappreciated in the metropole.[51] This dalliance with the far right in Algeria would haunt Soustelle through the remainder of his governorship and beyond as he became increasingly invested in and associated with violence. While a confusing muddle to his contemporaries, Soustelle's mixed bag of policies in Algeria in reality reflected his ethnological background and an effort to construct an idealized "native" he could then display to the world as the epitome of developmental colonialism.

Soustelle outlined his priorities for reform in January: "Bring back peace and order where they have been compromised, pursue and accelerate economic and social programs in order to create the resources necessary for a growing population, [and] give a new impetus to the progress of Algeria in all domains."[52] Soustelle soon moved further to the left with social reforms infused with lessons he had learned during his time in Mexico. Building on concepts initiated at low scale in 1951, Soustelle and Tillion targeted the illiterate and destitute via the *centres sociaux* to reform Algerian society from the bottom-up even as reforms took hold from the top-down.[53] In conversation with Algerian *evolué* politicians and intellectuals, Soustelle and his staff believed that basic literacy and French education would assist the lower classes in their movement into the modern world. Social centers, for all their idealist promise as places of assistance, still drew on the power inequalities in Algeria, placing rural Algerians at the command of a French educational system without real input into the curriculum.

Lyautey offered an historical model for social reform through close cooperation with native groups. Soustelle quoted the marshal's basic dictate that "the secret is the extended hand, not a condescending hand but the loyal man-to-man handshake made in an effort to understand each other," echoing that "trusting cooperation" served as the "essential base of all positive action."[54] The governor-general did not mimic Lyautey's rule by selected Moroccan tribal chiefs, instead maintaining the preexisting direct governance in conjunction with elected Algerian assemblies. He did not recognize that the time for "trusting cooperation" had passed for the core of the separatist movement.

Some contemporary French observers also criticized Soustelle's ethnological approach. One French delegate in the Algerian assembly railed against the "lack of contact" between Soustelle and the Algerian legislature. This delegate believed the governor-general, who "arrived with many diplomas and titles," did not understand the local political situation, instead believing himself the "holder of much knowledge [and] carrier of the democratic flame" who refused to consult the French elected officials already in place.[55] The new emphasis on ethnological investigation and policy threatened the power structures in place in Algeria. At the same time, they appealed to French officials in the countryside anxious to understand and to help their native charges with an eye toward preserving their own lives in the face of the FLN onslaught.[56] Indeed, this approach was firmly in line with the internal focus of the French colonial networks to which Soustelle was a prominent political heir, overlooking local reality in favor of an abstract, sociological, or ethnological understanding.

Although certainly concerned with the plight of his French subordinates in the countryside, Soustelle's focus remained on understanding the causes of rebellion. French Algerian social policy, in Soustelle's mind, had long relegated native Algerians to a backward status, judging them purely on technological achievement without considering the enormous intellectual potential already resident. He saw much of the ethnography of Algeria as employing easy binaries such as Berber/Arab or Colonial/Algerian; the reality was far more complex and deserving of study.[57] Ethnology provided the tools to dissect Algerian "society," but required direct contact with the population and a deliberate plan of examination.

The new governor-general thus based his government on ethnological principles. He criticized previous governments, notionally intent on republican principles of equality, as having overlooked the enormous administrative, social, and political inequities of the system. "A scientific knowledge of their [native] social structures" would help to alleviate this problem, he thought. Indeed, his government would use "ethnology, anthropology, [and] sociology" not only to inform but also to "guide public policy towards social and ethnic groups in overseas territories."[58] He expected his subordinates to follow these maxims. Soustelle thus assumed the part of social engineer as he ordered society administratively. He adhered to an "uncritical, unskeptical, and thus unscientifically optimistic" view of the possibility of progress given French scientific and industrial power.[59] Soustelle expected his colonial state to remake Algerian society on a local level, beginning in the countryside and in conversation with natives themselves. It was the choice of correspondents, however, that caused his administration to miss much of the real discontent in the colony. Localized discussion, in this case, did not reveal to him the terms and intellectual currents on which nationalists had constructed their program.

Hoping to gauge the opinion of the average Algerian, Soustelle directed his administrators to gather information not from dry staff meetings but from "conversation" with natives that he saw as "more edifying than a 100-page administrative report."[60] Soustelle believed that the "progress of Algeria" necessitated a dedicated corps of French administrators willing to conduct routine, unannounced trips into the country to engage in "human relations with the populace."[61] To that end Soustelle and his closest staff confidants, ethnologists Monteil, Tillion, and Jacques Juillet, embarked on numerous "study trips" to outlying Algerian regions to converse with local leaders and intellectuals. The trips also at times included Georgette Soustelle, who could gain the perspective of women and mothers when visiting hospitals, orphanages, and schools.[62]

Soustelle's regime employed women to a large degree. The governor-general believed that they would provide unique insight into the form and function of Algerian social structures. They offered Soustelle's government a perspective outside what many French analysts had perceived as a basically patriarchal system. Likely influenced by Monteil and Tillion, who had focused research in Uzbekistan, the Soviet Union, and Algeria on women, Soustelle came to view conversation with and education of women as crucial in understanding Algeria.[63] A gendered approach moved beyond the basic instrumentalization of sexual relations for control of chiefly lineages or access to native information, techniques employed at least in part by Delafosse and Faidherbe. When recognized as important contributors, women could shed light on one of the great mysteries for French Africanist scholars since at least Marty and Delafosse: the interconnection of genealogy, kinship, and history in the area that scholars saw as the foundation of Arab-Islamic civilization. Tillion and Georgette Soustelle were important players in both ethnological information gathering, as they had both proved during previous fieldwork, and in the formulation of native policy. They provided new access to previously unseen corners of Algerian social life as discussants with native women, though they struggled to escape from the limitations of their European, comparative backgrounds.[64]

For instance, Tillion found that in the "civilized" cities of Algeria women were pressed into servitude. These practices disrupted long-standing kinship ties with far-flung groups across the nomadic and seminomadic groups of the interior. Destroying the relationships of women with each other, in Tillion's view, fractured the basic social structure of Algerian groups and made the encroachment of modernity and industrialization even more destructive to peasants.[65] Tillion proposed that detailed examination of and conversation with the Algerian peasantry must stand as the first step in reform, as the rural population was the segment of Algerian society most targeted by the nascent FLN rebellion. For all of its promise, this analysis continued to compare Algerian women to their French counterparts, forever searching for a nuclear family and space for female liberation and failing to comprehend the complex dynamics of a society under colonial domination, based on a non-European socioeconomic foundation, and enduring wartime privations.[66] Soustelle and his team continued to misinterpret genealogies and the importance of an historical outlook to a people that he was freezing in place through direct study.

Soustelle relied on, though did not necessarily value, similar contributions across his key staff; he expected each to deliver a different perspective on local events. Of the 274 people employed by Soustelle on June 1, 1955, at his Algiers headquarters, 26 served as "key staff" in his civil and military cabinets, with most others dedicated to administrative tasks.[67] It was this smaller group that remained responsible for dialogue with native Algerians to understand and to stamp out revolt. They looked, most importantly, to Ferhat Abbas as a middleman who could deliver his conceptions of both the "average" Algerian and the revolutionary sentiment. Abbas was a French-educated, French-speaking native moderate who advocated for cooperation with France in a process culminating in independence; he was hardly a radical member of the FLN and thus not the best possible choice as liaison with revolutionary movements.

Nonetheless, Soustelle dispatched top-level staff to meet with Abbas on occasion as the best interlocutor with the disparate protest movements. The well-spoken intellectual characterized Soustelle's appointment of well-known scholars of Arab and Berber communities as critical to stemming discontent in the first months of his administration.[68] Abbas described the cabinet as having "among its personnel two men that Muslims know: Jacques Juillet and Commandant Vincent Monteil along with a woman of well-known courage and humanism, Germaine Tillion."[69] Abbas saw all three of these staff members as liberal and possessing significant ethnographic and linguistic expertise, a combination that offered him hope for the future. Monteil, who later authored an updated French translation of Ibn Khaldun and likely introduced some of the North African's civilizational ideas into the administration, tried to conduct oral interviews with FLN leaders but found resistance from Soustelle, who refused to "negotiate" in any sense with armed rebels, forming a schism with his ethnological cabinet from its earliest days.[70] Juillet's activity centered on altering the distribution of wealth and attacking social inequality at its economic roots.[71]

Most importantly, Tillion focused on socioeconomic class investigation and the inequalities of industrialization among the poor peasantry. A heroine of the MH circle of resistance during the Second World War, Tillion survived the camp at Ravensbruck and emerged as an important French scholar of North Africa.[72] She offered strong connections to metropolitan scholarly organizations, in particular the International Institute of African Languages and Cultures, which funded her North African research from 1934 to 1937; and the *Centre nationale de recherche scientifique* (CNRS) that funded her return trip in 1939–1940.[73] Her involvement in the administration thus brought credibility, in Soustelle's eyes, with both metropolitan thinkers and Berbers who were aware of her work with Chaouia tribes in the Aurès. She, in tandem with Monteil, opened the door to Arabic and Berber oral and written sources on local conditions. Her reliance first on governmental research funding and then on the colonial state, though, forced her to avoid any critical views on the nature of French governance in Algeria, particularly under Soustelle and his successor, Robert Lacoste.[74] She thus focused on an "objective" gathering of the facts of social life in Algeria.

Familiar with the works of classical Arab scholars on North Africa from her linguistic and ethnological training in France, Tillion consulted Ibn Khaldun, Leo Africanus, and numerous other North African sources for both background and analytical devices for use in deciphering the local civilizations. Her graduate thesis broke new ground by offering, in the words of her adviser, prominent Orientalist Louis Massignon, "for the first time to integrate different individuals, to sum up the social history" of a particular group.[75] She was primed for colonial investigation in war-torn North Africa.

Tillion arrived in Algeria first under a three-month CNRS mandate to study the socioeconomic causes of the uprising. Following a meeting with Soustelle in February 1955, Tillion entered the cabinet as *chargée de mission*, spending significant time on tours of the countryside in a methodical effort to understand the social realities far from Algiers.[76] In her examinations Tillion leaned heavily on ideas descended from "the great North African Ibn Khaldun," particularly his emphasis on the relationship between ideology and "the manner by which each [group] provides subsistence."[77] She described socioeconomic inequalities that owed much to the distribution of civilization in a process of rise and fall tied to the urban-rural dichotomy.

Tillion's ethnographies of Algerian populations provided Soustelle with what he believed was insight into the actual conditions of Algerian rural groups outside the day-to-day purview of French administrators. However, her approach was tainted by the nature of her research question, as it presupposed some basic social issues as the basis for revolt. Tillion located a social target for French reformers: the educational and economic conditions of the Algerian peasantry. When combined with the work of Monteil and Soustelle's own ethnological experience and understanding, Tillion's conclusions provided the foundation for reform of the Algerian rural populace in an effort to replace the FLN as the benevolent and knowledgeable power.[78] Key to defeating the insurgency, Tillion posited, was developing a counter to what she mistakenly interpreted as its secular and antireligious stance. Islam offered just such an institution.

Tillion observed that Islam, far from a source of "fanaticism and ferocity," instead acted as a "conducting medium" offering access to the accomplishments of both

Western and Eastern civilizations. "These ideas may have been transmitted by a sort of social osmosis," wrote Tillion in 1957, "from areas where the two communities [European and Muslim] were in contact."[79] She agreed with the conclusions of Marty, Delafosse, and others who had pointed to Islam as an important source of intellectual development in the colonies. The depiction of Islam as a progressive force enabled Soustelle to avoid, as much as possible, the dichotomizing language of "modern" France and "Islamic" Algeria in his administration. He instead described a policy of association, toleration, and ultimate integration of the Islamic way of life into the larger French polity, although he gave no sign that Algerians themselves would have the ability to shape the manner in which they would politically enter France.

Integration of Algerian Muslims into the French political structure, in Soustelle's opinion, required a detailed understanding of the unique social and legal norms introduced by Islam. Initially formed in 1935, the *Service des liaisons nord-africains* (SLNA) provided Soustelle and several of his predecessors with analyses that focused on religion as the defining aspect of Algerian life. Ultimately reoriented as the "Muslim policy section" of the civil cabinet, Soustelle expected SLNA staffers to avoid views of Islam as exotic or fanatical in favor of a balanced approach that emphasized Islamic toleration and learning.[80]

For example, a former French attaché in Istanbul sent a lengthy analysis of Islamic fatalism and failure to adapt to French methods to Soustelle in August of 1955. The author, a retired general, depicted Islam as "opposed to the spirit of progress." Colonel Paul Schoen, liberal proponent of Muslim rights, veteran of the native affairs bureau in Morocco, and the director of Soustelle's SLNA, countered by portraying cultural and intellectual achievements as very important in Islam, home to an advanced desire for "human progress."[81] Schoen nonetheless did agree that local Islamic groups needed to change to enter the modern Western world. Schoen concurred that the push to "secularize and modernize Algerian Islam" represented a "vital interest" for the French government in Algeria. His opinion, however, approached the problem from an Orientalist angle, as it overlooked the problem many Muslims would have with Western efforts to "reform" or "modernize" a religion based on the authority of dynastic rule and the power of appointed officials and judges. French reformers had no intellectual, political, or moral legitimacy to change Islamic structures.[82]

In the spirit of modernization, Schoen further advised Soustelle that failure to reduce polygamy and press the rights of women in marriage and childbirth could prove fatal not only to the colonial effort but to an Algerian society itself overcome by an exploding population and unable to produce enough food.[83] Even in an administration that for the first time considered the views of female staff members, Soustelle's key male subordinates caricatured women as silent partners in reproduction and social continuity. Very much products of their times, Schoen and Soustelle did not view women as important social players even as they gladly took their ethnographic inputs. Soustelle conceded that reform could occur only with the close cooperation of Algerians themselves, collaboration that began at the highest levels of government, included women, and extended to all colonial administrators, who were expected to learn local languages and received bonuses for strong results on language testing.[84] In reality, some of these Algerian women, such as Zohra Drif, were actively working to undermine the French presence through the use of FLN-connected social networks.[85] Soustelle's flawed investigative methodology thus caused him to miss opportunities for rapprochement.

Building on the experiences of Faidherbe and Lyautey, the governor-general found that ethnology in time of war primarily aided in understanding the opponent. By eliminating the sources of discontent, he thought the French would destroy socioeconomic and religious divisions that fueled the insurgency. He proposed to conduct these investigations in a "mission of peace" to better understand France's "Muslim sons" in a quest to "hasten the necessary evolution of this country in the direction of progress and of justice by honest and effective reforms."[86] Clearly paternalistic, Soustelle believed it was the responsibility of soldiers, administrators, and missionaries to collect information on colonial populations and to implement the requisite reforms. In Soustelle's mind, colonial functionaries in daily contact with the populations were in better position than governors, politicians, or local Algerian elites to change local circumstances. "These pioneers," Soustelle remembered in 1973, "showed themselves many times closer to Africans, more sensitive to their suffering, more determined to help them," a sentiment influenced at least in part by Mauss's emphasis on the importance of ethnological collection in tandem with people living among the subject population.[87] The low-level functionaries of colonial government could do the most to understand the world of the average Algerian; they helped the French government to react to and stamp out "agitation."[88] It was this reaction to political resistance that fueled violence and linked Soustelle not only to the violent conquests of Faidherbe and Lyautey but also to the right-wing elements among the settler population in Algeria. He never fully understood the causes of or remedies for sociopolitical discontent.

Soustelle, in part referring to his predecessors and political opponents, described revolution as the product of a loss of contact between population and government. He sought to restore that cooperation through intellectual exchange. The ethnological method of Delafosse and Marty, however, did not aid him in identifying intermediary authorities through whom to reestablish communication. Soustelle and his staff sought out both key Algerian political intellectuals and representative members of the rural poor as new contacts in this effort. In the process, he overlooked the importance of young, particularly university-trained elites who found little opportunity for employment in what they saw as a world dominated by France. Young intellectuals such as the teacher and author Mouloud Feraoun had grown by this time to appreciate the FLN, a movement that stood for some in Kabylia as "the guardian of all of our illusions, our extravagant hopes."[89] Ostensibly committed to ethnology conducted with the aid of Algerian intellectuals, Soustelle's administration engaged only with those already available in the political administration, bypassing the possibility of dialogue with people he discarded as terrorists and their sympathizers.

Algerian separatists noted that no form of continued political association with France would deliver the equality they sought, as colonialism inherently produced and relied on inequality. Soustelle and his staff missed the important issues raised by an American historian of France more than twenty years before: "What *does* happen when that superiority is not sufficiently recognized, and what *would* happen should it disappear through the success of European tutelage?" The historian answered his own query in tones that would later reverberate around the French colonial empire: "The association policy, called by whatever name, rests upon mutual interests, which may be temporary, and upon a fraternité that could hardly outlive them if French domination were still asserted."[90] It was power, not brotherhood, that held French Algeria together and tore it apart.

By the middle of 1955 the Algerian revolt still seemed limited to small bands operating in remote areas. Soustelle continued his program of reform not out of desperation, but from a deep-seated belief that his ethnological efforts would correct at least a half century of administrative and scientific neglect. Colonel Schoen advised Soustelle that comprehensive reform would succeed only following recognition of the fundamental misalignment of French and Algerian outlooks. In Schoen's view, the "schooling" of young Algerians, particularly girls, was of paramount importance. Any legislative action had to occur in a "climate of confidence" between the two sides, framed by "true Muslim policy," a coherence dreamed of by Marty and Delafosse in West Africa and never fully realized in practice anywhere in the French colonial system.[91] The "Plan Soustelle," which emerged from the ethnological examinations of the first four months of Soustelle's governor-generalship, therefore focused on three primary areas: land reform to accelerate industrialization, the instruction of Arabic in schools (alongside French), and citizenship for Muslim Algerians.[92] Soustelle did little to realize the first goal, as land reform required the reversal of over a century of policies designed to deliver the best parcels of land to French settlers while collectivizing "nomadic" Arab Algerians. His actual efforts thus focused on the second two pieces of his platform. Believing he had the support of political leaders in the metropole, Soustelle enacted a two-tiered approach to the "integration" of Algeria into France with what he thought was a full view of ethnological, geographic, and historical context.[93] Science thus informed Soustelle's rule in Algeria while also, at least in his mind, legitimizing his approach to his metropolitan superiors and to Algerian legislators.

In Soustelle's new Algeria, language was as a unifying factor for all Algerians regardless of national or ethnic origins. While French instruction would continue in all schools, Soustelle proposed to offer Arabic in two separate tracks. The "literary" or classical Arabic track focused on "Muslims," while its counterpart focused on the specific Algerian Arabic dialect and targeted all others, also referred to as "Europeans." Soustelle's plan did offer Europeans the opportunity to study classical Arabic if so inclined. The educational administration would then funnel the very best classical students, primarily native Muslims, to the French-controlled madrasas, reinvigorated as centers of higher Islamic learning under colonial tutelage.[94] As Marty had envisioned, Islam would serve in Soustelle's government as the educational gateway to African populations. French administrators could make use of its place at the center of local Islamic intellectual life by controlling the curriculum and infusing it with more "modern" ideas. Like his ethnological predecessors, Soustelle cultivated intellectual classes, in this case through their knowledge of classical Arabic, over their rural peers.

At the same time language stood as a bridge between the native divisions Soustelle saw as problematic in forging a unitary Algerian identity. The Berbers, many of whom had at least basic Arabic-speaking skills, stood apart from the colonial enterprise that had focused on controlling the Arab population since the early part of the twentieth century. The governor-general envisioned a "bilingual community" of Europeans, Berbers, and Arabs where the groups could engage in an exchange of the intellectual "treasures" of each "civilization."[95] Soustelle expected enhanced linguistic overlap to eliminate at least one source of friction, mutual intelligibility, and deliver a civilizational equilibrium founded on a common ability to communicate. Language acted as a unifying force, bringing together the disparate groups in Algeria in one or two common tongues. The policy, though, forced language education through French-controlled institutions, denying FLN separatists and other reformers one of their primary goals: control over cultural and linguistic expressions of Algerian identity.[96]

Bundled with measures designed to increase the educational level of Algerian Muslims (similar to American citizenship and civics classes), Soustelle's reform package rested on the increased employment of educated elites in the colonial structure. Unlike previous bills rejected for their ambiguity, Soustelle pushed for "social and intellectual levels" as requirements for government service, standards that would presumably be met (although he never provided a full description) at first by those with French-language skills and education. Through this new corps of civic-minded Muslims, he intended to spread participation to all Algerians over time as the educational system corrected centuries-old deficiencies. Soustelle expected the French to "accelerate the progress" of Algerian society so as to bring citizens of all civilizations to the same level.[97] These reforms necessitated an additional apparatus of practical political, administrative, and economic education designed to give way slowly to native Algerian administration as the population integrated fully into the French national state.

Soustelle turned to the colonial past and the examples of Bugeaud and Lyautey in designing a new integrative administrative device. Colonel Schoen took on the leadership of this effort. He and Soustelle collaborated on the creation of the *sections administratives specialisées* (SAS), an institution constructed on the example of the *bureaux arabes* and following the guidance of nineteenth-century colonial theorist and politician Albert de Broglie. In 1860, the prominent French statesman had advised French Algerian native affairs personnel "to penetrate ... [native] ideas on morality, justice, [and] social progress," a process important enough to form the "lynchpin of French conquest." Even after the *bureaux* slowly dissolved with the advent of civilian administration in Algeria in 1870, the idea persisted among colonists interested in social reform. Schoen quoted the most prominent of these thinkers, Lyautey, in calling for administrators with "no preconceived notions" about native populations. The colonial state needed military officers, said Schoen and Lyautey, who were "apt at understanding, feeling, judging, and divining needs" of their small communities.[98] Dissent, violence, and underdevelopment resulted not from fundamental defects of Islam or Arabic-Berber civilization, Schoen thought, but from a French "break in contact" with the population over the preceding 100 years.

In an effort to correct this gap, Soustelle and Schoen turned to the idea of ethnological native affairs officers adopted by Lyautey during his tenure in the Moroccan protectorate. By March 1955 Soustelle had convinced the French colonial and interior ministries to grant temporary transfer of several of these specially trained officers, who he called "elite elements" of the colonial service, to duty in the Aurès, the seat of revolt. Managed initially by the French army, Soustelle saw the "happy results" of their work, particularly their ability to react to local circumstances.[99] The program rapidly expanded by December 1955 to 196 SAS offices. Soustelle's "forward antenna of local authority" also included "medico-social" experts to help increase public confidence in the French ability to offer protection from rebel bands, as they were fluent in Arabic and also able to provide medical assistance when needed following FLN assaults.[100]

Officiers des affaires algériennes (OAA), topical experts with Arabic language skills, commanded SAS offices. Each SAS included an OAA acting as the "representative of central authority" and the "technical advisor of pacification." He had a staff including a noncommissioned officer or contractor and four technical specialists, including secretaries and interpreters. At times the staff increased with French and native Algerian women assisting in home medical care along with between thirty and fifty native security personnel also known as *makhzen*.[101] Women provided an important link to the hidden world of Algeria. Soustelle hoped that the use of SAS women, both French and Algerian, would help the government converse with Algerian groups in their own language, to convince them of the positive aspects of the French colonial state through direct intervention in one of what he saw as the key concerns of the daily life of an Algerian mother and wife: the health of her family. This newly converted corps of loyal French subjects, he thought, would exert influence on their family groups to support the French and reject the pan-Arab, pan-Islamic dogma of the FLN. Success in this approach, though, assumed a perfect set of SAS personnel with wide-ranging language skills, social understanding, and a willingness to risk their lives on long trips in the countryside. All of these factors, in fact, did not exist in most offices.[102]

Ignorant of these limitations, Soustelle expected his SAS offices to exercise "incessant activity" in "taking the population back in hand," particularly in rural areas "endowed with insufficient instruments of civilization." Comprising military, financial, and administrative aspects, the SAS model sought to reestablish what the governor-general called "national cohesion" to stamp out revolt from the ground up while also providing detailed ethnological examination.[103] In the words of Colonel Schoen, "true pacification is becoming that of hearts and minds." Winning over the local populace required a *"permanent investigation"* by an OAA operating as "topographer, geographer, ethnographer, agricultural engineer … and psychologist." The officers, educated on topics ranging from languages to Islamic jurisprudence, would produce a "monograph" on each sector intended to document their efforts and provide a strong baseline for future students of the area.[104] Above all, Schoen and Soustelle cautioned their field officers to avoid the power struggles and resistance to central government authority that doomed the *bureaux arabes*; they could not afford an emotionally involved "arabophilia," but had to remain both aloof and objective. SAS officers were thus caught in a vise between the integrationist ideal and the violent reality that put them in the middle of a poor administration, active rebels, a general resistance to change on all sides, and the widely divergent mind-sets of both European and Algerian activists.[105] While Soustelle recognized that the on-the-ground approach could cause a native backlash, generating complaints of paternalism, he stayed true to his model of civilizational development, calling for a measured approach that was "progressive" and "in good faith."[106] In his mind, the Algerian revolt stood no chance as long as the French gave proper attention to native concerns exposed by scientific examination and administration.

Soustelle's reforms that stimulated "contact" and development were perhaps the most durable of his short tenure as governor-general. "Implanted in the furthest reaches of the *bled* [Algerian near-desert], in the mountains or on the steppes," Soustelle told the Algerian assembly, SAS offices "devoted themselves body and soul to a noble task," an effort that expanded into the cities after Soustelle's departure in early 1956.[107] These offices, however, did not directly address the basic educational gap that Soustelle and his staff saw keeping the vast majority of native Algerians ignorant of and apart from the political franchise. In recognition of this problem, Tillion suggested that Soustelle create *centres sociaux* to provide supplementary education for native Algerians not able to access established schools. At the same time, she proposed these centers as tools to reduce rural poverty through specialized education in advanced agrarian techniques. Educational access, Tillion believed, gave rural natives at least an opportunity to escape cycles of poverty, malnourishment, and ignorance by giving them the intellectual tools to pursue better economic opportunities in the cities or even in France itself.[108]

Tillion recommended all the social centers operate under the direction of an experienced administrator, a man or woman with at least three years of colonial experience.[109] Not only central locations for ethnological and sociological study, Tillion expected the centers to act as meeting places for native French and Arabic speakers alike. Consequently, the sites offered a remedial French language sequence to accompany Soustelle's proposed Arabic language program for European colonists. Known as "français parlé," the curriculum presented elementary-level education to adolescents between fourteen and nineteen years of age five times a week over five months. Strictly limited to young males with prospective employment,[110] pre-professional language instruction worked hand-in-hand with the efforts of Soustelle and Tillion to create a class of French-literate elites able to take over the political and economic stewardship of Algeria. The centers produced bulletins with discussion on social topics from both French- and Arab-speaking authors printed in both languages.[111] Viewed by French Africanist scholars and soldiers as a hindrance to change since at least the time of Lyautey, the perceived subordination of Islamic women took center stage in the creation of Tillion's new curriculum that aimed at a "basic education" for all Algerians regardless of gender or status.[112] Equality of access to educational materials served as the primary purpose of these centers. The full integration of Algeria could happen only after the population gained a greater appreciation of European methods.

Soustelle thus charged the centers to support "all initiatives with the potential to improve the economic, social, and cultural progress of the population."[113] The governor-general and his ethnological aide envisioned them as sites of educational remediation and economic advancement. Tillion saw industrial and economic underdevelopment as the root cause of conflict and unrest in Algeria, creating a base inequality stemming from more than a century of colonial excess and repression.[114] Indeed, these centers echoed the efforts of Paul Marty to catalog genealogies and ideas in West Africa thirty years before while also building on the work of Mouloud Feraoun's failed *comité algérien pour l'éducation de base*.[115] All of these initiatives strove to ignite conversations and networks across societies, languages, and eras in the hope of a more benevolent and effective political collaboration. Soustelle described the centers in similar terms to the Algerian assembly in November 1955: "These centers constitute polyvalent organisms designed to ensure the accelerated development of under-developed collectivities towards material and moral well-being. Veritable cultural missions, they associate, at the personal level, the means and methods of education, health, professional training and agricultural modernization."[116] Moral development in this case implied a leveling of the educational opportunities across gender and age lines. Soustelle and Tillion had thus undertaken a comprehensive effort at social change and re-engineering that they hoped to achieve through the assistance of native elites. These reforms, however, relied on projected capabilities. Promises of future access to careers based on French language capability did not appeal to FLN supporters, who desired immediate access to the socioeconomic opportunities enjoyed by the citizens of France and the rest of the international community.[117]

Unfortunately for Soustelle and for France, these reforms stood little chance of success when opposed to compelling calls for the recovery of "national dignity" and a new "psycho-political union of all Algerians" from the FLN. Even moderate Algerian politicians by this time were forced to base their positions on a rejection of the French colonial presence if they hoped to maintain power.[118] Soustelle's ethnological efforts, linked to far-right settlers, based on dated colonial science, determinedly inward-looking, productive of political violence, and mired in a fundamental misreading of the sources of revolt and the ideological background of the FLN rebels, failed to assuage native social and political unrest or to address the larger nationalist, pan-Arab, and pan-Islamic sentiment moving through the region. Young, disaffected Algerian intellectuals, attuned to international events, rejected any French government that restricted their voice in the emerging Algerian nation and beyond. Soustelle's inability to perceive this sentiment at the root of unrest doomed his efforts to institute a cooperative Franco-Algerian government.

The failure of reform and the crash of ethnology

Soustelle saw progressive social policy as vital to Algeria's future, "the difference between life and death." He felt that only the work of dedicated scientists and policymakers such as Tillion could save Algeria from economic stagnation and ultimately social disintegration.[119] Beyond the resistance of FLN separatists, he found his efforts blocked at every turn by the ultra right-wing French colonists or the intransigence of Parisian politicians he had counted as supporters.[120] Fundamentally flawed and lacking real political coherence, Soustelle's ethnological approach appealed to no one. Revolutionary cadres posed the greatest danger to ethnologists in the field and also presented an enormous obstacle to Soustelle's programs. Although unknown to Soustelle at the time, the FLN, as the sole remaining revolutionary inheritor of earlier Algerian nationalist groups, represented the closest to a consolidated voice, announcing the real causes of unrest among the native Algerian population. SAS officers viewed the FLN as a worthy foe, countering state moves toward population control and reconstituting itself regardless of colonial action.[121]

Far from a passive opponent, the FLN and its military wing, the *armée de libération nationale* (ALN), focused on the SAS offices as their principal foes. For all of its limitations, Soustelle's ethnological approach threatened the FLN goal of intellectually and emotionally capturing the population so as to "transform the popular torrent into creative energy."[122] Recognizing elements of Maoist warfare that also constituted a core part of their own doctrine, FLN cadres sought to stop the "politico-administrative gymnastics" of SAS staffs. Although the OAA officers were still "novices," FLN leadership feared their ability to "acquire the people politically" if not stopped by deliberate methods of psychological warfare such as intimidation, carefully targeted violence, and propaganda.[123] French government offices in close contact with local populations threatened the FLN power base in the countryside. Revolutionary leaders thus looked to stop French methods of information collection that they perceived as another instrument of the oppressive colonial regime and a counter to the growing influence of revolutionary cadres. The revolutionaries saw a "permanent danger" in ethnological and administrative networks of native Algerian soldiers and their families. To the FLN, the actions of the SAS constituted open warfare.

While committed to violent attacks on French sympathizers and government officials, the FLN recognized the value of the SAS "hearts and minds" approach. The group sought to counter the reliance, in their eyes present as a deliberate policy since Lyautey, on doctors as "agents of pacification" by "conquering ignorance and misery." They instructed ALN fighters to destroy public confidence in French medicine by sabotaging their efforts as FLN-affiliated elites simultaneously offered effective medical and financial assistance to rural populations. Revolutionary leaders further directed their cadres to destroy French informational networks by attacking French-allied native Algerian military forces and offering an alternative educational system run by and for nationalist cadres working purely in Arabic.[124] French efforts at scientific examination and administration thus found significant roadblocks as the FLN at times menaced programs such as the ethnological work of Pierre Bourdieu and his team in eastern Algeria.[125]

The ethnological makeup of his cabinet placed Soustelle in a unique position to negotiate and converse with these rebel leaders in hopes of stemming the tide of rebellion. Tillion, Monteil, and Juillet had cultivated personal connections during their years of ethnographic fieldwork. They turned this expertise and supposed credibility with the native population they believed came from such close study into a means both to understand the causes of revolt and to mediate or reduce further acts of violence. Soustelle's view of the FLN as terrorists, however, limited their reach. Only after his reign, in 1957, was Tillion able to gain an audience with Saadi Yacef, FLN chief for Algiers, to curb the violence then occurring in the city.[126]

For his part, Soustelle met with Abbas several times beginning on April 2, 1955, to work on a solution to the violence. Abbas found Soustelle "a great man ... [who] did not lack good intentions." However, the turmoil of revolutionary Algeria needed more than that. Even in Abbas' mind, the time for reform had passed. It was a world where the "immobility" of French politics doomed any negotiated peace. Arab-Muslim leaders, recalled Abbas, agreed with Monteil and Juillet who "registered with anguish this immobility that justified, if such a thing was still necessary, the revolt of the oppressed."[127] This political stasis and policy incoherence doomed Soustelle's ethnological efforts and jaded Monteil, who scolded his superior: "I persist in not believing in the possibility of attempting both repression and 'reforms.' One must choose."[128] French Algerian governments had used torture and other extreme measures since 1954, a fact that certainly influenced the continued intransigence of some separatist leaders.[129] Soustelle's failure to rein in these brutal measures contributed to the disenchantment of his staff and emboldened his enemies who could turn such measures against the French in psychological warfare.

The resignation of both Monteil and Juillet in the summer of 1955 over these concerns offered FLN leaders, in Abbas' words, "new proof of the impotence of France."[130] With the loss of this "left wing" of Soustelle's cabinet, even Algerian moderates had to conclude that any possibility of true reform was gone; the right-wing elements of French colonial politics had ultimately won the day. Buoyed by increased support from disenchanted Algerian politicians, the FLN on August 20, 1955, launched a renewed wave of violence in the countryside. A failure in terms of dead and captured, the FLN could nonetheless claim victory in the "war of subversion," as they had created a deep trench between Europeans and native Algerians that would soon fill with "a river of blood," as Soustelle would later put it.[131] In the face of such violence the governor-general remained an idealist. Committed to his failed program, he continued to push for a political solution through the full incorporation of a unitary Algeria into the French state. By this time, however, discontent with the conduct of the war among French metropolitan elites had made such a goal politically untenable for Fourth Republic governments already on shaky ground. Soustelle did little to aid the French government, as his regime contributed to a long legacy of intrusive, directive French colonial policy in Algeria that did not account for the changing views of well-educated elites unwilling to accept a future of limited political rights.

As an ethnologist, Soustelle expected support from non-European Algerians in pushing for political integration. In his mind, the detailed scientific examinations of his staff set the stage for a properly tailored progression into the French state. He continued talks with Algerian leaders in the administration and expanded socioeconomic investigations in the countryside. These discussions came to naught, however, as the young nationalist leaders rejected Soustelle's proposed reliance on religious leaders in moving the state forward. While respectful of their elders, native nationalists called for greater roles for the young, well-educated secular elite and an incorporation of religious messages into a coherent Algerian national identity. By the end of September 1955, even the Muslim councils, composed largely of moderates, had rejected Soustelle's appeals for integration in favor of an as-yet ill-defined national model, one that fully dismissed any further role for France in Algeria's future.[132] In a twist replicated across the colonial world over the next twenty years, the people groomed by Soustelle to ease the transition into a new form of Franco-Algerian statehood discarded the model, instead opting for a future of national self-determination without French interference.

Conclusion

As the Fourth Republic teetered on the brink of collapse due in large part to the unpopularity of the Algerian war in France, Soustelle's position became untenable. He was recalled in January 1956, ironically now fêted by the settler community initially hostile to his appointment. Viewed as the sole voice for a continued *algérie française* by the French Algerian right-wing, his departure drew massive crowds (composed primarily of French settlers with very few native Algerians) to the docks to wish him well and call for his return as the only man still willing to keep Algeria French. He gave a final statement to the crowd, further stoking their hope for a reversal of fortune: "If you want me to continue to defend French Algeria then let me leave."[133] Now simply a member of the national assembly from Lyon, Soustelle kept his promise, returning to Algeria with de Gaulle in triumph in 1958 as the latter announced his return to politics and a continued *algérie française* in the new Fifth Republic.[134] However, Soustelle's renewed popularity in Gaullist circles dissipated with the revolt of military officers in Algeria and his reported complicity in the attempted putsch of 1961, a charge he denied until his death.[135] Even if not directly involved, Soustelle's political intransigence in the face of compelling social evidence had doomed him to a legacy as a right-wing colonial. Committed to ethnological and humanist ideals that were on the cutting-edge in the 1920s and 1930s, he seemed a relic by the 1950s.

Describing himself as "exiled and alone, spectator to a bloody drama that is destroying my country," Soustelle continued to press for Algerian integration until that country's independence in 1962.[136] Finally pardoned for his alleged role in the 1961 military revolt after de Gaulle's retirement in 1968, Soustelle went back to academic ethnology at EPHE and the MH, accompanying students on fieldwork in Mexico and creating an anthropological center in Lyon. Elected to the *Académie française* on June 2, 1983, Soustelle died of cancer on August 7, 1990, at his home in France.[137] His efforts to rein in Algerian political violence via a careful study of social life had failed.

Soustelle's administration ultimately represented the political culmination of more than a century of ethnological efforts to build a strong link between native and French understandings of difference in the colonies. The failure of his efforts revealed the weakness of science as policy; despite efforts to train his administrators to study the populace and consider their views, the project remained at its base paternalistic, developmental, and ignorant of the background and content of the separatist national movement. Soustelle's government continued the deeply internalized analysis of his predecessors, largely ignorant or dismissive of changes to the international or even transregional environment even if he did allow for some consideration of a Gamel Abdel Nasser-led pan-Arab conspiracy.[138] A flawed understanding of the Islamic nature of the revolt, and indeed of the power of Islamic genealogical and historical imaginaries in forming a nationalist conception, doomed his efforts to failure. His brand of ethnology, especially when based on concepts and techniques devised for West Africa in the first decades of the twentieth century, did not account for the relatively small but quite active group of disenchanted young Algerian intellectuals. These individuals had identities that simply did not fit with the French ethnological approach. They coded themselves not purely as Muslims, Kabyles, or Arabs, but as a combination of all of those things in an environment of national self-determination. No amount of sympathetic science could overcome a basic disrespect for the right to self-government, for the unwillingness to see the inherent violence of the colonial system.

From the cataclysm of the Algerian war emerged a new generation of social scientists repulsed by the excesses of colonial domination. Valuing a dialogue with native groups, these new thinkers dismissed political concerns and focused on the theoretical possibilities of science outside the metropole. Pierre Bourdieu, a young conscript working briefly in Soustelle's military cabinet and continuing on under Robert Lacoste, conducted ethnological and sociological studies of Algerian civilization in hopes of uncovering basic truths of social construction. Battling the powerful structural convention of Claude Lévi-Strauss then in vogue in French metropolitan theoretical circles, Bourdieu found in Soustelle's Algeria the optimum place for study oriented around the notion of individual contingency and variance. Ultimately, he worked under the model first given to Soustelle by Marcel Mauss: "He drew away, and drew us away as well, from the temptation to schematize that is built into the science of man."[139] Where Soustelle had failed, Bourdieu aimed to succeed.

6

Colonial Inheritance: Pierre Bourdieu and the Struggle for the Future of French Social Theory

As a wartime ethnologist in Algeria, Pierre Bourdieu worked with "extreme sadness and anxiety," risking personal safety in an effort to study Algerian society and aid its escape from the trap of Western colonial domination.[1] He practiced an engaged ethnological sociology concerned with the plight of its subjects and approaching scientific study as a "martial art ... to be used in self defense."[2] The preeminent French social critic and intellectual after the death of Michel Foucault in the 1980s, Bourdieu inherited the century-old debate on association. Disgusted by colonial excess, he worked to subvert the colonial political order through what he viewed as an appropriately inclusive form of social examination.

Working initially from a powerful empirical base developed in close cooperation with non-French residents of Algeria, Bourdieu offered an alternative to what he saw as the unimaginative structural approach that dominated French social science beginning in the 1950s. The young scholar reintroduced to social understanding and interaction the importance of context, local conditions, and individual variation by seeking no less than "a sort of Copernican revolution" through an active investigation of a society from its "interior." Bourdieu's approach encouraged social scientists to understand human collectivities "according to their own logic, norms and values,"[3] an idea derived in this French colonial tradition from Louis Faidherbe's initial intervention in Senegal and passed down through the ethnology of Maurice Delafosse and the sociology of Marcel Mauss, who Bourdieu frequently cited as among his most important influences.[4] In accepting that inheritance, however, he explicitly rejected the exploitation that came with colonial science and widened his lens to target the true source of malaise: the French colonial structure itself.

Basing his conclusions on data collected during his Algerian sojourn of 1955–1961 and included in publications into the early 1970s, Bourdieu returned the individual to discussions of social form and function while pressing for important dialogues between subjects and their foreign observers. From this position, he reconceptualized the collection and analysis of ethnological data and looked, with a weary and pessimistic eye, to the futures of Algeria and France. His Algerian experiences shaped his view of the world. The apparent hopelessness of a people crushed under the power of "modernity" and the onslaught of a market economy led him to theorize a basic disconnect between subjective and objective social structures.[5] Bourdieu thus upended the developmental concepts advanced by the French colonial ethnologists before him. More than an advocate for change according to a Western rubric, Bourdieu pushed Algerian Kabyles in particular to reappropriate their own identities, in the process escaping the time capsule in which colonialism had locked them.

In Bourdieu's experience, Algerian peasants took a different view of the horizon of experience and possibility than Europeans. "Different criteria of truthfulness are applied in the case of an event occurring within familiar space and in the case of a happening in the land of legends beginning at the very border of the directly experienced world," he wrote in 1963.[6] People, he thought, existed in multiple frames of reference simultaneously. The way in which they reconciled the differences between their everyday experiences and abstract beliefs revealed much about the forces that shaped social interaction. In this sense, Bourdieu agreed with the groundbreaking critique offered by Balandier in 1950, calling for a full consideration of societies before and after colonial contact in view of their specific "milieux."[7] Bourdieu could thus succeed where Mauss had failed and include the full range of historical elements that had influenced colonial societies.

Bourdieu's ethnological project built on Mauss's example with notable improvements introduced by reflexive and contextualized examinations. For instance, Bourdieu found that Kabyle "criteria of truthfulness" varied by individual circumstance. Such individual and group variations permitted Bourdieu to challenge the structural conclusions of Claude Lévi-Strauss by advocating a relativist approach to social experience anchored in personal history and the concept of the habitus, the accumulated influences on a person that formed the limits of his or her social experience and position. A detailed examination of Bourdieu's early writings, anchored in early Algerian empirical data gathered at first during military service, reveals his descent from the Delafosse–Mauss line of ethnological thought. Initially an agent of the state, he took an overtly anticolonial stance while extolling the importance of interested intellectuals in the interpretation of their own societal norms.

Never comfortable in rural peasant or metropolitan academic circles, Bourdieu, like so many others engaged in African ethnology, stood astride multiple worlds. Caught between the urban and the rural, the intellectual and the self-taught, and the modern and the traditional, Bourdieu devoted his life to challenging scholarly conventions.[8] He sought out colonial research subjects who lived on the edges of society, people to whom he could relate in a new spirit of sociology, one informed by and engaged with the lives of both subject and analyst. Societal change came not from the top-down or the bottom-up but from the margins in his mind, making those people resident on the outskirts of society prime subjects for ethnological investigation.

As other French ethnologists had suggested, Bourdieu found that migration and the movement of peoples over time altered modes of social interaction. Newcomers, heavily influenced by "the urban milieu and above all by their knowledge of the modern world and 'civilization,'" irrevocably modified the urban-rural interaction and Algerian society as a whole.[9] However, these new arrivals, for all their power as agents of change, did not immediately fit with the existing socioeconomic order, particularly that imposed by colonial rule. Many of them, Bourdieu posited, positioned themselves as intellectuals on the edges of "traditional" rural life, in the process becoming "organic" thinkers who renounced colonial allegiance through open conflict.[10] In this rupture Bourdieu saw opportunity for sociological study. It was this study that motivated him. It was this study that brought him to Algeria. It was this study that challenged the limited and internal ethnological narratives developed by his predecessors. It was this study that shaped the future of social theory in France and beyond.

Trapped between intellectual worlds: Bourdieu and Algerian fieldwork

Difference drove Bourdieu to understand the world around him. He saw himself as an awkward peg that did not fit in any particular opening. Experiences as the son of a white-collar worker in a blue-collar, largely agrarian part of southern France forced him to recognize his dissimilarity, as did his position as the country boy in schools of urban elites both in the small cities of southern France and later in Paris. In trying to define himself and his worldview, Bourdieu worked against most of the dominant intellectual paradigms of his time. He first rebelled against the Sartrean model of an "engaged" intellectual, striving instead for factual depth and extolling the power of empirical analysis and explanation as the true *raison d'être* for a modern French social scientist. He saw himself as an exemplar for a new generation of scientists who took full stock of their role in the life of subjects, but who also remained detached from the political sphere, a detachment he would find himself unable to maintain as he gained greater fame in France late in his life. Upon his arrival in Algeria, he found a world dominated by conservative politics and poor science in the Soustelle governorship. Instead, he described Algerian Islamic society as a unique and valuable social construction. All of Bourdieu's early work, though, attacked problems from the edges.

Born August 1, 1930, the young Bourdieu grew up as the son of a mailman. His family had entered the professional, nonagrarian world only recently, as his father came from sharecroppers and his mother from a relatively wealthy peasant family. The family thus did not enjoy even the little prominence that came with multigenerational occupation of official posts. Making his life even more difficult, Bourdieu's home Béarn region hosted primarily petty agriculture, making him something of a socioeconomic outcast, a white-collar child in a blue-collar world.[11] An outsider as a bourgeois among peasants, Bourdieu soon found himself even further outside the norm as a scholarship student at the provincial *lycée* in Pau, where his classmates did not recognize the name of his village and considered him rural and uneducated, a phenomenon that recurred even more forcefully when he later attended school in Paris.[12]

As a student at the famed *école normale superieure* (ENS) and *faculté des lettres*, Bourdieu confronted his otherness. He found himself at the highest levels of French academia but still very much on the outside of the university establishment.[13] In later writings he compared his position to the plight of the Algerian intellectual, who remained "a man, standing between two civilizations, who has been deeply stricken by all the tragedies of his people, and who quite often is himself inclined to a lukewarm or indifferent attitude in regard to religion."[14] He had problems coming to terms with the socioeconomic and class determinism that seemed to define the French academy, basic issues that would color his work for the entirety of his academic career. Understanding social structure and its components became central to his life. Difference drove him.

At the ENS from 1951 to 1954 and as a *lycée* teacher from 1954 to 1955, Bourdieu became familiar with the great works of sociology, particularly those of Emile Durkheim and Mauss. "There was a kind of horror of Durkheim," he recalled. "No one wanted to hear him spoken about." However, Bourdieu's teaching experience opened his eyes to the value of these early practitioners of sociology: "I had to read them [Durkheim's writings] in order to teach them, and it is then that I became interested in them since they helped me a lot in my empirical work … Mauss even more … I read pre-structuralist texts with a structuralist mode of thinking."[15] Like Mauss before him, Bourdieu sought the structures that lay under social formations. Again like his academic predecessor, he found that this search revealed only greater contextual complexity, one that he found himself better positioned to understand as colonial structures disintegrated.

In studying this complexity, Bourdieu entered an intellectual tradition in transition. Following the First World War, French philosophers discovered the work, in particular, of prominent German phenomenologist Edmund Husserl (1859–1938). As Michel Foucault has described, French thinkers who adapted Husserl's ideas broke into two distinct interpretations. The first, known as the "philosophy of the subject," found its strongest proponent in Jean-Paul Sartre. The explosion of existentialism after the Second World War as the most important Western European philosophy grew in part from its rhetoric of freedom, a message that appealed to European populations recently released from Nazi occupation.[16]

Foucault noted that another branch, often forgotten, also grew from the German tradition. Advanced most importantly by Georges Canguilhem, the "formalist" or "philosophy of knowledge" interpretation advocated a more theoretical and rational approach to the study of man, one based at least in part in the idea of the "universal deployment of reason" attributed to the Comtean positivist tradition, a powerful influence in its own right on French ethnology. In essence, Canguilhem explored the epistemology of Western understandings of truth-making. Truth, for Canguilhem and also later for Bourdieu, did not result purely from experience. In fact, the belief in a true/false dichotomy stemmed from what Canguilhem called "error." In Canguilhem's mind, existentialists committed a grave mistake in believing they could actually develop absolute "truth," a concept that was in his mind unattainable if considered from a rationalist point of view.[17] Bourdieu, in an article with Jean-Claude Passeron, discussed the effect of this belief in scientific truth: "Because empirical sociology in France was founded on the illusion of a first beginning and, by the same token, on ignorance of the epistemological problems posed by any scientific practice, as well as on a deliberate or unwitting disregard of the theoretical past of European science, it could not but succumb to positivist temptations."[18] Canguilhem's influence found its way to the very heart of Bourdieu's approach to science. Absolute truth was an expectation only for those who failed to see the error inherent in all human observation and analysis.

Lévi-Strauss and like-minded philosophers eventually followed Canguilhem's example, striking at an existential strawman that they saw as too focused on human experience and the variance introduced by individuals. Instead, they perceived the world through structure, concepts that shaped social interaction but that existed above and below the perceived and experienced surface of the world. Human actors in the daily performance of their social existence could not discern these structures. From this abstract perspective, Lévi-Strauss and his peers developed sophisticated models of the function of societal elements that remained fixed across time and space, often expressed in human experience as myths or legends. Fieldwork thus remained important in gathering these discernible expressions, but only insofar as the information gained aided the analyst in the divination of a theoretical model.[19]

While Lévi-Strauss had followed Mauss in basing his analysis on localized information, he, on the contrary, found little value in the history of "primitive societies" that offered "no lessons" to social anthropology.[20] Lévi-Straussian structuralism looked "beyond the empirical facts to the relations between them," which in Lévi-Strauss's words confirmed that "these relations are simpler and more intelligible than the things they interconnect," an approach that remained "resolutely teleological."[21] Sociological and anthropological truth, Lévi-Strauss theorized, was "not to be found among the elements of history." Instead, his brand of anthropology discerned structure through data that achieved "some degree of credibility because of their over-all coherence."[22] It was this structure that confronted and initially interested Bourdieu. Just as important, though, was the sociology of Marcel Mauss.

Viewing Mauss's writing as part of his "personal treasure," Bourdieu joined him in rejecting what the young thinker called "Lévy-Bruhl's mistake," or the creation of an "insurmountable distance between the anthropologist and those he takes as object." He modeled his scholarship on the writings of Mauss, who had described sociology as the study of "men of flesh and blood, living and having lived ... sociology like *human psychology* is part of this portion of biology that is anthropology, which is to say the accumulation of sciences considering man as a living being, conscious and sociable."[23] Ethnology, in this view, considered social interaction a uniquely human construction, one actively shaped and interpreted by the participants themselves. Sociologists and anthropologists could penetrate and explain this structure, in Bourdieu's mind, only when they considered their own views and backgrounds as part of this mixture.

Mauss's theories offered Bourdieu a way into structure, the ultimate aim of all sociologists. Bourdieu valued Mauss's work for its focus on specific civilizations and their constituent individuals, a profoundly humanist endeavor made easier by access to colonial subjects. Working against the currents of rigid structuralism and the continued strength of the aging, academically sedentary Durkheimians, Bourdieu sought out sociological study in the colonies. He hoped to profit there from a vast supply of empirical data without the stifling formalism of life in Parisian academia. In turning to sociology/ethnology and away from philosophy, Bourdieu rebelled against the French academic expectation that the finest theoretical minds would focus solely on abstract thought. While philosophers looked down on sociologists as "averagely empirical, lacking any theoretical or empirical inspiration," in Bourdieu's words, Durkheimian sociologists looked down on ethnologists who did not adopt their particular view of evolutionary social structures and elementary, universal forms.[24] Such a hierarchy of knowledge, Bourdieu believed, did little to honor Maussian relativism. Choosing Mauss over Durkheim, Bourdieu envisioned sociology as interdisciplinary, a science that incorporated the best of historical, ethnological, and economic data. An outsider by birth and nature, Bourdieu detested the idea of the intellectual elite developing theories far removed from the empirical source.

Local understanding, according to Bourdieu's model, depended on a full appreciation of context, a process that required self-analysis by the scientist himself or herself. Bourdieu's concern with science as self-critique grew in large part from his perception of existentialism. Sartre served as the face of this group, the personal culmination of the "mythology of the free intellectual." By the end of the Second World War, Sartre had parlayed his success as a philosopher and playwright to international fame, in the process establishing strong connections to international communism and in particular revolutionary movements. In Sartre's mind, the "authentic individual" carried an ethic of "permanent revolution"; he or she must wade into the middle of social movements in order to effect change.[25] Bourdieu, feeding off caricatures of existentialists as hedonists, positioned himself as the very opposite of a Sartrean free spirit, experiencing the world. Instead, he believed that philosophers must devote themselves to study, using their writings to inform and influence while avoiding involvement in the movements they described. Incorporation into political movements tainted the results of scientific or philosophical investigation.

Bourdieu considered knowledge generated by Sartre's concrete descriptions of the lived and experienced world as lacking in introspection. For Bourdieu, existential expositions became a pointless endeavor steeped in the exaltation of the researcher as a sort of philosopher-king not weighed down by evidentiary concerns. In the young social scientist's eyes, the existentialists lost sight of the most important scientific goal, an understanding of the rules, boundaries, and structures of social interaction. The Sartrean model of the total or ideal intellectual drove Bourdieu from the academic world: "I can say that I constructed myself, as I left the scholastic universe … against everything that the Sartrean enterprise represented for me."[26] Existentialism exerted an initial influence on Bourdieu through the emphasis on lived experience; however, the theory's failure to self-examine, to consider the sources of knowledge themselves made the philosophy less useful in the long run.[27] Dedicated to teaching and against the conceit of academic political activism, Bourdieu turned toward Canguilhem's epistemological approach as delivered in lectures at the EPHE and the *Collège de France*.[28] The young thinker immersed in the nontraditional academic milieux that had hosted Mauss for virtually his entire career, finding the inspiration for a new philosophy of science, one that would foreground the researcher.

Still groping for a theoretical approach to inform his own brand of sociology, Bourdieu turned to structuralism. He was drawn to the movement's efforts to "distinguish themselves from existentialism and all that it entailed in their eyes: that inspired 'humanism' that was prevalent, the preference for 'lived experience.'"[29] Also descended from phenomenology, Lévi-Straussian structuralism drew on Durkheim and Mauss, although Lévi-Strauss had never studied directly with either man. The structuralist paid homage to the AS, a "workshop where modern anthropology fashioned part of its tools and that we have abandoned, not so much out of disloyalty as out of the sad conviction that the task would prove too much for us."[30] What the AS movement had lacked, in Lévi-Strauss's view, was a coherent framework that could inform the explanation of social phenomena. Social analysis required a careful examination of each element's relation to the whole and to each other to discern the overall outline. In short, social reality was far too complex to boil down to a single, all-encompassing evolutionary portrait.

Lévi-Strauss and his followers took their views too far in Bourdieu's estimation. In assembling a "basic catalogue" of "simple elements and the laws governing their combination," Bourdieu believed the structuralists committed the cardinal sin of missing change and the contingencies introduced by time and history. Structuralist theory, he wrote, "leads to the placing of history between parentheses."[31] Instead, he turned back to Canguilhem and examined the sources of knowledge. By looking at social organization at its source, he hoped to understand the variance he saw in all human interactions. Algeria offered Bourdieu an opportunity to see variety and the importance of history firsthand. The ethnological investigations he conducted in Algeria revealed the impossibility of a structural description of an Algerian society enduring massive change as the colonial period drew to a bloody end.

Bourdieu gathered a large majority of the empirical materials for his writings on basic social forms and the clashes of civilizations during his time in Algeria from 1955 to 1961. The data he collected during this period formed the center of his views on education, cultural formation, time, development, and habitus.[32] Arriving in 1955 to serve his compulsory service in the French military, Bourdieu refused entry into the officer corps, opting instead to remain an enlisted man. Thanks to the intervention of a colonel from his native region, Bourdieu moved to the staff of the governor-general in Algiers in early 1956, an assignment that provided more opportunity for philosophical reflection and interaction with non-French Algerians themselves on a less confrontational (i.e., not as "pacification") basis. Little evidence remains to pinpoint his precise activities in this period, as most cabinet works did not contain authorial attribution. He may have participated in the editing of propaganda documents and in the creation of a compendium of French knowledge on Algeria.[33] In any case, he remained on the military staff as a clerk until 1957, when his military contract expired.

The young soldier spent his military years in Algiers profitably, working with the Social Secretariat, a reform organization originally founded by the Catholic Church to press ecumenical ideas in France's North African department.[34] Funding from this group enabled the young soldier-scholar to move into the rural interior and conduct a preliminary investigation of peasant life. They sponsored his first article-length publications and gave him time to write his initial ethnological monograph on Algeria. Although a mere private, Bourdieu enjoyed a large reputation thanks to his academic connections.

Following his discharge from military service, Bourdieu worked as an assistant professor of philosophy and sociology at the University of Algiers from 1958 to 1961. In that time Bourdieu enjoyed the assistance of not only metropolitan academics but also colonial scholars. A few local French archivists and historians "helped me considerably," and "guided my first steps," he recalled as he came to terms with the "transformations undergone by [the] peasant economy and society,"[35] as described by Germaine Tillion and the other ethnologists employed during Soustelle's governor-generalship. The focus by these ethnologists on modes of agrarian production and the possibilities of modernization and conversion to industrial production led Bourdieu to consult the works of Jacques Berque (1910–1995), the acclaimed scholar of North Africa who had grown up in Algeria and written on socioeconomic life in the region. Finding in Berque an "extraordinary guide for the young ethnologist-sociologist that I was," he relied on *Structures Sociales du Haut Atlas* (1955) for inspiration and as "a model of materialist methodology."[36] Berque's work taught him that North African groups worked according to their own logic; Bourdieu learned that each society had its own views that were important and valuable in their own right. Colonialism, however, had warped, exaggerated, and destroyed many of these forms. Viewing the problems in Algeria as resulting from a fundamental miscommunication of civilizations owing to unequal processes of modernization, Bourdieu incurred the wrath of most social scientists at the university and their French settler supporters. These groups saw the colonial world through a reactionary and synchronic lens designed to ensure their continued primacy in the colony. The young scholar thus quickly removed the right-wing yoke that had restricted and labeled Soustelle in the same period.

By the time Bourdieu arrived in Algeria, these university and settler communities had formed a relatively coherent bloc of ultra right-wing ideologues focused on the maintenance of *algérie française* at all costs. The few scientists conducting solid field research had little influence in a university that Bourdieu described as retaining an "intellectual quasi-autonomy" from metropolitan universities and "central science."[37] At the University of Algiers, social science in general, and ethnology in particular, required no fieldwork and generally adhered to preset conclusions exulting the power and importance of the French presence in enabling the advancement of Algeria into the modern world, a view not all that different from the conclusions reached by colonial ethnologists of West Africa in the early twentieth century. Dominated by the Marçais family, French Algerian ethnology and sociology held "knowledge of the Arabic language" as "sufficient for knowing society."[38] Ultimately, Bourdieu concluded that sociological studies of the rural population needed "a modern theory" to explain the vast inequalities of the system and the proper way forward.[39] In only a few years, he had reversed the inheritance of more than a century of French African ethnology.

Bourdieu and his colleagues thus also turned against *pied noir* Orientalist techniques and toward ethnography. By conducting oral interviews with interned FLN rebels and impoverished peasants and consulting the "ethnographic novels" of Algerian intellectuals, Bourdieu hoped to get closer to Algerian social structures. He reported that his approach to information gathering was so successful that, by the time of his departure in 1961, he had "found it all" in Algeria, enough to inform both ethnological analysis and sociological theory.[40] He had been successful, he thought, in large part due to close collaboration with native Algerians. Their views and insights formed an indispensable part of his repertoire. He saw them as important contributors to an empirically informed, theoretically described social reality. Bourdieu concluded that seeking out people willing to think about the way in which they interacted with others, whether educated or not, stood as the most profitable path to a deep understanding of society. In this way he walked on new ground, surpassing the ideas of Marty or Delafosse in moving beyond basic class distinctions, searching for a description of civilization wherever and in whomever it might occur, not only among the intellectual elite.

Grappling with associationist politics: Policies of development

Bourdieu's Algerian research agenda and analytical goals resembled those of Delafosse half a century before. The young sociologist-ethnologist searched for the strength and importance of "originary" Algerian society amid the excesses of colonialism. However, he recognized the fallacy of colonial development; he did not expect to reignite Algerian progress by a return to the past. Instead, he tried to understand the relationship of Algerians with their past so as to aid them in reappropriating lost identities, in the process putting them in a better position to confront industrial Europe.

At the same time, he strove to open the eyes of Algerian intellectuals, who, in his mind, followed Sartre and the radical anticolonial thinker Frantz Fanon in overlooking the plight of the common Algerian peasant in favor of a focus on the denigration and exploitation of Algerian elite classes by the colonial system. He teamed with well-established social scientists and writers such as Abdelmalek Sayed (1933–1998) and Mouloud Mammeri (1917–1989) in generating cutting-edge sociological and literary studies while working with them to understand local networks and repositories of knowledge. At the same time, he realized the French populace knew little regarding the state of affairs in the colonies; he thus set out to "tell the French, and especially people on the Left, what was really going on in a country about which they often knew next to nothing."[41] Bourdieu believed the establishment of a more equal Franco-Algerian scientific exchange would aid activist scientists and intellectuals such as Sayed and Mammeri in reclaiming their heritage and reengaging with the society from which they, like he in France, felt alienated.

Sociologie de l'Algérie, first published in 1958, emerged as Bourdieu's first effort to show both the contemporary conditions of life for what he saw as separate Algerian ethnic groups such as the "Arabic-speaking peoples" and Kabyle Berbers. At the same time, he practiced a form of salvage anthropology designed to recover and restore the lost, precolonial foundations of Algerian society.[42] Again, though evidencing no awareness of his contemporary's work, Bourdieu followed Balandier's admonition to conduct a "double history" of colonial societies that considered both original African structures and the assimilated hybrids generated by colonial domination.[43] An ethnological study that considered the state of Algerian society before the colonial incursion, he thought, exposed the excesses of foreign rule while calling for its immediate removal. Bourdieu felt his scholarship would also help social science, in a purely academic sense, to gain a greater appreciation for the structural "truth" of Algerian groups by willfully and consciously considering and removing the taint of colonial domination. Scientists, in other words, had to factor in the change wrought by years of French control when conducting sociological studies of native populations.[44] This consideration, overtly political and anticolonial on its face, in Bourdieu's mind led more importantly to increased scientific objectivity free from the exigencies of colonial rule. Bourdieu's early ethnographic efforts, still attached at times to structuralism and the standard tropes of French Algerian ethnography, nonetheless permitted him to reexamine the way in which scientists conducted social investigation.

Raymond Aron, in his preface to Bourdieu's work, praised the young scholar for opening the door for Algerians to enter a new world. He wrote, "Precisely because the struggle [with France] has given them an awareness of their own worth, the Muslims of Algeria henceforth are open to modern civilization."[45] Bourdieu, though, added a more somber note to the state of affairs in Algeria, lamenting the fate of a "society [Algeria] that is compelled to define itself by reference to another," in this case France. He continued, "Its drama is the acute conflict within an alienated conscience, locked in contradictions and craving for a way to re-establish its own identity, even by means of excess and violence."[46] Bourdieu considered himself an important player in this identity reestablishment, as he hoped to demonstrate to French and Algerian readers that only a shadow remained of precolonial Algerian society, in the process causing Algerians to adapt themselves to the modern world apart from the influence of France.

Bourdieu's description of "Arab-speaking" and Kabyle groups, however, fell at times into older French Algerian ethnographic stereotypes.[47] He concluded that North African social structures, whether Berber or Arab, were largely invariable, based on the family unit, and dominated by a powerful male figure.[48] In his mind, Arabs and Berbers had mixed for generations, making it difficult to distinguish between the groups any longer. "Everywhere," he wrote, "the Berber rock may be seen just beneath the surface of Muslim legislation."[49] Thus, Bourdieu, despite his best efforts, fell into colonial habits. In favoring Berber society as the basis for organization in Algeria, he elevated Kabyles to the place of distinguished predecessor, a key element of colonial social science that had denigrated the Arabs as backward. In this "Kabyle myth," Berbers stood as autochthones with a liberal democratic tradition, while the Arabs arrived as bloodthirsty bandits unable and unwilling to adapt to "modern" republican institutions.[50] While Bourdieu tried to distinguish Berber and Arab "traditions," he had difficulty in discerning the precolonial processes through which those modes of social interaction had appeared. A monolithic colonial state thus became the motor of change in Bourdieu's early, synchronic anthropology as he overlooked the internal fractures and disputes occurring within the French colonial state and Algerian Islamic societies.[51]

The French colonial state, he theorized, had upset the process of Arab-Berber mixing occurring since the success of Islamic conquerors in the seventh and eighth centuries. The arrival of Europeans had thrown this slow transition into chaos, Bourdieu thought, rigidifying the somewhat porous boundaries between Berber and Arab. He concluded that all Algerian groups found difficulty in maintaining even an "insecure and constantly threatened equilibrium" in the face of the Western advance.[52] He lamented the loss of many Algerian social structures destroyed by the French. Algeria, he thought, teetered on the edge of total collapse. The prospect of destruction, however, also served as an opportunity. Declaring ethnology a "colonial science" tainted by association with the structures of domination was a "great stupidity," Bourdieu noted. Still early in his development of a more comprehensive social science, Bourdieu missed the impact of scientific examination itself on its subjects. He found that colonialism had done much to ruin precolonial Algeria, but the science it introduced provided Algerians a way out of the colonial bind.

Along those lines, he described ethnology as the key to civilizational recovery in Algeria. The science stood as "a very important instrument of self-understanding, a sort of social psychoanalysis permitting one to pull together the cultural unconscious that all people born in a certain society have in their heads."[53] While much "cultural capital" came from the "implicit pedagogy" imparted by dominant social classes, people had an opportunity to take back some control of their fate via recognition of this fact. Although still enormously powerful, cultural norms faced a potent challenger in agents able to implement "explicit pedagogy" designed to produce a "habitus by the inculcation, methodically organized as such, of articulated and even formalized principles."[54] Ethnology, despite its introduction via colonialism, was most important as a stimulus to individual and group self-reflection.

Bourdieu expected this mass introspection, led by Algerian and outside scientists, to reveal the sociocultural fundamentals of the collectivity in question. Bourdieu believed ethnological analysis must occur in conversation with the subjects of analysis themselves, not solely via abstract and distant consideration of symbols. Engagement in such a "dialogue" enabled a "real comprehension" the investigator would not find elsewhere. As Lahouari Addi has noted, Bourdieu approached social analysis from "the point of view of the agent and not that of the researcher."[55] Kabyle researchers and informants played a vital role in gathering ethnographic information in Bourdieu's wartime Algerian methodology, as they were "situated in the social hierarchy" and thus recognizable to displaced villagers, impoverished peasantry, and FLN cadres alike. Emplacement in the social structure, even if on the edges, provided scientists with internal data not otherwise available.[56]

Bourdieu sought access to the disparate political and social entities in Algeria through communication with people in a position similar to the one in which he found himself. In his mind, native Algerians interested in scientific investigation were not common. He expected to encounter them only on the margins of society, ostracized in some cases as French sympathizers in the ongoing war. He thus sought people caught between war and peace, colonialism and national independence, "between two social conditions and two civilizations."[57] Natives who stood astride the French and Algerian worlds, who spanned the gap between underdeveloped rural and decaying urban lifestyles and mentalities, provided unique insight into their own particular social order. Only investigators sympathetic to the rigors of this sort of life, like Bourdieu, could in his mind hope to be effective in an atmosphere of transition where the privations of war struck everyone on a daily basis.

The young scientist thus recommended ethnological research teams comprised of both Frenchmen and natives. He expected these partnerships to operate with greater scientific credibility and ethnographic authority. While the French scientists delivered specialized, Western scientific input, only native Algerians could demonstrate relatedness, obvious links to Algerian society and the ability to speak the "language of loss" so widespread in the war-torn colony.[58] Ethnographic communication during conflict, Bourdieu theorized, required conversing in local metaphors and employing Algerian descriptions of reality. Language in both oral and written form offered a way into the society. "Oral improvisation" by the Franco-Algerian teams, Bourdieu thought, granted entry to the interworkings of the social group and gave "a pure meaning to the words of the tribe," particularly when considered in tandem with the written power of poetry penned by intellectual elites.[59] In a world with limited accessible written history, oral performance and literature provided the young scholar with what he thought was a penetrating view into civilizational norms.

Poetry and prose tantalized Bourdieu. Using literary texts to decipher a civilization, however, required him to do far more than a superficial reading. To be of any real worth, Bourdieu realized, his analysis required the assistance of skilled informants, preferably those with some sort of anthropological training. Mouloud Mammeri stood as perhaps the greatest example of this type of individual. A native Kabyle, he was a literary scholar of Berber as well as an acclaimed cultural critic, analyst, and author who was willing to work with French scholars in developing an intellectual way forward after colonialism. Mammeri had no affiliation with the FLN and, quite frankly, little to lose from a partnership with French scholars.[60]

Bourdieu and Mammeri found themselves in agreement on a number of issues, particularly regarding the fundamental misunderstandings between Algerian socioeconomic groups, divisions that they came to see as foundational to the violence that wracked the colony. When taken together, their writings offered a level of analysis approached by neither man alone.[61] Bourdieu hoped that such partnerships would serve as an example for ethnological examination. As a European scientist gained developmental insight, Bourdieu fully expected his Algerian colleague to "reappropriate his own identity" from the morass of colonial domination. Initiating the process of "reappropriation," however, required an understanding of the ways in which Algerians had lost their identities.

More than a century of colonial education, Bourdieu found, had forced many native Algerians to renounce portions of their maternal Arabic or Berber language, culture, and memory. Bourdieu hoped that a native ethnologist would rediscover these lost ideas through a detailed examination of social development over time. The process by which preceding French ethnologists had gathered information had been "odious," he thought. However, the "socioanalysis" conducted by joint research teams stood as a chance for the "dominated" to "liberate themselves."[62] Anthropology thus offered salvage of another kind: a retaking of the spirit of the society by its intellectuals for re-presentation to the populace at large, a conclusion that lay under Bourdieu's work from that point forward.[63] Native Algerians had to throw off the yoke of colonialism by accepting their current state and then moving to confront the West. Bourdieu believed that refuge in the past stunted, and would eventually deny, the Algerian ability to compete on the world stage.

Through it all Bourdieu recommended the ethnologist retain his distance. Development, while aided by external catalysts, ultimately had to come from within, from the native intellectual class engaged in societal examination. For Bourdieu, documenting this process of intellectual handover occurred not only in the form of ethnographic field notes but also via photography. Taking pictures enabled him to "intensify his gaze" on the subject society while providing a lasting record of an event or a person. He could feel sympathy for his subjects, but he remained mindful of the example of Germaine Tillion, who had retained some objective distance in her ethnographic surveys of death, if only for her own sanity, in the Ravensbruck work camp during the Second World War. This distance, for Bourdieu delivered both by his status as outside scientist and by the camera's lens, permitted an ethnologist to deal with the disappointment that came with observation of the vagaries of life in an oppressed society.[64] Poverty, illiteracy, and social destabilization brought on by more than 100 years of colonialism jarred even the most jaded observer. It was important to retain some separation from that cold reality even while describing it in the vivid terms Bourdieu thought necessary.

Nonetheless, removal of colonial pressure did not mean Bourdieu intended to return Algeria to the precolonial moment. The Algerian demographic and environmental contexts, at the very least, he realized had changed significantly in more than a century. Working with his native Algerian colleagues, he advised the population to acknowledge the unfortunate excesses of the colonial period, a legacy of exploitation that included misappropriation of land, demographic shifts, declining education, and the erasure of social structures, without giving in to them. In his analysis, social forms disintegrated with "the destruction of structural bases"; natives felt the effects "at all levels of social reality."[65] French colonialism had so infiltrated Algeria that the social forms present before its arrival had virtually ceased to exist; at best they had mutated beyond recognition.

Given this new reality, Bourdieu felt that the Algerian future depended on the society's recognition of the catastrophe of social destruction as well as its acceptance of the impossibility of a return to the *status quo antebellum*. Efforts by ethnologists to salvage what was left of Algerian society, he hoped, would aid in the creation of a new civilization, one built on the ruins of traditional structure combined with the "cultural disaggregation" wrought by the "clash" with the Occidental. This "original and coherent" society would then incorporate the best offered by the "Maghrebi world" and would be "animated by an original logic."[66] A new interpretation of the social and economic future required a novel viewpoint, one offered, in this view, by the salutary collaboration of native and French scientists in describing Algerian society. Offering an opportunity to start anew,[67] the Algerian world after the French departure required deliberate efforts by the new Algerian government to promote economic and social reform. Bourdieu agreed with the former Governor-General Soustelle in his call for a "degree of integration" into the extant world order by an Algeria cognizant of its "very low level" on the scale of development.[68] Unfortunately for the young scholar, he also emulated Soustelle in finding a limited audience for his ideas. In his own words, Bourdieu's first book "made no impact at all. It was the poor attempt of an outsider."[69]

For Bourdieu, science offered a means by which to escape the crushing weight of Western colonialism and industrial modernity. Like Soustelle, though, he failed to appreciate the full extent of ethnology's relationship with the unequal power relations of colonial domination. Most Algerians, regardless of the work of Mammeri or Sayed, had no desire to work arm-in-arm with Western specialists in removing the French yoke. Bourdieu's call for scientific cooperation in Algeria went largely unheeded, particularly in the 1960s as the new post-colonial Algerian governments increasingly focused on the elimination of those tainted by any scent of "collaboration" with French officials.[70] The new Algerian government undermined these scientific efforts in much the same way the French colonists had minimized Algerian contributions to state management and political affairs.

Much of this began in the 1950s. As the Franco-Algerian War entered a new phase with the onset of heavy urban warfare in Algiers in 1957, French settler efforts to maintain power grew more pronounced and sometimes violent. Still in the field as more French troops poured into the country in a broad policy of "pacification" through "quartering,"[71] Bourdieu's work brought him negative notoriety in French Algerian academic circles. The young scientist saw the "venomous and rancorous" attacks on his writings regarding the clash of civilizations and destruction of social structures as indicative of the importance of his conclusions. Angered by his dismissal of traditional disciplinary divisions and the civilized/primitive, observer/observed dichotomies in Algerian colonial life, Algerian right-wing political and academic figures increasingly targeted Bourdieu as an enemy of the regime.[72] Faced with the failure of his efforts to inject what he viewed as sufficient ethnological perspective into the Algerian war, and perhaps somewhat aware of his problematic position as an outsider in the midst of war, Bourdieu refocused his attention on the implications of his Algerian experiences and conclusions for sociology in general. In so doing he found himself opposing what was then the greatest name in French social science: Claude Lévi-Strauss. Advocating for a localized understanding of social structure, Bourdieu engaged in an intertextual battle with the great French anthropologist that would provide the framework for French social science for a generation.

Structure and the conduct of anthropology: Challenging Lévi-Strauss

Bourdieu and Lévi-Strauss, working from a common Maussian background, struggled to understand societies in flux as they encountered colonialism. They disagreed primarily over the role of the participant-observer, the importance and place of temporality, and most importantly the influence of primordial structure versus shared experience and unconscious acculturation in shaping social behavior. However, Bourdieu did not discount Lévi-Strauss's prominence in the study of man. The young scholar admired, but never employed, Lévi-Strauss's renaming of ethnology as "anthropology." Bourdieu thought the semantic change reinforced philosophical ties to Immanuel Kant. At the same time, the term evoked another vein of French science—the anthropology practiced by Paul Broca and his colleagues in the mid-nineteenth century. Through those connections, Bourdieu explored the combination of abstract theory and the "thoroughness and rigor" that marked physical sciences such as biology and physical anthropology, minus the racist approaches of its nineteenth-century practitioners.[73] At the same time, Lévi-Strauss's intervention gave the discipline new strength, as it rejected Lévy-Bruhl's theory of a specific "mythological mode of thought" among supposedly primitive peoples.[74] Several of Bourdieu's early articles approached Algeria from a structuralist perspective, but he realized by the mid-1960s that he needed to move beyond Lévi-Strauss's techniques in formulating his own approach.[75] Both men sought the basic societal forms that had served as the goal of sociology since Durkheim, but Bourdieu saw this structure as contingent rather than absolute and best discerned by dialogue rather than linguistic analysis. At the same time, Bourdieu's social studies included the rigorous and critical self-examination common in philosophy.[76]

Such self-examination as a tool to understand societies caused Bourdieu to reimagine the entire ethnological enterprise. In his mind, examining a society required assessment of the subject group by both its members and an outside ethnologist. At the same time, the ethnologist had to reflect on his or her own background. "The comprehensive ethnological examination that I have done on Algeria I can also cast on myself," he mused, extending the analysis "to the people of my country, to my parents, to my father's accent and that of my mother."[77] Bourdieu recognized that his own experiences and influences as a child colored his interpretations of Algerian peasant life. He thus introduced a new "multi-sited" ethnography that investigated both rural Algerians and the peasantry of his native region. More than just a comparative collection of notes, Bourdieu's early studies regarded areas as connected not to each other, but to the investigator himself or herself.[78]

When asked about the role of personal experience in research, Bourdieu replied, "it does play a role." He proposed that reflexive research must not focus purely on "raw personal experience." However, he thought scientific self-examination carried insight into contextual factors, including the passage of time, affecting social phenomena not visible from a distance. Bourdieu concluded, "I know what I thought 30 years ago and I know what I think now," a vital step in a process that required sociologists to "invent their own sociology, analyze themselves." Composed in direct response to the distant approach of Lévi-Straussian structuralism, Bourdieu's concept of participant "objectivation" made the ethnologist very much part of the analytical equation. In this version of sociology, proximity revealed flaws in methodology and conclusions while simultaneously opening up new avenues of thought.

In work on Kabylia, Bourdieu sought to "invert" or "reverse" Lévi-Strauss's *Tristes Tropiques*. In short, Bourdieu sought to "make the banal exotic." In the process Béarn offered a "control" for his sociological experiment while assisting in the transition from "indigenous" to "scholarly" lived experience.[79] Contrary to Lévi-Strauss's distant and powerless sadness at the disappearance of foreign societies, Bourdieu concluded that dissolution occurred as part of a larger process played out over time, involving both observed and observer. All conceptions of social construction, whether generated by native or foreign observer, were valuable in understanding the mechanics of human interaction. Analysis, then, was not limited to superstructure or mythic fundamentals. It was possible, in Bourdieu's view, for scientists to see the world from both native and foreign vantage points, deepening and sharpening their analysis by considering a wider range of comparative inputs.

In a phenomenological move, Bourdieu advocated a dissection of "the familiar relationship to the social world … to objectivate my relationship of familiarity with that object, and the difference that separates it from the scientific relationship that one arrives at, as I did in Kabylia."[80] Studying Béarn gave him insight into his own peasant and petty bourgeois background, a latent part of his perspective that he, at the very least unconsciously, transferred to his studies of rural peasantry in Kabylia. His position as a man between worlds placed him, in his words, "against the distance of cavalier positivism" while also keeping him away from "the sympathetic immersion of subjective intuitionism."[81] Said differently, he cautioned ethnologists to avoid the destructive tendency to identify with the native group under examination, although scientists had to gain some intimate involvement with a society in order to understand it. Bourdieu's work thus retained, at least in his mind, the empirical focus of a positivist approach but with deeper reflection into all possible interpretations of a social event from a native viewpoint.

Reflexivity, however, did not equal the glorification of the observer for Bourdieu. Hoping to avoid the "diary disease" that afflicted supposedly impartial and objective observers of foreign societies, like the author of *Tristes Tropiques*, Bourdieu called the entire process of ethnographic collection into question. He pressed for observers to "explore ... the social conditions of possibility—and therefore the effects and limits— of that experience and, more precisely, of the act of objectivation itself."[82] While Lévi-Strauss extolled the virtues of an approach in which "the ethnologist, unlike the philosopher, does not feel obliged to take the conditions in which his own thought operates, or the science peculiar to his society and his period, as a fundamental subject of reflection," Bourdieu responded with a call for a full consideration of the examiner's place within a particular "anthropological field."[83] Self-analysis, he proposed, must consider the influence of a national or regional tradition or practice, the structure of the academic community itself, and the academic background of the ethnologist him or herself. By acknowledging the origins and biases inherent in his or her work, Bourdieu thought the ethnologist would better isolate and understand the lived social experience of the subject of study. The conclusions that resulted from this deep examination, he hoped, aided the subject society in better adapting to the modern world.

Lévi-Strauss resisted such examination in part due to his personal temperament. Shy and self-effacing, the scientist did his best to avoid the limelight that came with intellectual celebrity in France.[84] At the same time, Lévi-Strauss and structuralism existed as a response to the public musings and persona of Sartre, the antihero for the academic generation that followed him. Lévi-Strauss's "hyper-empiricism" attracted many young sociologists and ethnologists, including Bourdieu. However, the father of French structural anthropology took his methodology a step further, pressing for the observer to "not only place himself above the values accepted by his own society or group, but ... [also to] adopt certain definite *methods of thought*." These thought patterns, useful for "all possible observers," he thought would enable a scientist to break completely from any traditions of which he might be a part. In fact, the scientist could almost ignore the precepts of the subject society, as his methods were airtight and not subject to local interpretation or adaptation. Moreover, Lévi-Strauss advocated for an anthropologist who "creates new mental categories and helps to introduce notions of space and time, opposition and contradiction, which are as foreign to traditional thought as the concepts met with today in certain branches of the natural sciences."[85] Lévi-Straussian analysts could thus completely distance themselves from research subjects while creating a new arm of the natural sciences speaking only in the language of scientific inquiry, not the subjective, humanistic approach previously in fashion in French ethnology.

Bourdieu rejected this separation as impossible; no observer engaged in "interpreting practices" could avoid the call of his own background. In Bourdieu's opinion, a scientist was instead "inclined to introduce into the object the principles of his relation to the object, as is attested by the special importance he assigns to communicative functions (whether in language, myth, or marriage)."[86] Lévi-Strauss's descriptions of basic oppositions as the foundation of social interaction among

American groups thus had a major flaw. Lévi-Strauss, Bourdieu thought, had reached conclusions that unconsciously reflected his own presuppositions, experiences, and upbringing. True "distance" from the object of study, Bourdieu thought, came not from placing the observer above the fray, so to speak, but by subjecting that observer to the analysis previously reserved only for those considered "other."

Reflexivity gave Bourdieu an opportunity to take his analysis in a novel direction. In a 1962 article on bachelors in rural France, he mused that "the primary task of sociology is perhaps to reconstitute the totality from which one can discover the unity of the subjective awareness that the individual has of the social system and of the objective structure of that system." The people under examination were themselves important sources as interpreters of their own cosmology, particularly insofar as their positions relative to the "dominant" social class revealed the influence of both their accumulated social capital and the unconscious activity of habitus. Individual awareness and perception could reflect the actuality of social structure, particularly when these perceptions accumulated into a larger, networked understanding of the rules that governed human interactions. This dual awareness, of both the subject's view of the social system and of the structure apparent to an outsider, delivered to Bourdieu the possibility of analytical finality and an approximation of objective truth for the outside scientist. Views of a society from both inside and outside brought humanity back to analysis, as in Bourdieu's mind the ethnologist had to "reconcile the truth of the objective 'given' that his analysis enables him to understand and the subjective certainty of those who live in it."[87] Frustrated by what he perceived as Lévi-Strauss's runaway dissociation from the groups subject to his analysis, Bourdieu sought to reincorporate some consideration of the humanity of native groups, be they in France or in Algeria.

Continuing in the tradition of Soustelle and Mauss, Bourdieu conducted his examinations in tandem with Algerians, thereby providing them with an insider/outsider view of their society and, Bourdieu hoped, enabling them to carry out the necessary reform to escape colonialism as capable participants cognizant of the forces unleashed by global forces. He had quickly moved beyond the pragmatic political hopes of his early ethnology to a more specific emphasis on understanding Algerian natives as humans. Association was impossible. More important was the humanity of scientific subjects, particularly their inability to understand the full objective truth of their own social constructions without the aid of an outside observer. Individual human beings, while intelligent interpreters of their reality, could not provide a full portrait of any all-encompassing structure: "They do not have in their heads the scientific truth of their practice that I am trying to extract from observation of their practice."[88] Ultimately, Bourdieu's ideal ethnologist could not expect any research subjects, even those with a positive approach toward scientific examination, to provide untainted, accurate information. Simple interviews and observation would not suffice.

In Bourdieu's estimation, groups would try to push investigators toward elders focused on the reputation of the group at large. Such an approach would skew those data; investigators needed to dig deeper and seek out lower-level members of the society.[89] Kabyle intellectuals, his partners in much of his scientific inquiry, were themselves alienated from their own, largely rural, society. However, they provided him with what he assessed as important and accurate perspectives that evaluated and dissected society in Kabylia from interesting angles. At the same time, they reappropriated their own social and political identities and destinies.

The memories and conclusions of elders were not sufficient in sketching social reality. More important was the notion of context. For Bourdieu, scientists would arrive at an accurate depiction of a society only when they considered the full range of economic and political factors that formed the history of each individual. Habitus shaped each person's practices, although individuals remained capable of shaping events through the flexible interaction of their accumulated influences with a constantly changing environment. In short, each actor ultimately engaged with his environment in a way both "sensible" and "reasonable" given his background. A full contextual understanding of individual participation in the larger society permitted the ethnologist to view, through the eyes of the native, the "objective, collective future" envisioned by members of the society, an idealized path subject to change.[90]

Structural analysis, in Bourdieu's view, did not consider the evolution of the socioeconomic worldview of research subjects over time. Rather, structuralists froze that view synchronically, analyzing social behavior through a sequence of isolated snapshots, not chronologically linked events. Likely influenced by the mistakes of Soustelle's brand of political ethnology, Bourdieu believed that Lévi-Strauss and his school "unwittingly" perpetuated the nefarious influence of "traditionalism" by creating "a system of oppositions and homologies" to represent that which was "by nature a succession."[91] For Bourdieu, "traditionalism" stood in the way of progress. A scientist who perpetuated a mode of thought that looked backward was irresponsible and locked the subjects of his study in a past moment, thereby removing any chance for conceptual or even political escape. This form of analysis reproduced the effects of colonialism in the guise of legitimate science.

Through an understanding of time, Bourdieu's ideal anthropologist discerned native manipulations of structure. For example, Bourdieu found that Kabyles altered the timeframes associated with Mauss's universal process of gift exchange. While he acknowledged Mauss had been correct in his description of gift-giving as a nearly universal act, Bourdieu refused to accept that the societal requirement for reciprocity controlled all the actions of individuals. In other words, it was the "strategy" of agents, not the action of a general "rule," that governed social interaction, a process best evaluated side-by-side with "time" and "its rhythm, its orientation, its irreversibility."[92] Bourdieu thus advocated for social study focused first on the individual. The background that informed the manner in which each person dealt with changing circumstances came from local context. Bourdieu proposed that an ethnologist must, in a method previously demonstrated by Marty and Delafosse, consult the research subjects themselves to gain a complete appreciation for contextual changes over time. An historical and diachronic approach to social study enabled comprehension of the actions of the individual and the collective as interrelated and mutually constituting, neither sufficient in its own right in forming final ethnological conclusions.

In his early writings, even Lévi-Strauss acceded to the importance of some context in conducting ethnological analysis. He cautioned that "by taking as our inspiration a model outside time and place we are certainly running a risk: we may be underestimating the reality of progress."[93] Societies could and did change, at least in the anthropologist's early thought. As a minimum, civilizations existed across a broad spectrum of possible stages, although their movements were not evolutionary but "progressive, acquisitive." While societies might appear "stationary" from one perspective, from another they might demonstrate "important changes."[94] Lévi-Strauss ultimately concluded, however, that these progressions and distinctions exerted minimal influence on social structure.

Railing against Europeans who looked at societal age as an indicator of relative importance, Lévi-Strauss ultimately declared he was "happy to adapt myself to a system with no temporal dimensions in order to interpret a different form of civilization."[95] He believed that the synchronic approach offered the objectivity desired by all anthropologists. This method avoided the search for progress and development that hampered much of French colonial ethnology by completely disentangling the European, firmly anchored in the linear movement of time and civilization, from the untranslatable musings of an alien society. Lévi-Strauss found what he thought was a theoretical alternative to colonial techniques in structural anthropology. He described his approach as an analytical endeavor by which a scientist "examines those differences and changes in mankind that have a meaning for all men, and excludes those particular to a single civilization, which dissolves into nothingness under the gaze of the outside observer."[96] Only through generalization and universal application would anthropology have a significant impact outside the matrix of colonial domination. Meaning existed for Lévi-Strauss only at the level of abstraction, well above and beyond any particular society.

Both Bourdieu and Lévi-Strauss sought to understand difference through an examination of a social "totality," derived from a "form that is common to the various manifestations of social life."[97] Understanding these structures and their "non-accidental"[98] operation linked both thinkers back to their intellectual predecessors, particularly Mauss. However, Lévi-Strauss rejected his mentor's relativism. In Bourdieu's words, structural analysis "purported to rid ethnology" of "the subject and her lived experience." In the upstart's eyes Lévi-Strauss's "profoundly dehistoricized vision of social reality" made the acclaimed scholar "unsympathetic" to Bourdieu's concept of the habitus, or "history turned into nature."[99] Time and its passage were crucial to social understanding and analysis, particularly in tumultuous times.

While the destruction of "traditional" societies filled Bourdieu and Lévi-Strauss with regret and sadness, it also offered opportunity. Both men believed the "transformations" wrought by the onset of modernity and the clash of civilizations revealed the internal controls regulating each system.[100] Lévi-Strauss viewed these ruptures, arising from the fall of colonial empires, as windows through which to "abstract the structure that underlies the many manifestations and remains permanent through a succession of events."[101] In his mind, underlying forms controlled future social manifestations in a powerful teleology. Societal distinctions, he thought, existed only on the surface, with each undergirded by fundamental structures that did not vary. Operating from another angle, Bourdieu sought to assist the politically disadvantaged through social reform after first understanding the collectivity's fundamentals. He expected his approach to deliver a more complete view of groups and the individuals that composed them as shaped by localized experience and host to enormous variance.

Bourdieu reintroduced local context as a basic form and boundary for social interactions without admitting the presence of absolute, universal forms. He credited Mauss for this concept. More than just the accumulated experiences of individuals, Mauss had described powerful contextual influences as habitus, a collective structure that changed in form "between societies, educations, proprieties and fashions, prestiges" and combined social, psychological, and biological elements.[102] Bourdieu gave the idea, also previously mentioned by Lyautey, more concrete form and substance. He defined the concept as a "durably installed generative principle of regulated improvisations" that comprised the "immanent law, *lex insita*, laid down in each agent by his earliest upbringing."[103] In other words, Bourdieu's version of habitus influenced all actions of an individual. Habitus acted differently for each person, shaping his or her social activity as a sort of behavioral law; it emerged from the unique combination of lived experiences and family examples in each person's background. In a move reminiscent of his call for reflexive analysis, Bourdieu saw this habitus as both creating social boundaries and reflecting those borders in a mutually sustaining process.

Habitus thus encased structure and antistructure, the culmination of Lévi-Strauss's quest for unifying forms and the precise antithesis of the universal binaries the senior scholar described. In Bourdieu's words, "Through the habitus, the structure that has produced it governs practice, not by the processes of a mechanistic determinism, but through the mediation of the orientations and limits it assigns to the habitus' operations of invention." Individuals did not constantly remake the social environment; rather, they existed in a dialogic relationship with that environment. They could not describe the impact their collected influences and cultural capital had on their lives. They could only demonstrate that impact by the ways in which they engaged in social interaction given changing circumstances. Habitus existed not only to shape the views of individuals but also those tied to a specific "group or class," thereby making the influences and history shaping each individual a "structural variant" of the similar forces that formed his or her nuclear social unit.[104] Social classes, particularly those at the top of hierarchies, engaged in "cultural reproduction" through the articulation, often implicit, of social and cultural norms through education. In this way they recreated a "cultural arbitrary" by means of a process that was "the equivalent, in the cultural order, of the transmission of genetic capital in the biological order."[105] Society passed down through generations in the form of accumulated capital tied to the habitus in an almost chromosomal inheritance.

Bourdieu provided an early example in his work on Islam in Algeria. He represented the great religion as reproduced in many individual "religious profiles." Each man or woman's personal expression of and interaction with Islam revealed "the hierarchical integration in each individual of the different levels, the importance of which would vary with his way of life, his education, and his aspirations."[106] It was this emphasis on communication between elements, conducted largely unconsciously from the point of view of the individual, and the possibility of structural dialogue and mutation that set Bourdieu apart from his older and more experienced rival.

For his part, Lévi-Strauss also reduced social forms down to "an ideal repertoire that it should be possible to define." This model agreed with Bourdieu's conclusion that each individual habitus remained bounded within a larger, less flexible set of behavioral possibilities constructed by the society as a whole. However, Lévi-Strauss took the analysis a step further, once again searching for "a sort of table, like that of the chemical elements, in which all actual or hypothetical customs would be grouped in families so that one could see at a glance which customs a particular society had in fact adopted."[107] Far from constituted by a specific society composed of particular individuals, Lévi-Strauss's version of reducible types spread across all societies, confined to a basic boilerplate restricted by human nature. He pushed analysis beyond the structural functionalism of Radcliffe-Brown, finding that the "relations between the terms," not the definitions attached to those terms, were most important in understanding the rules governing behavior. "In order to understand the avunculate [relationship between nephew and mother's brother]," wrote Lévi-Strauss, "we must treat it as one relationship within a system, while the system itself must be considered as a whole in order to grasp its structure."[108] The total, he concluded, was more than the sum of its parts; a scientist had to understand both the relationship between the components and their appearance as a coherent structure.

Bourdieu saw this argument as incomplete, as it lacked "the study of the relations between the agents and these relations," or the agency of the individuals as they injected variance or interpretation into any system. He determined that failure to consider the actions of smaller units in the formation of social norms reified the observer's analysis and led to "the [analytical] realism of the structures."[109] Incomplete analysis, in other words, made subject actions appear part of a larger theoretical construct. Bourdieu concluded that no structure was so solid. Conversely, social convention existed in the mind of each individual, the product of formative experiences and norms imbued by the society of which he or she was a member; no two people had precisely the same habitus.

In contrast, Lévi-Strauss described "human knowledge" as a "closed system." He portrayed the myth-making and telling process as a "simultaneous production of myths themselves, by the mind that generates them and, by the myths, of an image of the world that is already inherent in the structure of the mind." Built from cultural remnants expressed as "signs" or "symbols," myths emerged from the hands of a "bricoleur" who worked "in an already established semantic environment."[110] Lévi-Strauss thus saw this knowledge operating in a Newtonian space where it could be neither created nor destroyed, but recycled and refashioned in the hands of a skilled craftsman. Human social organizations made little progress, he thought, instead, sliding between oppositional positions. Revealed by ethnographic observation, these binaries, such as raw/cooked and fresh/decayed, operated as "two poles around which accumulate complex combinations of emotions, sentiments and memories." This same "dualism" shaped human life in a dialectical existence down to the most basic Shakespearean expression: to be or not to be, to exist or not to exist.[111]

Basic social forms governed the unconscious in Lévi-Strauss's model. Discerning those basic divisions revealed to the structuralist, "these forms are fundamentally the same for all minds—ancient and modern, primitive and civilized." Anthropologists could thus apply those ideas to other societies.[112] Basic psychological formations controlled human interaction and remained present beneath any "illusions of liberty" held by individuals, he posited.[113] Lévi-Strauss searched for these basic structures across the Americas from his earliest expedition in the 1930s, focusing on the Nambikwara Indians of Brazil. He saw no need to go beyond a synchronic method, as the group had no history. "I had been looking for a society reduced to its simplest expression," he explained, "that of the Nambikwara was so truly simple that all I could find in it was individual human beings."[114] From these most basic components of the group Lévi-Strauss ascertained the basic psychological tools and divisions that guided behavior. From this analysis Lévi-Strauss formulated more general theories, the oppositions noted above, to describe man at his most basic and untainted by European-invented notions of development or evolution.

Bourdieu rejected this stance by returning "real-life actors" to the equation. He believed that individuals were more than "regulated automatons" who existed as "epiphenomena of structures." Instead, he postulated that men universally "manipulated social reality" by creating "an infinity of practices adapted to endlessly changing situations" built from "a small batch of schemes" common to all groups.[115] Conducted from the ground in close cooperation with research subjects and with a self-critical eye, Bourdieu's method of ethnological examination opposed the "bird's eye" approach of Lévi-Strauss's all-seeing ethnologist. Bourdieu thought the artificiality of Lévi-Strauss's "laboratory" left out a key question to informants: why?[116] It was important, he concluded in words similar to those of Delafosse a half-century before, to let subjects describe in their own words the reasons that lay under the behavioral decisions they made. The answers that informants provided could not, of course, describe the untranslatable actions of their habitus, but they were important to understanding the behavior of individual actors in response to changing circumstances.

When Bourdieu's ethnologist had completed the collection of data, he or she had also to subject to a rigorous self-analysis, thereby avoiding both the "exoticism" of distance and the possibility of statistical "fetishism" brought on by the belief that conclusions informed by a sort of ethnological algebra formed all-powerful "truth." Only then, equipped with the productive combination of abstract theory and detailed dialogical data, would the ethnologist arrive at the height of social science, the intersection of sociology and ethnology.[117] It was only at this overlap of the positivist and the theoretical, the empirical and the abstract that social scientists could hope to understand and assist others.

Conclusion

Following a brief bout with cancer, Bourdieu died on January 23, 2002, leaving behind 40 books, more than 500 articles, and the most important school of sociological thought in contemporary France.[118] Founder of the Center for European Sociology and the journal *Actes de la recherche en sciences sociales*, Bourdieu's work earned translation in five languages by the time of his death. Consequently, his influence spread across the globe, influencing American anthropological scholars in particular, many of whom were looking for alternatives to structuralism.[119] Indeed, British and American anthropology went through a reflexive turn in part due to Bourdieu's influence, reconsidering the definitions of observer, objectivity, subjectivity, and even the field itself. He was most important not for his Algerian ethnographies, writings that still employed some of the colonial racial vulgate. Rather, he reformulated the practice of social analysis through a consideration of his Algerian field data, in the process disputing the findings of French structural anthropology.

Though he arrived at this engaged ethno-sociology through efforts to extricate Algeria from its associationist political trap, Bourdieu avoided most direct political involvement. His descriptions of the actions of oppressive modern states found a large audience in French student movements beginning in 1968, but he refused to take part in demonstrations until offering his support to a rail worker strike in 1995.[120] The critical and commercial successes of his work, particularly his later investigations of French academia and gender relations, earned him the Gold Medal for outstanding contributions to social science research from the *Conseil national de recherche scientifique* in 1993, ironically the first person so honored since Lévi-Strauss in 1968.[121] Bourdieu eventually took on the mantle of leading social intellectual and activist through efforts to translate academic work into the vernacular, making it accessible to people both inside and outside the academy. As an "organic intellectual of humanity," Bourdieu saw his role later in life as "denaturalizing and defatalizing human existence," reintroducing context and circumstance as important players in any social development.[122]

Bourdieu agreed with Mauss that comprehending any social groups, including those in Africa, required on-site observation and interaction with natives of those groups. Drawing "native" intellectuals into Delafossian interdisciplinary investigations of social forms enabled Africans to take back some control of their development through a close partnership with French scientists. Humans, in this rendering, were important not only as scientific objects but as intelligent, thinking members of societies, much as described by Mauss.

At the same time, Bourdieu went beyond many of the conclusions of those who preceded him. Most importantly, due in large part to the period and environment in which he worked, the ethnologist-sociologist worked from an anticolonial viewpoint. He did not see ethnology as fundamentally developmental, as the French colonial state in Algeria had destroyed much of what it had encountered and observed. History was a constant process of acculturation, of the influence of accumulated events and teachings on the social predispositions of individual actors. Dominated for over a century by the French colonial state, Algerians had to recognize that their positions had been inscribed and reinscribed over generations by a social order that sought its own reproduction above all else. Bourdieu thus brought pessimism to the study of Algeria that his predecessors did not carry. He escaped the sadness brought on by the seeming inevitability of oppression by advocating for the importance of individuals in science and society. Recognition of the efforts of a dominant social group to control lower classes, he theorized, was the first step in a move to overturn those norms and reestablish some measure of equality. In a move unthinkable in a colonial framework, even the ethnological approach of Jacques Soustelle, Bourdieu followed Marcel Mauss in developing a counter to what he called the "coarse analyses of the most vulgar, common, and collective dimensions of human existence" that characterized modern French sociology.[123]

Plying a trade that approached people not as "puppets" of a monolithic structure but instead as agents who could, at least in part, understand the "meaning of their actions,"[124] Bourdieu changed French sociology from the bottom up, from the outside in, from the margins of the French empire to the metropole itself. His work escaped the trap of colonialism not through ethnographic innovation, but instead through the eventual application of these Algerian-grounded concepts to larger problems relating to the conduct of science itself, calling into question the role of the scientist-observer.

Conclusion

From the 1840s to the 1960s, select colonial and metropolitan soldiers, scholars, and administrators grew to understand Africa in large part through ethnological conversations, both textual and oral, with native Africans. The men and women featured in this study conducted their investigations with the support of the colonial state and with an eye toward the improvement of colonial rule. In their minds, colonial government would benefit from a deeper and more complete comprehension of African social, intellectual, and political life. The perspectives of native Africans themselves grew more important as legitimate sources of information, though in the unequal colonial power dynamic they did not often earn status as originators of important ideas. That was left to the French scholars themselves, perpetuating the colonial system and hardening the surface of colonial governance as it introduced greater weakness in the underlying structures. The manner in which French colonial scholars described African societies derived in large measure from the translated French understanding of selected words of native Africans. Importantly, these French Africanists harnessed these ideas, however limited and flawed in translation, and turned them to additional scholarly ends in the growing discussions on the fundamental building blocks of human collectivities. In the process, these scholars profoundly changed the French sociological method.

Reform, French colonial scholars cautioned, was not possible in a policy vacuum. It took a concerted dialogue between French colonial intellectuals such as Maurice Delafosse, Paul Marty, or Pierre Bourdieu and native African thinkers such as Sahelian Islamic scholar Saad Buh or Kabyle poet Mouloud Mammeri. Together, these Franco-African ethnologists would both describe social reality and develop a comprehensive plan to hasten the arrival of a more advanced social and political condition. It was important to French Africanists to avoid the pull of "tradition," the ultimate hindrance to progress. Better than those who preceded them, these French thinkers until Bourdieu nonetheless focused internally, believing the colonial state a self-perpetuating organism moving and growing according to its own logic. They paid little mind to external events and focused instead on important truths divined from ethnological investigation, turning those back on the structure itself. Such an incestuous approach sowed the seeds of its own destruction. French thinkers never fully understood the societies they examined because they struggled to capture change. Their efforts to graft a new political structure atop such a flawed understanding were thus doomed to failure.

In conducting these investigations, French scholars encountered a more fluid conception of time, where history and lived experience overlapped. As one native thinker, the late-colonial and postcolonial writer and historian Amadou Hampâté Bâ (1901–1991), explained, "The past is relived like present experience, outside of time in some way …. We move there at our pleasure as fish do in the sea or water molecules combine to form life."[1] This uniquely African sense of time, so different from European conceptions of the path to "modernity," confused French scholars unable to compare colonial events to anything but the European experience. As they struggled to understand and make use of this fluidity between the past and present, French scholars located similar ideas in texts, some written as early as the fourteenth century, which employed a complex combination of family, religion, genealogy, and mobility in composite portraits of African life. Reconciling these concepts became the most important goal of French Africanist scholarship.

French Africanists, especially by the second decade of the twentieth century, tapped into a long African historical tradition. Since the tenth century, Arabic-language chroniclers had recorded interactions across the Sahara, building on long-standing techniques of genealogy and oral history. The 1830 arrival of French forces in Algeria brought a concerted European effort to understand this history. However, most colonial ethnographers of the early- and mid-nineteenth-century phases of conquest and consolidation considered Africa in synchronic terms, hopelessly locked in a backward state and perhaps even populated by a different species of humans

In attempting to maintain African political and social structures, though, French scholars in truth acted in opposition to their stated humanistic intentions. Delafosse, Marty, and their peers sought to isolate the moments of greatness in the African past. Although they intended their discussions, at least in part, to indicate the complexity and importance of African civilizations, French Africanists implicitly rejected the present as irrelevant and backward while they simultaneously limited their descriptions of that complexity. In their choice of sources and translation, these scholars limited the reach of Africans. French ethnological studies froze Africans in the past and disregarded the dynamic nature of African life. At the same time, French Africanists, whether scholars, soldiers, or administrators, privileged the views of elites who, in many cases, had something to gain from collaboration with the militarily and economically powerful colonial state. The imbalances of power in a colonial situation did not occur to men who were, in truth, working against the grain of overt exploitation and the idea of making the world "French." Their ideas, grounded in empirical investigation, slowly turned the tide not only of colonial policymaking, but also of theoretical formulation in the metropole.

In the end, ethnologists, regardless of language or even intent, participated in colonial science with the goal, again until Bourdieu, of furthering French reach and power in Africa. They submitted analyses designed to facilitate a French Empire more in tune with the needs of its inhabitants, both metropolitan and colonial, and poised to reemerge as a great power as the twentieth century progressed. Ultimately, these conclusions, given great credence at the time by peers, seem to have done little to solidify French rule. However, they did have an important and lasting effect in Africa, among Africans. The French colonial form of ethnology as seen in this study required the input of informed intellectual elites from among the African populations. Several of these native African scholars, at first acting simply as assistants, ultimately became successful scholars in their own right, publishing in academic journals beginning in the early twentieth century. Colonial ethnologists hoped to provide a more human form of rule in the colonies through scientific examination. In the end, they gave native Africans the tools to dismantle that very structure. The ethnological rhizome cultivated for so long by these officials remained beyond the end of the colonial era, maintained and expanded by African intellectuals themselves.

Notes

Introduction

1. For a foundational discussion of these concepts as found in French metropolitan theory, see Raymond Betts, *Assimilation and Association in French Colonial Theory, 1890–1914* (New York, 1961).
2. Chinua Achebe, "An Image of Africa," *Research in African Literatures* 9, 1 (Spring 1978), 13. The article is a reproduction of a 1977 address.
3. Martin Thomas, *Empires of Intelligence: Security Services and Colonial Disorder after 1914* (Berkeley: University of California Press, 2008), 3, 8.
4. Michel Foucault, *The Order of Things: An Archaeology of the Human Sciences* (New York, 1970 [1966]), 51–54.
5. Helen Tilley, *Africa as a Living Laboratory: Empire, Development, and the Problem of Scientific Knowledge, 1870–1950* (Chicago, 2011), 15, 328; and Jonathan Wyrtzen, *Making Morocco: Colonial Intervention and the Politics of Identity* (Ithaca, NY: Cornell University Press, 2015), 13.
6. Charles Tilly, *Coercion, Capital, and European States, AD 990–1992* (Malden, MA, 1992), 100–101.
7. Tilley, *Africa as a Living Laboratory*, 218 and Chapter 5, *passim*.
8. This work builds on an interesting vein of scholarship regarding the role of soldiers as knowledge producers. See, for example, Mary Renda, *Taking Haiti: Military Occupation and the Culture of US Imperialism, 1915–1940* (Chapel Hill, 2000); Paul Kramer, *The Blood of Government: Race, Empire, the United States, and the Philippines* (Chapel Hill, 2006); and Paul W. Foos, *A Short, Offhand Killing Affair: Soldiers and Social Conflict during the Mexican-American War* (Chapel Hill, 2002).
9. Camille Lefebvre, "Le temps des lettres: Echanges diplomatiques entre sultans, émirs et officiers français, Niger 1899–1903," *Monde(s)* 5 (May 2014), 63–64. See also Tilley, *Africa as a Living Laboratory*, 26–27.
10. James Clifford, *The Predicament of Culture: Twentieth-Century Ethnography, Literature, and Art* (Cambridge, MA, 1988), 4.
11. Arjun Appadurai, *Modernity at Large: Cultural Dimensions of Globalization* (Minneapolis, 1996), 1–3.
12. Catherine Coquery-Vidrovitch and Henri Moniot, *L'Afrique noire de 1800 à nos jours*, 3rd ed. (Paris, 1992), 185–186; Claudine Cotte, "Géopolitique de la colonisation," in *L'Afrique occidentale au temps des français: Colonisateurs et colonisés, c. 1860–1960*, ed. Catherine Coquery-Vidrovitch and Odile Goerg (Paris, 1992), 90; Edmund Burke III, *The Ethnographic State: France and the Invention of Moroccan Islam* (Berkeley, 2014), 6.
13. Michel Foucault, *Dits et écrits* (Paris, 1994), IV, 828. Thanks to John Martin for this reference.

14 For an introduction to the enormous literature on these and related thinkers, see, for instance, Quentin Skinner, *The Foundations of Modern Political Thought, Volume 2: The Age of Reformation* (New York, 1978); Michèle Duchet, *Anthropologie et histoire au siècle des Lumières: Buffon, Voltaire, Rousseau, Helvétius, Diderot*, 2nd ed. (Paris, 1977); and Anthony Pagden, *The Fall of Natural Man: The American Indian and the Origins of Comparative Ethnology* (Cambridge, 1982). See also Michael P. Banton, *Racial Theories*, 2nd ed. (Cambridge, 1998), for the best overall description of the movement from ideas of "race as lineage" to "race as type." Banton's description of racial ideas owes much to Thomas Kuhn's *The Structure of Scientific Revolutions* (Chicago, 1962) and the concept of paradigm shifts.
15 Jennifer Pitts, *A Turn to Empire: The Rise of Imperial Liberalism in Britain and France* (Princeton, 2005), 11; Pagden, *The Fall of Natural Man*, 223. See also Theodore Koditschek, *Liberalism, Imperialism, and the Historical Imagination: Nineteenth-Century Visions of a Greater Britain* (Cambridge, 2011).
16 C.A. Bayly, *Empire and Information: Intelligence Gathering and Social Communication in India, 1780–1870* (Cambridge, 1996), 2, 7, 142, 366 (quote on 142).
17 See Emmanuelle Sibeud, *Une science impériale pour l'Afrique? La construction des savoirs africanistes, 1878–1930* (Paris, 2002) for some exposition of these networks. Alice Conklin's work, *A Mission to Civilize: The Republican Idea of Empire in France and West Africa, 1895–1930* (Stanford, 1997), is an important example of the "great man" style of analysis anchored in Parisian policy circles. She broke new ground in exposing the contributions, even if depicted as relatively minor, of ethnologist-administrators in the colonies, particularly Maurice Delafosse. However, she stopped at the level of the governors-general for the most part, rarely tracing the genesis of republican ideas of African reality back to practitioners in the field.
18 Wyrtzen, *Making Morocco*, 7.
19 Gary Wilder, *The French Imperial Nation-State: Negritude and Colonial Humanism between the Two World Wars* (Chicago, 2005), 20–21. He described his work as an incorporation of Marx, Arendt, and Foucault "into a modified Marxian framework for understanding the noneconomic dimensions of our political modernity through an imperial optic," 14–15. See also his "Colonial Ethnology and Political Rationality in French West Africa," *History and Anthropology* 14, 3 (2003), 20–21.
20 Kuhn, *The Structure of Scientific Revolutions*, 3.
21 Bruno Latour, *Science in Action: How to Follow Scientists and Engineers through Society* (Cambridge, MA, 1987), 180. See also Arthur O. Lovejoy, *The Great Chain of Being: A Study of the History of an Idea* (New Brunswick, NJ, 2009 [1936]).
22 Tilley, *Africa as a Living Laboratory*, 10.
23 Matei Candea, *Corsican Fragments: Difference, Knowledge, and Fieldwork* (Bloomington, 2010), 6, 80–81.
24 Claude Markovits, *The Global World of Indian Merchants, 1750–1947: Traders of Sind from Bukhara to Panama* (Cambridge, 2008), proposed a wheel and spoke model; and Tony Ballantyne, *Orientalism and Race: Aryanism in the British Empire* (New York, 2002), adhered to a more static but wide-ranging model of a web of connections.
25 Gilles Deleuze and Félix Guattari, *A Thousand Plateaus: Capitalism and Schizophrenia*, trans. Brian Massumi (Minneapolis, 1987 [1980]), 8.
26 Ibid., 7–8.
27 Ibid., 25.

Chapter 1

1. Charles Manso, "A la statue du general Faidherbe, inaugurée à Lille, le 25 Octobre 1896" (Lille, 1896). Originally produced as part of pamphlet to accompany statue dedication in Lille. Translated as "Honor: you carry it everywhere, General/it was your sacred good, it was your ideal/it guided you like a star/and you kept it there, this pure and costly honor/just as you kept it in the desert/under your rough canvas tent." Lines refer, in particular, to Faidherbe's service in the north of France during the Franco-Prussian War.
2. Letters between William Ponty (governor-general Afrique Occidentale française), sculptor Georges Bareau, and minister of colonies (Georges Trouillot) beginning November 6, 1909, and continuing into 1911, FM/SG/AOF/X/4, Archives Nationales d'Outre-Mer, Aix-en-Provence, France (hereafter ANOM). The government of Senegal removed the statue in 1983.
3. Sibeud, *Une Science Impériale pour l'Afrique?*, 26–27.
4. "280eme séance, 8 Jan 1874," *Bulletins de la Société d'anthropologie de Paris*, IIe série, 9 (1874), 4.
5. "301eme séance, 7 Jan 1875," *Bulletins de la Société d'anthropologie de Paris*, IIe série, 10 (1875), 1. This devotion extended even to Faidherbe's will, when he donated his skull to the Broca physical anthropology laboratory. See "502eme séance, 3 Oct 1889," *Bulletins de la Société d'anthropologie de Paris*, 12, 1 (1889), n.p. (454–455).
6. "502eme séance, 3 Oct 1889," *Bulletins de la Société d'anthropologie de Paris*, 12, 1 (1889), 456.
7. Ibid., 452.
8. "280eme Séance, 8 Jan 1874," *Bulletins de la Société d'anthropologie de Paris*, IIe série, 9 (1874), 2.
9. Thomas, *Empires of Intelligence*, 2.
10. Coquery-Vidrovitch and Moniot, *L'Afrique noire*, 176; and Lefebvre, "Le temps des lettres," 59–60.
11. Kimberly Bowler offers strong analysis of these *bureaux*, in particular demonstrating their position as opponents of civilian settlers on land reform and the form of political rule: K.A. Bowler, "'It Is Not in a Day that a Man Abandons His Morals and Habits': The Arab Bureau, Land Policy, and the Doineau Trial in Algeria, 1830–1870" (PhD Dissertation, Duke University, 2011). For a wider political and intellectual history of the tortured path of the *bureaux*, see Osama Abi-Mershed, *Apostles of Modernity: Saint-Simonians and the Civilizing Mission in Algeria* (Stanford, 2010); or an older example, Xavier Yacono, *Les Bureaux arabes et l'évolution des genres de vie indigènes dans l'ouest du Tell algérois (Dahra, Chélif, Oursenis, Sersou)* (Paris, 1953). For a first-hand account, see Ferdinand Hugonnet, *Souvenirs d'un chef de bureau arabe* (Paris, 1858).
12. "Certificat de Service" dated 21 Germinale An X (April 11, 1802), AP/113APOM/1, ANOM.
13. Quotation in Terry Nichols Clark, *Prophets and Patrons: The French University and the Emergence of the Social Sciences* (Cambridge, MA, 1973), 34. No detailed biography of Faidherbe exists, particularly with respect to his family background. See, for instance, Georges Hardy, *Faidherbe* (Paris, 1947); Barnett Singer and John Langdon, *Cultured Force: Makers and Defenders of the French Colonial Empire* (Madison, 2004); and Leland C. Barrows, "General Faidherbe, the Maurel and Prom

Company, and French Expansion in Senegal" (PhD Dissertation, University of California at Los Angeles, 1974) or "Louis Léon César Faidherbe (1818–1889)" in *African Proconsuls: European Governors in Africa*, ed. L.H. Gann and Peter Duignan (New York, 1978), 51–79. At the *école* he entered as 57/130 students. See Préfecture du Nord to Minister of War, June 10, 1838, and October 17, 1838; "Demande de bourse," n.d.; "Renseignements concernant la demande d'une bourse à l'Ecole polytechnique faite en faveur du jeune Faidherbe, Louis Leon César," May 29, 1838, in Faidherbe Dossier 7Yd1515, Société Historique de la Défense, Chateau de Vincennes, Paris, France (hereafter SHD); and Section des Ecoles militaires of the Minister of War to Faidherbe family, October 24, 1938, in AP/113APOM/2, ANOM. See also Barrows, "General Faidherbe," 89–92.

14 Enfantin to Pichard, February 2, 1826, *Oeuvres de Saint-Simon et d'Enfantin*, 2nd ed., ed. E. Dentu (Paris, 1865–1878), I, 165.

15 In particular, Faidherbe encountered the explorer Henri Duveyrier, whose father was an ardent Saint-Simonian, and the physician/politician Auguste Warnier, who drafted the 1873 law that encouraged colonial seizures of native land. See Michael Heffernan, "The Limits of Utopia: Henri Duveyrier and the Exploration of the Sahara in the Nineteenth Century," *The Geographical Journal* 155, 3 (1989) for a discussion of the connection of these Saint-Simonians in Algeria. See Abi-Mershed, *Disciples of Modernity*, 26–27 and *passim*; and Marcel Emerit, *Les Saint-Simoniens en Algérie* (Paris, 1941) for a discussion of the Saint-Simonian efforts in France, Algeria, and Egypt.

16 Barrows makes this point explicitly, "General Faidherbe," 52.

17 General Vaillant, Ecole Polytechnique Evaluation, October 15, 1840, in Faidherbe dossier, SHD.

18 Patricia M.E. Lorcin, *Imperial Identities: Stereotyping, Prejudice, and Race in Colonial Algeria* (New York, 1995), 115–116.

19 Anthony Thrall Sullivan, *Thomas-Robert Bugeaud: France and Algeria, 1784–1849—Politics, Power, and the Good Society* (Hamden, CT, 1983), 105–106.

20 Faidherbe to mother, n.d., quoted in Barrows, "General Faidherbe," 92–93. I was unable to find these letters in ANOM.

21 Louis Faidherbe, *Le Sénégal: La France dans l'Afrique occidentale* (Paris, 1889), dedication page. Hardy and other biographers offer little information regarding the possibility of a meeting during this period, although Barrows remarks that no evidence exists either way. Barrows, "General Faidherbe," 94–97. Interestingly, Schoelcher also had links to Saint-Simonians, particularly Michel Chevalier, through discussion in the Paris *société d'ethnologie* (founded 1839), where Schoelcher argued that racial deficiencies stemmed from a history of oppression, not biological characteristics, a counter to the European racial supremacy advanced by Chevalier. See Philippe Regnier, "Du côté de chez Saint-Simon: Question raciale, question sociale et question religieuse," *Romantisme* 4, 130 (2005), 31–32.

22 Evaluation of 1847 (n.d.); Evaluation of October 31, 1848, Basse Terre, Faidherbe dossier, SHD.

23 Language Study Books (black, blue, looseleaf), AP/113APOM/5, ANOM. The languages included in the books (as labeled by Faidherbe): Arabic, Spanish, Italian, English, Latin, Portuguese, Greek, German, Hebrew, Breton, Corsican, Aramaic, Patois Créole, fifteenth/sixteenth-century French, Mallorcan, idiome Barbaresque, Romane of Richard the Lionheart, Languedocien, Normand, Guadeloupian

Créole, Limousin, Picard, Bressan, Bourguignon, Béarnais, Dauphinois, Lorrain, Bourbonnais, Gascon, Auvergnat.

24 Evaluation of September 3, 1849, Faidherbe dossier, SHD.
25 This "Kabyle Myth" or "Berber Vulgate" held up the Berbers as more ready for assimilation to the French way by virtue of democratic political institutions and only superficial adherence to Islam, and was a critical component of efforts to "divide and rule." The best study of this effect in Algeria specifically is Lorcin, *Imperial Identities*, although like most such studies, it offers little insight into the role played by Arabic or Berber notables. See also Kabyle Berbers, *Arab Studies Quarterly* 5, 4 (1983): 380–395; and the histories of Jacques Berque, for example, *Maghreb, Histoire et Sociétés* (Gembloux, 1975). On the role of Algerian Islamic intellectuals in the perception and the shaping of colonial policy, see James McDougall, *History and the Culture of Nationalism in Algeria* (Cambridge, 2006).
26 Lorcin, *Imperial Identities*, 140.
27 Nomination for Chevalier de la Légion d'Honneur, August 20, 1851, Faidherbe dossier, SHD.
28 On the codes of honor and civility in nineteenth-century France, see Robert A. Nye, *Masculinity and Male Codes of Honor in Modern France* (Oxford, 1993), in particular chapter 7. On the importance of charisma to the European colonial project in Africa, particularly in its role as enabler of elevated social status for conquerors and governors, see Edward Berenson, *Heroes of Empire: Five Charismatic Men and the Conquest of Africa* (Berkeley, 2011).
29 Faidherbe to mother, March 18, 1850; June 30, 1851; September 22, 1851, AP/113APOM/3, ANOM; and also Faidherbe to mother, May 11, 1851, and September 11, 1851, quoted in Barrows, "General Faidherbe," 103 (I could not locate these letters in ANOM).
30 Barrows, "General Faidherbe," 924.
31 For more on French raiding methods, often employing native troops, see Douglas Porch, *The Conquest of the Sahara* (New York, 1984); Benjamin Brower, *A Desert Named Peace: The Violence of France's Empire in the Algerian Sahara, 1844–1902* (New York, 2009); and Julia Clancy-Smith, *Rebel and Saint: Muslim Notables, Populist Protest, Colonial Encounters (Algeria and Tunisia, 1800–1904)* (Berkeley, 1994).
32 Faidherbe to mother, March 18, 1850, AP/113APOM/3, ANOM.
33 The first full European translation of one component of Ibn Khaldun's universal history, the *kitab al-ibar*, appeared as *Histoire des Berbères et des dynasties Musulmans de l'Afrique septentrionale [kitab al-ibar]*, 4 vol., ed. Paul Casanova, trans. Baron de Slane (Algiers, 1847–1851). Ibn Khaldun's more detailed depiction of civilizational movement, which also served as a methodological introduction to his seven-volume work, was translated as *Les Prolégomènes*, ed. and trans. Baron de Slane (Paris, 1863), also offering the most complete source for examination of French interaction with Khaldunian concepts. Faidherbe's first oblique references to consultation of Islamic sources occur in an 1854 notebook hand-titled *Notice sur les Maures du Sénégal et sur les noirs de la Sénégambie*, Number 58, AP/113APOM/6, ANOM.
34 Ibn Khaldun, *Les Prolégomènes*, I, 258.
35 Ibid., I, 256, 290–291.
36 Ibid., II, 294.
37 Ibid., I, 260; II, 300, 306.
38 Louis Faidherbe, "Les Berbères et les Arabes des bords du Sénégal," *Bulletin de la Société de Géographie* (February 1854), AP/113APOM/6, ANOM.

39 Handwritten comments in Ibid., 104.
40 "Populations noires des bassins du Sénégal et du haut Niger," in notebook *Notice sur les Maures*, ANOM, 281.
41 Ibid., 283–284; Louis Faidherbe, "Renseignements géographiques sur la partie du Sahara comprise entre l'oued noun et le Soudan," *Nouvelles annales des voyages, de la géographie et de l'histoire* Série 6, 19 (August 1859), 132; Louis Faidherbe, "L'avenir du Sahara et du Soudan," *Revue Maritime et Coloniale* (June 1863), 223.
42 Faidherbe, "L'avenir du Sahara," 227–229.
43 Edmund Burke III, "The Sociology of Islam: The French Tradition," in *Genealogies of Orientalism: History, Theory, Politics*, ed. Edmund Burke III and David Prochaska (Lincoln, 2008), 161. See, for example, Octave Depont and Xavier Coppolani, *Les confréries religieuses musulmanes: publié sous le patronage de M. Jules Cambon, Gouverneur général de l'Algérie* (Algiers, 1897). For further analysis of the writings of Depont and Coppolani, see George R. Trumbull IV, *An Empire of Facts: Colonial Power, Cultural Knowledge, and Islam in Algeria, 1870–1914* (Cambridge, 2009).
44 Abi-Mershed, *Apostles of Modernity*, 5, 18.
45 For more on the *royaume arabe* and the ideas of Ismayl Urbain and Louis-Napoleon (Napoleon III), see Abi-Mershed, *Apostles of Modernity*, Chapter 6; Annie Rey-Goldzeiguer, *Le royaume arabe: La politique algérienne de Napoléon III, 1861–1870* (Algiers, 1977); and Georges Spillmann, *Napoléon III et le royaume arabe d'Algérie* (Paris, 1975).
46 Tamba Eadric M'bayo, "African Interpreters, Mediation, and the Production of Knowledge in Colonial Senegal: The Lower and Middle Senegal Valley, ca. 1850s to ca. 1920s" (PhD Dissertation, Michigan State University, 2009), 130.
47 Minister of Marine and Colonies (Théodore Ducos) to Minister of War (Jean Vaillant), October 23, 1854, Faidherbe dossier, SHD, and Barrows, "General Faidherbe," 104, 202. Barrows provides the only complete discussion of the patronage process that went into Faidherbe's assumption of control in 1854, which he developed from a close examination of the papers of the Maurel Company in Bordeaux.
48 Oumar Ba, *La Pénétration française au Cayor* (Dakar, 1976), 24. "N'Diaye" is a common surname in Senegal among the Wolof community. Interestingly, it is translated as "commerce, sale, or merchandise," perhaps a reference both to Faidherbe's commercial sponsorship as governor and his belief in progress as linked to economic development. Jean-Léopold Diouf, *Dictionnaire wolof-français et français-wolof* (Paris, 2003), 255.
49 Yves-Jean Saint-Martin, *Le Sénégal sous le Second Empire: Naissance d'un Empire Colonial (1850–1871)* (Paris, 1989), 268.
50 On the power of sexual concubinage in the colonial world, see in particular Ann Laura Stoler, *Carnal Knowledge and Imperial Power: Race and the Intimate in Colonial Rule* (Berkeley, 2002).
51 Louis Faidherbe, *Notice sur la Colonie du Sénégal et sur les pays qui sont en relation avec elle* (Paris, 1859), 14–16.
52 Saint-Martin, *Sénégal sous le Second Empire*, 241. The Minister of the Navy also served as the Minister of the Colonies during this period. For a full list of the articles published under Faidherbe's watch, including those by native subordinates such as Bou al Mogdad, see "Table alphabétique et analytique des matières contenues dans les 24 volumes de la *Revue maritime et coloniale* de 1861 à 1868 et dans les 3 volumes de la *Revue algérienne et coloniale*, 1859 et 1860" (Paris, 1870).
53 Barrows, "Louis Faidherbe," 65, 68.

54 William B. Cohen, *The French Encounter with Africans: White Response to Blacks, 1530–1880* (Bloomington, 1980), 257.
55 Faidherbe, "Speech of 14 July 1860," in Delavignette, *op cit*, 247.
56 Louis Faidherbe, *Le Sénégal: La France dans l'Afrique Occidentale* (Paris, 1889), 366.
57 M'bayo, "African Interpreters," 150.
58 Faidherbe, *Le Sénégal*, 370.
59 Ibid., 369.
60 Saint-Martin, *Sénégal sous le Second Empire*, 269–270. For more detailed biographies of Faidherbe's corps of translators, see M'bayo, "African Interpreters," 233–288.
61 M'bayo, "African Interpreters," 134.
62 M'bayo, "African interpreters," 151.
63 See Henri Gaden, "Légendes et coutumes sénégalaises: Cahiers de Yoro Diao," *Revue d'ethnographie et de sociologie* 3 (1912): 119–137, 191–202; Delafosse and Van Gennep served as editors for the journal. Faidherbe named Diao's father chief of Ouâlo when he supported the French against the rebellious Emir of Trarza (later analyzed by Paul Marty) in 1855. See also Jean-Hervé Jezequel, "Maurice Delafosse et l'émergence d'un littérature africaine à vocation scientifique," in *Maurice Delafosse: Entre orientalisme et ethnographie. L'itineraire d'un africaniste (1870–1926)*, ed. Jean-Loup Amselle and Emmanuelle Sibeud (Paris, 1998), 93.
64 On the native-generated rubrics of "white" and "black" distinction along the Sahel, particularly in what would become Mali and Mauritania (but also applying to similar areas in Senegal), see Bruce S. Hall, *A History of Race in Muslim West Africa, 1600–1960* (Cambridge, 2011), Chapter 1.
65 Louis Faidherbe, "Lettre de M. Faidherbe à Monsieur le Président de la commission centrale de la société de géographie, Saint-Louis, le 12 Mars 1853," *Bulletin de la société de géographie*, Série 4, 7, 37 (February 1854): 129–130. On this process of subjugation, see Abdel Wedoud Ould Cheikh, "Nomadisme, Islam et pouvoir politique dans la société maure précoloniale (XIème siècle-XIXème siècle): Essai sur quelques aspects du tribalisme" (PhD Dissertation, University of Paris V, 1985), I, chapters 1 and 2; and H.T. Norris, *The Arab Conquest of the Western Sahara* (Harlow, Essex, 1986).
66 Ibn Khaldun, *Les Prolégomènes*, I, 169.
67 Ibid., I, 273, 310–312.
68 Faidherbe, "Les Berbères et les Arabes," 90.
69 Louis Faidherbe, "Populations Noires des bassins du Sénégal et du Haut Niger," in 1854 notebook hand-titled *Notice sur les Maures du Sénégal et sur les noirs de la Sénégambie*, Number 58, AP/113APOM/6, ANOM, 288. Article was written August 30, 1855, and may have appeared in the May–June 1856 edition of the *Bulletin de la société de géographie*.
70 Faidherbe, "L'avenir du Sahara," 223 and "Récit de la bataille d'Isly," in notebook *Notice sur les Maures*, ANOM, 272.
71 Faidherbe, "L'avenir," 230, 244–245.
72 Faidherbe, "Bataille d'Isly," 276–279.
73 Faidherbe, "L'avenir," 221. The specific reference is to Spahi sublieutenant "Alioun-Sal" for his work resisting the West African jihadist el-Hajj Umar Tal. See also Faidherbe, "Renseignements géographiques," 129, for specific attribution of native oral sources.
74 Louis Faidherbe, "Speech of 14 July 1860, Saint Louis, Senegal," printed in the *Moniteur du Sénégal*, July 17, 1860; reproduced in Robert Delavignette and Charles-Andre Julien, *Les Constructeurs de la France d'Outre-Mer* (Paris, 1946), 248–249.

75 Paul Topinard, *L'anthropologie*, 5th ed. (Paris, 1895), 12. See Lorcin, *Imperial Identities* and Abi-Mershed, *Apostles of Modernity* for further discussion of racialized assimilation policy in Algeria.
76 For basic discussion of this intellectual trend across Europe, see Carole Reynaud-Paligot, *De l'identité nationale: Science, race et politique en Europe et aux Etats-Unis, XIXe-XXe siècles* (Paris, 2011), Chapters 1–5.
77 Paul Broca, "Histoire des Progrés des Etudes Anthropologiques depuis la fondation de la Société: Compte rendu décennal," July 8, 1869, *Bulletins et Mémoires de la Société d'Anthropologie de Paris*, IIeme Série, Tome 4 (1869): cx–cxi. On the development of this group, see in particular Martin Staum, "Nature and Nurture in French Ethnography and Anthropology, 1859–1914," *Journal of the History of Ideas* 65, 3 (2004), 475–495.
78 Broca, "Histoire des Progrés des Etudes Anthropologiques," cxxiv.
79 "280eme Séance, 8 Jan 1874," *Bulletins de la Société d'anthropologie de Paris*, IIe série, 9 (1874), 3.
80 "283eme Séance, 19 Feb 1874," *Bulletins de la Société d'anthropologie de Paris*, IIe série, 9 (1874), 141.
81 See Michael Heffernan, "A State Scholarship: The Political Geography of French International Science during the Nineteenth Century," *Transactions of the Institute of British Geographers* New Series 19, 1 (1994), 21–45; Elizabeth A. Williams, "Anthropological Institutions in Nineteenth Century France," *Isis* 76, 3 (1985), 331–348; Sibeud, *Une Science Impériale*, 43–44; and Anne Godlewska, "Traditions, Crisis, and New Paradigms in the Rise of the Modern French Discipline of Geography 1760–1850," *Annals of the Association of American Geographers* 79, 2 (1989), 192–213, for more discussion of institutionalization.
82 Faidherbe, explorer Henri Duveyrier, and naturalist Adrien Berbrugger gained entrance to the Royal Geographic Society of London in 1864. Lorcin, *Imperial Identities*, 143.
83 Louis Faidherbe, "Sur l'ethnologie canarienne et sur les Tamahou," *Bulletins de la Société d'anthropologie de Paris*, IIe série, 9 (1874), 141–145.
84 "502eme Séance," *Bulletins de la Société d'anthropologie de Paris*, 459.
85 Louis Faidherbe and Paul Topinard, *Instructions sur l'anthropologie de l'Algérie* (Paris, 1874), 27.
86 Ibid., 32.
87 Ibid., 5.
88 Louis Faidherbe, "Sur les dolmens d'Afrique," *Bulletins de la Société d'anthropologie de Paris*, IIe série, 8 (1873), 118–119.
89 Louis Faidherbe, "Voyage de Cinq Nasamons d'Hérodote dans l'intérieur de la Libye," *Revue Africaine. Journal des travaux de la Société historique algérienne*, 1 (1867): 55–71, *passim*.
90 Sibeud has described metropolitan opinions of ethnographic narratives as "easy to write" and thus not worthy of serious consideration in *Une science impériale*, 43–44.
91 Minister of War to Commander, Algiers, September 17, 1870; Minister of War to Faidherbe, April 24, 1871; Note of May 26, 1883, Faidherbe dossier, SHD.
92 Faidherbe dedicated his final work to several of these officers: Ancelle (who edited a book on him), Bizard, and his son-in-law Lieutenant Brosselard. Faidherbe, *Le Sénégal*, 10.
93 Henri Labouret, *Monteil: Explorateur et Soldat* (Paris, 1937), 23–24, 105.
94 Joseph Gallieni, *Voyage au Soudan français (Haut-Niger et pays de Ségou), 1879–1881* (Paris, 1885), 464.

95 "Rôle colonisateur du chemin de fer," *Journal officiel de Madagascar*, October 31, 1904, in Joseph Gallieni, *Gallieni Pacificateur: Ecrits coloniaux de Gallieni*, ed. Hubert Deschamps and Paul Chauvet (Paris, 1949), 359; Faidherbe, *Le Sénégal*, 10.
96 Gallieni, *Voyage au Soudan français*, 5; Joseph Gallieni, *Deux campagnes au Soudan français, 1886–1888* (Paris, 1891), 633.
97 "Cours d'Hamy" in "Notes d'anthropologie," 2AP8A2, Fonds Maurice Delafosse, Muséum National d'histoire naturelle, Paris, France (MNHN); Ismael Hamet, "La civilisation Arabe en Afrique Centrale," *Revue du Monde Musulman* 14, 5 (April 1911), 33.
98 William A. Hoisington, Jr., *Lyautey and the French Conquest of Morocco* (New York, 1995), 1–2.
99 Xavier Coppolani was the most prominent inheritor of this tradition spanning North and West Africa, although Robert Arnaud also participated. See Robinson, "French Africans," 32–35; Trumbull, *Empire of Facts*, 26; and FM/SG/MRT/IV/1 and FM/SG/SOUD/III/4, ANOM for details of Coppolani's efforts, which ultimately included the 1900 foundation of the *Revue Franco-Musulmane et Saharienne* as an additional outlet for French and native studies.

Chapter 2

1 Hubert Lyautey to father, July 10, 1881, in Hubert Lyautey, *Un Lyautey inconnu: Correspondance et journal inédits, 1874–1934*, ed. André Le Révérend (Paris, 1980), 104–105. Lyautey reported the café owner as one Sidi Abdallah.
2 Lyautey to mother, July 1, 1881, in Lyautey, *Un Lyautey inconnu*, ed. Le Révérend, 100–101.
3 Ibid., 101. Lyautey named Major Coyne, whom he described as "an archaeologist, an artist and a savant" with significant expertise on Saharan Algeria, serving as the chief of the political affairs bureau for southern Algeria, as his primary colleague in these expeditions.
4 Lyautey to Joseph de la Bouillerie, May 1, 1882, in Lyautey, *Un Lyautey inconnu*, ed. Le Révérend, 120–121.
5 See André Le Révérend, "Lyautey écrivain, 1854–1934" (PhD Dissertation, University of Montpellier III, 1974) for a detailed analysis of the romanticism in certain elements of Lyautey's writings, which included correspondence with as many as 600 different people and organizations.
6 See Lyautey to E.M. de Vogüé, February 26, 1897, in Hubert Lyautey, *Choix de Lettres, 1882–1919*, ed. Lieutenant-Colonel Ponton d'Amécourt (Paris, 1947), 146–148.
7 Hubert Lyautey, "Réception de M. Lyautey: Discours prononcé dans la séance publique le jeudi 8 Juillet 1920, Institut de France," www.academie-francaise.fr/immortels/index.html, accessed December 1, 2010.
8 Evaluation of first half, 1898, signed by Joseph Gallieni, in Lyautey dossier 9Yd453, SHD.
9 Hubert Lyautey, "Le rôle colonial de l'armée," *Revue des Deux Mondes* 70, 1 (January 15, 1900), 309, 311; Lyautey to E.M. de Vogüé, February 26, 1897, in Lyautey, *Choix de Lettres*, ed. Ponton d'Amécourt, 148.
10 Raymond Betts argued that Faidherbe, Gallieni, and Lyautey served as the greatest proponents of the political notion of "association" with natives, particularly because their "practice seemed to be preceding theory," Betts, *Assimilation and Association*, 120. For varying perspectives on Lyautey and his influence, see Alan Scham, *Lyautey*

in Morocco: Protectorate Administration, 1912–1925 (Berkeley, 1970), which follows in the tradition of, for instance, former Lyautey subordinate Georges Hardy's *Portrait de Lyautey* (Paris, 1949) in a hagiographic treatment. For a more balanced perspective, see William A. Hoisington, Jr., *Lyautey and the French Conquest of Morocco* (New York, 1995); Daniel Rivet, *Lyautey et l'institution du protectorat français au Maroc*, 3 vol. (Paris, 1988); and Spencer Segalla, *The Moroccan Soul: French Education, Colonial Ethnology, and Muslim Resistance, 1912–1956* (Lincoln, NE, 2009). Le Révérend, "Lyautey l'écrivain," provides useful literary analysis of the full corpus of Lyautey's writings, paying particular attention to unpublished letters and diaries. Le Révérend's subsequent biography, *Lyautey* (Paris, 1983), is far less detailed and suffers at times from a lack of documentation. By far the best documented and argued account of Lyautey's early life is Pascal Venier, *Lyautey avant Lyautey* (Paris, 1997).

11 "Discours de M. le Maréchal de France Lyautey," *Hespéris: Archives berbères et bulletin de l'Institut des Hautes Etudes Marocaines* 2, 4 (1922), 433.
12 "Célébration du dixième anniversaire du premier débarquement des troups françaises à Casablanca, le 5 Aout 1907," in Hubert Lyautey, *Paroles d'action: Madagascar-Sud-Oranais-Oran-Maroc (1900–1926)*, 5th ed. (Paris, 1948), 229. See also "Ouverture de la Foire d'Echantillons de Fez," October 15, 1916, in Lyautey, *Paroles d'Action*, 198.
13 Paul Rabinow, *French Modern: Norms and Forms of the Social Environment* (Chicago, 1995 [1989]), 278, 285, 287. Rabinow also notes that local Muslim notables on whom Lyautey relied actually resisted any architectural "modernization" in an effort to retain some uniquely Moroccan characteristics.
14 Wyrtzen, *Making Morocco*, 17–18.
15 Lyautey to sister, February 20, 1895, in Lyautey, *Choix de Lettres*, ed. Ponton d'Amécourt, 69.
16 Douglas Porch, "Bugeaud, Gallieni, Lyautey: The Development of French Colonial Warfare," in *Makers of Modern Strategy from Machiavelli to the Nuclear Age*, ed. Peter Paret (Princeton, 1986), 387. On the rise of the pro-colonial lobby, see Betts, *Assimilation and Association*, 5.
17 Quoted in Maurice Durosoy, *Avec Lyautey: Homme de guerre, homme de paix* (Paris, 1976), 92.
18 Le Révérend, *Lyautey*, 11–20. The best Lyautey genealogist was Hubert Lyautey himself, who did exhaustive research on his family. See 475AP/1–9, Archives Privées Lyautey, Archives Nationales, Paris, France (hereafter AN).
19 Le Révérend, *Lyautey*, 19; Barnett Singer and John Langdon, *Cultured Force: Makers and Defenders of the French Colonial Empire* (Madison, 2004), 182.
20 Hardy, *Portrait de Lyautey*, 185.
21 Singer and Langdon, *Cultured Force*, 183.
22 While these early periods with Lyautey were prior to his publishing career, de Mun was later quite productive and entered the Académie française in 1897. He authored, among other works, *La question ouvrière* (Paris, 1885); and *Ma Vocation Sociale* (Paris, 1908). Besides his own testimony, the Lyautey papers contain an invitation to a meeting of de Mun's *Cercle* from March of 1876. 475AP/10, AN.
23 "Notes Quotidiennes," April 18, 1875, in Hubert Lyautey, *Rayonnement de Lyautey*, ed. Patrick Heidseick (Paris, 1941), 31.
24 Venier, *Lyautey avant Lyautey*, 32–33.
25 "Notes de voyage en Algérie," in Lyautey, *Un Lyautey inconnu*, ed. Le Révérend, 42.
26 Notebook entitled "Algérie 78" in 475AP/230, AN.
27 "Notes de voyage en Algérie," in Lyautey, *Un Lyautey inconnu*, ed. Le Révérend, 44–48, 59.

28 Ibid., 57.
29 Evaluation of August 1, 1881, Lyautey dossier, SHD; Lyautey was inducted into his first scholarly society, the Société Dunoise d'archéologie, histoire, sciences et arts on January 6, 1879, while still a lieutenant. Certificate of induction, 475AP/13, AN.
30 Lyautey to Antonin de Margerie, November 30, 1882, in Lyautey, *Choix de lettres*, ed. Ponton d'Amécourt, 6–7.
31 Lyautey to father, December 14, 1880, in Lyautey, *Un Lyautey inconnu*, ed. Le Révérend, 74. The *bureaux* had been officially suppressed as of the accession of civilian control of Algeria in 1871, but change took time, as many of these officers remained in place in the 1880s. Lyautey maintained correspondence with several local Arab notables until as late as 1888, exchanging holiday wishes and brief postcards. See 475AP/261, AN, and Lyautey to Joseph de la Bouillerie, March 12, 1883 in Hubert Lyautey, *Lettres de jeunesse: Italie-1883, Danube-Grèce-Italie-1893* (Paris, 1931), 17.
32 "Inauguration du monument du Général de Lamoricière," Teniet, May 8, 1910, in Lyautey, *Paroles d'action*, 57–59.
33 On the centrality of Algeria for Lyautey, see "Ouverture de la première conférence nord-africaine," Algiers, February 6, 1923, where he describes the colony as a place to which he had "so many links, so many work personal friendships," in Lyautey, *Paroles d'action*, 383.
34 Chief of Staff, Ministry of War to Lyautey, February 17, 1881, Lyautey dossier, SHD; Chief of Staff, Ministry of War to Lyautey, December 24, 1883, 475AP/13, AN.
35 See Société d'économie sociale de la société bibliographique des unions de la paix sociale, "Bulletin de la société d'économie sociale, Session de 1881," *La Réforme Sociale* 1, 1 (1881), I–IV. for a discussion of the group's goals and founding ideas.
36 *La Réforme sociale, Bulletin de la société d'economie sociale et des unions de la paix sociale* (January 1892), 32 lists Lyautey as group member for "Seine-et-Oise, sub-section Saint-Germain-en-Laye," while a captain in the 4th Chasseurs regiment. Venier, *Lyautey avant Lyautey*, 44, discusses Lyautey's presence at numerous Parisian salons run by influential women in the 1890s. See also Lyautey to Henry Bordeaux, July 16, 1924, where he describes his early development "nourished by Le Play," in Hubert Lyautey, *Les plus belles lettres de Lyautey*, ed. Pierre Lyautey (Paris, 1962), 134.
37 For de Vogüé's connections to the pro-colonial lobby, see Charles-Robert Ageron, *France coloniale ou parti colonial?* (Paris, 1978), 136 and chapter 4. Venier indicates Lyautey may have published anonymously in *Le Gaulois, Le journal des débats*, and *Revue de cavalerie* as well as *Revue des Deux Mondes* (see below). Venier, *Lyautey avant Lyautey*, 46–47 fn4.
38 Lyautey to E.M. de Vogüé, June 15, 1900, in Hubert Lyautey, *Lettres du sud de Madagascar, 1900–1902* (Paris, 1935), 17.
39 Lyautey to E.M. de Vogüé, February 14, 1895, in Hubert Lyautey, *Lettres du Tonkin et de Madagascar (1894–1899)*, 2nd ed., ed. Max Leclerc (Paris, 1921), 128.
40 For a more detailed exposition of French defense policy and the looming specter of German defeat and future combat, see Allan Mitchell, *Victors and Vanquished: The German Influence on Army and Church in France after 1870* (Chapel Hill, 1984), especially chapter 5, where he discusses the almost oxymoronic state of military education (offensive emphasis) and strategic thinking (entirely defensive) until 1900; and Robert A. Doughty, *Pyrrhic Victory: French Strategy and Operations in the Great War* (Cambridge, MA, 2005), chapter 1.
41 Lyautey to sister, December 25, 1894, in Lyautey, *Lettres du Tonkin et de Madagascar*, 90.

42 Lyautey to sister, November 16, 1894, in Lyautey, *Choix de lettres*, ed. Ponton d'Amécourt, 39-40. The governor-general of Indochina on Lyautey's arrival was Jean de Lanessan, who gained some renown as a colonial theorist in his own right; see his *Colonisation française en Indochine* (Paris, 1895). See Carole Reynaud Paligot, *La république raciale: Paradigme racial et idéologie républicaine (1860-1930)* (Paris, 2006), 69-76 for more on de Lanessan.
43 Lyautey to sister, November 16, 1894, in Lyautey, *Choix de lettres*, ed. Ponton d'Amécourt, 41.
44 Evaluation of 1896 signed by Boisdeffre (although apparently written by General Duchemin), Lyautey dossier, SHD. Lyautey worked as chief of staff for Boisdeffre, the former army chief of staff and now governor-general of Indochina, from June 1896.
45 Gallieni had led an expedition to negotiate with and pacify the resistance that remained from el-Hajj Umar Tal's jihadist movement of the 1850s. He and his team were held captive for almost a year by Shaykh Ahmadu, Sultan of Segou, Umar's son and successor. Gallieni describes the event in *Voyage au Soudan français*.
46 Gallieni to Eugène Etienne, January 16, 1888, and Gallieni to Louis Archinard, August 5, 1888, cited in A.S. Kanya-Forstner, *The Conquest of the Western Sudan: A Study in French Military Imperialism* (Cambridge, 1969), 143. The best biography is Marc Michel, *Gallieni* (Paris, 1989). See also Jacques Bernhard, *Gallieni: le destin inachevé* (Paris, 1991); and Pierre Lyautey, *Gallieni* (Paris, 1959).
47 F. Charles-Roux and G. Grandidier, "Avant-Propos," in Joseph Gallieni, *Lettres de Madagascar, 1896-1905*, ed. F. Charles-Roux and G. Grandidier (Paris, 1928), 8-9.
48 Michel, *Gallieni*, 71, 74-75 (quotation on 75).
49 Joseph Gallieni, *Neuf ans à Madagascar* (Paris, 1908), 323.
50 Letter to Governor of Senegal, April 17, 1887, and Rapport, May 10, 1887, cited in Kanya-Forstner, *Conquest of the Western Sudan*, 150.
51 Joseph Gallieni, *Une colonne dans le Soudan français, 1886-1887* (Paris, 1888), 42-44; Michel, *Gallieni*, 89.
52 See Gallieni, *Deux campagnes au Soudan français, 1886-1888*, in particular the discussion of the work of Lieutenant Radisson, 557. See also Gallieni's later description of the collection of vital ethnographic information in his letter to Joseph Chailley, secretary-general of the union française, April 27, 1898, in Gallieni, *Lettres de Madagascar*, ed. Charles-Roux and Grandidier, 28.
53 See the account of J. Vallière, "Notice géographique sur le Soudan français," *Bulletin de la Société de géographie de Paris* 8, 4 (1887), 486-521 (quote on 520).
54 Lyautey to sister, November 17, 1900, in Lyautey, *Lettres du sud de Madagascar*, 43.
55 Lyautey, *Gallieni*, 178-179. Lyautey expressed this reluctance in a letter to "A Parisian friend," February 2, 1899, in Lyautey, *Lettres du Tonkin et de Madagascar*, 625. Lyautey's friend and mentor, Albert de Mun, also an ardent Catholic, emerged as a leading anti-Dreyfusard during this event, likely leading Lyautey to keep some public distance between them. See Ruth Harris, *Dreyfus: Politics, Emotion, and the Scandal of the Century* (New York, 2010), for more discussion of de Mun's place in these events.
56 They visited the *Société de géographie commerciale de Paris* and of Marseille; the Sorbonne; the *Comité de Madagascar*; the *Union colonial française*, the chambers of commerce of Marseille, Lyon, and Rouen; and the *Ecole de la paix sociale*, a Le Play group in Paris. The two officers gained induction into a number of geographic societies at the same time. See Venier, *Lyautey avant Lyautey*, 128; Hoisington, *Lyautey and the French Conquest of Morocco*, 17 fn83; and 475AP/13, AN.

57 Hubert Lyautey and Joseph Gallieni, "La France à Madagascar," *La Réforme sociale* 4eme série, 9 (January 16, 1900), 113–139 (quote on 131). The meeting included a number of intellectual luminaries such as colonial theorist Anatole Leroy-Beaulieu; fellow members of the *Institut de France* Georges Picot and Eugène Rostard; Senator Albert Le Play; and a number of government officials. Leroy-Beaulieu, in his introductory remarks, described the group's mission as handed down by Le Play: "To show an interest in all peoples, all races, even to peoples that we call primitive, that some treat as barbarians. We believe that the study of human races is profitable for social science," 114.

58 Betts, *Assimilation and Association*, 5, 7–8; Ageron, *France coloniale*, 137. By this time the Chamber of Deputies in Paris included a powerful pro-colonial group headed by the deputy from Oran (Algeria), Eugène Etienne, who rejected the idea of assimilation and instead pushed for association. See below for more details, but Etienne remained a confidant and correspondent of Lyautey throughout the early twentieth century, particularly during Lyautey's time in the Algerian-Moroccan borderlands.

59 "Instructions à MM. les administrateurs civils et militaires chefs de province, au sujet du programme de pacification à poursuivre à Madagascar," *Journal Officiel de Madagascar* (JOM), May 22, 1898, reproduced in Gallieni, *Gallieni Pacificateur*, 241–242.

60 "Conclusions d'une tournée autour de l'île: la politique des races," *JOM*, February 25, 1902, in Gallieni, *Gallieni Pacificateur*, 325. Gallieni referred to these social groups at times as "races," at others as "ethnicities."

61 Virgil Matthew explicitly discusses Gallieni's adherence to the social evolutionary doctrine most famously espoused in the nineteenth century by Herbert Spencer. Virgil L. Matthew, Jr., "Joseph Simon Gallieni (1849–1916)," in *African Proconsuls: European Governors in Africa*, ed. L.H. Gann and Peter Duignan (New York, 1978), 103.

62 Gallieni, *Neuf ans*, 49; Gallieni to Chailley, December 26, 1903, in Gallieni, *Lettres de Madagascar*, ed. Charles-Roux and Grandidier, 138.

63 The academy included 18 titular members, with 2 of them natives. The group also numbered 30 associates. Gallieni, *Neuf ans*, 217; and Gallieni, *Gallieni pacificateur*, 343 fn2.

64 Gallieni to Lyautey, May 2, 1902, 475AP/13, AN.

65 For a general description of the international intrigue surrounding Morocco, see Hoisington, *Lyautey and the French Conquest of Morocco*; Douglas Porch, *The Conquest of Morocco* (New York, 1983); William McDowell, "From Entente Cordiale to Algeciras Conference: The Interplay of German Foreign and Domestic Policy during the First Moroccan Crisis" (PhD Dissertation, University of Edinburgh, 1984); and K. Wilson, "The Making and Putative Implementation of a British Foreign Policy of Gesture, December 1905 to August 1914: The Anglo-French Entente Revisited," *Canadian Journal of History* 31, 2 (1996), 227–255.

66 Lyautey to Eugène Etienne (Senator from Oran), October 27, 1904, in Lyautey, *Vers le Maroc*, 124–125. On strategy formulation in Morocco during the First World War, see William T. Dean III, "Strategic Dilemmas of Colonization: France and Morocco during the Great War," *The Historian* 73, 4 (December 2011), 730–746.

67 "Rapport d'ensemble sur l'organisation de la zône limitrophe Algéro-Marocaine," n.d., 475AP/66, AN. A *glacis* is a slope in front of a traditional European fortress that leaves invaders exposed to fire.

68 Ibid.
69 Burke, *The Ethnographic State*, 177–178.
70 Hubert Lyautey, "Bureau arabe subdivision d'Aïn Sefra," 475AP/58, AN.
71 Ibid., and letter to sister, June 14, 1905, in Lyautey, *Choix de lettres*, ed. Ponton d'Amécourt, 238–245.
72 Lyautey, "Bureau arabe."
73 Lyautey to sister, June 14, 1905, in Lyautey, *Choix de lettres*, ed. Ponton d'Amécourt, 246. This letter also indicated Lyautey's receipt of Paul Desjardins' latest work, *Catholicisme et critique*, which he considered "le plus évolutif" in full contrast with his surroundings.
74 Lyautey to E.M. de Vogüé, October 10, 1907, in Hubert Lyautey, "Lettres de Rabat," *Revue des Deux Mondes* 6, 64 (July 15, 1924), 283.
75 This is not to suggest that Lyautey was alone in this misinterpretation, which was typical of Western scholars, who considered Ibn Khaldun's work as theoretical rather than grounded in specific historical circumstances. Aziz al-Azmeh, *Ibn Khaldun in Modern Scholarship: A Study in Orientalism* (London, 1981), 180–181.
76 Ibn Khaldun, *Les Prolégomènes*, II, 238, 359.
77 Ibid., 267.
78 Ibid., 89, 46–47.
79 Abdellah Hammoudi, *Master and Disciple: The Cultural Foundations of Moroccan Authoritarianism* (Chicago, 1997), 110.
80 Lyautey to Monsieur Delcassé (foreign affairs minister), June 15, 1915, in Hubert Lyautey, *Lyautey l'Africain: Textes et lettres du Maréchal Lyautey*, ed. Pierre Lyautey (Paris, 1953–1957), III, 64–68.
81 "Au retour à Rabat du Sultan Moulay Youssef," Rabat, October 20, 1912, in Lyautey, *Paroles d'action*, 71.
82 Lyautey to Millerand (minister of war), June 16, 1915, in Lyautey, *Lyautey l'Africain*, ed. P. Lyautey, III, 27.
83 Rivet, *Lyautey et l'institution du protectorat*, I, 184–186.
84 Wyrtzen, *Making Morocco*, 50–51.
85 Lyautey to Gallieni, November 20, 1915, in Lyautey, *Les plus belles lettres*, ed. P. Lyautey, 121.
86 Burke, *The Ethnographic State*, 118–124, 136.
87 Hoisington, *Lyautey and the French Conquest of Morocco*, 206; and Rabinow, *French Modern*, 317–318.
88 Thomas, *Empires of Intelligence*, 80. See also Wyrtzen, *Making Morocco*, 52.
89 On the implications of Lyautey's editing of his letters, see Berenson, *Heroes of Empire*, 232; and Rabinow, *French Modern*, chapter 9.
90 On native communication, see, for example, Bou Amana to Lyautey, October 27, 1903, in 475AP/58, AN. This file contains numerous other letters in similar condition, with both Arabic and French writing intended for Lyautey while he still commanded the sub-division on the Algerian-Moroccan frontier. Lyautey regularly took part in Moroccan campaigns of "pacification" from 1903 to 1911 from his positions in Algeria. On Lyautey's belief in the power of French academic achievement, see "Ouverture de l'Exposition de Casablanca," September 5, 1915, in Lyautey, *Paroles d'action*, 143. Hammoudi agrees with Lyautey's assessment of the power of French scientific achievement, as he documents numerous examples of rebellious nationalist cadres who nonetheless admired the intellectual achievements of the protectorate; Hammoudi, *Master and Disciple*, 122.
91 "Situation politique et militaire," June 27, 1913, in Lyautey, *Lyautey l'africain*, ed. P. Lyautey, I, 236.

92   Rivet, *Lyautey et l'institution du protectorat*, I, 195–196.
93   Segalla, *The Moroccan Soul*, 28, 59. Hardy was reportedly dismissed from the AOF staff in 1919 for a conflict with the assimilationist camp of Blaise Diagne and others, a conflict that also involved Delafosse. See also Spencer Segalla, "Georges Hardy and Educational Ethnology in French Morocco, 1920–1926," *French Colonial History* 4 (2003), 172, 182. Segalla's work remains the only substantial biography of Hardy, but see also the short discussion by Albert Charton, "Georges Hardy," *Annuaire des anciens élèves de l'école normale supérieure,* 1974, in 684Mi (Correspondence of Hardy and Lyautey), AN.
94   Georges Hardy, "L'éducation française au Maroc," *Revue de Paris* 28, 2 (April 15, 1921), 773.
95   Georges Hardy, "Le congrès de la société indigène," *Outre-Mer* 3, 4 (December 1931), 472.
96   Georges Hardy, *Mon frère le loup: Plaidoyer pour une science vivante* (Paris, 1925), 52.
97   Lyautey to Albert de Mun, June 16, 1912, in Lyautey, *Choix de lettres*, ed. Ponton d'Amécourt, 290.
98   "Au lendemain de la libération de Fès: programme politique," June 10, 1912, *Lyautey l'Africain*, ed. P. Lyautey, I, 183. For a first-hand account of service in these units, see Jean-Dominique Carrère, *Missionaires en burnous bleu: Au service de renseignements durant l'épopée marocaine* (Limoges, 1973). Much of Lyautey's language in developing these institutions would reappear in Algeria under Jacques Soustelle in 1955.
99   Lyautey to minister of war, January 24, 1913, 475AP/137, AN.
100 "Aux obsèques du Colonel Berriau, Directeur du service des affairs indigènes," December 19, 1918, in Lyautey, *Paroles d'action*, 275–276.
101 Rivet, *Lyautey et l'institution du protectorat*, II, 46–47.
102 Henrys to Lyautey, December 12, 1914, 475AP/109, AN.
103 "Horaire des cours et conférences," Cours de perfectionnement des officiers de renseignements, November 1, 1920–January 31, 1921, Direction des affaires indigènes et Service des renseignements, 475AP/137, AN. See also Segalla, "Georges Hardy and Educational Ethnology," 172.
104 "Le service des Beaux arts au Maroc," Cours de perfectionnement des officiers de renseignements, November 1, 1920–January 31, 1921, Direction des affaires indigènes et Service des renseignements, 475AP/137, AN.
105 See William A. Hoisington, Jr., "Designing Morocco's Future: France and the Native Policy Council, 1921–25," *Journal of North African Studies* 5, 1 (2000), 63–108 for more detail on the interworkings of the council.
106 Segalla, "Georges Hardy and Educational Ethnology," 173; Rivet, *Lyautey et l'institution du protectorat*, II, 252.
107 Burke, *The Ethnographic State*, 125.
108 Paul Marty, *Le Maroc de demain* (Paris, 1925), 253; Segalla, "Georges Hardy and Educational Ethnology," 173.
109 "Au Congres des Hautes-Etudes Marocaines," Rabat, May 26, 1921, in Lyautey, *Paroles d'action*, 342.
110 See Hoisington, *Lyautey and the French Conquest of Morocco*, chapters 6 and 7, for strong analysis of the failure of indirect rule in Rabat, Casablanca, and among the Chaouia. See also Scham, *Lyautey in Morocco*, 195–202; and Rivet, *Lyautey et l'institution du protectorat*, III, 195–197, 203–212, where he describes the French administration as a "leviathan."
111 Hoisington, *Lyautey and the Conquest of Morocco*, chapter 7.

112 "Au Congrès des Hautes-Etudes Marocaines," May 26, 1921, Rabat, in Lyautey, *Paroles d'action*, 341–343.
113 Hamet was cited specifically by the IHEM for his pioneering work with eighteenth- and nineteenth-century Sultanate documents. See "Séance du 27 Mai 1921," *Hespéris: Archives Berbères et bulletin de l'Institut des Hautes Etudes Marocaines* 1, 4 (1921), 441–442. Hamet also worked heavily with similar documents in West Africa, collaborating in particular with Delafosse.
114 "Aperçu historique," submitted as part of voyage d'étude March 24, 1921, 475AP/137, AN.
115 "Séance du jeudi 20 Octobre 1921," *Hespéris: Archives Berbères et bulletin de l'Institut des Hautes Etudes Marocaines* 1, 4 (1921), 469. This particular visit included Ch. Diel and E. Mâle, members of the Institut de France; Stèphane Gsell, prominent Orientalist at the Collège de France; and Augustin Bernard, a professor at the Sorbonne.
116 "Au Congrès des hautes études marocaines," December 7, 1922, Rabat, in Lyautey, *Paroles d'action*, 375–377; "Séance du samedi 9 Decembre," *Hespéris: Archives Berbères et bulletin de l'Institut des Hautes Etudes Marocaines* 2, 4 (1922), 435.
117 Segalla, *The Moroccan Soul*, 73; Maurice Delafosse, "La leçon des faits: C'est des institutions des indigènes qu'il faut nous inspirer pour déterminer l'orientation à donner à leur évolution," *La Dépeche coloniale et maritime*, February 28, 1924, 1.
118 "Discours prononcé à l'occasion du transfert aux Invalides des cendres du Maréchal Lyautey," May 10, 1961, in Charles de Gaulle, *Discours et messages, Volume 3: Avec le renouveau, Mai 1958-Juillet 1962* (Paris, 1962), 315. Tombstone cited in Hardy, *Portrait de Lyautey*, 252.

Chapter 3

1 Paul Marty, *Etudes sur l'Islam en Côte d'Ivoire* (Paris, 1922), 4 fn1.
2 Lefebvre, "Le temps des lettres," 58–59, 71–72.
3 James C. Scott, *Seeing Like a State: How Certain Schemes to Improve the Human Condition Have Failed* (New Haven, 1998), 13. See also Camille Lefebvre, "We have tailored Africa: French colonialism and the 'artificiality' of Africa's borders in the interwar period," *Journal of Historical Geography* 37 (2011), 197.
4 Hamidou Diallo, "Pouvoir colonial, islam et première guerre mondiale en AOF," in *AOF: réalités et héritages. Sociétés ouest-africaines et ordre colonial, 1855-1960*, ed. Charles Becker, Saliou Mbaye, and Ibrahim Thioub (Dakar, 1997), I, 408, 416.
5 Marty credits Colonel Mangeot, his coauthor on "Les Touareg de la boucle du Niger," *Bulletin du Comité des études historiques et scientifiques de l'Afrique occidentale française* 3-4 (1918), with significant assistance in tandem with "les troupes coloniales" in *Etudes sur l'Islam et les tribus du Soudan* (Paris, 1920), III, 468. Marty and Delafosse each published at least one book with the *Comité de l'Afrique française*, a powerful pro-colonial lobby in France led by, among others, Charles Jonnart, Ernest Roume, and Eugène Etienne (the powerful deputy from Oran). See Marty, *Le Maroc de demain*, back matter; and Mamadi Aïssa, *Traditions historiques et légendaires du Soudan occidental*, ed. and trans. Maurice Delafosse (Paris, 1913), back matter.
6 Hamet, "La civilisation Arabe en Afrique centrale," 6 fn1. An example of the items collected by Henri Gaden is "Fétoun de Ahmadou Bamba," translated by Bou el Moghdad December 29, 1910, in Saint-Louis, which argued that the French were indeed a civilizing force (as Saad Buh also argued in his contemporary letter to

his jihadist brother Ma' al-Ainin). See AP/15APC/1 (fonds Gaden), ANOM. On a particular alliance with missionary Auguste Dupuis-Yakouba in Timbuktu, see Owen White, "The Decivilizing Mission: Auguste Dupuis-Yakouba and French Timbuktu," *French Historical Studies* 27, 3 (2004), 545–546, 553–554 fn66, and 556. White quotes Delafosse from his preface to Dupuis-Yakouba, *Les Gow* (Paris, 1911), i–ii.

7   Paul Marty, *L'Islam en Mauritanie et au Sénégal* (Paris, 1916), 6-7.
8   Maurice Delafosse, "Etude préparatoire d'un programme de mesures à prendre en vue d'améliorer la situation des indigènes au double point de vue administratif et social, 1 Mai 1919," in Marc Michel, "Un programme réformiste en 1919: Maurice Delafosse et la 'politique indigène' en AOF," *Cahiers d'Etudes Africaines* 15, Cahier 68 (1975), 324; Maurice Delafosse, *Haut-Sénégal-Niger* (Paris, 1972 [1912]), I, 109–112.
9   Maurice Delafosse, "L'assimilation ou le phénix colonial: Un essai de mise au point," *La Dépêche Coloniale et Maritime*, January 5, 1923, 1; Marty, *Le Maroc de demain*, 115; and *L'Islam en Guinée: Fouta-Diallon* (Paris, 1921), 451. On Delafosse's specific criteria for evaluating the proper level of French involvement in a native society, see "Etude préparatoire," 321 and "Ce qu'on peut leur demander," *La Dépêche Coloniale et maritime*, October 1, 1924, 1.
10 Betts, *Assimilation and Association*, 20.
11 Lefebvre, "Le temps des lettres," 64.
12 Jean-Louis Triaud, "L'Islam sous le régime colonial," *L'Afrique occidentale au temps des français*, 152.
13 Marty, *Etudes sur l'Islam et les tribus du Soudan*, II, 259.
14 Marty included appendices of such writings, often copies of letters with ethnographic information or transcriptions of genealogies, in most of his larger works, particularly *Etudes sur l'Islam au Sénégal* (Paris, 1917); and *Etudes sur l'Islam et les tribus du Soudan*. On these documents in general, see Bruce S. Hall and Charles C. Stewart, "The Historic 'Core Curriculum' and the Book Market in Islamic West Africa," in *The Trans-Saharan Book Trade: Arabic Literacy, Manuscript Culture, and Intellectual History in Islamic History*, ed. Graziano Kratti and Ghislaine Lydon (Leiden, 2011), 147; and Norris, *The Arab Conquest of the Western Sahara*, 72–73. I owe the use of the term "gatekeeper" to conversations with Fahad Bishara.
15 Certificates of study and Evaluation of 1907, Paul Marty Dossier 6Ye 49900, SHD. His Arabic degree came from the Ecole des Lettres d'Alger (later the University of Algiers), his history degree from the Faculté d'Aix-en-Provence, and his certificate in secondary education from the Académie d'Alger.
16 Evaluation of 1908 (signature illegible, possibly Cuisset); and 1909 evaluation (unsigned), Marty dossier, SHD.
17 Evaluation of 1909, Marty dossier, SHD.
18 Evaluation of 1911, Marty dossier, SHD.
19 Paul Marty, "Les institutions israélites au Maroc," *Revue des études Islamiques* 4, Cahier 3 (1930), 329.
20 On the relationship between Delafosse and Houdas, see Maurice Delafosse, "Le Gâna et le Mali et l'emplacement de leurs capitales," *Bulletin du comité d'études historiques et scientifiques de l'Afrique occidentale française* 7 (1924), 482. On Houdas' call for documentation, see, for example, Georges de Gironcourt, "Les inscriptions de la nécropole de Bentia (avec extraits d'une note de M. Houdas)," *Comptes-rendus des séances de l'Académie des Inscriptions et Belles-Lettres* 55, 2 (1911), 202–203.
21 Catherine Coquery-Vidrovitch, "Les changements sociaux," *L'Afrique occidentale au temps des français*, 25.

22 See the instructions in two notebooks entitled, "Instructions générales du 1er Aout 1904 mises à jour au 30 Juin 1905 par M. Delafosse, administrateur de la cercle de Korhogo," in 2AP8B2, Fonds Maurice Delafosse (2AP8), Fonds du Patrimoine, Bibliothèque du musée de l'homme, Muséum national d'histoire naturelle (hereafter MNHN).
23 Marty, *L'Islam en Guinée*, 342 and *Etudes sur l'Islam en Côte d'Ivoire*, 77. See also Delafosse notebook entitled "Dialecte du district de Boromo Haute Volta" 2AP8A1, MNHN. The notebook contains Arabic and West African grammars as well as writings entitled "Textes peuls du Fouta Sénégalais" and "Textes Peuls du Massina," listed as collected at Djenné by M. Lurlousaien (?) and another by M. d'Arbousier.
24 David Robinson, *Paths of Accommodation: Muslim Societies and French Colonial Authorities in Senegal and Mauritania, 1880-1920* (Athens, OH, 2000), 39; "Fiches de renseignements," 14MIOM/895 (AOF 13G69), Archives Nationales du Sénégal (ANS), housed at ANOM; "Demande de renseignement," 14MIOM/784 (AOF 5G64), ANS, ANOM.
25 See, for example, Commandant de Cercle du Sine-Saloum, Sénégal, to Marty, June 21, 1915, where the commandant refers to his desire to read Marty's latest book (perhaps Marty's *Islam en Mauritanie et au Sénégal*, first published in the *Revue du monde musulman* in that year), 14MIOM/895 (AOF 13G69), ANS, ANOM.
26 Maurice Delafosse, *Les Nègres* (Paris, 1927), 68.
27 Ibid., 69.
28 Musa Kamara to Delafosse, November 15, 1924, quoted in David Robinson, "Un historien et anthropologue sénégalais: Sheikh Musa Kamara," *Cahiers d'études Africaines* 28, Cahier 109 (1988), 99.
29 Jean Schmitz, "L'historiographie des Peuls musulmans de l'Afrique de l'ouest: Shaykh Musa Kamara (1864-1945), saint et savant," in *AOF: réalités et héritages*, ed. Becker, Mbaye, and Thioub, II, 862.
30 Marty, *Etudes sur l'Islam et les tribus du Soudan*, 336-338. As another example, Marty wrote a section of his earlier work, *Etudes sur l'Islam au Sénégal*, I, 262-279, with the assistance of documentary and oral accounts provided by followers of Amadu Bamba (1853-1927).
31 This description of colonial reform triangulates between the descriptions of colonial reformers in Gary Wilder, *The French Imperial Nation-State*; the "accommodation" model advanced by David Robinson in *Paths of Accommodation*; and the intellectual transmission portrayed by Bruce Hall in *A History of Race*.
32 Hall and Stewart, "The Historic 'Core Curriculum,'" 144.
33 Chouki el Hamel, *La vie intellectuelle Islamique dans le Sahel Ouest Africain: Une étude sociale de l'enseignement Islamique en Mauritanie et au Nord du Mali (XVIe-XIX3 siècles) et traduction annotée de Fath ash-shakur d'al-Bartili al-Walati (mort en 1805)* (Paris, 2002), 153.
34 The explorer in this case was Georges de Gironcourt; see *Missions de Gironcourt en Afrique occidentale, 1908-1909; 1911-1912: Documents scientifiques*, ed. Georges de Gironcourt (Paris, 1920), 147-149.
35 See Hall, *A History of Race*, 225, for a description of Shaykh Bay's views in this regard.
36 See Abdel Wedoud ould Cheikh, *Eléments d'histoire de la Mauritanie* (Nouakchott, 1991), 38, for a discussion of one such example, where Sahelian elites controlled the flow of fifteenth-century chronicles so as to suggest to Marty that the warrior-clerical divide in West Africa was of more recent vintage.
37 Marty, *Islam en Mauritanie et au Sénégal*, 139, 210-218; he also cultivated relations with Saad Buh's rival, Shaykh Sidiyya (d. 1926), whom he saw as a perfect

collaborator, 105. See also Maurice Delafosse, "Le clergé musulman de l'Afrique occidentale," *Revue du monde musulman* 11, 6 (June 1910), 183; "Notice de Cheikh Saad Bouh," in *Chroniques de la Mauritanie Sénégalaise, Nacer Eddine*, ed. and trans. Ismael Hamet (Paris, 1911), 264–270; and Robinson, *Paths of Accommodation*, 50.

38 Triaud, "L'Islam sous le régime colonial," 141.
39 Ibid., 147.
40 For more details on this period, see Glen McLaughlin, "Sufi, Saint, Sharif: Muhammad Fadil Wuld Mamin, His Spiritual Legacy and the Political Economy of the Sacred in Nineteenth Century Mauritania" (PhD Dissertation, Northwestern University, 1997), 62–66; and Robinson, *Paths of Accommodation*, 162–176.
41 Cheikh Saad Bouh to Ma-al-Ainin, 1909 in FM/SG/MRT/VI/1, ANOM. The letter was reproduced in *l'Afrique française*, a publishing organ of a French pro-colonial lobby, in November 1909; see Dedoud ould Abdallah, "Guerre sainte ou sédition blâmable? Nasiba de Shaikh Sa'd Bu contre le jihad de son frère shaikh Ma al-Ainin," in *Le temps des marabouts: Itinéraires et stratégies islamiques en Afrique occidentale française v. 1880–1960*, ed. David Robinson and Jean-Louis Triaud (Paris, 1997), 125–126 and fn20. See also governor-general AOF (William Ponty) to minister of colonies (Georges Trouillot), September 7, 1909, and minister of colonies to minister of foreign affairs (Stéphan Pichon), September 30, 1909, FM/SG/MRT/VI/1, ANOM.
42 Robinson has described such wide-ranging links for Saad Buh, particularly in his influence on religious authorities such as Shaykh Musa Kamara. See *Paths of Accommodation*, 168.
43 Delafosse, *Haut-Sénégal-Niger*, I, 32–33.
44 Maurice Delafosse, *L'âme nègre* (Paris, 1922), 12–13, 15.
45 Paul Marty, "Folklore Tunisien: L'onomastique des noms propres de personne," *Revue des études Islamiques* 10, Cahier 4 (1936), 393.
46 Hamet, "La civilisation Arabe," 34; Hamet, "*Nour el-Eulab* (Lumière des Coeurs) de Chëikh Otmane ben Mohammed ben Otmane dit Ibn-Foudiou," *Revue Africaine* 41 (1897), 81.
47 Marty, *Etudes sur l'Islam et les tribus du Soudan*, II, 328 (annex 10).
48 Hamet, "Littérature arabe saharienne," *Revue du monde musulman* 12, 11 (November 1910), 405. The full article is in 12, 10 (October 1910), 194–213 and 12, 11 (November 1910), 380–405.
49 Louis Massignon, "Une bibliothèque saharienne," *Revue du monde musulman* 8 (May–June 1909), 409, 411.
50 Marty, *L'Islam en Guinée*, 1–2.
51 See Conklin, *A Mission to Civilize* for a discussion of the interaction of these governors-general with metropolitan officials and their staffs regarding ethnological investigation and the implications of republican governance. On the official relationship between the colonies, see AOF governor-general (Ernest Roume) to Algeria governor-general (Charles Jonnart), November 21, 1903, in ALG/GGA/28H/2, ANOM.
52 *Missions de Gironcourt*, 1, 2, 150. See also the discussion and reproduction of several of these documents in Charles Grémont, *Les Touaregs Iwellemmedan, 1647–1896: Un ensemble politique de la boucle du Niger* (Paris, 2010).
53 See note by Bonnel de Mezières, April 13, 1913, in FM/SG/AOF/X/6, ANOM regarding his acquisitions in Timbuktu. See also Maurice Delafosse, "Découvertes de M. Bonnel de Mezières dans la région de Tombouctou," *Revue d'ethnographie*

et de sociologie 5, 5–6 (May–June 1914), 203–205. See, for example, Marty, *Etudes sur l'Islam et les tribus du Soudan*, II, 88–89 and I, 352–354 for discussions of the importance of these sources.

54 For example, Xavier Coppolani conducted expeditions to the Mauritanian Sahel and was eventually tasked with the conquest of the area before his 1905 assassination. On the Coppolani expeditions, see his reports and correspondence contained in FM/SG/MRT/IV/1, ANOM, and also the discussion in *Democracy and Development in Mali*, ed. R. James Bingin, David Robinson, and John M. Staatz (East Lansing, 2000). Robert Arnaud, administrator in Algeria, also conducted an expedition to West Africa. See AOF governor-general (Roume) to minister of colonies (Georges Leygues), March 29, 1906, and Roume to Robert Arnaud, March 24, 1906, in FM/SG/AOF/III/3, ANOM.

55 See, for example, Shaykh Bay al-Kunti, "Notes sur d'anciennes tribus touareg," in Grémont, *Les Touaregs Iwellemmedan*, 517.

56 Houdas and Delafosse provide an excellent view into this process in their preface to Mahmoûd Kâti ben el-Hâdj el-Motaouakkel Kâti, *Tarikh el-Fettach, ou chronique du chercheur pour servir à l'histoire des villes, des armées, et des principaux personnages de Tekrour* (TF), ed. and trans. Octave Houdas and Maurice Delafosse (Paris, 1964 [1913–1914]). Explorers such as Mungo Park and René Caillié made vague references to the documentary history of the area, but German explorer Heinrich Barth reportedly saw a manuscript fragment of this document during his voyages in West Africa. See his *Travels and Discoveries in North-Central Africa; being a journal of an expedition undertaken under the auspices of H.B.M.'s government in the years 1849–1855* (London, 1857–1858). See also the preface to Abderrahim ben Abdallah ben 'Imran ben 'Amir es-Sa'di, *Tarikh es-Soudan* (TS) ed. and trans. Octave Houdas with Edm. Benoist (Paris, 1964 [1898–1900]).

57 Houdas acquired partial copies from Louis Archinard, colonial soldier and explorer in Mali, and Félix Dubois, historian of Timbuktu. He received the best copy from Orientalist René Basset of the Ecole des lettres d'Alger, who got the 1792 manuscript copy from a Dr. Tautain. Preface to es-Sa'di, TS, XIV–XV.

58 John O. Hunwick, *Timbuktu and the Songhay Empire: Al-Sa'di's Tarikh al-Sudan down to 1613 and other contemporary documents* (Boston, 1999), lxiv.

59 Houdas, preface to TS, II, V.

60 Ibid., 308–319.

61 See Paul Marty, "L'Islam et les tribus dans la colonie du Niger," *Revue des Etudes Islamiques* 4, Cahier 3 (1930), 346 (the full article is in *REI* 4, 3 (1930), 333–432 and 5, 2 (1931), 139–240); *Etudes sur l'Islam et les tribus du Soudan*, I, 181–193; and numerous examples in *L'Islam en Mauritanie et au Sénégal; Etudes sur l'Islam et les tribus Maures: Les Brakna* (Paris, 1921); and *L'Islam en Guinée*.

62 Félix Dubois, quoted in preface to Mahmoûd Kâti, TF, VII.

63 Preface to TF, VIII–XI. Bonnel de Mezières reportedly found a partial copy in Timbuktu in 1911 in the personal library of Sidi Muhammad al-Imam bin al-Soyuti, later a professor at the city's madrasa. Clozel found a more complete copy in the possession of Abdoulaye Waly Bah, a Muslim scholar in Haut-Sénégal-Niger, in 1912.

64 See preface, TF, XIV, XIX. Nehemia Levtzion has persuasively argued that heavy portions of the recovered TF manuscript were altered under the nineteenth-century direction of Shehu Amadu of Massina, who inserted justification for his imperial claims as the thirteenth Caliph of Islam. See Nehemia Levtzion, "A Seventeenth-Century Chronicle by Ibn al-Mukhtar: A Critical Study of 'Ta'rikh al-fattash,'"

Bulletin of the School of Oriental and African Studies, University of London 34, 3 (1971), 571–593. The editors considered the possibility of multiple authors but did not document the possibility of later political manipulation.

65 P. Joseph Brun, "Notes sur le *Tarikh el-Fettach*," *Anthropos* 9 (1914), 593. Brun was the first to doubt the Houdas-Delafosse conception of authorship in print, but stopped short of Levtzion's conclusions.
66 TF, appendix 2, 328.
67 TF, 75–79, and appendix 2, 326–333. The editors proposed that the fragment listed as appendix 2 may have originally formed the opening of the work. Subsequent analysts have agreed that it may have been removed at some point in the later editing/forging process.
68 Delafosse, "Découvertes de M. Bonnel de Mezières," 305, and "Le Gâna et le Mali," 486–493, 498, 519–520. Delafosse references Ibn Khaldun as the best of these Arab sources, but also uses Ibn Hawqal, Ibn Battuta, and al Bekri.
69 P.F. de Moraes Farias, *Arabic Medieval Inscriptions from the Republic of Mali: Epigraphy, Chronicles, and Songhay-Tuareg History* (Oxford, 2003), xxxvi–xxxviii, lv–lvi.
70 Ibid., chapter 2, section 2, lxix–lxxxv.
71 Siré-Abbas-Soh, *Chroniques du Foûta Sénégalais*, ed. and trans. Maurice Delafosse with Henri Gaden (Paris, 1913), 2, 5, 28, 46. Siré-Abbas-Soh reportedly penned the collection of stories from his memory in only 15 days. Henri Gaden aided the effort by offering translation and orthographic services as well as connections with locals to gain supporting documentation for verification. For a similar methodology, see Aïssa, *Traditions historiques et légendaires du Soudan Occidental*; and *Chroniques de la Mauritanie Sénégalaise*.
72 Hamet, "Littérature arabe," 195.
73 Maurice Delafosse, "Traditions Musulmans relatives à l'origine des Peuls," *Revue du monde musulman* 20 (September 1912), 264. A fragment of this same history appeared in an appendix of *Tedzkiret en-Nisian fi akhbâr moulouk es-Soudan*, ed. and trans. Octave Houdas (Paris, 1966 [1913–1914]).
74 On "historical reconstruction" using multiple sources, see Marty, *Etudes sur l'Islam et les tribus Maures*, 2. For the appropriation of Kunta language of race, see Marty, *Etudes sur l'Islam et les tribus du Soudan*, I, 2–3, 65, 154, and III, 157; and Hamet, "Littérature arabe," 197, 402–403. For a detailed analysis of this Kunta/Tuareg language, see Hall, *A History of Race*, chapter 1.
75 Maurice Delafosse, "Les Hamites de l'Afrique occidentale," *L'Anthropologie* V (1894), 157–172. Note that Delafosse later discounted the "Hamitic hypothesis" as a "purely artificial" linguistic entity in "Sur l'unité des langues négro-africaines," *Revue d'ethnographie et des traditions populaires* I (1920), 124–126.
76 See, for instance, Delafosse's discussion of Peul origins in *Missions de Gironcourt*, 105–108, and Marty, *Etudes sur l'Islam et les tribus du Soudan*, III, 3.
77 Ibn Khaldun, *Les Prolégomènes*, II, 272–273.
78 "Lettre de Cheikh Sid Mohammed ben Cheikh Ahmed ben Suleimane," *Chroniques de la Mauritanie Sénégalaise*, 157.
79 Timothy Cleaveland, *Becoming Walata: A History of Saharan Social Formation and Transformation* (Portsmouth, NH, 2002), 37–38, 58, 64–65, 193 (quote on 65). See also and Bruce S. Hall, "The Question of 'Race' in the Pre-Colonial Southern Sahara," *Journal of North African Studies* 10, 3 (2005), 348–349.
80 M'hammad ibn Ahmad Yura al-Daymani, *Ikhbar al-ahbar bi akhbar al-abar (Renseignements des lettrés sur l'histoire des puits)*, trans. Paul Marty (Rabat, 1991), 9–11; Siré-Abbas-Soh, *Chroniques du Foûta Sénégalais*, 15.

81 Maurice Delafosse, *Sur des traces probables de civilisation égyptienne et d'hommes de race blanche à la Côte d'Ivoire* (Paris, 1901), 53–54; Delafosse, "Traditions Musulmans relatives à l'origine des Peuls," 242–257.
82 Delafosse, "Le Gâna et le Mali," 480.
83 Norris, *Arab Conquest of the Western Sahara*, 12–16, 45; Farias, *Arabic Medieval Inscriptions*, cxxxvii–cxxxviii; and ould Cheikh, *Eléments d'histoire de la Mauritanie*, 19, 21, 59. ould Cheikh also offers a detailed portrait of genealogical appropriation in Mauritania in "La tribu comme volonté et comme représentation. Le facteur religieux dans l'organisation d'un tribu maure: les Awlâd Abyayri," in *Al-Ansâb: La quête des origines. Anthropologique historique de la société tribale arabe*, ed. Pierre Bonte, Edouard Conte, Constant Hamès, and Abdel Wedoud Ould Cheikh (Paris, 1991), 218–222. See Tarif Khalidi, *Arabic Historical Thought in the Classical Period* (Cambridge, 1994) for a discussion of the progression of genealogy and history through the phases of Arab-Islamic state development.
84 Note that this discussion is limited only to the intra-African practice of slavery, and not the trans-Atlantic slave trade, which was a different institution altogether.
85 On Tuareg warrior and clerical genealogies, see Hall, *A History of Race*, 58–66. On the strength of religious/political authority via "charismatic capital," see Abdel Wedoud ould Cheikh, "Nomadisme, Islam, et pouvoir politique dans la société maure précoloniale (XIème-XIXème siècle): Essai sur quelques aspects du tribalisme" (PhD Dissertation, University of Paris V, 1985), III, 885–904.
86 Marty, *L'Islam en Guinée*, 272.
87 Hall, *A History of Race*, 230–231.
88 Marty, *Etudes sur l'Islam en Côte d'Ivoire*, 368.
89 Delafosse, "L'animisme nègre et sa résistance à l'Islamisation en Afrique occidentale," *Revue du monde musulman* (March 1922), 157.
90 Delafosse, *Haut-Sénégal-Niger*, 94, 126–127.
91 Maurice Delafosse, "Des soi-disant clans totémiques de l'Afrique occidentale," *Revue d'ethnographie et des traditions populaires* 1 (1920), 106–107; and *Les Noirs de l'Afrique*, 2nd ed. (Paris, 1941 [1922]), 138. Marty provides significant analysis of clerical genealogies in virtually all of his works, but see in particular *Etudes sur l'Islam au Sénégal*, I, 15–68, where he dissects the interrelationship of many of the prominent Islamic clerics.
92 Delafosse, "L'animisme nègre," 144; and "Etude préparatoire," 324.
93 Delafosse, *Les Nègres*, 38–39. Delafosse in particular advocated for a policy similar to Lyautey's sponsorship of the grands caids. See also Hardy, "Le congrès de la société indigène," 481 for a later discussion of this same theme.
94 James L.A. Webb, Jr., *Desert Frontier: Ecological and Economic Change along the Western Sahel, 1600–1850* (Madison, 1995), xvi, 15–17. See also Abdel Wedoud Ould Cheikh, "Nomadisme, Islam et pouvoir politique," chapters 1 and 2; and Hall, *A History of Race*, 37–39.
95 Ibn Khaldun, *Les Prolégomènes*, I, 170–171, 174–175.
96 Ibid., I, 257, 271.
97 Maurice Delafosse, "Les populations noirs de l'Afrique," *La Géographie* 37 (1922), 452–463 (Côte d'Ivoire), 463–465 (Sahel).
98 Delafosse, *Sur des traces probables de civilisation égyptienne et d'hommes de race blanche à la Côte d'Ivoire*, 2. Delafosse defended the Egyptian thesis throughout his career, although he later admitted that supposed archaeological evidence of Egyptian residents (particularly in the form of jewelry) was in fact explained through local manufacture or movement across trans-Saharan trade routes.

99   Ibn Khaldun, *Les Prolégomènes*, I, 13–14, 350–351; II, 299, 362.
100 Ibn Khaldun, *Histoire des Berbères et des dynasties musulmans de l'Afrique septentrionale*, I, 167.
101 Marty, *Etudes sur l'Islam et les tribus du Soudan*, I, 251–252.
102 Delafosse, "Les populations noires de l'Afrique," 463–464.
103 Marty, *Etudes sur l'Islam et les tribus Maures*, 8.
104 Ibn Khaldun, *Histoire des Berbères*, I, 167, 34; II, 1.
105 Delafosse described multiple waves of invasion across the desert. The first, composed of Hilalien Arabs in the eleventh century, was relatively small. The larger and more permanent invasion of the fourteenth century actually consisted of the Beni Hassan of Yemeni extraction. See Delafosse, *Haut-Sénégal-Niger*, I, 188–190. For Marty's part, he also considered these separate waves in different works, in particular his four-volume *Etudes sur l'Islam et les tribus du Soudan*.
106 Marty, *Etudes sur l'Islam et les tribus du Soudan*, I, 180–181.
107 "Rapport au Gouverneur," January 22, 1902, Niabley; Piece 62, 2AP8D49, MNHN.
108 Delafosse, *Haut-Sénégal-Niger*, I, 347. Delafosse offers similar, although less positive, reviews of other West African groups in the same volume.
109 Marty, *Etudes sur l'Islam et les tribus du Soudan*, III, 464–465.
110 Ibid., IV, 47–48.
111 Ibid., II, 37–38.
112 Delafosse, *Les civilisations Négro-africaines* (Paris, 1925), 69–74. Delafosse's understanding of castes in West Africa generally jibes with that found in more recent scholarship. See, for example, Tal Tamari, "The Development of Caste Systems in West Africa," *Journal of African History* 32, 2 (1991), 223–224.
113 Maurice Delafosse, "Juxtaposition, assimilation, association," *La Dépêche coloniale*, June 21, 1924, 1.
114 René Verneau, the celebrated physical anthropologist, focused on physiometric measurement in the style of Paul Broca, and Paul Topinard taught Delafosse at the Muséum, as did the director of the anthropology lab, E.T. Hamy. See René Verneau, "Nécrologie—Maurice Delafosse," *L'Anthropologie* (1926), 595.
115 "Cours d'Hamy: Anthropologie" in 2AP8A2, "Notes d'anthropologie," MNHN.
116 Marty, *L'Islam en Guinée*, 9, 511. See also ould Cheikh, "Nomadisme, Islam et pouvoir politique" for a detailed discussion of these caste structures since the eleventh century.
117 Maurice Delafosse, Article 3, entitled "Musulmans" in chapter 1, "Service Général et affaires politiques" of his "Instructions générales du 1er Aout 1904 mises à jour au 30 Juin 1905 par M. Delafosse, administrateur de la cercle de Korhogo," in 2AP8B2, MNHN.
118 Catherine Coquery-Vidrovitch, "Du territoire à l'Etat-nation," *AOF: réalités et héritages*, ed. Becker, Mbaye, and Thioub, 24–25; and Claudine Cotte, "Géopolitique de la colonization," *L'Afrique occidentale au temps des français*, 88.
119 Maurice Delafosse, "L'état actuel de l'Islam dans l'Afrique occidentale française," *Revue du monde musulman* 11 (May–August 1910), 53.
120 Marty, *Etudes sur l'Islam au Sénégal*, I, 10. Here Marty refers not only to Faidherbe and Gallieni but also to AOF governors-general William Ponty (r. 1908–1915) and Francois-Joseph Clozel (r. 1915–1917).
121 Marty, *L'Islam en Guinée*, 512; *Etudes sur l'Islam et les tribus du Soudan*, III, 232.
122 Marty, *Etudes sur l'Islam et les tribus du Soudan*, II, 260.
123 Marty, *Etudes sur l'Islam au Sénégal*, I, 286.

124 Hall, *A History of Race*, 193–194.
125 Marty, *Etudes sur l'Islam en Côte d'Ivoire*, 222. Ivor Wilks identifies one such individual as "Sa'id Kunardi" in "The Transmission of Islamic Learning in the Western Sudan," in *Literacy in Traditional Societies*, ed. Jack Goody (Cambridge, 1968), 189.
126 Marty, *L'Islam en Mauritanie et au Sénégal*, 105.
127 See typed copies of biographical sketches of Senegalese marabouts in FM/SG/AOF/X/6, ANOM, which also includes collective breakdowns by order, affiliation, number of students, and crossover with French schools.
128 For a description of the Hamallist controversy, see Christopher Harrison, *France and Islam in West Africa, 1860–1960* (Cambridge, 1988), 171–180; Louis Brenner, *Controlling Knowledge: Religion, Power and Schooling in a West African Muslim Society* (Bloomington, IN, 2001), 33–34, 162; Robinson, *Paths of Accommodation*, 155, 160; and Hanretta, *Islam and Social Change*, which gives an excellent description of a related dispute involving Yacouba Sylla, a former Hamallah follower.
129 The best discussion of the development and reach of the colonial Murid order is Cheikh Anta Babou, *Fighting the Greater Jihad: Amadu Bamba and the Founding of Muridiyya in Senegal, 1853–1913* (Athens, OH, 2007).
130 Marty, *Etudes sur l'Islam au Sénégal*, I, 272.
131 Ibid., I, 280–281. On Marty's manipulation of these divisions, see Donal Cruise O'Brien, "Les négociations du contrat social sénégalais," in *La construction de l'état au Sénégal*, ed. Donal Cruise O'Brien, Momar-Coumba Diop, and Mamadou Diouf (Paris, 2002), 84–85.
132 Marty, "L'Islam et les tribus dans la colonie du Niger," 343.
133 Paul Marty, *Etudes sur l'Islam au Dahomey: Le bas-Dahomey, Le haut-Dahomey* (Paris, 1926), 168.
134 Marty, *Etudes sur l'Islam et les tribus du Soudan*, II, 136. Marty cites Ibn Battuta for accounts of these Islamic missionaries.
135 Marty, *Etudes sur l'Islam en Côte d'Ivoire*, 444–445.
136 Marty, *Etudes sur l'Islam au Sénégal*, I, 4.
137 Delafosse, *Haut-Sénégal-Niger*, III, 187.
138 Delafosse, *Haut-Sénégal-Niger*, I, 347–348; Delafosse, "L'animisme nègre," 160.
139 Hamet, "La civilisation Arabe en Afrique centrale," 31.
140 Marty, *Etudes sur l'Islam en Côte d'Ivoire*, 272–273.
141 Delafosse, "Les populations noirs de l'Afrique," 467.
142 Delafosse, "L'état actuel de l'Islam," 37.
143 Marty, *Etudes sur l'Islam et les tribus du Soudan*, II, 261.
144 Delafosse, "L'animisme nègre," 146.
145 Marty, *Etudes sur l'Islam et les tribus du Soudan*, II, 3.
146 Delafosse, *Les Nègres*, 10–11.
147 Marty, *Le Maroc de demain*, 142–143.
148 Ibid., 86.
149 Marty, *L'Islam en Guinée*, 514.
150 Ibid., 362; Paul Marty, "Vingt ans de politique algérienne. Le départ de M. Luciani," *Revue du monde musulman* 40–41 (September–December 1920), 3; Marty, *Etudes sur l'Islam et les tribus du Soudan*, II, 85, 92–93. The Saint Louis madrasa, for instance, featured a director selected from among Arabic-speaking professors in Algeria (could be either native or French, although usually French), 2 French

instructors, 1 Algerian instructor, and 2 black African instructors; Marty, *Etudes sur l'Islam au Sénégal*, II, 114.
151 Hamet, "La civilisation Arabe en Afrique Centrale," 33.
152 Preface to *Tedzkiret en-Nisian*, VI-VII.
153 Jean-Hervé Jezequel, "Maurice Delafosse et l'emergence d'un littérature africaine à vocation scientifique," in *Maurice Delafosse: Entre Orientalisme et ethnographie*, 94. Jezequel discusses publications in the 1916 and 1919 editions of the journal, and Delafosse's publication of an ethnographic work by Diguy Kante in the educational bulletin of the AOF in 1918. See also Jézéquel, "'Collecting Customary Law': Educated Africans, Ethnographic Writings, and Colonial Justice in French West Africa," in *Intermediaries, Interpreters, and Clerks: African Employees in the Making of Colonial Africa*, ed. Benjamin Lawrance, Emily Lynn Osborn, and Richard L. Roberts (Madison, 2006), 139-158; and Delafosse, *Les civilisations Négro-africaines*, 127-129 and "Le clergé musulman," 187 for glowing praise of African language development in isolation.
154 Delafosse, *Les états d'âme d'un colonial* (Paris, 1909), 70.
155 Oualid Eddimany, "Amr el Oualy Nacer Eddine," copied by Saad Buh, in Hamet, *Chroniques de la Mauritanie Sénégalaise*, 177.
156 Louise Delafosse, *Maurice Delafosse, le Berrichon conquis par l'Afrique* (Paris, 1976), 95-96, 106, 116-117. Delafosse owed his new position to the sponsorship of both Houdas and E.T. Hamy, who provided him with a new boss and a future mentor in Louis-Gustave Binger, then the governor of Côte d'Ivoire and a former guest lecturer at the Sorbonne. Delafosse made contact in the colony with Colonel Louis-Parfait Monteil, a colonial officer and commander; and his brother Charles (father of later Ibn Khaldun scholar and Jacques Soustelle collaborator Vincent), a colonial administrator and linguist, who assisted in the collection of local documents and oral interviews. Delafosse also served as the administrator of the cercle of Baoulé in 1896.
157 In 1899 Delafosse turned down a grant from the école des langues orientales vivantes, as he had left his brief assignment in Liberia to return to Côte d'Ivoire. See Administrator, Ecole spéciale des langues orientales vivantes to minister of colonies (Antoine Guillain), March 15, 1899; minister of colonies to governor, Côte d'Ivoire, March 20, 1899; Delafosse to governor, Côte d'Ivoire, March 21, 1899; and governor, Côte d'Ivoire, to minister of colonies, March 22, 1899, that show the full sequence of events. FM/SG/CIV/III/4, ANOM.
158 Albert Decrais (minister of colonies), "Instructions ministerielles," October 31, 1901, Piece 8 in 2AP8D3B, MNHN.
159 François-Joseph Clozel and Roger Villamur, *Les coutumes indigènes de la Côte d'Ivoire* (Paris, 1902), 536. These comments follow the reproduction of a Delafosse letter from June 1902 regarding an ethnographic examination of Bondoukou, then Delafosse's duty station. Delafosse later pointed back to the ethnographic questionnaire published in this work as the definitive guide to such study. See "Instructions générales du 1er Aout 1904 mises à jour au 30 Juin 1905 par M. Delafosse, administrateur de la cercle de Korhogo," in 2AP8B2, MNHN.
160 See, for example, "Le M" (presumably minister of colonies) to governor general, AOF, March 8, 1902, where the minister provides 15 copies of a recent Houdas publication regarding Arabic writings among the Trarza Moors and the possibility of a greater civilization than previously realized along the Sahel, FM/SG/AOF/II/1, ANOM. The Houdas publication attached was *Note sur une inscription arabe trouvée chez les Maures Trarza*, published by the National Press in 1901.

161 Delafosse to director of African affairs, Ministry of Colonies, June 18, 1903; Louis-Gustave Binger to 2eme Bureau, Ministry of Colonies, June 23, 1903; chief of Cabinet to minister of colonies, September 3, 1903, FM/SG/CIV/III/4, ANOM.
162 Evaluation of October 3, 1914, signed by François Clozel, Feuillet du Personnel, 1938, Marty Dossier 6Ye 49900, SHD.
163 Harrison, *France and Islam*, 135. Harrison based this conclusion on a purchase record he found in the colonial archive; I could find no corroborating archival evidence, but the purchase fits with the pattern, although on a larger scale, seen in the dissemination of Houdas' work.
164 Evaluation of 1934, Marty dossier, SHD. The supervisor only vaguely referred to his work as "Islam en AOF." It is unclear whether he received prizes for any specific book; only his work on Niger appeared in the 1930s, with all others completed between 1916 and 1922. He left AOF in 1925 for Morocco and later Tunisia, the foci of his later publications.
165 Conklin, *Mission to Civilize*, 176–179.
166 "Notes d'après-guerre," Feuillet individuel de campagne 1937; Feuillet spécial, August 23, 1920; Feuillet spécial, November 13, 1918; Feuillet spécial, May 10, 1921, Marty dossier, SHD.
167 See, for example, Issa Kane, "Ould Deid, Emir du Trarza de 1930 à 1944," *Bulletin hebdomadaire d'informations locales*, January 15–21, 1945, 5, ALG/GGA/28H/1, ANOM. The author cites Marty as the definitive reference on Islamic warrior and clerical lineages in Adrar beginning in 1910.
168 Marty, "Vingt ans de politique algérienne," 7–8.
169 Paul Marty, *Etudes sur l'Islam au Sénégal*, I, 288.
170 On political sponsorship, see Michel, "Un programme réformiste," 315. See Ageron, *France coloniale ou parti colonial?*, 162–164 for more on circulation numbers. For more on dissemination of colonial scholarship, see Raoul Girardet, *L'idée coloniale en France de 1871 à 1962* (Paris, 1972), particularly chapters 3 and 4; and Betts, *Assimilation and Association*, chapters 6–8. On the need for "evolution" by association, see Maurice Delafosse, "Civilisation, assimilation, association, autant de termes qu'il importe de définir," *La Dépêche coloniale et maritime*, January 16, 1923, 1.
171 Delafosse, "Civilisation, assimilation, association," 1. On the perception of a return of assimilation as a colonial doctrine, see Delafosse, "L'assimilation ou le phénix colonial," 1.
172 Georges Hardy, "Maurice Delafosse," *La Revue indigène* (1930), 237.
173 Henri Labouret, "Questions de politique indigène africaine: Protectorat ou administration directe," *Outre-Mer* 1, 1 (March 1929), 88–89.
174 Tilley, *Africa as a Living Laboratory*, 263–264.
175 Delafosse, "La leçon des faits," 1.
176 Louise Delafosse, *Le Berrichon*, 389; Lord Frederick D. Lugard, "The International Institute of African Languages and Cultures," *Africa* 1, 1 (January 1928), 7. Labouret describes Nigeria as the site where "the protectorate method was brilliantly applied," producing "the most advanced" African society. Labouret, "Questions de politique indigène," 82.
177 Lugard, "International Institute," 2, 4.
178 Anne Piriou, "Indigénisme et changement social: Le cas de la revue *Outre-Mer*," in *L'Africanisme en questions*, ed. Anne Piriou and Emmaneulle Sibeud (Paris, 1997), 47; Hardy, "Maurice Delafosse," 22; Anna Pondopoulu, "Approche à l'étude des sociétés africaines dans le Bulletin du Comité d'Etudes Historiques et Scientifiques de l'Afrique Occidentale Française," *AOF: réalités et héritages*, ed. Becker, Mbaye, and Thioub, II, 724.

179 Ed Van Hoven, "Representing Social Hierarchy. Administrators-Ethnographers in the French Soudan: Delafosse, Monteil and Labouret," *Cahiers d'Etudes Africaines* 30, Cahier 118 (1990), 182; Piriou, "Indigénisme et changement social," 53. Reformers also published in *L'Afrique française*, the mouthpiece of the powerful *Comité de l'Afrique française* and associated with Lyautey, among others. See Wilder, *The French Imperial Nation-State*, 59–60.

180 Labouret preface to Moussa Travélé, "Le Komo ou Koma," *Outre-Mer* 1, 2 (June 1929), 127; "Le prix d'outre-mer," *Outre-Mer* 2, 1 (March 1930), 93. Anna Pondopoulo has also pointed out the journal editors' focus on "unedited work" for publication, "Approche à l'étude des sociétés africaines," 725.

181 Piriou, "Indigénisme et changement social," 63, 68. Piriou provides an exhaustive list of native *Outre-Mer* contributors: Mamby Sidibé (1929, 1931, 1932, 1935); Moussa Travélé (1929, 1931); A. Dim Delobson (1929, 1930); Dominique Traoré (1932); Guillaume Cyrille (1932, 1933); Amadou Mapaté Diagne (1933); M. Montrat (1935); Robert Ouattara (1936); and Balde Saikou (1937). The journal folded in 1937.

182 Jézéquel, "Collecting Customary Law,"150; Jézéquel, "Maurice Delafosse et l'émergence d'un littérature africaine à vocation scientifique," 95; François Manchuelle, "Assimilés ou patriotes africains? Naissance du nationalisme culturel en Afrique française (1853–1931)," *Cahiers d'études africaines* 35, Cahier 138/139 (1995), 354.

183 Jézéquel lists Sidibé, Amadou Mapaté Diagne, and Moussa Travélé as among the contributors to the journal. See "Collecting customary law," 142.

184 See Manchuelle, "Assimilés ou patriotes africains?"; and McDougall, *History and the Culture of Nationalism*.

185 Bou Haqq, "Noirs et blancs au confins du désert," *Bulletin du comité d'études historiques et scientifiques de l'AOF* 21 (1938), 480–489 (quote on 488). The editors described the author only as "a personality who traveled for many years in the Sahel" who had decided to use the pseudonym Bou Haqq, as it translated to "friend of the truth."

186 Maurice Delafosse, *Les états d'âme d'un colonial* (Paris, 1909), 8–9.

187 René Maunier, "Maurice Delafosse (1870–1926)," *Revue d'ethnographie et des traditions populaires* 7, 27–28 (1926), 189. See also Jean-Loup Amselle and Emmanuelle Sibeud, "Introduction," in *Maurice Delafosse: Entre orientalisme et ethnographie. L'itineraire d'un africaniste (1870–1926)*, ed. Jean-Loup Amselle and Emmanuelle Sibeud (Paris, 1998), 10.

188 Auguste Terrier to Delafosse, March 25, 1924. Terrier, writing in his role on the Comité de l'Afrique française, attached a copy of an Arabic manuscript and asked Delafosse to aid in interpreting and translating. In a note added March 28, 1926, Delafosse indicated he gave the piece to a student to translate. 2AP8C6h, MNHN.

189 "Discours de M. Lévy-Bruhl, Membre de l'Institut," in *Maurice Delafosse, 1870–1926*, ed. André You (Paris, 1928), n.p.

190 Mauss to Métraux, May 27, 1927, Folder Métraux, Lettres de Marcel Mauss (MAS 20), Fonds Marcel Mauss, Archives de Collège de France, Institut Mémoires de l'Edition Contemporaine, Caen, France (hereafter MAS).

191 Marty, *Etudes sur l'Islam en Côte d'Ivoire*, 40.

192 Delafosse, *Haut-Sénégal-Niger*, III, 1.

193 Ibid., III, 2.

194 Ibid., III, 109, parentheses in original.

195 Maurice Delafosse, "Terminologie religieuse au Soudan," L'anthropologie 24 (1924), 371.
196 It is important to note that this stance was explicitly rejected later by European cultural and social anthropologists. Claude Lévi-Strauss in particular argued that mythological structures were universal, but it was the relationships between the terms used to describe these myths that were most important. Thus, these relationships, unchanged by the act of translation, served as the subject of his analysis. See Claude Lévi-Strauss, *The Raw and the Cooked: Introduction to a Science of Mythology, Volume 1*, trans. John Weightman and Doreen Weightman (New York, 1969 [1964]).
197 Maurice Delafosse, "Les langues d'Afrique," L'anthropologie 20 (1920), 547.
198 Maurice Delafosse, "Les classes nominales négro-africaines: Leur disparition graduelle," *Bulletin et mémoires de la société de linguistique de Paris* 27 (1926), 49–50; and Delafosse, "Les langues d'Afrique," 547–549.
199 Delafosse, *Haut-Sénégal-Niger*, III, 178.
200 Marty, *Etudes sur l'Islam au Sénégal*, I, 284.
201 Delafosse, *Les Civilisations Négro-africaines*, 9.
202 Delafosse, "Des soi-disant clans totémiques," 88. See also Delafosse, "Terminologie religieuse au Soudan," 372–373 for a discussion of the terms "fetish" and "gris-gris" in French scientific usage. Marty described figurative "fetishist vomiting" that could be cured only with the ministrations of Islamic marabouts in Zinder in "L'Islam et les tribus dans la colonie du Niger," 393. He also commented on fetishes as a Western construction in *Etudes sur l'Islam en Côte d'Ivoire*, 38.
203 Delafosse, "Des soi-disant clans totémiques," 109.
204 On Delafosse's last days, see Delafosse, *Le Berrichon*, 398. On Marty, see Report of March 15, 1938, by Doctor-Lieutenant Colonel Gaulrier, Marty dossier, SHD, which discusses his death in a military hospital in Tunis. Reassigned to Morocco in 1925, Marty found himself ejected from the country in 1930 after accusations of Christian proselytization by the Sultan's staff. This proselytization may have come from his efforts to pass out Arabic translations of Ernest Renan's *Vie de Jésus* (1863)—see Segalla, *The Moroccan Soul*, 230.
205 Pondopoulo, "Approche à l'étude des sociétés africaines," 730.
206 Ibn Khaldun, *Les Prolégomènes*, I, 308, 142. For more on the concept of force and domination by the state in Ibn Khaldun's theories, see, for example, Moncef M'halla, *Lire la Muqaddima d'Ibn Khaldun: Deux concepts-clés de la théorie khaldunienne, asabiya et taghallub (force et domination)* (Tunis, 2007); Aziz al-Azmeh, *Ibn Khaldun: An Essay in Reinterpretation* (London, 1982); and Abdelghani Megherbi, *La pensée sociologique d'Ibn Khaldoun* (Algiers, 2010).
207 Léopold Sédar Senghor, afterword to Louise Delafosse, *Le Berrichon*, 401–402.

Chapter 4

1 By 1914 Paul Broca's *société d'anthropologie de Paris*, the fading seat of physical anthropological thinking, was surpassed in membership by the *Institut ethnographique international de Paris*, founded by Maurice Delafosse and Arnold van Gennep and focused on colonial ethnographic information gathering. See Emmanuelle Sibeud, "The Elusive Bureau of Colonial Ethnography in France,

1907–1925," in *Ordering Africa: Anthropology, European Imperialism, and the Politics of Knowledge*, ed. Helen Tilley and Robert J. Gordon (New York, 2007), 59–60.

2 Emile Durkheim, "Préface," *Année Sociologique* 1, 1 (1896), iv.

3 Anthony R. Gringeri, Jr., "Twilight of the Sun Kings: French Anthropology from Modernism to Postmodernism, 1925–50" (PhD Dissertation, University of California, Berkeley, 1990), 28. On the anticolonial nature of the work of Marcel Mauss and Paul Rivet, see Alice Conklin, *In the Museum of Man: Race, Anthropology, and Empire in France, 1850–1950* (Ithaca, NY, 2013), 192, 235.

4 E. Rabaud; H. Breuil; R. Lantiu; and M. Mauss, "Les origins de la société," 1931 debate reproduced in Marcel Mauss, *Oeuvres*, ed. V. Karady (Paris, 1968–1969), II, 486.

5 Gringeri argued that Mauss founded modern French anthropology based on Durkheimian primitivism and a new emphasis on ethnography, "Twilight of the Sun Kings," 25–26.

6 George Weisz, *The Emergence of Modern Universities in France, 1863–1914* (Princeton, 1983), 161, 167.

7 Lévi-Strauss discussed this phenomenon, particularly the impact of theories on gift-giving, in "French Sociology," *Twentieth Century Sociology*, ed. Georges Gurvitch and Wilbert E. Moore (New York, 1945), 512.

8 Georges Balandier, "La situation colonial: Approche théorique," ed. Jean Copans, *Cahiers internationaux de sociologie* 110 (2001), 10. The original appears in *Cahiers internationaux de sociologie* 11 (1951), 44–79.

9 See, for example, undated "Questionnaire ethnographique" in Folder 34.7, MAS, which is quite similar to the list Delafosse compiled in 1901–1902. The questionnaire in Mauss's files requested information on "clothing, personal ornamentation, coloring and tattooing, drawing and sculptures, cooking, braiding, weaving, basketry, pottery, dyeing and painting, metallurgy, machines, construction, invention, spirit of preservation, housing, fire, foods, cannibalism, drug use, hunting and fishing, nomadic and pastoral life, agriculture, education, mental faculties, writing, astronomy, arithmetic, money and securities, weights and measures, commerce, property, succession, slavery, government, justice, crimes, social organization, kinship, marriage, family, widows, morals, sexual relations, death, funeral ceremonies, paths/oaths/ordeals, taboos, sacred animals, religion, mythology, magic and magicians, history, initiation ceremonies, circumcision, music, games, swimming, navigation, war, customs, stone tools, reproduction, abnormal characters, artificial deformities, medicine and surgery."

10 See Marcel Mauss, "Essai sur le don: Forme et raison de l'échange dans les sociétés archaïques," *Année Sociologique* Nouvelle série, I (1923–1924), 30–186. In this chapter I will refer to the reproduction of this article in Marcel Mauss, *Sociologie et anthropologie*, ed. Georges Gurvitch (Paris, 1968 [1950]), 145–279.

11 On this point, see also Conklin, *In the Museum of Man*, 191.

12 See Folder 1.78, Franz Boas; Folder Evans-Pritchard in MAS 18, Folder Labouret in MAS 19, and Folders Malinowski, Professor Gunn, and Radcliffe-Brown in MAS 20.

13 Claude Lévi-Strauss, *Introduction to the Work of Marcel Mauss*, trans. Felicity Baker (London, 1987 [1950]), 1.

14 Interviews with students and colleagues collected in Marcel Fournier, *Marcel Mauss: A Biography*, trans. Jane Marie Todd (Princeton, 2006 [1994]), 279–280.

15 Denise Paulme, introduction to Marcel Mauss, *Manuel d'ethnographie*, 2nd ed. (Paris, 1967 [1947]), 5.

16 Mauss, "Essai sur le don," 275–276.
17 George Weisz, "Education and the Civil Utility of Social Science," *Minerva* 16, 3 (1978), 453. Jules Ferry, at various times minister of education, foreign affairs, and prime minister in the 1880s, enacted serious education reform that made schooling free, obligatory, and secular. He also, in his guise as foreign minister, advocated for colonial expansion to Indochina, an effort which, while ultimately successful, pushed him out of government for a time.
18 Pierre Bourdieu, *The State Nobility: Elite Schools in the Field of Power*, trans. Lauretta C. Clough (Stanford, 1996 [1989]), 6.
19 Weisz, *The Emergence of Modern Universities*, 291–292; Weisz, "Education and the Civil Utility of Social Science," 453. Carole Reynaud Paligot has argued that race theorist/anthropologist Charles Letourneau was a key transitional figure between the anatomist-anthropologists (such as Paul Broca) of the mid-nineteenth century and Durkheim, as Letourneau focused on the intellectual and psychological consequences of physical distinctions between the races. See Paligot, *La république raciale*, 84–86. On the struggles of historians to redefine the discipline as based on social and economic analysis in this same period, see Laurent Mucchielli, "Aux origines de la nouvelle histoire en France: L'évolution intellectuelle et la formation du champ des sciences sociales (1880–1930)," *Revue de synthèse* 4, 1 (January–March 1995), 55-98. For an overview of the combat of Durkheim and his followers with other French social theorists, see Laurent Mucchielli, *Mythes et histoire des sciences humaines* (Paris, 2004).
20 Fournier, *Marcel Mauss*, 9–16; Jean Poirier, "Marcel Mauss et l'élaboration de la science ethnologique," *Journal de la société des océanistes* 6 (1950), 212.
21 Datta, *Birth of a National Icon: The Literary Avant-Garde and the Origins of the Intellectual in France* (Albany, 1999), 86–87.
22 On this period in French academia, see Weisz, *The Emergence of Modern Universities in France*, 294; Christophe Charle, *La république des universitaires, 1870–1940* (Paris, 1994), 190–191; and Clark, *Prophets and Patrons*, 180–195.
23 Pierre Bourdieu and Jean-Claude Passeron, "Sociology and Philosophy in France since 1945: Death and Resurrection of a Philosophy without Subject," *Social Research* 34, 1 (1967), 166.
24 Philippe Besnard, "La formation de l'équipe de l'Année Sociologique," *Revue française de sociologie* 20, 1 (January–March 1979), 17.
25 Marcel Mauss, "L'oeuvre de Mauss par lui-même," *Revue française de sociologie* 20, 1 (January–March 1979), 210. This piece reportedly came from Mauss's letter of candidacy to the Collège de France in 1930.
26 Mauss, "L'oeuvre de Mauss," 209; Marcel Mauss, "Les civilisations: éléments et formes," in *Civilisation. Le mot et l'idée* (Paris, 1930), reproduced in *Oeuvres*, II, 468.
27 Emile Durkheim and Marcel Mauss, "Note sur la notion de civilisation," *Année Sociologique* 12 (1913), reproduced in *Oeuvres*, II, 455.
28 Balandier was among the first to call out this contradiction in "La situation coloniale," 11.
29 Sibeud, "The Elusive Bureau," 60.
30 Marcel Mauss, "L'ethnographie en France et à l'étranger," *Revue de Paris* 20, 5 (September–October 1913), 821; *Manuel d'ethnographie*, 13.
31 Fournier, *Marcel Mauss*, 21, 28 fn103. See also "CV Mauss," MAS 38.10, where he referred to some of his scholarships as "for services at the same level as the ECOLE NORMALE" (caps in original).

32 "CV Mauss," MAS 38.10; Fournier, *Marcel Mauss*, 37, 44, 85–86, 89.
33 Sibeud, *Une science impériale pour l'Afrique?*, 222; Besnard, "La formation de l'équipe," 17.
34 Datta, *Birth of a National Icon*, 65 fn4, 67. See also Christophe Charle, *Naissance des "intellectuels": 1880–1910* (Paris, 1990), 11–13.
35 Besnard, "La formation de l'équipe," 19; Fournier, *Marcel Mauss*, 123. Mauss's contacts included a young Jean Jaurès, the famed socialist leader who would remain among Mauss's closest political friends until his death.
36 Born in Paris on April 10, 1857 (d. March 13, 1939), Lévy-Bruhl had a brilliant academic career, including graduation from the *école normale supérieure* in 1876 and an 1884 doctoral degree. See Jean Cazeneuve, *Lucien Lévy-Bruhl*, trans. Peter Rivière (New York, 1972 [1963]), ix–xvi; and Gringeri, "Twilight of the Sun Kings," 58–66. Missionary-ethnographer Maurice Leenhardt was another such unconventional scholar who pushed Lévy-Bruhl in a productive give-and-take on the complexity of the "primitive" mind. See James Clifford, *Person and Myth: Maurice Leenhardt in the Melanesian World* (Durham, NC, 1992 [1982]), 200–206; and "Dossier Nécrologique," Folder 22.16, IMEC, Archives de Collège de France, Fonds Lucien Lévy-Bruhl (hereafter LVB), for a description of the connection between the two men.
37 Lucien Lévy-Bruhl, *Primitive Mentality*, trans. Lilian A. Clare (New York, 1923 [1922]), 384.
38 Jules Brévié to Lévy-Bruhl, October 15, 1923; Brévié to Lévy-Bruhl, December 4, 1931, LVB 3. On his death the *Monde Colonial* extolled Lévy-Bruhl's role as patron of colonial scientific investigation. See "Deuil dans notre comité de patronage," *Monde Colonial*, April 1939, LVB 22.16.
39 Mauss's decorations included the croix de guerre with 2 bronze stars; croix de la victoire; croix militaire anglaise; medaille interallié, croix du combatant, croix du combatant engagé, and the medaille de la victoire. See "CV Mauss," MAS 38.10 and "Décoration de la croix militaire anglaise," MAS 38.9.
40 Mauss, "L'oeuvre de Mauss," 219.
41 Clark, *Prophets and Patrons*, 200–201, 218–219. Célestin Bouglé (1870–1940) led the teaching side of sociology, particularly in the late 1920s and 1930s. W. Paul Vogt has described Bouglé as caught between two wings of ethnology in the period: the linguistic emphasis of Mauss and his followers, and the statistical approach of Maurice Halbwachs (1877–1945) and others. See his, "Un durkheimien ambivalent: Célestin Bouglé, 1870–1940," *Revue française de sociologie* XX, 1 (1979), 124–125. See also Robert Leroux, *Histoire et sociologie en France: De l'histoire-science à la sociologie durkheimienne* (Paris, 1998).
42 Born April 23, 1873, in the German state of Wurtemberg, van Gennep moved with his mother to Lyon at age 6. Brilliant with languages, he graduated from the école des langues orientales and EPHE and taught in Poland and Switzerland before assuming a life as a poor scholar in France beginning in the First World War. He was excluded from the AS and from other French universities in part due to his withering attacks on the publications of others and his dislike for metropolitan theory. He reportedly had skill in French, Dutch, German, English, Italian, Spanish, Portuguese, Russian, various Slavic languages, and several "Eastern languages" and could read numerous Scandinavian languages. See Ketty Van Gennep, *Bibliographie des oeuvres d'Arnold van Gennep* (Paris, 1964); Rosemary Zumwalt, *The Enigma of Arnold Van Gennep (1873–1957): Master of French Folklore and Hermit of Bourg-la-Reine* (Helsinki, 1988); and Nicole Belmont, *Arnold Van Gennep: The Creator of French Ethnography*, trans. Derek Coltman (Chicago, 1979).

43 See van Gennep to Mauss, February 28, 1902, MAS 13.20; Zumwalt, *The Enigma of Arnold van Gennep*, 50–51.
44 Arnold van Gennep, "Etudes Ethnographiques," in *Religions, Moeurs et légendes: Essais d'ethnographie et de linguistique* (Paris, 1908–1909), I, 187; van Gennep to Mauss, February 5, 1907, and May 18, 1907, MAS 13.20.
45 Mauss, "L'ethnographie en France et à l'étranger," 538.
46 Arnold van Gennep, *En Algérie* (Paris, 1914), 8, 20–21, 129.
47 Delafosse to Mauss, May 13, 1920, MAS 6.45; Christine Laurière, *Paul Rivet: Le savant et le politique* (Paris, 2008), 351–352; Jacques Soustelle, "Discours prononcé dans la séance publique le jeudi 24 Mai 1984," www.academie-francaise.fr/immortels/index.html, accessed December 1, 2010.
48 Lucien Lévy-Bruhl, "L'Institut d'Ethnologie de l'Université de Paris," *Annales de l'Université de Paris* 1 (1926), 206.
49 "Pour la création de l'Institut d'Ethnologie," addressed to "Monsieur le ministre," n.d., MAS 40.21. The document concluded with recognition of the importance of funding from "the state, colonial governments, and the specific donations that it will perhaps be possible to solicit." For an earlier expression of a similar institutional idea, see Mauss, "L'ethnographie en France," 820.
50 Marcel Mauss, "Notices biographiques," *Année Sociologique* Nouvelle série, 2 (1924–1925), 6–7. See also Lucette Valensi, "Le Maghreb vu du centre: Sa place dans l'école sociologique française," in *Connaissances du Maghreb: Sciences sociales et colonisation*, ed. Jean-Claude Vatin (Paris, 1984), 231.
51 Mauss, "L'ethnographie en France," 550.
52 Marcel Mauss, "Fragment d'un plan de sociologie générale descriptive," *Annales Sociologiques* 1 (1934), reproduced in *Oeuvres*, III, 353–354.
53 Lucien Lévy-Bruhl to Mauss, June 27, 1925, MAS 8.10.
54 Labouret to Mauss, June 12, 1921, MAS 7.2.
55 Lévy-Bruhl, "L'Institut d'Ethnologie de l'Université de Paris," 208–209.
56 Mauss to Bronislaw Malinowski, January 28, 1930, Folder Malinowski, MAS 20. For more on the brief Moroccan fieldwork, see Mauss to Lecoeur, February 17, 1930, and July 9, 1931, Folder Lecoeur, MAS 19.
57 Delafosse to Mauss, May 13 and May 28, 1920, MAS 6.45.
58 Lucien Lévy-Bruhl, "L'Institut d'Ethnologie pendant l'année scolaire 1925–1926," *Annales de l'Université de Paris* 2 (1927), 94.
59 Ibid., 91; Lucien Lévy-Bruhl, "L'Institut d'Ethnologie de l'Université de Paris," *Annales de l'Université de Paris* II (1927), 207.
60 Mauss to Resident General, Morocco, December 30, 1925, entitled "Note sur l'institut d'ethnologie de l'université de Paris," MAS 40.22; Printed extract of *Revue d'ethnographie et des traditions populaires* (3–4 trimesters, 1925), 23–24 in LVB 10.3.
61 Louis Finot to Mauss, October 14, 1925, MAS 4.24. Also cited in Alice Conklin, "The New 'Ethnology' and 'La Situation Coloniale' in Interwar France," *French Politics, Culture, and Society* 20, 2 (2002), 37–38.
62 Jacques Soustelle, *The Four Suns: Recollections and Reflections of an Ethnologist in Mexico*, trans. E. Ross (New York, 1971 [1967]), 10–11.
63 See, for example, "Rapport présenté par le docteur Rivet, professeur au Muséum, Directeur du musée d'ethnographie du Trocadéro," January 22, 1931, MAS 11.20, which discusses funding intended to procure additional ethnographic displays.
64 Labouret to Mauss, July 31, 1931, MAS 6.49.
65 Mauss to chairman, Rockefeller Foundation, September 29, 1930, Folder chairman, MAS 18; Fournier, *Marcel Mauss*, 247, 293.

66 Lévy-Bruhl, "L'institut d'ethnologie pendant 1925–1926," 92.
67 Mauss, *Manuel d'ethnographie*, 14.
68 Griaule (1898–1956) served as a lieutenant in the French aviation corps from 1917 to 1924, when he reinitiated studies at the école des langues orientales and the école pratique des hautes études. His previous mission went to Abyssinia in August 1928 with Mauss's support for 100–150,000 francs of French governmental sponsorship to collect "documents, manuscripts, ethnographic information and archeological monuments." See "Note au sujet d'une mission en Abyssinie confiée à M. Griaule," n.d., Folder Griaule, MAS 18; Jean-Paul Lebeuf, "Marcel Griaule," in *Ethnologiques: Hommages à Marcel Griaule*, ed. Solange de Ganay, Annie Lebeuf, and Jean-Paul Lebeuf (Paris, 1987), XXI–XXII; and Alice Conklin, "Civil Society, Science, and Empire in Late Republican France: The Foundation of Paris's Museum of Man," *Osiris* 17 (2002), 285.
69 Georges-Henri Rivière, "Témoignage," in *Ethnologiques*, ed. de Ganay, Lebeuf and Lebeuf, XI; Paul Rivet and Georges-Henri Rivière, "La mission ethnographique et linguistique Dakar-Djibouti," *Minotaure* 1, 2 (April 1933), 3. Rivière, as the codirector of the Trocadero ethnographic museum, acted as a primary link between the research team and the French museum and academic communities.
70 Conklin, *In the Museum of Man*, 211.
71 Marcel Griaule, "Introduction méthodologique," *Minotaure* 1, 2 (April 1933), 7–8. Griaule authored numerous studies relating to his time in West Africa as his career continued, focusing in particular on the Dogon. See his *Conversations with Ogotemmêli*, trans. Ralph Butler with Audrey I. Richards and Beatrice Hooke (Oxford, 1965 [1948]).
72 Jean Lacouture, *Le témoignage est un combat: une biographie de Germaine Tillion* (Paris, 2000), 36.
73 Germaine Tillion, *Il était une fois l'ethnographie* (Paris, 2000), 47, which also features Tillion's description of IE coursework. See Mauss evaluation in "Rapport sur le travail fourni au M.E.T. [*musée d'ethnographie du Trocadéro*] par les etudiants en 1932," MAS 11.22; Evaluation by Marcel Mauss in ALG/GGA/11CAB/62, ANOM, also reproduced as Marcel Mauss to Directeur de la recherche scientifique, March 25, 1942, in Tzvetan Todorov ed., *Le Siècle de Germaine Tillion* (Paris, 2007), 269.
74 "Report of 6 March 1937," MAS 12.63. The "Oueld Abderrahmane" is a specific lineage of Kabyles in the Aurès, chosen by the young fieldworkers for their apparent openness for study. Interestingly, Tillion complained of working "without direction" in a letter to Mauss of January 4, 1937, MAS 12.63. Mauss's reply is lost to history, but likely contained some specific instructions to Tillion and her research partner, the sister of prominent museum curator Georges-Henri Rivière.
75 Germaine Tillion, "Report of 6 March 1937," MAS 12.63.
76 Lévi-Strauss, "French Sociology," 522 fn62.
77 The letters offer no detail on the specific conclusions, apparently discussed in a previous letter from Mauss but no longer in evidence in the archives. Lévi-Strauss to Mauss, October 4, 1931; Lévi-Strauss to Mauss, March 14, 1936; Lévi-Strauss to Mauss, December 5 [1938?], MAS 8.3. On the results of this research, Lévi-Strauss's only detailed ethnographic mission, see Claude Lévi-Strauss, *La vie familiale et sociale des Indiens Nambikwara* (Paris, 1948).
78 Mauss to Radcliffe-Brown, December 6, 1924, Folder Radcliffe-Browne [sic], MAS 20.
79 Lévi-Strauss, "French Sociology," 527.
80 Mauss to Alfred Métraux, April 7, 1927, Folder Métraux, MAS 20.

81 Mauss, "Les civilisations," 471; Marcel Mauss, "Divisions et proportions des divisions de la sociologie," *Année Sociologique* Nouvelle série, 2 (1924), 171–172.
82 Mauss, *Manuel d'ethnographie*, 23–24.
83 Mauss, "L'ethnographie en France," 539–540.
84 Mauss, *Manuel d'ethnographie*, 201. Mauss approvingly references Delafosse's collection *L'âme nègre* (Paris, 1922) as a perfect example.
85 Mauss, "L'oeuvre de Mauss," 215. See also Mauss, "L'âme, le nom et la personne," *Bulletin de la société française de philosophie* 29 (1929), reproduced in *Oeuvres*, II, 134, for Mauss's views on Leenhardt's analysis of the interrelationship between personality and society and a refutation of Lévy-Bruhl's early notions on "mystical" and "prelogical" native thought processes.
86 Mauss, "Essai sur le don," 147.
87 Lévi-Strauss, *Introduction to the Work of Marcel Mauss*, 26.
88 Mauss, "Essai sur le don," 275.
89 Ibid., 264, 278.
90 Marcel Mauss and Henri Hubert, "Esquisse d'une théorie générale de la magie" [1902–1903], in *Sociologie et anthropologie*, 137.
91 See, for example, Sir James Frazer, *The Golden Bough: A Study in Magic and Religion* (Oxford, 1994 [1890]); *Totemism and Exogamy: A Treatise on Certain Early Forms of Superstition and Society* (London, 1910).
92 Marcel Mauss, "La problème des classifications en Afrique occidentale," *Année Sociologique* X (1907), reproduced in *Oeuvres*, II, 244–245.
93 Mauss, "Divisions et proportions," 125. See also his earlier discussions in Marcel Mauss, "Typologie des races et des peuples," *Année Sociologique* IV (1901), reproduced in *Oeuvres*, III, 363; and Emile Durkheim and Marcel Mauss, "De quelques formes primitives de classification: contribution à l'étude des représentations collectives," *Année Sociologique* VI (1903), 17.
94 Durkheim and Mauss, "Note sur la notion de civilisation," 454. Italics in original.
95 Mauss, "Les civilisations," 456–457; Marcel Mauss, "Note sur le totémisme," *Année Sociologique* VIII (1905), reproduced in *Oeuvres*, I, 164; Marcel Mauss, "Mentalité primitive et participation," *Bulletin de la société française de philosophie* 23 (1923), reproduced in *Oeuvres*, II, 128.
96 Fournier, *Marcel Mauss*, 349. Fournier cites Denise Paulme as witness to the light funeral turnout.
97 Wendy James, "The Treatment of African Ethnography in 'L'Année Sociologique'" *Année Sociologique* Série 3, 48, 1 (1998), 199–201.
98 Wendy James, "Mauss in Africa: On time, History, and Politics," in *Marcel Mauss: A Centenary Tribute*, ed. Wendy James and N.J. Allen (New York, 1998), 227, 240.
99 Lebeuf, "Marcel Griaule," XXIV.
100 Marcel Griaule, speech of July 1, 1949, in *Marcel Griaule, conseiller de l'union française*, ed. Maurice Demark (Paris, 1957), 60–61. See also speech of August 19, 1954, 144; and Marcel Griaule, *Méthode de l'Ethnographie*, ed. Geneviève Calame-Griaule (Paris, 1957), 5.
101 See, for example, Adandé Alexaure, secretary of the Dakar Museum to Paul Rivet, December 4, 1937, MAS 11.20. The presence of this letter in Mauss's files is a mystery; perhaps, Rivet passed it to him as the IE's expert on African ethnographic collection (through his students) and as a man desirous of detailed contact with African intellectuals as sources of ethnological knowledge. Alexaure proposed correspondence courses or travel funding for native African intellectuals to attend the IE.

102 Léopold Sédar Senghor, "Préface," in *Ethnologiques*, ed. de Ganay, Lebeuf and Lebeuf, V–VII.
103 Durkheim and Mauss, "De quelques formes primitives de classification," 86.
104 Lévi-Strauss, *Introduction to the Work of Marcel Mauss*, 61.
105 Abdellah Hammoudi, like Bourdieu, has found that ethnography can serve as a precursor to the higher level of analysis found in sociology. For Hammoudi, it is important to focus first on "situational encounters" and then move to "a second stage, into a metalanguage, with the aim of constructing a synoptic view of things. Otherwise, we may be stuck with languages of the traditions themselves." See Abdellah Hammoudi, "Textualism and Anthropology: On the Ethnographic Encounter, or an Experience in the Hajj," in *Being There: The Fieldwork Encounter and the Making of Truth*, ed. John Borneman and Abdellah Hammoudi (Berkeley, 2009), 32.

Chapter 5

1 Germaine Tillion, "Conflits de civilisation," in *Le siècle de Germaine Tillion*, ed. Tzvetan Todorov (Paris, 2007), 281.
2 Alice Conklin, "L'ethnologie militante de l'entre-deux-guerres," in *Le siècle de Germaine Tillion*, ed. Todorov, 56.
3 Jacques Soustelle, *Vingt-huit ans de Gaullisme* (Paris, 1968), 286.
4 Neil MacMaster, *Burning the Veil: The Algerian War and the "Emancipation" of Muslim Women, 1954–62* (Manchester, 2009), 4.
5 Balandier, "La situation coloniale," 22.
6 See Matthew Connelly, *A Diplomatic Revolution: Algeria's Fight for Independence and the Origin of the Post-Cold War Era* (Oxford, 2002), chapters 2 and 3 for discussion of the sophistication of the Algerian approach that sought international recognition and resources from the early 1950s. See also James Le Sueur, *Uncivil War: Intellectuals and Identity Politics during the Decolonization of Algeria*, 2nd ed. (Lincoln, 2005 [2001]), 12, for a discussion of these disconnects and misunderstandings among French intellectuals.
7 Course on Islam delivered by Captain Jacques Carret, Service des Liaisons Nord-Africains (SLNA), part of "Stage d'orientation" for officiers des affaires algériennes (OAA), December 6, 1955, ALG/SAS/DOC/3, ANOM. The course notes serve as a model of the previous orientation courses given to new SAS and OAA officers in late 1954 and early 1955 (during Soustelle's tenure), for which little documentation remains beyond basic outlines.
8 McDougall, *History and the Culture of Nationalism in Algeria*.
9 Thomas, *Empires of Intelligence*, 76.
10 Grégor Mathias, *Les section administratives spécialisées en Algérie: Entre ideal et réalité (1955–1962)* (Paris, 1998), 13, 52 (quote on 13).
11 On this point, see Connelly, *A Diplomatic Revolution*, 78, where he recounts that the FLN killed 6.5 times more Algerians than did the French from 1954 to 1957, particularly in mid-1955, when the FLN target set expanded to include civilians.
12 Ferhat Abbas, *Autopsie d'une guerre: l'aurore* (Paris, 1980). See also Henri Grimal, *Decolonization, the British, French, Dutch, and Belgian Empires, 1919–1963*, trans. Stephan De Vos (Boulder, 1978 [1965]), 386.
13 See, for example, Frederick Cooper, *Decolonization and African Society: The Labor Question in French and British Africa* (Cambridge, 1996), 392, 395, 423;

Gert Oostindie and Inge Klinkers, *Decolonising the Caribbean: Dutch Policies in a Comparative Perspective* (Amsterdam, 2003), 67, for a discussion of international trends. On the problems of such linear, if not synchronic, assumptions in African political and social development, see the strong critique of Mahmood Mamdani's work in Frederick Cooper, *Colonialism in Question: Theory, Knowledge, History* (Berkeley, 2005), 17-18.

14 Melanie White, "The Liberal Character of Ethnological Governance," *Economy and Society* 34, 3 (2005), 474-494, also employs this term in a related way, but in a different context (that of nineteenth- and early-twentieth-century US and UK politics). She defines the approach as "the set of practices that is organized by a developmental notion of human conduct (i.e. character) that operates as a standard of liberal government and serves as an index for the responsible exercise of freedom," 476.

15 Rabinow, *French Modern*, chapter 10, esp. 321-322; John Kent, *The Internationalization of Colonialism: Britain, France, and Black Africa, 1939–1956* (Oxford, 1992), 1-2; Cooper, *Decolonization and African Society*, 389, 392, 402, 406.

16 Speech, June 28, 1955, 8 PM on Radio Algiers, FM/81F/641, ANOM; also in Jacques Soustelle, *Aimée et souffrante Algérie* (Paris, 1956), 108-109.

17 Todd Shepard, *The Invention of Decolonization: The Algerian War and the Remaking of France* (Ithaca, NY, 2008), 47.

18 Balandier, "La situation coloniale," 9.

19 Hassan Remaoun, "La politique coloniale française et la structuration du projet nationalitaire en Algérie, à propos de l'idéologie du FLN, puis de l'état national," in *La guerre d'Algérie: Au miroir des décolonisations françaises, Actes du colloque international*, ed. Société française d'histoire d'outre-mer (Paris, 2000), 272.

20 Scott, *Seeing Like a State*, 4-5, 94.

21 On Soustelle's view of time in civilizational development, see Soustelle, *The Four Suns*, 218; Soustelle, "La genèse des civilisations," 52; Jacques Soustelle, "Discours prononcé dans la séance publique le jeudi 24 Mai 1984," www.academie-francaise.fr/immortels/index.html, accessed December 1, 2010.

22 Soustelle, *The Four Suns*, 3.

23 Bernard Ullmann, *Jacques Soustelle, le mal aimé* (Paris, 1995), 11, 13-20. The two were married on August 5, 1931. Georgette (1909-1999) outlived her husband by 8 years. For more on Georgette, see Jacqueline de Durand-Forest, "Georgette Soustelle (1909-1999)," *Journal de la Société des Américanistes* 85 (1999): 428-432.

24 Ullmann, *Jacques Soustelle*, 16-17; Elizabeth Murphrey, "Jacques Soustelle and the Passing of French Algeria" (PhD Dissertation, Duke University, 1976), 10-17.

25 Soustelle, *The Four Suns*, 6.

26 Ibid., 7. Parenthetical reference in original.

27 Murphrey indicates Soustelle met Lévy-Bruhl at the Trocadero in "Jacques Soustelle," 14-15. Their association continued until Lévy-Bruhl's death in 1939; Soustelle helped the great scholar to consolidate his late publication of *Morceaux Choisis* (Paris, 1936), where Lévy-Bruhl wrote of his error, at least in part, in coming to the notion of the "primitive mind." Soustelle authored an obituary of Lévy-Bruhl as well: "Lucien Lévy-Bruhl," *Europe* 49, 196 (April 1939): 533-535.

28 Jacques Soustelle, *Mexique, terre indienne* (Paris, 1936), 7, 10.

29 Jacques Soustelle, *La famille Otomi-Pame du Mexique central* (Paris, 1937), VI.

30 Ibid., 34, 91-93.

31 Soustelle, *La famille Otomi-Pame*, 549; Jacques Soustelle, "La culture matérielle des Indiens Lacandons," *Journal de la Société des Américanistes* V (1937), 85-86.

32 Murphrey, "Jacques Soustelle," 24–25; Mauss to Lecoeur, February 8, 1937, MAS 19, Folder Lecoeur.
33 Jean Marin and Jacques Soustelle, "Les français parlent aux français," Radio address of June 11, 1942, 2149 hours, in *Les voix de liberté: Ici Londres, 1940–1944, vol. 2: Le monde en feu, 8 December 1941–7 November 1942* (Paris, 1975), 137. Alice Conklin strongly argues the importance of this moment as a search for alternatives to racism, *In the Museum of Man*, 18.
34 Jacques Soustelle, "Musées vivants pour une culture populaire," *Vendredi* 34 (June 26, 1936), 1.
35 Soustelle, *Mexique, terre indienne*, 153.
36 Soustelle, *Four Suns*, 97.
37 Soustelle, *Mexique, terre indienne*, 268; Soustelle, *La famille Otomi-Pame*, 104.
38 See Denis Rolland, "Jacques Soustelle, de l'ethnologie à la politique," *Revue d'histoire moderne et contemporaine* 43, 1 (January–March 1996), 139–140; Roger Faligot and Pascal Krop, *La Piscine: The French Secret Service since 1944*, trans. W.D. Halls (New York, 1989 [1985]), 29; and Soustelle, *Vingt-huit ans de Gaullisme*, 22–23.
39 Jacques Soustelle, *L'espérance trahie (1958–1961)* (Paris, 1962), 255; Jacques Soustelle, "Nous sommes en présence en Algérie d'une entreprise aggressive de panarabisme à direction égyptienne," *Le Monde*, March 3, 1956, 1; Soustelle, *Aimée et souffrante Algérie*, 6–7. Soustelle reported in his memoir that Algerian Constantine Deputy Abdelmadjid Ourabah called for him to duplicate his "precious stone" approach to culture in Algeria as the deputy had read in *Mexique, terre indienne*.
40 Marin and Soustelle, "Les français parlent aux français," 137. The MH witnessed the execution (of Boris Vildé and Anatole Levitsky) and deportation of numerous affiliated faculty and students in this period, including the exile of Rivet to South America.
41 Sébastien Albertelli, *Les services sécrets du Général de Gaulle: le BCRA, 1940–1944* (Paris, 2009), 371; Ullmann, *Jacques Soustelle*, 102; Jacques Soustelle, *Envers et contre tout* (Paris, 1947–1950), II, 271. On these networks of intelligence operatives, largely controlled by American and British forces, see Jacques Valette, "Guerre Mondiale et Decolonisation: le cas du Maroc en 1945," *Revue française d'histoire d'outre-mer* 70, 260–261 (1983), 133–150; T.C. Wales, "The 'Massingham' Mission and the Secret 'Special Relationship': Cooperation and Rivalry between the Anglo-American Clandestine Services in French North Africa, November 1942–May 1943," in *The Politics and Strategy of Clandestine War: Special Operations Executive, 1940–1946*, ed. Neville Wylie (New York, 2007); and, for a unique description of the vague lines between forces in the period, Carleton S. Coon, *A North African Story: The Anthropologist as OSS Agent, 1941–1943* (Ipswich, MA, 1980).
42 "Séance du 23 Mars 1946," *Annales de l'assemblée nationale constituante elue le 21 Octobre 1945: Débats* (Paris, 1946), III, 1034. For a complete listing of Soustelle's wartime and immediate postwar employment, see R.B., "M. Jacques Soustelle," *Le Monde*, January 27, 1955, 3.
43 Mathias, *Les sections administratives spécialisées en Algérie*, 17.
44 "Discours prononcé à Brazzaville le 30 Janvier 1944 lors de l'ouverture de la conférence africaine," in Soustelle, *Vingt-huit ans de Gaullisme*, 430–431. I have used this copy of de Gaulle's speech specifically because it was reproduced by Soustelle in his book; whether accurate representations of de Gaulle's actual words or not, it is this wording that Soustelle attributed to his superior.
45 Decree of February 1, 1955, FM/81F/641, ANOM.

46 MacMaster, *Burning the Veil*, 11.
47 Cooper, *Colonialism in Question*, 25–26, 209, 215–216, 218; Cooper, *Decolonization and African Society*, 401, 425, 432, 439; Grimal, *Decolonization*, 287–290.
48 McDougall, *History and the Culture of Nationalism*, 138, 140; Charles-Robert Ageron, *De l'Algérie française à l'Algérie algérienne* (Saint-Denis, 2005), 449, 453; Henry F. Jackson, *The FLN in Algeria: Party Development in a Revolutionary Society* (Westport, CT, 1977), 22–30; and Front de Liberation Nationale, "Plateforme," III, 3, in *La révolution algérienne par les textes*, ed. André Mandouze (Paris, 1961), 31.
49 Soustelle, *Aimée et souffrante Algérie*, 1.
50 Decree of July 21, 1955, FM/81F/641, ANOM.
51 "L'Algérie ... ce serait Sedan," delivered at French National Assembly, March 9, 1956, FM/81F/24, ANOM.
52 "M. Soustelle: j'entends donner une impulsion nouvelle au progres de l'Algérie dans tous les domaines," *Le Monde*, January 30–31, 1955, 3.
53 MacMaster, *Burning the Veil*, 77.
54 *Pour l'Algérie*, 81, ALG/SAS/DOC/1, ANOM.
55 Gabriel Lambert to Maurice Bourgès-Maunoury (minister of the interior), September 27, 1955, FM/81F/641, ANOM.
56 See, for example, Paul Biliquey, director of Boys' School of Adrar, to Soustelle, October 25, 1955, ALG/GGA/11CAB/5, ANOM.
57 Soustelle in *The Four Suns*, 73–74, accuses Western governments of assessing civilizations on the basis of one aspect, for instance, technology, at the expense of enormous achievements in other areas. See also Soustelle's speech to the UN, February 6, 1957, FM/81F/24, ANOM.
58 Soustelle, *Aimée et souffrante Algérie*, 26–27; Soustelle, *Vingt-huit ans de Gaullisme*, 291.
59 Scott, *Seeing Like a State*, 4–5. See also Michael Adas, *Machines as the Measure of Men: Science, Technology, and Ideologies of Western Dominance* (Ithaca, NY, 1989), for a discussion of the place of technological superiority as ideology for colonial domination and expansion.
60 Christian Desbordes, "Jacques Soustelle et la défense de l'Occident" (PhD Dissertation, University of Auvergne, 2000), 337.
61 Circulars 4.684CC and 4.685CC, June 15, 1955, in *Pour l'Algérie, pour la France: Directives aux autorités locales (Avril 1956)* (Algiers, 1956), 19–23, ALG/SAS/DOC/1, ANOM.
62 Report of Colonel Constans (director of the Military Cabinet) on governor-general trip to Kabylia, March 7, 1955; Report of Vincent Monteil (chief of the Military Cabinet) on governor-general trip to Boufarik, March 14, 1955, ALG/GGA/11CAB/29, ANOM.
63 MacMaster, *Burning the Veil*, 74–75.
64 MacMaster, *Burning the Veil*, 3.
65 Tillion, *Il était une fois l'ethnographie*, 261; Alison Rice, "Déchiffrer le silence: A conversation with Germaine Tillion," *Research in African Literatures* 35, 1 (Spring 2004), 163–164.
66 MacMaster, *Burning the Veil*, 12, 16, 18–19.
67 "Effectif de la Direction des Cabinets Civil et Militaire," June 1, 1955, ALG/GGA/11CAB/1, ANOM.
68 This is not to suggest that Abbas was the only anticolonial figure in Algeria at the time, or even necessarily the most important. The best analysis of the competing Algerian revolutionary groups and their interrelationship is Mohammed Harbi, *Le F.L.N.: Mirage et Réalité* (Paris, 1980).

69 Abbas, *Autopsie d'une guerre*, 67–68, 73.
70 Fabien Sacriste, *Germaine Tillion, Jacques Berque, Jean Servier et Pierre Bourdieu: Des ethnologues dans la guerre d'indépendance algérienne* (Paris, 2011), 60.
71 Soustelle did not initially select Tillion as his research attaché, at first preferring Jean Servier, a more celebrated (and also conservative) scholar and war hero who ultimately did not get the job for reasons that remain obscure. See Arrete, February 15, 1955, and Soustelle to Lamassoure, n.d. (February 1955), ALG/GGA/11CAB/1, ANOM. Monteil's translation appeared as *Discours sur l'histoire universelle (Al-Muqaddima)*, ed. and trans. Vincent Monteil (Beirut, 1967–1968). It became the definitive French translation (surpassing that of de Slane), although in much of the non-Arabic-speaking world, it was perhaps bested by Franz Rosenthal's English translation.
72 A 1932 graduate of IE, Tillion also received a diploma in noncivilized religion from EPHE (1939) and in Berber from the école des langues orientales in 1942. Her two doctoral theses disappeared during her time in the Ravensbruck camp, taken by her Nazi captors. See Tillion CV, ALG/GGA/11CAB/62, ANOM; Rice, "Déchiffrer le silence," 172–173; and Nelly Forget and Nancy Wood, "Notice biographique," in *Le siècle de Germaine Tillion*, ed. Todorov, 11–31.
73 Forget and Wood, "Notice biographique," 12–13; Tillion CV, ALG/GGA/11CAB/62, ANOM. See also Tillion, *Il était une fois l'ethnographie*, 13, where she described the CNRS decision that the Aurès would be an outstanding field site and that a woman could work there profitably. This book was Tillion's late effort to recapture, in monograph form, her ethnographic fieldwork in Algeria from 1934 to 1956.
74 On the implications of state-funded research and its effect on anthropological introspection and criticism, see Sally Falk Moore, "Encounter and Suspicion in Tanzania," in *Being There: The Fieldwork Encounter and the Making of Truth*, ed. John Borneman and Abdellah Hammoudi (Berkeley, 2009), 152–153.
75 Tillion, *Il était une fois l'ethnographie*, 15; Evaluation by Louis Massignon, ALG/GGA/11CAB/62, ANOM.
76 Forget and Wood, "Notice biographique," 21–22; Rice, "Déchiffrer le silence," 167; Arrete, March 2, 1955; G. Dupovy (director, CNRS) to Soustelle, September 14, 1955; Lamassone to Soustelle, June 11, 1955, ALG/GGA/11CAB/62, ANOM. Louis Massignon, in conjunction with François Mitterrand, first asked her to travel to Algeria in early 1955. CNRS paid Tillion until April 1, 1956, at which time the French Algerian government took over administrative responsibility for her research.
77 Tillion, *Il était une fois l'ethnographie*, 110.
78 Soustelle, *Aimée et souffrante Algérie*, 83–84.
79 Germaine Tillion, *Algeria: The Realities*, trans. Ronald Matthews (New York, 1958), 9–10.
80 Circular 2.281NA, August 29, 1950, *Pour l'Algérie*, ALG/SAS/DOC/1.
81 General Sarrou to Soustelle, August 22, 1955; Soustelle to Sarrou, September 20, 1955; Jacques Barbier (deputy director of Civil Cabinet) to Colonel Schoen, September 13, 1955; Sarrou paper with SLNA annotations, "Sur l'adaptation de l'Islamisme à la civilisation occidentale," 1 fn3 and 23 fn1, ALG/GGA/11CAB/79, ANOM. For more on Colonel Schoen and the SLNA, see Maurice Faivre, "Le Colonel Paul Schoen du SLNA au Comité Paradi," *Guerres mondiales et conflits contemporains* 208 (October–December 2002), 69–89.
82 See Hammoudi, *Master and Disciple* for a discussion of the power of the political-religious relationship, and its inversion, in governance of Muslim states.

83 Schoen to Soustelle, October 14, 1955, ALG/GGA/11CAB/79, ANOM. The focus on female colonial subjects was not entirely new, as the interwar period, particularly in West Africa, saw a heavy focus on eugenics and the reproduction of both a colonial workforce and a French population to serve as administrators. See Alice Conklin, "'Faire Naître' vs 'Faire du Noir': Race Regeneration in France and West Africa, 1895–1930," in *Promoting the Colonial Idea: Propaganda and Visions of Empire in France*, ed. Tony Chafer and Amanda Sackur (New York, 2002), 143–155.

84 See Soustelle to Deputies and Senators, March 17, 1955, where he requests that all Algerian legislators, particularly those of native Arab or Berber origin, work closely with the governor-general's office prior to submitting ideas to the French national assembly in Paris. See also the responses of Ahmed Ait Ali (March 23, 1955), Amar Naroum (March 24) and Mahdi (n.d.), ALG/GGA/11CAB/2. On languages, see Soustelle, *Aimée et souffrante Algérie*, 80, where he discusses these inducements for administrators.

85 MacMaster, *Burning the Veil*, 323.

86 Soustelle radio address, October 28, 1955, FM/81F/641, ANOM. See also Circular 2.385CC, April 5, 1955, *Pour l'Algérie*, ALG/SAS/DOC/1.

87 Jacques Soustelle, *Lettre ouverte aux victimes de la décolonisation* (Paris, 1973), 47.

88 Lamassoure to prefects of Algiers, Oran, Constantine, southern territories, April 1, 1955, ALG/GGA/11CAB/2, ANOM.

89 Tillion warned of the problem of disillusioned university students in June 1955, a group whose job requirements were eventually subsumed in the *centres sociaux*; Sacriste, *Des ethnologues dans la guerre*, 60. Mouloud Feraoun, *Journal, 1955–1962: Reflections on the French-Algerian War*, ed. James D. LeSueur, trans. Mary Ellen Wolf and Claude Fouillade (Lincoln, 2000 [1962]), Entry for November–December 1955, 49. Feraoun (1913–1962) was a leading Algerian writer and correspondent of famed French Algerian writer Albert Camus, who also worked in Tillion's *centres sociaux* from 1960 to 1962. He was assassinated in 1962 by a right-wing French OAS gunman only four days before the signing of the Evian Accords ended the war. For examples of his writing, see most notably *Le fils du pauvre* (Paris, 1954); and *La terre et le sang* (Paris, 1953).

90 Italics in original. M.M. Knight, "French Colonial Policy—The Decline of 'Association'" *Journal of Modern History* 5, 2 (June 1933), 215; parts also cited in Rabinow, *French Modern*, 277–278.

91 Schoen to Soustelle, October 14, 1955, ALG/GGA/11CAB/79, ANOM. On the lack of coherence in French Muslim policy in West Africa, see Gregory Mann, "Fetishizing Religion: Allah Koura and French 'Islamic Policy' in Late Colonial French Soudan (Mali)," *Journal of African History* 44, 2 (2003), 263–282; and David Robinson, "France as a Muslim Power in West Africa," *Africa Today* 46, 3/4 (Summer 1999), 105–127.

92 Memorandum, Direction d'affaires d'Algérie (Ministry of the Interior), December 8, 1955, FM/81F/24, ANOM. This memorandum, apparently created for internal metropolitan consumption, offers the simplest and most straight-forward description of Soustelle's broad plans for reform.

93 Stephen Tyre, "From Algérie française to France musulmane: Jacques Soustelle and the Myths and Realities of 'Integration,' 1955–1962," *French History* 20, 3 (2006), 288; Desbordes, "Jacques Soustelle et la défense de l'Occident," 342; Soustelle, *Aimée et souffrante Algérie*, 36.

94 "Projet de décision relatif à l'enseignement de la langue arabe en Algérie," n.d (1955), FM/81F/24, ANOM.

95 Soustelle, *Aimée et souffrante Algérie*, 88.
96 On this point see Remaoun, "La politique coloniale française," 275; and Mohammed Harbi, *L'Algérie et son destin: Croyants ou citoyens* (Paris, 1992).
97 "Avant-projet de loi édictant des mesures destinées à favoriser l'accès à la fonction publique des citoyens français musulmans et leur emploi dans les services semi-publics d'Algérie," ALG/GGA/11CAB/78, ANOM. The proposal noted that legal equality had existed in name since September 20, 1947, but had never been properly applied due to low levels of economic and social development and problematic wording. See also "Note pour Monsieur Lamassoure," June 22, 1955 (signature illegible, perhaps V. Monteil), which points to the proposed 1936 Blum-Violette reforms and other bills as too vague to enforce.
98 Colonel Schoen, "Quelques conseils," November 19, 1955, in *Pour l'Algérie*, 45–46, ALG/SAS/DOC/1, ANOM.
99 Soustelle to Resident-General, Morocco, March 26, 1955, ALG/SAS/DOC/5 and "Notice provisoire sur le service des affaires algériennes," ALG/SAS/DOC/1, ANOM; Soustelle, *Aimée et souffrante Algérie*, 51; Mathias, *Les sections administratives spécialisés en Algérie*, 19–20.
100 Note from chief of service of Administrative and Economic Action to secretary-general of civil cabinet, November 21, 1955, ALG/SAS/DOC/5. This note was intended to provide historical and policy background in preparation for a Soustelle speech to the Algerian assembly in November 1955. See also Jacques Soustelle, *Lettre d'un intellectuel à quelques autres à propos de l'Algérie* (Algiers, 1955), 11–12.
101 Pamphlet entitled "Français et Françaises de bonne volonté! L'Algérie a besoin de vous" (Paris, 1957), ALG/SAS/DOC/1, ANOM.
102 Mathias, *Les sections administratives spécialisées en Algérie*, 29–31, 45.
103 "Notice provisoire sur le service des affaires algériennes (1ere partie): Mission-Organisation-Personnels," December 1955; Circular 1783CM, October 4, 1955; note to accompany Arrete of September 5, 1955; Soustelle to Vrolyk (Chief of SAS), September 6, 1955, ALG/SAS/DOC/1, ANOM. For a later restatement, see pamphlet "L'action des SAS dans les domaines social, économique et culturel" (Algiers, 1958), ALG/SAS/DOC/3, ANOM.
104 Italics in original. On this educational program, see "Programme du stage d'orientation des officiers des affaires algériennes et des administrateurs des services civils contractuels, stage du 5 au 24 décembre 1955," ALG/SAS/DOC/3, ANOM. Most of the specific presentations for that course no longer exist in the French archives, but similar courses from 1956 remain in printed form, including most notably Captain Jacques Carret's "Introduction à l'étude du maraboutisme et des confréries religieuses en Algérie," January 23, 1956; and M. Letourneau's "Le passé de l'Afrique du Nord dans ses rapports avec le présent," April 16, 1956, which includes significant discussion of the temporal component of Berber and Arab-Bedouin civilizations as roughly equivalent to middle-ages Europe. For an analogous Russian effort to subsume Islam, see Robert D. Crews, *For Prophet and Tsar: Islam and Empire in Russia and Central Asia* (Cambridge, MA, 2006).
105 Mathias, *Les sections administratives spécialisées en Algérie*, 12–13.
106 Schoen, "Quelques conseils," in *Pour l'Algérie*, 47–59, ALG/SAS/DOC/1.
107 Soustelle to Algerian assembly, 3rd session, November 29, 1955, FM/81F/641, ANOM; Desbordes, "Jacques Soustelle," 383. Robert Lacoste, Soustelle's successor, created the *sections administratives urbaines* (SAU) in 1956 to find the sources of revolt in the cities, particularly Algiers.

108 Tillion, *Il était une fois l'ethnographie*, 20; Arrete, October 27, 1955 in *Journal officiel de l'Algérie*, November 4, 1955, FM/81F/24, ANOM.
109 Forget, "Le service des centres sociaux," 41–42.
110 Pamphlet "Français Parlé," Service des centres sociaux d'Alger, ALG/SAS/DOC/4, ANOM.
111 Forget, "Le service des centres sociaux," 41–42 fn23.
112 "L'action des SAS," ALG/SAS/DOC/3, ANOM; Nelly Forget, "Le service des centres sociaux en Algérie," *Matériaux pour l'histoire de notre temps* 26 (1992), 41.
113 Arrete, October 27, 1955, *Journal Officiel de l'Algérie*, November 4, 1955, FM/81F/24, ANOM; "L'action des SAS dans les domaines social, économique et culturel," ALG/SAS/DOC/3, ANOM. Although the brains behind the concept, Tillion did not direct the centres sociaux; that responsibility fell to Charles Aguesse.
114 See Tillion, *Algeria: The Realities*, passim, for more discussion of this underdevelopment.
115 Le Sueur, *Uncivil War*, 64.
116 Soustelle speech to Algerian assembly, November 29, 1955, FM/81F/641, ANOM.
117 Harbi commented that "elite nationalists" took inspiration in this sense not only from Islamic culture and Arabic language but also from "rational scientific philosophy expressed in French," *L'Algérie et son destin*, quoted in Remaoun, "La politique coloniale française," 275.
118 Front de libération nationale, "Plateforme," I, A, a in *La révolution algérienne par les textes*; Connelly, *A Diplomatic Revolution*, 95. See Ageron, *De l'Algérie française*, 449, for the example of moderate Algerian politician Dr. Bensalem, who was forced in early 1955 to accede the necessity of an exclusively "Algerian citizenship." See Cooper, *Colonialism in Question*, 204–205, 230 for this point in a larger colonial milieu.
119 Jacques Soustelle, *Le drame Algérien et la décadence française: Réponse à Raymond Aron* (Paris, 1957), 33–34.
120 Soustelle, *Vingt-huit ans de Gaullisme*, 116–117.
121 Mathias cites in particular C. Dufresnoy, C. Hary, and C. Pothier in this conclusion; *Les sections administratives spécialisées en Algérie*, 119.
122 Front de Libération nationale, "Plateforme," III, 3, in *La revolution algérienne par les textes*, 31.
123 FLN/ALN Wilaya d'Oran (5), Service de renseignements et de liaisons, "Le SAS: Leur politique, rôle et méthodes," 1 (Algiers?, 1958), 6–7, 15–18, ALG/SAS/DOC/5, ANOM. This document was written in French and perhaps intended for the French-educated elites of the cities. Many FLN/ALN manifestos of the period appeared first in French and only later in Arabic, owing in part to the elite origins of several of the founding members of the nationalist movements in the area.
124 FLN/ALN Wilaya d'Oran (5), Service de renseignements et de liaisons, "Le SAS: Leurs dangers et les moyens de les combattre," 2 (Algiers?, 1958), 7–9, 12–16.
125 See, for example, Pierre Bourdieu, "Algerian Landing," trans. Loïc Wacquant, *Ethnography* 5, 4 (2005), 415–443; "Entre amis," *Awal* 21 (2000), 5–10.
126 Forget and Wood, "Notice biographique," 24–25. For a compelling account of this encounter, which Yacef claimed he instigated to argue against the use of torture, see Germaine Tillion, *Les ennemis complémentaires* (Paris, 1960), 40–51; and Saadi Yacef, *Souvenirs de la bataille d'Alger* (Paris, 1962).
127 Abbas, *Autopsie d'une guerre*, 74–75.
128 Reproduced in Desbordes, "Jacques Soustelle," 490. Monteil also reportedly said in 1955 that oppressive French tactics were founded on race and brought a "war

unaccountable and merciless," with the tacit acceptance of torture hastening his resignation; Connelly, *A Diplomatic Revolution*, 87.

129   Murphrey, "Jacques Soustelle," 115. François Mitterrand ordered Roger Wuillaume to examine the use of torture in Algeria prior to Soustelle's appointment in early 1955. In a report delivered to Soustelle in March of that year, Wuillaume recommended "raising the veil of hypocrisy" that hid torture in police operations by approving the use of such measures in exigent circumstances by specially trained paratroop regiments. "Le rapport de M. Roger Wuillaume, Inspecteur General de l'Administration, 2 Mars 1955," in *La Raison d'état: Textes publiés par le comité Maurice Audin*, ed. Pierre Vidal-Nacquet (Paris, 1962), 55, 57, 68.

130   Abbas, *Autopsie d'une guerre*, 109, 111–112.

131   Soustelle, *Aimée et souffrante Algérie*, 125.

132   Me Ould-Aoudia, "Aperçu sur la situation en Algérie," October 15, 1955, ALG/GGA/11CAB/78, ANOM; Chef du service de l'action administrative et économique (signature illegible) to Soustelle, November 22, 1955, ALG/GGA/11CAB/2, ANOM; McDougall, *History and the Culture of Nationalism*, 140.

133   Soustelle, *Aimée et souffrante Algérie*, 253–258 (quotation on 258); "La manifestation européene de sympathie à l'égard de Jacques Soustelle," *Le Monde*, February 4, 1956, 4.

134   Soustelle, *Vingt-huit ans de Gaullisme*, 145–147; Soustelle, *Aimée et souffrante Algérie*, 192.

135   Jacques Soustelle, *La page n'est pas tournée* (Paris, 1965), 76–77; Murphrey, "Jacques Soustelle," 253.

136   Soustelle, *L'espérance trahie (1958–1961)*, 11.

137   Ullmann, *Jacques Soustelle*, 372, 389–390, 409; "Jacques Soustelle," www.academie-francaise.fr/immortels/index.html, accessed December 1, 2010.

138   See Soustelle, "The Algerian Tragedy," 330; Soustelle, *Vingt-huit ans de Gaullisme*, 130; and Soustelle, "Entreprise aggressive de panarabisme," 1.

139   Soustelle, *The Four Suns*, 8.

Chapter 6

1   Bourdieu, "Algerian Landing," 424.

2   From radio interview in *La sociologie est un sport de combat*, VHS, directed by Pierre Carles (New York, 2001). With respect to his time in Algeria, Bourdieu always called his practice "ethnology" rather than "anthropology," a term that he reserved for Claude Lévi-Strauss. However, he also applied elements of Maussian sociology, which leads me to the term "ethnological sociology."

3   Pierre Bourdieu, "Logique interne de la civilisation traditionelle," in *Le sous-développement en Algérie*, ed. Secretariat Social d'Algérie (Algiers, 1959), 41.

4   Perhaps the most important single scholarly contribution by Mauss to Bourdieu's ethnological theories came in "Les techniques du corps," [1936] in Mauss, *Sociologie et anthropologie*, 365–386, where Mauss used the term "habitus" to describe unconsciously inherited and understood patterns of physical movement.

5   Lahouari Addi, "Pierre Bourdieu, l'Algérie et la pessimisme anthropologique," *Petits déjeuners de la MOM* [Maison de l'Orient de la Mediterrannée], April 19, 2007, www.mom.fr/IMG/pdf/Ptdej_Lahouari.pdf, accessed January 13, 2012, 1, 2, 4; Addi, *Sociologie et anthropologie chez Pierre Bourdieu: Le paradigme anthropologique kabyle*

et ses conséquences théoriques (Paris, 2002), 47; Fabien Sacriste, *Des ethnologues dans la guerre d'indépendance algérienne*, 315, 325.

6 Pierre Bourdieu, "The Attitude of the Algerian Peasant toward Time" [1963], trans. Gerald E. Williams, in *Mediterranean Countrymen: Essays in the Social Anthropology of the Mediterranean*, ed. Julian Pitt-Rivers (New York, 1973), 60–61.

7 Balandier, "La situation coloniale," 29.

8 Bourdieu considered himself well-educated in philosophy (via the école normale) but an autodidact in ethnology, with coursework coming in that discipline only after his return from Algeria in 1961. Axel Honneth, Hermann Kocyba, and Bernd Schwibs with Pierre Bourdieu, "The Struggle for Symbolic Order: An Interview with Pierre Bourdieu," trans. J. Bleicher, *Theory, Culture and Society* 3, 3 (1986), 39.

9 Pierre Bourdieu and Abdelmalek Sayed, "Paysans déracinés: Bouleversements morphologiques et changements culturels en Algérie," *Etudes Rurales* 12 (January–March 1964), 62.

10 Pierre Bourdieu, "Révolution dans la révolution," *Esprit* Nouvelle série 29, 1 (January 1961), 32.

11 Pierre Bourdieu, *Sketch for a Self-Analysis*, trans. Richard Nice (Cambridge, 2007 [2004]), 86–88.

12 Pierre Bourdieu, "J'avais 15 ans ... Pierre par Bourdieu," *Le Nouvel Observateur*, January 31, 2002, 30; *La sociologie est un sport de combat*. Bourdieu spent a year of preparatory school following his time in Pau at the prestigious lycée Louis-le-Grand in Paris before moving on to higher education at ENS.

13 David Swartz, "In Memoriam: Pierre Bourdieu 1930–2002," *Theory and Society* 31, 4 (August 2002), 548.

14 Pierre Bourdieu, *The Algerians*, trans. Alan C.M. Ross (Boston, 1962 [1958]), 118. See also Deborah Reed-Danahay, " 'Tristes Paysans': Bourdieu's Early Ethnography in Béarn and Kabylia," *Anthropological Quarterly* 77, 1 (Winter 2004), 92–93.

15 Quoting interview with Bourdieu in 1994–1995, Michael Grenfell, *Pierre Bourdieu, Agent Provocateur* (New York, 2004), 15–16. On Bourdieu's links to *Année Sociologique*, see also David L. Swartz, "Drawing Inspiration from Bourdieu's Sociology of Symbolic Power," *Theory and Society* 32, 5–6 (2003), 521; Erwin Dianteill, "Pierre Bourdieu et la religion. Synthèse critique d'une synthèse critique," *Archives des sciences sociales des religions* 118 (2002), 5–19; and "Pierre Bourdieu and the Sociology of Religion: A Central and Peripheral Concern," *Theory and Society* 32, 5–6 (2003), 529–549.

16 Michel Foucault, "La vie: L'expérience et la science," *Revue de métaphysique et de morale* 90, 1 (January–March 1985), 4. Foucault points in particular to Husserl's *Cartesianische Meditationem und pariser Voträge*, which appeared in France as *Méditations cartésiennes* in 1929, as the key text that led French philosophers to adopt a more phenomenological tone. On the importance of the postwar moment to existentialism, see David Drake, *Sartre* (London, 2005), 64. See also Alan D. Schrift, *Twentieth Century French Philosophy: Key Themes and Thinkers* (Oxford, 2006), 20.

17 Foucault, "La vie," 6, 14.

18 Bourdieu and Passeron, "Sociology and Philosophy in France since 1945," 184.

19 Schrift, *Twentieth Century French Philosophy*, 36–47. The most prominent structuralist colleagues of Lévi-Strauss in France were Louis Althusser (1918–1990), Roland Barthes (1915–1980), and Jacques Lacan (1901–1981).

20 James A. Boon, *Other Tribes, Other Scribes: Symbolic Anthropology in the Comparative Study of Cultures, Histories, Religions, and Texts* (New York, 1982), 57;

Claude Lévi-Strauss, "L'anthropologie sociale devant l'histoire," *Annales. Histoire, sciences sociales* 15, 4 (July–August 1960), 631.

21 Claude Lévi-Strauss, *The Naked Man: Introduction to a Science of Mythology, Volume 4*, trans. John Weightman and Doreen Weightman (New York, 1981 [1971]), 687.

22 Lévi-Strauss, *The Raw and the Cooked*, 13.

23 Marcel Fournier, "Pierre Bourdieu: La sociologie est un sport de haut niveau," *Awal: Cahiers d'études berbères* 27/28 (2003), 58; Pierre Bourdieu, "Participant Objectivation," trans. Loïc Wacquant, *Journal of the Royal Anthropological Institute* 9, 2 (June 2003), 286; Marcel Mauss, "Rapports réels et pratiques de la psychologie et de la sociologie" [1924], in Mauss, *Sociologie et anthropologie*, 285. Italics in original.

24 Honneth et al., "The Struggle for Symbolic Order," 37. Bourdieu in particular disliked Georges Davy, the last remaining active member of the original *Année sociologique* and a member of the board for the *agrégation* in philosophy.

25 Norman H. Greene, *Jean-Paul Sartre: The Existentialist Ethic* (Ann Arbor, 1960), 3, 173. Greene's work offers a contemporary, but not collaborative, depiction of Sartrean philosophy. For a basic introduction to Sartre, see Drake, *Sartre*. The best account of Sartre's early years is John Gerassi, *Jean-Paul Sartre: Hated Conscience of His Century* (Chicago, 1989). The most complete biography is Annie Cohen-Solal, *Sartre, 1905–1980* (Paris, 1999).

26 Bourdieu, *Sketch for a Self-Analysis*, 10–11.

27 Honneth et al., "The Struggle for Symbolic Order," 35. Bourdieu also read some Marxism, particularly the early work of Marx himself (such as the *Theses on Feuerbach*), but fought against Stalinism while at ENS; as a result, Emmanuel Le Roy Ladurie (later an acclaimed Annalist historian) denounced Bourdieu, Derrida, and several like-minded classmates as "social traitors." Luc Ferry and Alain Renaut, however, depicted Bourdieu as a Marxist who denied the model in an effort to make himself appear unique, a common approach for the period in their view. Luc Ferry and Alain Renaut, *French Philosophy of the Sixties: An Essay on Antihumanism*, trans. Mary H.S. Cattani (Amherst, 1990 [1985]), 183–184 and chapter 5.

28 Bourdieu, *Sketch for a Self-Analysis*, 23, 27–28. Canguilhem mentored Bourdieu as he emerged from ENS, though they had a brief falling-out when Bourdieu accepted a teaching position at Moulins instead of Canguilhem's preferred post at Toulouse. They ultimately reconciled and Bourdieu considered working under Canguilhem for his doctorate in the late 1950s, a pursuit he ultimately abandoned.

29 Ibid., 36.

30 Dedication to Emile Durkheim in Claude Lévi-Strauss, *Structural Anthropology*, trans. Claire Jacobson and Brook Grundfest Schoepf (New York, 1963 [1958]). Lévi-Strauss mentions his "dialogue" with Maurice Merleau-Ponty and Simone de Beauvoir in Claude Lévi-Strauss, *The Savage Mind*, trans. George Weidenfeld and Nicolson Limited (Chicago, 1966 [1962]), front matter and xi.

31 Bourdieu and Passeron, "Sociology and Philosophy in France," 201.

32 See Swartz, "Drawing Inspiration," 522; Tassadit Yacine, "Pierre Bourdieu in Algeria at War: Notes on the Birth of an Engaged Ethnosociology," trans. Loïc Wacquant and James Ingram, *Ethnography* 5, 4 (2004), 488; and Frédéric Lebaron, "Pierre Bourdieu: Economic Models against Economism," *Theory and Society* 32, 5–6 (2003), 551–565; Bourdieu, "Algerian Landing," 423.

33 Yacine, "Pierre Bourdieu in Algeria at War," 492; Sacriste, *Des ethnologues dans la guerre*, 286 fn4.
34 The group was led, during Bourdieu's time, by Father Henri Sanson. For more on the group's relationship with Bourdieu, see H. Sanson, "C'était un esprit curieux," *Awal* 27/28 (2003), 279–286.
35 Bourdieu, "Entre amis," 6; Pierre Bourdieu, *The Logic of Practice*, trans. Richard Nice (Stanford, 1990 [1980]), 3; Yacine, "Pierre Bourdieu in Algeria at War," 490–492.
36 Bourdieu, "Entre amis," 7; Jacques Berque, *Structures Sociales du Haut-Atlas* (Paris, 1955). Indeed, Berque came from a family long involved in colonial administration, as his father Augustin worked in Algeria during the Second World War, and Berque himself had experience as a colonial administrator in Morocco. See his "Entrée dans le bureau arabe," in *Nomades et vagabonds* (Paris, 1975). Bourdieu was also highly impressed by Berque's articles, "Qu'est-ce qu'une tribu nord-africaine," in *L'éventail de l'histoire vivante, hommage à Lucien Febvre* (Paris, 1953); and "Cent-vingt ans de sociologie maghrébine," *Annales. Economies, Sociétés, Civilisations* 11, 3 (1956), 296–324, which gave him "countless starting points and invaluable points of reference."
37 Bourdieu, "Entre amis," 6–7.
38 Ibid., 6; André Nouschi, "Autour de *Sociologie de l'Algérie*," *Awal* 27/28 (2003), 32. Yacine, "Pierre Bourdieu in Algeria at War," 496; Sacriste, *Des ethnologues dans la guerre*, 220–221.
39 Hafid Adnani and Tassadit Yacine, "L'autre Bourdieu," *Awal* 27/28 (2003), 232.
40 Bourdieu, "Entre amis," 7; "Pierre Bourdieu et l'anthropologie," *Actes de la recherche en sciences sociales* 150 (2003), 6; Yacine, "Pierre Bourdieu in Algeria at War," 492. Yacine reports that Bourdieu accelerated his departure in 1961 for fear of an impending assassination attempt by right-wing settlers, a legitimate fear given that one of the students working with Bourdieu and Sayed, Moula Henine, was killed by OAS extremists; Sacriste, *Des ethnologues dans la guerre*, 309 fn2.
41 Bourdieu, "Algerian Landing," 419; Bourdieu "Entre amis," 7. For Fanon's calls to action during the Algerian revolution, see most importantly *Les damnés de la terre* (Paris, 1961). See also Sartre's preface to Fanon's work and the collection *Situations V: Colonialisme et néo-colonialisme* (Paris, 1964).
42 Bourdieu, *The Algerians*, x. In this work, a translation of *Sociologie de l'Algérie*, he broke Algeria into "Arabic-speaking peoples," Kabyles, Shawia (Chaouia), and Mozabites. See also Jane E. Goodman and Paul A. Silverstein, "Introduction," in *Bourdieu in Algeria: Colonial Politics, Ethnographic Practices, Theoretical Developments*, ed. Jane E. Goodman and Paul A. Silverstein (Lincoln, 2009), 3, 12.
43 Balandier, "La situation coloniale," 13.
44 Pierre Bourdieu with Alain Darbel, Jean-Claude Rivet and Claude Seibel, *Travail et Travailleurs en Algérie* (Paris, 1963), 257–258. See also Jane E. Goodman, "The Proverbial Bourdieu: Habitus and the Politics of Representation in the Ethnography of Kabylia," in *Bourdieu in Algeria*, ed. Goodman and Silverstein, 118.
45 Aron preface to Bourdieu, *The Algerians*, vi.
46 Bourdieu, *The Algerians*, xiv.
47 On this point, see also Abdellah Hammoudi, "Phenomenology and Ethnography: On Kabyle *Habitus* in the Work of Pierre Bourdieu," in *Bourdieu in Algeria*, ed. Goodman and Silverstein, 200–201.
48 Bourdieu, *The Algerians*, 3, 83, 85, 97.
49 Ibid., 92. Balandier made a similar argument about hybrid colonial societies, breaking them into white colonial, white foreigner, mixed people of color, and

native categories with a basic assumption of white colonial superiority, "La situation coloniale," 19.
50 For more on this myth, see Lorcin, *Imperial Identities*.
51 See Hammoudi, "Phenomenology and Ethnography," 200–201, 229; and Goodman, "The Proverbial Bourdieu," 100.
52 Bourdieu, *The Algerians*, 13, 16, 56–57, 73.
53 Pierre Bourdieu and Mouloud Mammeri, "Du bon usage de l'ethnologie," *Actes de la recherche en sciences sociales* 150 (2003), 15.
54 Pierre Bourdieu and Jean-Claude Passeron, *Reproduction in Education, Society, and Culture*, 2nd ed., trans. Richard Nice (London, 1990 [1970]), 47.
55 Bourdieu et al., *Travail et Travailleurs*, 260–261; Addi, *Sociologie et anthropologie chez Pierre Bourdieu*, 21–22. Bourdieu credited Maurice Halbwachs' *Les Causes du Suicide* (Paris, 1930) as the inspiration for his interior research method.
56 Paul Rabinow has also commented on the importance of informants on the margins as points of entry for ethnographic research. See *Reflections on Fieldwork in Morocco* (Berkeley, 1977).
57 Pierre Bourdieu, "Pour Abdelmalek Sayed" [1998] in Pierre Bourdieu, *Esquisses algériennes*, ed. Tassadit Yacine (Paris, 2008), 357; Bourdieu, "Algerian Landing," 429–431; Bourdieu et al., *Travail et Travailleurs*, 262. For a strongly ethnographic study of Algerian villagers, see Pierre Bourdieu, "The Sense of Honour" [1966] in *Algeria 1960*, trans. Richard Nice (Cambridge, 1979), 95–132.
58 Bourdieu et al., *Travail et Travailleurs*, 13, 262–263; Paul A. Silverstein, "Of Rooting and Uprooting: Kabyle Habitus, Domesticity and Structural Nostalgia," *Ethnography* 5, 4 (2004), 562.
59 Mouloud Mammeri and Pierre Bourdieu, "Dialogue sur la poésie orale en Kabylie," *Actes de la recherche en sciences sociales* 23 (September 1978), 51, 57.
60 Mammeri attended the same Parisian lycée (Louis-le-grand) as Bourdieu, but had to stop his application to ENS to enter military service in 1939. He ultimately attended university in Algiers, later teaching and founding associations for the study of the Berber language and the journal *Awal*. Tassadit Yacine has written that Mammeri and some of his French-speaking colleagues such as Mouloud Feraoun were viewed as "traitors" to the nationalist cause by some members of the FLN, an interesting contrast considering Feraoun was assassinated by OAS Frenchmen; Tassadit Yacine, "Rapports de genres et littératures postcoloniales chez Mouloud Feraoun et Mouloud Mammeri," *Awal: Cahiers d'études berbères* 38 (2008), 16. Mammeri authored, most notably, *La colline oubliée* (Paris, 1952) and *Le sommeil du juste* (Paris, 1955) in the 1950s. See also Aomar Ait Aider, *Mammeri a dit* (Tizi-Ouzou, Algeria, 2009).
61 See, for example, Mouloud Mammeri, *L'Opium et le bâton* (Paris, 1965), for discussion of the different forms and views of violence in war-time Algeria.
62 Pierre Bourdieu, "La réappropriation de la culture reniée: à propos de Mouloud Mammeri," in *Amour, phantasmes et sociétés en Afrique du nord et au sahara*, ed. Tassadit Yacine (Paris, 1992), 17, 18, 21.
63 See, for example, *The Weight of the World: Social Suffering in Contemporary Society*, trans. Pricilla Parkhurst Ferguson (Stanford, 1999); *La domination masculine* (Paris, 1998); *Homo Academicus*, trans. Peter Collier (Stanford, 1988); and *Distinction: A Social Critique of the Judgment of Taste*, trans. Richard Nice (Cambridge, MA, 1984).
64 Pierre Bourdieu, *Images d'Algérie: Une affinité élective*, ed. Franz Schultheis and Christine Frisinghelli (Arles, 2003), 24, 29. Tillion's work inspired Bourdieu in a number of ways, from its focus on economic disequilibrium brought on by

colonialism to the realization of the importance of collectivity in North African thought processes and social structures. He particularly found interesting her *Algérie en 1957*; and "Dans l'Aurès: Le drame des civilisations archaïques," *Annales. Histoire, sciences sociales* 12, 3 (July–September 1957), 393–402. See Pierre Bourdieu, "Choc des civilisations," in *Le Sous-développement en Algérie*, 56; and Bourdieu, *The Algerians*, 202–203.

65 Bourdieu and Mammeri, "Du bon usage de l'ethnologie," 16; Bourdieu and Sayed, "Paysans déracinés," 57.

66 Pierre Bourdieu, "Révolution dans la révolution," *Esprit* Nouvelle série, 20, 1 (January 1961), 36; Bourdieu and Sayed, "Paysans déracinés," 58; Bourdieu, *The Algerians*, xi fn1; Pierre Bourdieu, "De la guerre révolutionnaire à la révolution," in *L'Algérie de demain*, ed. François Perroux (Paris, 1962), 7; Bourdieu, "Choc des civilisations," 58.

67 Bourdieu, "De la guerre révolutionnaire à la révolution," 11.

68 Bourdieu, "Logique interne de la civilisation traditionelle," 43.

69 Honneth et al., "The Struggle for Symbolic Order," 39.

70 On the emphasis on Arab identity and the move against perceived French collaborators in postcolonial Algeria, see McDougall, *History and the Culture of Nationalism in Algeria*; J.N.C. Hill, *Identity in Algerian Politics: The Legacy of Colonial Rule* (Boulder, 2009); and Jean Galland, *L'indépendance, un combat qui continue* (Paris, 2007).

71 The most renowned first-hand description of French tactical and operational techniques in Algeria remains David Galula, *Pacification in Algeria, 1956–1958* (Santa Monica, CA, 2006 [1963]).

72 Bourdieu to André Nouschi, cited in Yacine, "Pierre Bourdieu in Algeria at War," 497–498.

73 Honneth et al., "The Struggle for Symbolic Order," 38; Bourdieu, "Algerian Landing," 419. See also Martin Enrique-Criado, *Les deux Algéries de Pierre Bourdieu*, trans. Hélène Bretin (Bellecombe-en-Bauges, 2008), 80, for a discussion of Bourdieu's affinity for Lévi-Strauss's work as a counter to ethnocentrism.

74 Bourdieu, *The Logic of Practice*, 5.

75 For Bourdieu's structural phase, see his "The Berber House or the World Reversed," *Social Science Information* 9 (1970), 151–170; and, to a lesser extent, "The Sentiment of Honour in Kabyle Society," trans. Philip Sharrard, in *Honour and Shame: The Values of Mediterranean Society*, ed. John G. Peristiany (Chicago, 1966), 192–211.

76 Honneth et al., "The Struggle for Symbolic Order," 38. For a very helpful and concise juxtaposition of Bourdieu's early work and Lévi-Strauss's employment of the linguistic theory of Ferdinand de Saussure (1857–1913), see Enrique-Criado, *Les deux Algéries*, 77–99.

77 Bourdieu, *Images d'Algérie*, 42.

78 Loïc Wacquant, "Following Pierre Bourdieu into the Field," *Ethnography* 5, 4 (2004), 396–397. Bourdieu's movement toward "reflexivity" influenced numerous Western anthropologists, including Johannes Fabian, who in 1983 acknowledged his debt to Bourdieu for his idea of "coevalness" in anthropological observation. See Johannes Fabian, *Time and the Other: How Anthropology Makes Its Object* (New York, 1983), xi–xii. For another example of such influence, see Appadurai, *Modernity at Large*, chapters 2 and 3 for a discussion of the "product of representation."

79 *La Sociologie est un sport de combat*.

80   Bourdieu, "Algerian Landing," 435–436.
81   Bourdieu, "Entre amis," 9.
82   Bourdieu, "Participant Objectivation," 282.
83   Lévi-Strauss, *The Raw and the Cooked*, 10–11; Bourdieu, "Participant Objectivation," 283. Some in American anthropology by the 1980s had also labeled *Tristes Tropiques* as "self-referential," a heroic tale of "anthropologist as seeker" expressed in almost mythic terms. See Clifford Geertz, *Works and Lives: The Anthropologist as Author* (Stanford, 1988), 28, 45.
84   Christopher Johnson, "Anthropology and the *Sciences Humaines*: The Voice of Lévi-Strauss," *History of the Human Sciences* 10, 3 (1997), 124. Lévi-Strauss initially studied law in Paris before passing the *agrégation* in philosophy in 1931 and moving on to ethnographic research in Brazil in the early 1930s. For more on Lévi-Strauss's background, see Christopher Johnson, *Claude Lévi-Strauss: The Formative Years* (Cambridge, 2003); and Denis Bertholet, *Claude Lévi-Strauss* (Paris, 2003). A more complete biographical treatment is Patrick Wilcken, *Claude Lévi-Strauss: The Poet in the Laboratory* (New York, 2010).
85   Bourdieu, "Algerian Landing," 436; Claude Lévi-Strauss, "The Place of Anthropology in the Social Sciences and Problems Raised in Teaching It," in *Structural Anthropology*, 364, emphasis in original.
86   Pierre Bourdieu, *Outline of a Theory of Practice* (Cambridge, 1977 [1972]), 2. Emphasis in original.
87   Pierre Bourdieu, "Bachelorhood and the Peasant Condition" [1962], in Pierre Bourdieu, *The Bachelor's Ball: The Crisis of Peasant Society in Béarn*, trans. Richard Nice (Cambridge, 2008 [2002]), 94.
88   Bourdieu, "Participant Objectivation," 288.
89   Bourdieu and Mammeri, "Du bon usage de l'ethnologie," 12.
90   Bourdieu, *Outline of a Theory of Practice*, 79; Pierre Bourdieu, "The Disenchantment of the World," in Pierre Bourdieu, *Algeria 1960*, trans. Richard Nice (Cambridge, 1979 [1963]), 64.
91   Bourdieu, "Disenchantment of the World," 29.
92   Bourdieu, *Outline of a Theory of Practice*, 5–7, 9.
93   Claude Lévi-Strauss, *Tristes Tropiques*, trans. John Weightman and Doreen Weightman (New York, 1974 [1955]), 312.
94   Claude Lévi-Strauss, *Race and History* (Paris, 1961 [1958]), 19, 37.
95   Lévi-Strauss, *Tristes Tropiques*, 95.
96   Ibid., 58.
97   Lévi-Strauss, "The Place of Anthropology in the Social Sciences," 365. See also Lévi-Strauss, *The Savage Mind*, 10; and Lévi-Strauss, *The Naked Man*, 626.
98   Adnani and Yacine, "L'autre Bourdieu," 236.
99   Bourdieu, "Algerian Landing," 423; Bourdieu, *Outline of a Theory of Practice*, 78.
100 Lévi-Strauss, "L'anthropologie sociale devant l'histoire," 636–637. Lévi-Strauss frames his discussion as strong agreement with Radcliffe-Brown on this point.
101 Claude Lévi-Strauss, "Introduction: History and Anthropology," in *Structural Anthropology*, 21.
102 Marcel Mauss, "Body Techniques," in Marcel Mauss, *Sociology and Psychology: Essays*, trans. Ben Brewster (Boston, 1979 [1950]), 101. Mauss's analysis focused on the similar forms of physical movement in social and cultural groups, not on the full scope of social behavior. On Lyautey's vision of habitus as collected and

expected behavior in a colonial context, see Lyautey to E.M. de Vogüé, October 20, 1907, in Hubert Lyautey, "Lettres de Rabat," *Revue des Deux Mondes* Période 6, 64 (July 15, 1924), 299.
103 Bourdieu, *Outline of a Theory of Practice*, 78, 81–82. Bourdieu's first description of habitus, although lacking that label, appeared in his earliest ethnography: "One must nevertheless admit that everything seems to indicate that every civilization, at each period of its development, 'was making a choice,' by reference to the system of its fundamental choices (a culture being a system of choices which no one *makes*)," italics in original. Bourdieu, *The Algerians*, 111.
104 Bourdieu, *Outline of a Theory of Practice*, 95, 86–87.
105 Bourdieu and Passeron, *Reproduction*, 23, 32, 47, 99 (quotes on 32 and 47).
106 Bourdieu, *The Algerians*, 117.
107 Lévi-Strauss, *Tristes Tropiques*, 178.
108 Claude Lévi-Strauss, "Structural Analysis in Linguistics and Anthropology," in *Structural Anthropology*, 46. See also Claude Lévi-Strauss, "Social Structure," in *Structural Anthropology*, 312. In this case Lévi-Strauss is offering his take on Radcliffe-Brown's famous study of the importance of the mother's brother in South Africa. See A.R. Radcliffe-Brown, *Structure and Function in Primitive Societies: Essays and Addresses* (Glencoe, IL, 1952), chapter 1.
109 Pierre Bourdieu, "Structuralism and Theory of Sociological Knowledge," trans. Angela Zanotti-Karp, *Social Research* 35, 4 (1968), 705.
110 Lévi-Strauss, *The Savage Mind*, 17–21, 269; Lévi-Strauss, *The Raw and the Cooked*, 8, 341.
111 Lévi-Strauss, *The Raw and the Cooked*, 143; Lévi-Strauss, *La vie familiale et sociale*, 126–128; Lévi-Strauss, *The Naked Man*, 694; Claude Lévi-Strauss, *The Origin of Table Manners: Introduction to a Science of Mythology, Volume 3*, trans. John Weightman and Doreen Weightman (New York, 1978 [1968]), 469.
112 Lévi-Strauss, "Introduction: History and Anthropology," 17, 21. See also Lévi-Strauss, *The Origin of Table Manners*, 18.
113 Lévi-Strauss, *The Raw and the Cooked*, 10.
114 Lévi-Strauss, *Tristes Tropiques*, 317.
115 Honneth et al., "The Struggle for Symbolic Order," 41; Bourdieu and Mammeri, "Du bon usage de l'ethnologie," 15; Bourdieu, *Outline of a Theory of Practice*, 16.
116 Honneth et al., "The Struggle for Symbolic Order," 44–45; Bourdieu and Passeron, "Sociology and Philosophy in France since 1945," 198. On Lévi-Strauss's views of models preceding laboratory work, see Lévi-Strauss, *Tristes Tropiques*, 57.
117 Bourdieu et al., *Travail et Travailleurs*, 9; Bourdieu and Mammeri, "Du bon usage de l'ethnologie," 14. See also Honneth et al., "The Struggle for Symbolic Order," 39.
118 Swartz, "In Memoriam," 547, 550.
119 Deborah Reed-Danahay, *Locating Bourdieu* (Bloomington, 2005), 83. On reflexivity in anthropology, particularly in the United States, see, for example, Sherry Ortner, *Anthropology and Social Theory: Culture, Power, and the Acting Subject* (Durham, NC, 2006); James L. Peacock, *The Anthropological Lens: Harsh Light, Soft Focus*, 2nd ed. (Cambridge, 2001 [1986]); James Clifford, "On Ethnographic Authority," *Representations* 2 (Spring 1983), 118–146; and the collected essays in *Writing Culture: The Poetics and Politics of Ethnography*, ed. James Clifford and George E. Marcus (Berkeley, 1986).
120 Addi, "Pierre Bourdieu, l'Algérie et le pessimisme anthropologique," 7.
121 Swartz, "In Memoriam," 550.

122 Grenfell, *Agent Provocateur*, 198; Bourdieu, "Entre amis," 10.
123 Bourdieu, *Sketch for a Self-Analysis*, 17.
124 Bourdieu, "Bachelorhood and the Peasant Condition," 95.

Conclusion

1 Amadou Hampâté Bâ, *Amkoullel, l'enfant Peul: Mémoires* (Arles, 1991), 14.

Bibliography

Archival Collections

Archives Nationales, Paris, France (AN)
    475AP—Archives Privées Lyautey
        475AP10
        475AP13
        475AP58
        475AP66
        475AP73
        475AP76
        475AP109
        475AP137
        475AP208
        475AP215
        475AP226
        475AP230
        475AP243
        475AP261
    684Mi—Correspondance Georges Hardy

Archives Nationales d'Outre-Mer (ANOM)—Aix-en-Provence, France
    Fonds d'Algérie (ALG)
    Gouvernment Général d'Algérie (GGA)
        11CAB (Cabinet Civil Soustelle)
            11CAB/1
            11CAB/2
            11CAB/15
            11CAB/29
            11CAB/35
            11CAB/62
            11CAB/78
            11CAB/79
            28H/1-3

    Sections administratives spécialisées (SAS), Documentation (DOC)
        SAS/DOC/1-5

    Fonds Ministèriels (FM)
        81F
            81F/24
            81F/641

Séries géographiques (SG)
    Afrique Occidentale Française (AOF)
        AOF/II/1
        AOF/III/3
        AOF/IV/6
        AOF/X/4
        AOF/X/6
    Côte d'Ivoire (CIV)
        CIV/III/4
    Mauritanie (MRT)
        MRT/IV/1
        MRT/VI/1
    Soudan (SOUD)
        SOUD/III/4
Fonds Privées (FP)
    Fonds Gaden (15APC/1-2)
    Fonds Faidherbe (113APOM/1-6)

Archives du Sénégal, Archives du Gouvernement Général de l'AOF (14MIOM)
    14MIOM/784 (AOF 5G64)
    14MIOM/895 (AOF 13G69)
    14MIOM/1812 (AOF 2G39-70)

Institut Mémoires de l'édition contemporaine (IMEC)—L'abbaye d'Ardenne, Caen, France
    Archives de Collége de France (CDF)
        Fonds Lucien Lévy-Bruhl (LVB)
            LVB 3
            LVB 22.16
            LVB 10.3
        Fonds Marcel Mauss (MAS)
            MAS 1.27
            MAS 4.24
            MAS 6.45
            MAS 6.49
            MAS 7.2
            MAS 7.45
            MAS 8.3
            MAS 8.10
            MAS 11.20
            MAS 11.22
            MAS 12.63
            MAS 13.20
            MAS 17.4
            MAS 18
            MAS 19
            MAS 20
            MAS 21.20
            MAS 21.37
            MAS 38.9

MAS 38.10
MAS 40.21
MAS 40.22
Muséum National d'Histoire Naturelle, Paris, France (MNHN)
   Bibliothèque du Musée de l'homme
      Fonds du Patrimoine
         2AP 8—Fonds Delafosse

Société Historique de la Défense, Chateau de Vincennes, Paris, France (SHD)
   6Ye49900—Dossier Paul Marty
   7Yd1515—Dossier Louis Léon César Faidherbe
   9Yd453—Dossier Louis Hubert Gonzalve Lyautey

Published Primary Sources—Journals, Newspapers, Proceedings

Actes de la recherche en sciences sociales

Africa

Afrique et l'Asie

American Opinion

Annales de l'Assemblée Nationale Constituante elue le 21 Octobre 1945

Annales de l'Université de Paris

Annales. Histoire, Sciences Sociales

L'Année Sociologique

L'anthropologie

Archives de sociologie des religions

Awal

Bulletin du comité de l'Afrique française

Bulletin du comité des etudes historiques et scientifiques de l'Afrique Occidentale française

Bulletin de l'enseignement de l'Afrique Occidentale française

Bulletin de la société de géographie

Bulletin de la société de géographie commerciale de Paris

Bulletin et mémoires de la société d'anthropologie de Paris

Bulletin de la société d'ethnographie de Paris, later *Ethnographie*

Bulletin et mémoires de la société de linguistique de Paris

Cahiers internationaux de sociologie

La Dépêche Coloniale et Maritime

Documents

Esprit

Ethnography

Etudes rurales

Europe

L'Express

Le Figaro magazine

Foreign Affairs

La Géographie

Hespéris: Archives Berbères et Bulletin de l'Institut des Hautes Etudes Marocaines

Journal of Modern History

Journal of the Royal Anthropological Institute

Journal de la Société des Africanistes

Journal de la Société des Américanistes

Minotaure

Le Monde

Newsweek

Notes africaines

Le Nouvel Observateur

Nouvelles annales des voyages, de la géographie et de l'histoire

Outre-Mer

La Réforme Sociale

Revue Africaine. Bulletin des travaux de la société historique algérienne

Revue coloniale

Revue des deux mondes

Revue d'ethnographie et de sociologie

Revue d'Ethnographie et des Traditions Populaires

Revue des Etudes Ethnographiques et Sociologiques

Revue des Etudes Islamiques

Revue française de sociologie

La Revue hebdomadaire

Revue indigène

Revue de Madagascar

Revue maritime et coloniale

Revue du Monde Musulman

Revue de Paris

Revue politique et parlementaire

Revue de synthèse

Revue Tunisienne

Social Research

Theory, Culture and Society

Vendredi

The World Today

Published Primary Sources—Books/Articles

Aïssa, Mamadi. *Traditions historiques et légendaires du Soudan occidental*, manuscript copy by Mamadou Sallana, ed. and trans. Maurice Delafosse. Paris: Comité de l'Afrique française, 1913.
Alleg, Henri. *La Question*. Paris: Editions de Minuit, 1961 [1958].
Ancelle, J. *Les Explorations au Sénégal et dans les contrées voisines depuis l'antiquité jusqu'à nos jours*. Paris: Maisonneuve frères et C. LeClerc, 1886.
Aussaresses, Paul. *Services Spéciaux: Algérie, 1955-1957*. Paris: Perrin, 2001.
Azzedine, Commandant. *Les fellaghas*, 2nd ed. Algiers: ENAG, 1997 [1976].
Bâ, Amadou Hampaté. *Amkoullel, l'enfant peul: mémoires*. Arles: Actes Sud, 1991.
Balandier, Georges. "La situation coloniale: Approche théorique," *Cahiers Internationaux de Sociologie* Nouvelle Série, 110 (January–June 2001): 9–29.
Bartholomew, J.G. *A Literary and Historical Atlas of Africa and Australasia*. London: J.M. Dent and Sons, 1913.
Berque, Jacques. *Structures Sociales du Haut-Atlas*. Paris: Presses Universitaires de France, 1955.
Berque, Jacques. "Cent-vingt ans de sociologie maghrébine," *Annales. Economies, Sociétés, Civilisations* 11, 3 (1956): 296–324.
Berque, Jacques. *Nomades et vagabonds*. Paris: Union générale d'éditions, 1975.
Berque, Jacques et al., *Eventail de l'histoire vivante, hommage à Lucien Febvre*. Paris: A. Colin, 1953.
Bidault, Jules. *L'horticulture dans les écoles primaires*. Paris: F. Tandou, 1864.
Bidault, Jules and Paul Hennequin. *Histoire populaire de l'empire napoléonienne depuis son établissement jusqu'à nos jours, livre de lecture courante à l'usage des écoles primaires*. Paris: E. Just Bernard, 1854.
Biobaku, Saburi. "Les responsabilités de l'historien africain en ce qui concerne l'histoire et l'Afrique," *Présence africaine* 27–28 (August–November 1959): 96–99.
Bou Haqq. "Noirs et blancs au confins du désert," *Bulletin du Comité d'études historiques et scientifiques de l'AOF* 21 (1938): 480–487.

Bourdieu, Pierre. "Choc des civilisations," in *Le Sous-Développement en Algérie*. Algiers: Editions du Secretariat Social d'Alger, 1959: 53–64.
Bourdieu, Pierre. "Logique interne de la civilisation traditionnelle," in *Le Sous-Développement en Algérie*. Algiers: Editions du Secretariat Social d'Alger, 1959: 41–51.
Bourdieu, Pierre. "Révolution dans la révolution," *Esprit* Nouvelle Série, 29, 1 (January 1961): 27–40.
Bourdieu, Pierre. *The Algerians*, trans. Alan C.M. Ross. Boston: Beacon Press, 1962.
Bourdieu, Pierre. "Célibat et condition paysanne," *Etudes Rurales* 5–6 (April–September 1962): 32–135.
Bourdieu, Pierre. "The Sentiment of Honour in Kabyle Society," trans. Philip Sharrard, in *Honour and Shame: The Values of Mediterranean Society*, ed. John G. Peristiany. Chicago: University of Chicago Press, 1966: 192–211.
Bourdieu, Pierre. "Structuralism and Theory of Sociological Knowledge," trans. Angela Zanotti-Karp, *Social Research* 35, 4 (1968): 681–706.
Bourdieu, Pierre. "The Berber House or the World Reversed," *Social Science Information* 9 (1970): 151–170.
Bourdieu, Pierre. "The Attitude of the Algerian Peasant toward Time," trans. Gerald E. Williams, in *Mediterranean Countrymen: Essays in the Social Anthropology of the Mediterranean*, ed. Julian Pitt-Rivers. New York: Greenwood Press, 1973 [1963]: 55–72.
Bourdieu, Pierre. *Outline of a Theory of Practice*, trans. Richard Nice. Cambridge: Cambridge University Press, 1977 [1972].
Bourdieu, Pierre. *Algeria 1960*, trans. Richard Nice. Cambridge: Cambridge University Press, 1979 [1963].
Bourdieu, Pierre. *The Logic of Practice*, trans. Richard Nice. Stanford: Stanford University Press, 1990 [1980].
Bourdieu, Pierre. "Sur les rapports entre la sociologie et l'histoire en Allemagne et en France," *Actes de la recherche en sciences sociales* 106–107 (March 1995): 108–122.
Bourdieu, Pierre. "Entre Amis," *Awal* 21 (2000): 5–10.
Bourdieu, Pierre. "J'avais 15 ans ... Pierre par Bourdieu," *Le Nouvel Observateur*, January 31, 2002: 30–31.
Bourdieu, Pierre. *Images d'Algérie: une affinité élective*, ed. Franz Schultheis and Christine Frisinghelli. Arles: Actes Sud, 2003.
Bourdieu, Pierre. "Participant Objectivation," *The Journal of the Royal AnthropologicalInstitute* 9, 2 (June 2003): 281–294.
Bourdieu, Pierre. "Algerian Landing," trans. Loïc Wacquant. *Ethnography* 5, 4 (2004): 415–443.
Bourdieu, Pierre. "The Odyssey of Reappropriation," trans. Loic Wacquant. *Ethnography* 5, 4 (2004): 617–621.
Bourdieu, Pierre. *Sketch for a Self-Analysis*, trans. Richard Nice. Cambridge: Polity, 2007.
Bourdieu, Pierre. *The Bachelor's Ball: The Crisis of Peasant Society in Béarn*, trans. Richard Nice. Cambridge: Polity, 2008 [2002].
Bourdieu, Pierre. *Esquisses algériennes*, ed. Tassadit Yacine. Paris: Seuil, 2008.
Bourdieu, Pierre and Mouloud Mammeri. "Du bon usage de l'ethnologie," *Actes de la Recherche en sciences sociales* 150 (2003): 9–18.
Bourdieu, Pierre and Jean-Claude Passeron. "Sociology and Philosophy in France since 1945: Death and Resurrection of a Philosophy without Subject," *Social Research* 34, 1 (1967): 162–212.
Bourdieu, Pierre and Jean-Claude Passeron. *Reproduction in Education, Society, and Culture*, 2nd ed., trans. Richard Nice. London: Sage Publications, 1990 [1970].

Bourdieu, Pierre and Abdelmalek Sayed. *Le Déracinement: la crise de l'agriculture traditionelle en Algérie*. Paris: Minuit, 1964.

Bourdieu, Pierre and Abdelmalek Sayed. "Paysans Déracinés: Bouleversements morphologiques et changements culturels en Algérie," *Etudes Rurales* 12 (January-March 1964): 56–94.

Bourdieu, Pierre and Antoine Spire. *"Si le monde social m'est supportable, c'est parce que je peux m'indigner."* Paris: Aube, 2002.

Bourdieu, Pierre and Loïc Wacquant. "The Organic Ethnologist of Algerian Migration," *Ethnography* 1, 2 (2000): 173–182.

Bourdieu, Pierre with Alain Darbel, Jean-Claude Rivet, and Claude Seibel. *Travail et Travailleurs en Algérie*. Paris: Mouton, 1963.

Brévié, Jules. *Islamisme contre naturisme au Soudan français*. Paris: Editions Leroux, 1923.

Broca, Paul. *Histoire des progrès des études anthropologiques depuis la fondation de la Société: Compte rendu décennal (1859–1869) lu dans la séance solenelle du 8 Juillet 1869*. Paris: A. Hennuyer, 1870.

Brun, P. Joseph. "Notes sur le *Tarikh-el-Fettach*," *Anthropos* 9 (1914): 590–596.

Carpenter, Frank G. *From Tangier to Tripoli: Morocco, Algeria, Tunisia, Tripoli, and the Sahara*. New York: Doubleday, Page and Company, 1925.

Carrère, Jean-Dominique. *Missionaires en burnous bleu: Au service de renseignements durant l'épopée marocaine*. Limoges: Charles Lavauzelle, 1973.

Charles-Roux, J. "Le Général Gallieni," *Revue de Madagascar* 1, 1 (July 1899): 7–23.

Chroniques de la Mauritanie Sénégalaise, Nacer Eddine, ed. and trans. Ismael Hamet. Paris: E. Leroux, 1911.

Clozel, François-Joseph and Roger Villamur. *Les coutumes indigènes de la Côte d'Ivoire*. Paris: A. Challamel, 1902.

Comte, Auguste. *Auguste Comte and Positivism: The Essential Writings*, ed. Gertrud Lenzer. New York: Harper and Row, 1975.

Coon, Carleton S. *A North African Story: The Anthropologist as OSS Agent, 1941–1943*. Ipswich, MA: Gambit, 1980.

Crémieux-Brillac, Jean-Louis, ed. *Voix de la liberté: Ici Londres, Vol 2: Le Monde en feu*. Paris: Documentation française, 1975–1976.

ad-Daymani, M'Hammad ibn Ahmad Yura. *Ikhbar al-ahbar bi akhbar al-abar (Renseignements des lettrés sur l'histoire des puits)*, trans. Paul Marty. Rabat: Institut des Etudes Africaines, 1991.

de Gaulle, Charles. "Discours prononcé à l'accession du transfert aux Invalides des cendres du Maréchal Lyautey," May 10, 1961, in *Discours et Messages, Volume 3: Avec le renouveau, Mai 1958-Juillet 1962*. Paris: Plon, 1970, 315–317.

de Gironcourt, Georges R. "Les inscriptions de la nécropole de Bentia (avec extraits d'une note de M. Houdas)," *Comptes-rendus des séances de l'Académie des Inscriptions et Belles-Lettres* 55, 2 (1911): 198–206.

de Gironcourt, Georges R. *Missions de Gironcourt en Afrique occidentale, 1908/1909-1911/1912; documents scientifiques*. Paris: Société de géographie, 1920.

de Gobineau, Arthur. *The Inequality of the Human Races*, trans. Adrian Collins. London: William Heineman, 1915.

Delafosse, Maurice. "Les Hamites de l'Afrique occidentale," *L'Anthropologie* V (1894): 157–172.

Delafosse, Maurice. *Sur des traces probables de civilisation égyptienne et des hommes de race blanche à la Côte d'Ivoire*. Paris: Masson, 1901.

Delafosse, Maurice. *Les états d'âme d'un colonial*. Paris: Comité de l'Afrique française, 1909.

Delafosse, Maurice. "Le clergé musulman de l'Afrique occidentale," *Revue du Monde Musulman* 11 (June 1910): 177–206.

Delafosse, Maurice. "L'état actuel de l'Islam dans l'Afrique occidentale française," *Revue du Monde Musulman* 11 (May–August 1910): 32–53.

Delafosse, Maurice. "L'âme d'un peuple africain: les bambara," *Revue d'ethnographie et de Sociologie* 2, 1–2 (1911): 10–14.

Delafosse, Maurice. "Compte rendu d'Ismael Hamet, ed. and trans., *Chroniques de la Mauritanie sénégalaise*," *Revue d'ethnographie et de sociologie* 3 (1912): 73–74.

Delafosse, Maurice. "Traditions musulmans relatives à l'origine des Peuls," *Revue du Monde Musulman* 20 (September 1912): 242–268.

Delafosse, Maurice. "Découvertes de M. Bonnel de Mézières dans la région de Tombouctou," *Revue d'ethnographie et de sociologie* 5, 5–6 (May–June 1914): 203–205.

Delafosse, Maurice. "Des soi-disant clans totémiques de l'Afrique occidentale," *Revue d'Ethnographie et des traditions populaires* 1 (1920): 87–109.

Delafosse, Maurice. "Les langues d'Afrique," *L'Anthropologie* (1920): 545–549.

Delafosse, Maurice. "Sur l'unité des langues négro-africaines," *Revue d'Ethnographie et des traditions populaires* 1 (1920): 123–128.

Delafosse, Maurice. "Compte rendu d'Arnold Van Gennep, *L'état actuel du problème totémique*," *Revue d'Ethnographie et des traditions populaires* 2 (1921): 145–147.

Delafosse, Maurice. *L'âme nègre*. Paris: Payot, 1922.

Delafosse, Maurice. "L'animisme nègre et sa résistance à l'Islamisation en Afrique Occidentale," *Revue du Monde Musulman*, March 1922: 121–163.

Delafosse, Maurice. "Compte rendu de Georges Hardy, *Les éléments de l'histoire coloniale*," *Bulletin du comité d'études historiques et scientifiques de l'Afrique occidentale française* 1922: 153–154.

Delafosse, Maurice. "Langage secret et langage conventionnel dans l'Afrique noire," *L'Anthropologie* 22 (1922): 83–92.

Delafosse, Maurice. "Les populations noirs de l'Afrique," *La Géographie* 37 (1922): 451–467.

Delafosse, Maurice. "L'affectation des élèves-administrateurs," *La Dépêche Coloniale et Maritime* 14–15 January 1923, 1–2.

Delafosse, Maurice. "L'assimilation ou le phénix colonial: Un essai de mise au point," *La Dépêche Coloniale et Maritime*, January 5, 1923, 1.

Delafosse, Maurice. "Civilisation, assimilation, association, autant de termes qu'il importe de définir," *La Dépêche Coloniale et Maritime*, January 16, 1923, 1.

Delafosse, Maurice. "Ce qu'on peut leur demander," *La Dépêche Coloniale et Maritime*, October 1, 1924, 1.

Delafosse, Maurice. "Juxtaposition, assimilation, association," *La Dépêche Coloniale et Maritime*, June 21, 1924, 1.

Delafosse, Maurice. "La leçon des faits: C'est des institutions des indigénes qu'il faut nous inspirer pour déterminer l'orientation à donner à leur évolution," *La Dépêche Coloniale et Maritime*, February 28, 1924, 1.

Delafosse, Maurice. "Le Gâna et le Mali et l'emplacement de leurs capitales," *Bulletin du Comité d'Etudes historiques et scientifiques de l'AOF* 7 (1924): 479–542.

Delafosse, Maurice. "Terminologie religieuse au Soudan," *L'Anthropologie* 24 (1924): 371–383.

Delafosse, Maurice. *Les civilisations négro-africaines*. Paris: Stock, 1925.

Delafosse, Maurice. "Les classes nominales négro-africaines: Leur disparition graduelle," *Bulletin et mémoires de la Société de linguistique de Paris* 27 (1926): 43–50.
Delafosse, Maurice. *Les Nègres.* Paris: F. Rieder, 1927.
Delafosse, Maurice. "Maurice Delafosse," *Africa* 1, 1 (January 1928): 112–115.
Delafosse, Maurice. *Histoire de l'Afrique Occidentale française*, ed. J.L. Monod, 2nd ed. Paris: Delagrave, 1931 [1925].
Delafosse, Maurice. *Les Noirs de l'Afrique*, 2nd ed. Paris: Payot, 1941 [1922].
Delafosse, Maurice. *Haut-Sénégal-Niger*, 3 vol. Paris: Maisonneuve et Larose, 1972 [1912].
Delafosse, Maurice and Lucien Hubert. *Tombouctou: Son histoire, sa conquête.* Paris: Guillaumin, 1894.
de Lanessan, Jean-Marie Antoine. *La colonisation française en Indo-Chine.* Paris: F. Alcan, 1895.
Delavignette, Robert. *Les constructeurs de la France d'Outre-Mer.* Paris: Corrêa, 1946.
de Mun, Albert. *La question ouvrière.* Paris: J. Lecoffre, 1885.
de Mun, Albert. *Ma vocation sociale: Souvenirs de la fondation de l'oeuvre des cercles catholiques d'ouvriers.* Paris: P. Lethellieux, 1908.
Depont, Octave and Xavier Coppolani. *Les confréries religieuses musulmanes: publié sous le patronage de M. Jules Cambon, Gouverneur général de l'Algérie.* Algiers: Adolphe Jourdan, 1897.
Descamps, Paul, Marcel Mauss, and Paul Rivet. "Ethnographie et Ethnologie," *Revue de Synthèse* 1, 6 (April–June 1931): 195–203.
de Slane, Baron William MacGuckin. *Catalogue des manuscripts Arabes, Bibliothèque Nationale, Département des manuscripts.* Paris: Imprimerie Nationale, 1883–1895.
de Tocqueville, Alexis. *Writings on Empire and Slavery*, ed. and trans. Jennifer Pitts. Baltimore: The Johns Hopkins University Press, 2001.
Dieterlen, Germaine. "Les résultats des missions Griaule au Soudan français (1931–1956)," *Archives de sociologie des religions* 2, 3 (January–June 1957): 137–142.
Diop, Cheikh Anta. *Antériorité des civilisations nègres: Mythe ou verité historique?* Paris: Présence africaine, 1967.
Diop, Cheikh Anta. *Precolonial Black Africa: A Comparative Study of the Political and Social Systems of Europe and Black Africa, from Antiquity to the Formation of Modern States*, trans. Harold J. Salemson. Trenton, NJ: Africa World Press, 1987 [1960].
Doutté, Edmond. *Magie et religion dans l'Afrique du Nord.* Algiers: A. Jourdan, 1908.
Exposition Coloniale Internationale: Guide Officiel, text by André Demaison. Paris: Mayeux, 1931.
Faidherbe, Louis. "Lettre de M. Faidherbe à Monsieur le Président de la Commission Centrale de la Société de géographie, Saint-Louis, le 12 Mars 1853," *Bulletin de la Société de Géographie* Série 4, 7, 37 (February 1854): 129–130.
Faidherbe, Louis. *Notice sur la colonie de Sénégal et sur les pays qui sont en relation avec elle.* Paris: A. Bertrand, 1859.
Faidherbe, Louis. "Rensignements géographiques sur la partie du Sahara comprise entre l'Oued Noun et le Soudan," *Nouvelles annales des voyages, de la géographie et de l'histoire* Série 6, 19 (August 1859): 129–156.
Faidherbe, Louis. "L'avenir du Sahara et du Soudan," *Revue maritime et coloniale* (June 1863): 221–248.
Faidherbe, Louis. "Voyage des Cinq Nasamons d'Hérodote dans l'intérieur de la Libye," *Revue Africaine. Journal des travaux de la société historique algérienne* 1 (1867): 55–71.
Faidherbe, Louis. "Sur l'ethnographie du nord de l'Afrique," *Bulletins de la Société d'anthropologie de Paris*, IIe série, 5 (1870): 48–57.

Faidherbe, Louis. "Sur le prognathisme artificial des Mauresques du Sénégal" *Bulletins de la Société d'anthropologie de Paris*, IIe série, 7 (1872): 766–768.

Faidherbe, Louis. "Epigraphie Phénicienne et Numidique (Libyque)," *Revue Africaine. Journal des travaux de la société historique algérienne* XVII (1873): 57–65.

Faidherbe, Louis. "Sur les dolmens d'Afrique," *Bulletins de la Société d'anthropologie de Paris*, IIe série, 8 (1873): 118–122.

Faidherbe, Louis. "Découverte d'une Inscription Libyque aux Canaries," *Revue Africaine. Journal des travaux de la société historique algérienne* XVIII, 103 (1874): 33–37.

Faidherbe, Louis. "Sur l'ethnologie canarienne et sur les Tamahou," *Bulletins de la Société d'anthropologie de Paris*, IIe série, 9 (1874): 141–145.

Faidherbe, Louis. *Le Sénégal: La France dans l'Afrique Occidentale*. Paris: Hachette, 1889.

Faidherbe, Louis and Paul Topinard. *Instructions sur l'anthropologie de l'Algérie*. Paris: A. Hennuyer, 1874.

Fanon, Frantz. *Les damnés de la terre*. Paris: La Découverte, 2002 [1961].

Feraoun, Mouloud. *Le fils du pauvre*. Paris: Editions du Seuil, 1954.

Feraoun, Mouloud. *Journal, 1955–1962: Reflections on the French-Algerian War*, ed. James D. LeSueur, trans. Mary Ellen Wolf and Claude Fouillade. Lincoln: University of Nebraska Press, 2000 [1962].

Feraoun, Mouloud. *La terre et le sang*. Algiers: ENAG, 2006 [1953].

Frazer, Sir James George. *The Golden Bough: A Study in Magic and Religion*. Oxford: Oxford University Press, 1994 [1890].

Frazer, Sir James George. *Totemism and Exogamy: A Treatise on Certain Early Forms of Superstition and Society*. London: Macmillan, 1910.

Gaden, Henri. "Légendes et coutumes sénégalaises: Cahiers de Yoro Diao," *Revue d'ethnographie et de sociologie* 3 (1912): 119–137; 191–202.

Gallieni, Joseph. *Voyage au Soudan français (Haut-Niger et pays de Ségou), 1879–1881*. Paris: Hachette, 1885.

Gallieni, Joseph. "Le Soudan français," *Bulletin de la Société de géographie commerciale de Paris* 10 (1887): 695–698.

Gallieni, Joseph. "La Conquête commerciale du Soudan français," *Bulletin de la Société de Géographie commerciale de Paris* 11 (1888): 288–294.

Gallieni, Joseph. *Une Colonne dans le Soudan français, 1886–1887*. Paris: Baudouin, 1888.

Gallieni, Joseph. *Deux campagnes au Soudan français*. Paris: Hachette, 1891.

Gallieni, Joseph. *Neuf ans à Madagascar*. Paris: Librairie Hachette, 1908.

Gallieni, Joseph. *Lettres de Madagascar, 1886–1905*, ed. F. Charles-Roux and G. Grandidier. Paris: Société des éditions géographiques, maritimes et coloniales, 1928.

Gallieni, Joseph. *Les Carnets de Gallieni*, ed. Gaëtan Gallieni and P.B. Gheusi. Paris: A. Michel, 1932.

Gallieni, Joseph. *Gallieni Pacificateur: écrits coloniaux de Gallieni*, ed. Hubert Deschamps and Paul Chauvet. Paris: Presses Universitaires de France, 1949.

Gallieni, Joseph. "Pages inédites des carnets du Maréchal Gallieni: Inspections en Afrique du Nord," ed. Joseph Valynseale, *L'intermédiaire des Chercheurs et Curieux* 32 (1982): 767–772, 1243–1248.

Galula, David. *Pacification in Algeria, 1956–1958*. Santa Monica, CA: RAND Corporation, 2006 [1963].

Gouvernement Général de l'Afrique Occidentale Française. *Annuaire du Gouvernement Général de l'Afrique occidentale française*. Paris: Dubois and Bauer, 1922.

Griaule, Marcel. *Conseiller de l'union française*, ed. Maurice Demarle. Paris: Nouvelles editions Latines, 1957.

Griaule, Marcel. *Méthode de l'Ethnographie*, ed. Geneviève Calame-Griaule. Paris: Presses Universitaires de France, 1957.
Griaule, Marcel. *Conversations with Ogotemmêli*, trans. Ralph Butler with Audrey I. Richards and Beatrice Hooke. London: Oxford University Press, 1965 [1948].
Gurvitch, George and Wilbert E. Moore, ed. *Twentieth Century Sociology*. New York: The Philosophical Library, 1945.
el Hamel, Chouki. *La vie intellectuelle Islamique dans le Sahel Ouest Africain: Une étude sociale de l'enseignement islamique en Mauritanie et au nord du Mali (XVIe–XIXe siècles) et traduction annotée de Fath ash-Shakur d'al-Bartili al- Walati (mort en 1805)*. Paris: L'Harmattan, 2002.
Hamet, Ismaël. "*Nour el-Eulab* (Lumière des Coeurs) de Cheïkh Otmane ben Mohammed ben Otmane dit Ibn-Foudiou," *Revue Africaine* 41, 227 (1897): 297–320; and 42, 228 (1898): 58–81.
Hamet, Ismaël. "Littérature arabe saharienne," *Revue du Monde Musulman* 12, 10 (October 1910): 194–213; and 12, 11 (November 1910): 380–405.
Hamet, Ismaël. "La civilisation Arabe en Afrique Centrale," *Revue du Monde Musulman* 14, 4 (April 1911): 1–35.
Hanoteau, A. and A. Letourneux. *La Kabylie et les coutumes Kabyles*, 2nd ed. 3 vol. Paris: Editions Bouchene, 2003 [1872].
Hardy, Georges. *Une Conquête morale: L'enseignement en AOF*. Paris: A. Colin, 1917.
Hardy, Georges. "L'education française au Maroc," *Revue de Paris* 28, 2 (April 15, 1921): 773–788.
Hardy, Georges. *Mon frère le loup: Plaidoyer pour une science vivante*. Paris: Emile Larose, 1925.
Hardy, Georges. "Maurice Delafosse," *La Revue Indigéne*, 1930: 22–26; 110–112; 206–212; 234–240.
Hardy, Georges. "Le congrès de la société indigène," *Outre-mer* 3, 4 (December 1931): 468–492.
Hardy, Georges. *Faidherbe*. Paris: Editions de l'Encyclopédie de l'Empire français, 1947.
Hardy, Georges. *Portrait de Lyautey*. Paris: Bloud et Gay, 1949.
Honneth, Axel; Hermann Kocyba and Bernd Schwebs with Pierre Bourdieu. "The Struggle for Symbolic Order: An Interview with Pierre Bourdieu," trans. J. Bleicher. *Theory, Culture and Society* 3, 3 (1986): 35–51.
Houdas, Octave. *Ethnographie de l'Algérie*. Paris: Maissonneuve Frères et Charles LeClerc, 1886.
Hough, Walter. "University of Paris," *American Anthropologist* New Series 28, 2 (April 1926): 451–452.
Hugonnet, Ferdinand. *Souvenirs d'un chef de bureau arabe*. Paris: Michel Lévy frères, 1858.
Ibn Khaldun. *Les Prolégomènes*, 3 vol., ed. and trans. Baron de Slane. Paris: Imprimerie Impériale, 1863.
Ibn Khaldun. *Histoire des Berbéres et des dynasties musulmans de l'Afrique septentrionale [Kitab al-Ibar]*, 4 vol., ed. Paul Casanova, trans. Baron de Slane. Paris: Paul Geuthner, 1925 [Algiers, 1847–1851].
Ibn Khaldun. *Discours sur l'histoire universelle (Al-Muqaddima)*, ed. and trans. Vincent Monteil. Beirut: Commission internationale pour la traduction des chefs-d'oeuvre, 1967–1968.
Institut français d'anthropologie. "Assemblée générale du 21 Mai 1930," *L'Anthropologie* 40 (1930): 453–456.

Keller, Conrad. *Madagascar, Mauritius and the Other East-African Islands*. London: S. Sonnenschein and Company, 1901.

Knight, M.M. "French Colonial Policy—The Decline of 'Association,'" *Journal of Modern History* 5, 2 (June 1933): 208–224.

Labouret, Henri. "Questions de politique indigène africaine: protectorat ou administration directe," *Outre-mer* 1, 1 (1929): 82–93.

Labouret, Henri. *Monteil: Explorateur et Soldat*. Paris: Burger-Levrault, 1937.

Labouret, Henri. *Colonisation, colonialisme, décolonisation*. Paris: Larose, 1952.

Lavisse, Ernest. "Une méthode coloniale: l'armée et la colonisation," *La Revue de Paris* 6, 3 (June 1899): 681–698.

Lavisse, Ernest. "Une méthode coloniale: politique et gouvernement," *La Revue de Paris* 6, 4 (July 1899): 54–70.

Le Play, Frédéric. *Frédéric Le Play on Family, Work, and Social Change*, ed. and trans. Catherine Bodard Silver. Chicago: University of Chicago Press, 1982.

Les Chroniques de Oualata et de Nema (Soudan Français), ed. and trans. Paul Marty. Paris: Librairie Orientaliste Paul Geuthner, 1927.

Lévi-Strauss, Claude. *La vie familiale et sociale des Indiens Nambikwara*. Paris: Société des Américanistes, 1948.

Lévi-Strauss, Claude. "L'anthropologie sociale devant l'histoire," *Annales. Histoire, Sciences Sociales* 15, 4 (July–August 1960): 625–637.

Lévi-Strauss, Claude. *Race and History*. Paris: UNESCO, 1961 [1958].

Lévi-Strauss, Claude. "Les discontinuités culturelles et le developpement économique et social," *Social Science Information* 2, 7 (1963): 7–15.

Lévi-Strauss, Claude. *Structural Anthropology*, trans. Claire Jacobson and Brooke Grundfest Schoepf. New York: Basic Books, 1963 [1958].

Lévi-Strauss, Claude. *Totemism*, trans. Rodney Needham. Boston: Beacon Press, 1963 [1962].

Lévi-Strauss, Claude. "Anthropology: Its Achievements and Future," *Current Anthropology* 7, 2 (April 1966): 124–127.

Lévi-Strauss, Claude. *The Savage Mind*, trans. George Weidenfeld and Nicolson, Ltd. Chicago: University of Chicago Press, 1966 [1962].

Lévi-Strauss, Claude. *Les structures élémentaires de la parenté*. Paris: Mouton, 1967 [1949].

Lévi-Strauss, Claude. *The Raw and the Cooked: Introduction to a Science of Mythology, Volume 1*, trans. John and Doreen Weightman. New York: Harper and Row, 1969 [1964].

Lévi-Strauss, Claude. *From Honey to Ashes: Introduction to a Science of Mythology, Volume 2*, trans. John Weightman and Doreen Weightman. New York: Harper and Row, 1973 [1966].

Lévi-Strauss, Claude. *Tristes Tropiques*, trans. John and Doreen Weightman. New York: Atheneum, 1974 [1955].

Lévi-Strauss, Claude. *The Origin of Table Manners: Introduction to a Science of Mythology, Volume 3*, trans. John Weightman and Doreen Weightman. New York: Harper and Row, 1978 [1968].

Lévi-Strauss, Claude. *The Naked Man: Introduction to a Science of Mythology, Volume 4*, trans. John and Doreen Weightman. New York: Harper and Row, 1981 [1971].

Lévi-Strauss, Claude. *The View from Afar*, trans. Joachim Neugroschel and Phoebe Hoss. New York: Basic Books, 1985 [1983].

Lévi-Strauss, Claude. *Introduction to the Work of Marcel Mauss*, trans. Felicity Baker. London: Routledge and Kegan Paul, 1987 [1950].

Lévy-Bruhl, Henri. "In Memoriam, Marcel Mauss," *Année Sociologique* 3eme série, 1 (1948–1949): 1–4.
Lévy-Bruhl, Lucien. *Les Carnets de Lucien Lévy-Bruhl*. Paris: Presses Universitaires de France, 1949.
Lévy-Bruhl, Lucien. *How Natives Think*, trans. Lilian A. Clare. London: George Allen and Unwin, 1926 [1910].
Lévy-Bruhl, Lucien. "L'Institut d'Ethnologie de l'Université de Paris," *Annales de l'Université de Paris* (1926): 205–209.
Lévy-Bruhl, Lucien. "L'Institut d'Ethnologie pendant l'année scolaire 1925–1926," *Annales de l'Université de Paris* (1927): 90–94.
Lévy-Bruhl, Lucien. *Morceaux Choisis*. Paris: Gallimard, 1936.
Lévy-Bruhl, Lucien. *The Philosophy of Auguste Comte*, trans. Kathleen de Beaumont-Klein. New York: G.P. Putnam's Sons, 1903 [1900].
Lévy-Bruhl, Lucien. *Primitive Mentality*, trans. Lilian A. Clare. New York: The Macmillan Company, 1923 [1922].
Lévy-Bruhl, Lucien. *The Soul of the Primitive*, trans. Lilian A. Clare. London: George Allen and Unwin, 1928 [1927].
London Daily News. *The Men of the Third Republic, or the Present Leaders of France*. Philadelphia: Porter and Coates, 1873.
Lugard, Lord Frederick D. "The International Institute of African Languages and Cultures," *Africa* 1, 1 (January 1928): 1–12.
Lyautey, Hubert. "Du rôle social de l'officier," *Revue des deux mondes* 61, 3 (March 15, 1891): 443–459.
Lyautey, Hubert and Joseph Gallieni. "La France à Madagascar, 20 November 1899," *La Réforme Sociale*, 4eme série, 9 (January 16, 1900): 113–139.
Lyautey, Hubert. "Le rôle colonial de l'armée," *Revue des deux mondes* 70, 1 (January 15, 1900): 309–328.
Lyautey, Hubert. "Lettres de Rabat," *Revue des deux mondes* 64, 4 (July–August 1921): 273–304.
Lyautey, Hubert. *Lettres du Tonkin et de Madagascar (1894–1899)*, 2nd ed., ed. Max Leclerc. Paris: A. Colin, 1921.
Lyautey, Hubert. "E.-M. De Vogüé," in *Le livre du centenaire: cent ans de vie française à la Revue des Deux Mondes*. Paris: Hachette, 1929: 429–444.
Lyautey, Hubert. "Eloge de l'élite," *La Revue hebdomadaire* (July 12, 1930): 212–220.
Lyautey, Hubert. *Lettres de jeunesse: Italie-1883, Danube-Grèce-Italie-1893*. Paris: Bernard Gresset, 1931.
Lyautey, Hubert. *Lettres du sud de Madagascar, 1900–1902*. Paris: A. Colin, 1935.
Lyautey, Hubert. *Vers le Maroc: lettres du Sud-Oranais, 1903–1906*, ed. Pierre Lyautey. Paris: A. Colin, 1937.
Lyautey, Hubert. *Rayonnement de Lyautey*, ed. Patrick Heidseick. Paris: Gallimard, 1941.
Lyautey, Hubert. *Choix de lettres, 1882–1919*, ed. Paul de Ponton, Comte d'Amécourt. Paris: A. Colin, 1947.
Lyautey, Hubert. *Lyautey l'africain: textes et lettres de Maréchal Lyautey*, 4 vol., ed. Pierre Lyautey. Paris: Plon, 1953–1957.
Lyautey, Hubert. *Les plus belles lettres de Lyautey*, ed. Pierre Lyautey. Paris: Calmann- Lévy, 1962.
Lyautey, Hubert. *Un Lyautey inconnu: correspondance et journals inédits, 1874–1934*, ed. André Le Révérend. Paris: Perrin, 1980.
Lyautey, Hubert. *Paroles d'action*, ed. Jean Louis Miège. Paris: Imprimerie nationale, 1995 [1927].

Lyautey, Hubert. "Réception de M. Lyautey: Discours prononcé dans la séance publique le jeudi 8 juillet 1920, Institut de France," www.academie-francaise.fr/immortels/index.html, accessed January 12, 2010.
Mammeri, Mouloud. *La colline oubliée*. Paris: Plon, 1952.
Mammeri, Mouloud. *Le sommeil du juste*. Paris: Plon, 1955.
Mammeri, Mouloud. *L'opium et le bâton*. Paris: Plon, 1965.
Mammeri, Mouloud and Pierre Bourdieu. "Dialogue sur la poésie orale en Kabylie," *Actes de la Recherche en sciences sociales* 23 (September 1978): 51–66.
Manso, Charles. *A la statue du général Faidherbe*, inaugurée à Lille, le 25 octobre 1896.
Marty, Paul. *L'Islam en Mauritanie et au Sénégal*. Paris: E. Leroux, 1916.
Marty, Paul. *Etudes sur l'Islam au Sénégal*, 2 vol. Paris: E. Leroux, 1917.
Marty, Paul. "Vingt ans de politique algérienne. Le départ de M. Luciani," *Revue du Monde Musulman* 40–41 (September–December 1920): 1–9.
Marty, Paul. *Etudes sur l'Islam et les tribus du Soudan*, 4 vol. Paris: E. Leroux, 1920–1921.
Marty, Paul. *Etudes sur l'Islam et les tribus maures: les Brakna*. Paris: E. Leroux, 1921.
Marty, Paul. *L'Islam en Guinée: Fouta-Diallon*. Paris: E. Leroux, 1921.
Marty, Paul. *Etudes sur l'Islam en Côte d'Ivoire*. Paris: E. Leroux, 1922.
Marty, Paul. *Le Maroc de demain*. Paris: Comité de l'Afrique française, 1925.
Marty, Paul. *Etudes sur l'Islam au Dahomey: le bas Dahomey, le haut Dahomey*. Paris: E. Leroux, 1926.
Marty, Paul. "L'art des Beni M'Tir," *Revue des Etudes Islamiques* 2, Cahier 4 (1928): 481–511.
Marty, Paul. "Les institutions israélites au Maroc," *Revue des Etudes Islamiques* 4, Cahier 3 (1930): 297–332.
Marty, Paul. "L'Islam et les tribus dans la colonie du Niger," *Revue des Etudes Islamiques* 4, Cahier 3 (1930): 333–432; and 5, Cahier 2 (1931): 139–240.
Marty, Paul. "Historique de la mission militaire française en Tunisie (1827–1882)," *Revue Tunisienne* 23–24 (1935): 171–207, 309–346.
Marty, Paul. "L'année liturgique musulmane à Tunis," *Revue des Etudes Islamiques* 9, Cahier 1 (1935): 1–38.
Marty, Paul. "Folklore Tunisien: L'onomastique des noms propres de personne," *Revue des Etudes Islamiques* 10, Cahier 4 (1936): 363–434.
Marty, Paul and Colonel Mangeot. "Les Touareg de la Boucle du Niger," *Bulletin du Comité des études historiques et scientifiques de l'Afrique occidentale française* 3–4 (1918): 87–136, 257–288, 432–475.
Massignon, Louis. "Une bibliothèque saharienne," *Revue du Monde Musulman* 8 (May–June 1909): 409–418.
Maunier, René. "Maurice Delafosse (1870–1926)," *Revue d'Ethnographie et des Tradtions populaires* 7, 27–28 (1926): 189–193.
Maunier, René. *Mélanges de sociologie nord-africaine*. Paris: Félix Alcan, 1930.
Mauss, Marcel. "L'ethnographie en France et à l'étranger," *Revue de Paris* 20, 5 (September–October 1913): 537–560 and 815–837.
Mauss, Marcel. "Essai sur le don: Forme et raison de l'échange dans les societies archaïques," *Année Sociologique* Nouvelle série, 1 (1923–1924): 30–186.
Mauss, Marcel. "In Memoriam: L'oeuvre inédite de Durkheim et de ses collaborateurs," *Année Sociologique* Nouvelle série, 1 (1923): 7–29.
Mauss, Marcel. "Divisions et proportions des divisions de la sociologie," *Année Sociologique* Nouvelle série, 2 (1924): 98–173.
Mauss, Marcel. "M. Marcel Mauss ... " *Documents* 2, 3 (1930): 177.

Mauss, Marcel. *Manuel d'ethnographie*. Paris: Payot, 1967 [1947].
Mauss, Marcel. *Oeuvres*, 3 vol., ed. V. Karady. Paris: Editions de Minuit, 1968–1969.
Mauss, Marcel. *Sociologie et Anthropologie*, ed. Georges Gurvitch. Paris: Presses Universitaires de France, 1968 [1950].
Mauss, Marcel. "L'oeuvre de Mauss par lui-même," *Revue française de sociologie* 20, 1 (January–March 1979): 209–220.
Mauss, Marcel. *Sociology and Psychology: Essays*, trans. Ben Brewster. London: Routledge and Kegan Paul, 1979 [1950].
Mauss, Marcel. "Notices biographiques," *Année Sociologique* Nouvelle Série, 2
el-Motaouakkel Kâti, Mahmoûd Kâti ben el-Hâdj [Ibn el-Mukhtar?]. *Tarikh el-Fettach, ou Chronique du chercheur pour servir à l'histoire des villes, des armées, et des principaux personnages de Tekrour*, ed. and trans. Octave Houdas and Maurice Delafosse. Paris: Adrien-Maissonneuve, 1964 [1913–1914].
Newsweek. "Soustelle: If de Gaulle fails ... " December 19, 1960, 32–34.
Olivier, Marcel. "Les origins et les buts de l'Exposition Coloniale," *Revue des Deux Mondes* 101, 8 (May 1, 1931): 46–57.
Olivier, Marcel. "Philosophie de l'Exposition Coloniale," *Revue des Deux Mondes* 101, 8 (November 15, 1931): 278–293.
Perroux, François, ed. *L'Algérie de demain*. Paris: Presses Universitaires de France, 1962.
Pinon, René. *L'empire de la méditerranée*. Paris: Perrin et cie, 1912.
Pitt-Rivers, Julien, ed. *Mediterranean Countrymen: Essays in the Social Anthropology of the Mediterranean*. New York: Greenwood Press, 1973.
Randau, Robert. *Le chef des porte-plum: Roman de la vie coloniale*. Paris: Harmattan, 2005 [1922].
Randau, Robert. *Les colons: Roman de la patrie algérienne*. Paris: Harmattan, 2007 [1907].
La République française. *Annales de l'Assemblée Nationale Constituante elue le 21 Octobre 1945, Débats*, vol. 3. Paris: Imprimerie des journaux officiels, 1946.
Roume, Ernest. "Avant Propos," *Outre-mer* 1, 1 (1929): 4–6.
es-Sa'di, Abderrahim ben Abdallah ben 'Imran ben 'Amir. *Tarikh es-Soudan*, ed. and trans. Octave Houdas with Edm. Benoist. Paris: Adrien-Maisonneuve, 1964 [1898–1900].
Saint-Simon, Henri. *Henri Saint-Simon (1760–1825): Selected Writings on Science, Industry and Social Organisation*, ed. and trans. Keith Taylor. New York: Holmes and Meier, 1975.
Saint-Simon, Henri. *The Political Thought of Saint-Simon*, ed. and trans. Ghita Ionescu. Oxford: Oxford University Press, 1976.
Saint-Simon, Henri and Prosper Enfantin. *Oeuvres de Saint-Simon et d'Enfantin*, 2nd ed., 47 vol., ed. E. Dentu. Paris: Librairie de la société des gens de lettres, 1865–1878.
Sartre, Jean-Paul. *Situations V: Colonialisme et néo-colonialisme*. Paris: Gallimard, 1964.
Secretariat Social d'Algérie. *Le sous-développement en Algérie*. Algiers: Editions du Secretariat Social, 1959.
Sloane, William M. *Greater France in Africa*. London: C. Scribner's Sons, 1924.
La sociologie est un sport de combat. VHS. Directed by Pierre Carles. New York: First Run/Icarus Films, 2001.
Soh, Siré Abbas. *Chroniques du Foûta Sénégalais*, ed. and trans. Maurice Delafosse with Henri Gaden. Paris: E. Leroux, 1913.
Soustelle, Jacques. "La mythologie primitive d'après M. Lévy-Bruhl," *Revue de Synthèse* 9 (February 1935): 159–161.
Soustelle, Jacques. *Mexique, terre indienne*. Paris: B. Grasset, 1936.

Soustelle, Jacques. "Musées vivants pour une culture populaire," *Vendredi* 34 (June 26, 1936): 1, 7.
Soustelle, Jacques. "La culture matérielle des Indiens Lacandons," *Journal de la Société des Américanistes* (1937): 1–95.
Soustelle, Jacques. *La famille Otomi-Pame du Mexique central*. Paris: Institut d'ethnologie, 1937.
Soustelle, Jacques. "Racisme et Colonisation," *Europe* 46 (Febuary 15, 1938): 270–276.
Soustelle, Jacques. "Lucien Lévy-Bruhl," *Europe* 49, 196 (April 1939): 533–535.
Soustelle, Jacques. *Envers et contre tout: souvenirs et documents sur la France libre*, 2 vol. Paris: R. Laffont, 1947–1950.
Soustelle, Jacques. "France, Europe and Peace," *Foreign Affairs* 26, 3 (April 1948): 497–504.
Soustelle, Jacques. "Indo-China and Korea: One Front," *Foreign Affairs* 29, 1 (October 1950): 56–66.
Soustelle, Jacques. *Lettre d'un intellectuel à quelques autres à propos de l'Algérie*. Algiers: Imprimerie officielle du gouvernement general de l'Algérie, 1955.
Soustelle, Jacques. *Aimée et souffrante Algérie*. Paris: Plon, 1956.
Soustelle, Jacques. "Nous sommes en présence en Algérie d'une entreprise aggressive de panarabisme à direction égyptienne," *Le Monde*, March 3, 1956: 1.
Soustelle, Jacques. "The Algerian Tragedy and Problems of Africa," *The World Today* 13, 8 (August 1957): 321–330.
Soustelle, Jacques. *Le Drame algérien et la décadence française: réponse au Raymond Aron*. Paris: Plon, 1957.
Soustelle, Jacques. "The Wealth of the Sahara," *Foreign Affairs* 37, 4 (July 1959): 626–636.
Soustelle, Jacques. "Algeria: An Appeal to American Opinion," Letter of June 1962, *American Opinion* 5, 7 (July–August 1962): 68.
Soustelle, Jacques. *L'espérance trahie*. Paris: L'Alma, 1962.
Soustelle, Jacques. *La page n'est pas tournée*. Paris: La Table Ronde, 1965.
Soustelle, Jacques. *Vingt-huit ans de Gaullisme*. Paris: La Table Ronde, 1968.
Soustelle, Jacques. *Progrès et liberté*. Paris: La Table Ronde, 1970.
Soustelle, Jacques. *The Four Suns: Recollections and Reflections of an Ethnologist in Mexico*, trans. E. Ross. New York: Grossman Publishers, 1971 [1967].
Soustelle, Jacques. "Les services spéciaux," *Revue Politique et Parlementaire* 74, 829 (February 1972): 54–61.
Soustelle, Jacques. *Lettre ouverte aux victimes de la décolonisation*. Paris: A. Michel, 1973.
Soustelle, Jacques. "Discours prononcé dans la séance publique le jeudi 24 Mai 1984," www.academie-francaise.fr/immortels/index.html (Jacques Soustelle), accessed December 1, 2010.
Tedzkiret en-Nisian fi akhbâr moulouk es-Soudan, ed. and trans. Octave Houdas. Paris: Adrien Maisonneuve, 1966 [1913–1914].
Tillion, Germaine. "Dans l'Aurès: Le drame des civilisations archaïques," *Annales. Histoire, Sciences Sociales* 12, 3 (July–September 1957): 393–402.
Tillion, Germaine. *Algeria: The Realities*, trans. Ronald Matthews. New York: Knopf, 1958.
Tillion, Germaine. *Les ennemis complémentaires*. Paris: Minuit, 1960.
Tillion, Germaine. *Le harem et les cousins*. Paris: Editions du Seuil, 1966.
Tillion, Germaine. *Il était une fois l'ethnographie*. Paris: Editions du Seuil, 2000.
Topinard, Paul. *L'Anthropologie* (5 édition). Paris: C. Reinwald, 1895.
Vallière, J. "Notice géographique sur le Soudan français," *Bulletin de la Société de Géographie de Paris* 8, 4 (1887): 486–521.
Van Gennep, Arnold. *Religions, moeurs et légendes: Essais d'ethnographie et de linguistique*, 2 vol. Paris: Société du Mercure de France, 1908–1909.

Van Gennep, Arnold. *Etudes d'ethnographie algérienne*. Paris: Leroux, 1911.
Van Gennep, Arnold. *En Algérie*. Paris: Mercure de France, 1914.
Van Gennep, Arnold. *L'état actuel du problème totémique*. Paris: E. Leroux, 1920.
Van Gennep, Arnold. *Traité comparatif des nationalités*. Paris: Payot et Cie, 1922.
Van Gennep, Arnold. *Le Folklore du Dauphiné*, vol. 1. Paris: Librairie Orientale et Américaine, 1932.
Van Gennep, Arnold. *The Semi-Scholars*, trans. Rodney Needham. London: Routledge and Paul, 1967.
Verneau, René. "Nécrologie—Maurice Delafosse," *L'Anthropologie* (1926): 595–597.
Vidal-Naquet, Pierre, ed. *La raison d'état: Textes publiés par le comité Maurice Audin*. Paris: Minuit, 1962.
Yacef, Saadi. *Souvenirs de la bataille d'Alger*. Paris: Julliard, 1962.
You, André [les amis de Maurice Delafosse]. *Maurice Delafosse, 1870–1926*. Paris: Société d'Editions Géographiques, Maritimes et Coloniales, 1928.

Secondary Sources—Books and Articles

Abi-Mershed, Obama. *Apostles of Modernity: Saint-Simonians and the Civilizing Mission in Algeria*. Stanford: Stanford University Press, 2010.
Achebe, Chinua. "An Image of Africa," *Research in African Literatures* 9, 1 (Spring 1978): 1–15.
Adas, Michael. *Machines as the Measure of Men: Science, Technology and Ideologies of Western Dominance*. Ithaca, NY: Cornell University Press, 1989.
Addi, Lahouari. *Sociologie et anthropologie chez Pierre Bourdieu. Le paradigm anthropologique kabyle et ses conséquences théoriques*. Paris: La Découverte, 2002.
Addi, Lahouari. "Pierre Bourdieu, l'Algérie et le pessimisme anthropologique," *Petits déjeuners de la MOM* [Maison de l'Orient de la Mediterrannée], April 19, 2007, www.mom.fr/IMG/pdf/Ptdej_Lahouari.pdf, accessed January 13, 2012.
Adnani, Hafid and Tassadit Yacine. "L'autre Bourdieu," *Awal* 27/28 (2003): 229–247.
Ageron, Charles-Robert. *Histoire de l'Algérie contemporaine (1830–1966)*. Paris: Presses Universitaires de France, 1966.
Ageron, Charles-Robert. *France coloniale ou parti colonial?* Paris: Presses Universitaires de France, 1978.
Ageron, Charles-Robert. *De l'Algérie française à l'Algérie algérienne*. Saint-Denis: Bouchène, 2005.
Ageron, Charles-Robert. *Genèse de l'Algérie algérienne*. Saint-Denis: Bouchène, 2005.
Ahmad, Zaid. *The Epistemology of Ibn Khaldun*. New York: Routledge Curzon, 2003.
Ait Aider, Aomar. *Mammeri a dit*. Tizi Ouzou, Algeria: Editions l'Odyssée, 2009.
Albertelli, Sébastien. *Les services secrets du Général de Gaulle: le BCRA, 1940–1944*. Paris: Perrin, 2009.
Amselle, Jean-Loup and Emmanuelle Sibeud, ed. *Maurice Delafosse: Entre orientalisme et ethnographie. L'itineraire d'un africaniste (1870–1926)*. Paris: Maisonneuve et Larose, 1998.
Appadurai, Arjun. *Modernity at Large: Cultural Dimensions of Globalization*. Minneapolis: University of Minnesota Press, 1996.
Arthur, W. Brian. "Competing Technologies, Increasing Returns, and Lock-In by Historical Events," *The Economic Journal* 99, 394 (March 1989): 116–131
Austen, Ralph and Jan Jansen. "History, Oral Transmission and Structure in Ibn Khaldun's Chronology of Mali Rulers," *History in Africa* 23 (1996): 17–28.

al-Azmeh, Aziz. *Ibn Khaldun in Modern Scholarship: A Study in Orientalism*. London: Third World Centre for Research and Publishing, 1981.

al-Azmeh, Aziz. *Ibn Khaldun: An Essay in Reinterpretation*. London: Frank Cass, 1982.

Ba, Oumar. *La pénétration française au Cayor du régne de Birima N'Goné Latyr à l' Intronisation de Madiodo Déguéne Codou*. Dakar: Published by the author, 1976.

Baali, Fuad. *Society, State, and Urbanism: Ibn Khaldun's Sociological Thought*. Albany: State University of New York Press, 1988.

Babou, Cheikh Anta. *Fighting the Greater Jihad: Amadu Bamba and the Founding of the Muridiyya of Senegal, 1853-1913*. Athens, OH: Ohio University Press, 2007.

Bandau, Anna, Marcel Dorigny, and Rebekka von Mallinckrodt, ed. *Les mondes coloniaux à Paris au XVIIIe siècle: Circulation et enchevêtrement des savoirs*. Paris: Karthala, 2011.

Banton, Michael. *Racial Theories*, 2nd ed. Cambridge: Cambridge University Press, 1998.

Barrows, Leland C. "General Faidherbe, the Maurel and Prom Company, and French Expansion in Senegal." PhD Dissertation, University of California at Los Angeles, 1974.

Barth, Henrik; Andre Gingrich, Robert Parkin, and Sydel Silverman. *One Discipline, Four Ways: British, German, French, and American Anthropology*. Chicago: University of Chicago Press, 2005.

Bayly, C.A. *Empire and Information: Intelligence Gathering and Social Communications in India, 1780-1870*. Cambridge: Cambridge University Press, 1996.

Bazin, René. *Charles de Foucauld: Explorateur du Maroc, ermite au Sahara*. Paris: Plon-Nourrit et cie, 1921.

Becker, Charles, Saliou Mbaye, and Ibrahima Thioub, ed. *AOF: réalités et héritages. Sociétés oust-africaines et ordre colonial, 1895-1960*. Dakar: Direction des Archives du Sénégal, 1997.

Belmont, Nicole. *Arnold Van Gennep: The Creator of French Ethnography*, trans. Derek Coltman. Chicago: University of Chicago Press, 1979.

Ben Hamouche, Mustapha. *Dar es-Sultân: l'algérois à l'époque ottomane: gestion urbaine et aménagement du territoire*. Algiers: Dar el-bassair, 2009

Bercher, L. "Paul Marty, 1882-1938: Necrologie," *Revue Tunisienne* 33-34 (1938): 15-17.

Berenson, Edward. *Heroes of Empire: Five Charismatic Men and the Conquest of Africa*. Berkeley: University of California Press, 2011.

Berndt, Jeremy. "Closer than Your Jugular Vein: Muslim Intellectuals in a Malian Village, 1900 to the 1960s," PhD Dissertation, Northwestern University, 2008.

Bernhard, Jacques. *Gallieni: le destin inachevé*. Vagney: G. Louis, 1991.

Berque, Jacques. *Maghreb, Histoire et Sociétés*. Gembloux: Duculot, 1974.

Bertholet, Denis. *Claude Lévi-Strauss*. Paris: Plon, 2003.

Besnard, Philippe. "La formation de l'équipe de l'Année Sociologique," *Revue française de sociologie* 20, 1 (January-March 1979): 7-31.

Betts, Raymond. *Assimilation and Association in French Colonial Theory, 1890-1914*. New York: Columbia University Press, 1961.

Bingin, R. James; David Robinson, and John M. Staatz, ed. *Democracy and Development in Mali*. East Lansing: Michigan State University Press, 2000.

Blanchard, Pascal and Sandrine Lemaire, ed. *Culture Coloniale: La France conquise par son empire, 1871-1931*. Paris: Editions Autrement, 2003.

Blanckaert, Claude, ed. *Les politiques de l'anthropologie: Discours et pratiques en France (1860-1940)*. Paris: Harmattan, 2001.

Bonte, Pierre, Edouard Conte, Constant Hamès, and Abdel Wedoud Ould Cheikh, ed. *Al-Ansâb: La quête des origines. Anthropologie historique de la société tribale arabe*. Paris: Editions de la maison des sciences de l'homme, 1991.
Boon, James A. *Other Tribes, Other Scribes: Symbolic Anthropology in the Comparative Study of Cultures, Histories, religions, and texts*. New York: Cambridge University Press, 1982.
Borneman, John and Abdellah Hammoudi, ed. *Being There: The Fieldwork Encounter and the Meaning of Truth*. Berkeley: University of California Press, 2009.
Bourdieu, Pierre. *The State Nobility: Elite Schools in the Field of Power*, trans. Lauretta C. Clough. Stanford: Stanford University Press, 1996 [1989].
Bouveresse, Jacques. *Bourdieu: savant et politique*. Marseilles: Agone, 2003.
Bowler, Kimberly A. "'It Is Not in a Day that a Man Abandons His Morals and Habits': The Arab Bureau, Land Policy, and the Doineau Trial in Algeria, 1830–1870." PhD Dissertation, Duke University, 2011.
Brenner, Louis. *Controlling Knowledge: Religion, Power and Schooling in a West African Muslim Society*. Bloomington: Indiana University Press, 2001.
Brocheux, Pierre and Daniel Hémery. *Indochina: An Ambiguous Colonization, 1858–1954*, trans. Ly Lan Dill-Klein with Eric Jennings, Nora Taylor, and Noémi Tousignant. Berkeley: University of California Press, 2009.
Bromberger, Christian and Tzvetan Todorov. *Germaine Tillion, une ethnologue dans le siècle*. Arles: Actes Sud, 2002.
Brower, Benjamin C. *A Desert Named Peace: The Violence of France's Empire in the Algerian Sahara, 1844–1902*. New York: Columbia University Press, 2009.
Burke, Edmund III. *The Ethnographic State: France and the Invention of Moroccan Islam*. Berkeley: University of California Press, 2014.
Burke, Edmund III and David Prochaska, ed. *Genealogies of Orientalism: History, Theory, Politics*. Lincoln: University of Nebraska Press, 2008.
Candea, Matti. *Corsican Fragments: Difference, Knowledge, and Fieldwork*. Bloomington: Indiana University Press, 2010.
Cazeneuve, Jean. *Lucien Lévy-Bruhl*, trans. Peter Rivière. New York: Harper and Row, 1972.
Chafer, Tony and Amanda Sackur, ed. *Promoting the Colonial Idea: Propaganda and Visions of Empire in France*. New York: Palgrave, 2002.
Chakrabarty, Dipesh. *Provincializing Europe: Postcolonial Thought and Historical Difference*. Princeton: Princeton University Press, 2000.
Chaturvedi, Vinayak, ed. *Mapping Subaltern Studies and the Postcolonial*. London: Verso, 2000.
Charle, Christophe. *Naissance des "intellectuels": 1880–1910*. Paris: Minuit, 1990.
Charle, Christophe. *La république des universitaires, 1870–1940*. Paris: Seuil, 1994.
Christelow, Allen. *Muslim Law Courts and the French Colonial State in Algeria*. Princeton: Princeton University Press, 1985.
Clancy-Smith, Julia. *Rebel and Saint: Muslim Notables, Populist Protest, Colonial Encounters (Algeria and Tunisia, 1800–1904)*. Berkeley: University of California Press, 1994.
Clark, Terry N. *Prophets and Patrons: The French University and the Emergence of the Social Sciences*. Cambridge, MA: Harvard University Press, 1973.
Cleaveland, Timothy. *Becoming Walata: A History of Saharan Social Formation and Transformation*. Portsmouth, NH: Heinemann, 2002.
Clifford, James. "On Ethnographic Authority," *Representations* 2 (Spring 1983): 118–146.

Clifford, James. *The Predicament of Culture: Twentieth-Century Ethnography, Literature, and Art*. Cambridge, MA: Harvard University Press, 1988.
Clifford, James. *Person and Myth: Maurice Leenhardt in the Melanesian World*. Durham, NC: Duke University Press, 1992 [1982].
Clifford, James and George E. Marcus, ed. *Writing Culture: The Poetics and Politics of Ethnography*. Berkeley: University of California Press, 1986.
Cohen, William B. *Rulers of Empire: The French Colonial Service in Africa*. Stanford: Hoover Institution Press, 1971.
Cohen, William B. *The French Encounter with Africans: White Response to Blacks, 1530–1880*. Bloomington: Indiana University Press, 1980.
Cohen-Solal, Annie. *Sartre, 1905–1980*. Paris: Gallimard, 1999.
Colin-Jenvoine, Emmanuelle and Stéphane Derozier. *Le financement du FLN pendant la guerre d'Algérie, 1954–1962*. Saint-Denis: Bouchène, 2008.
Conklin, Alice. *A Mission to Civilize: The Republican Ideal of Empire in France and West Africa, 1895–1930*. Palo Alto: Stanford University Press, 1997.
Conklin, Alice. "Civil Society, Science, and Empire in Late Republican France: The Foundation of Paris's Museum of Man," *Osiris* 17 (2002): 255–292.
Conklin, Alice. "The New 'Ethnology' and 'La Situation Coloniale' in Interwar France," *French Politics, Culture and Society* 20, 2 (2002): 29–46.
Conklin, Alice. *In the Museum of Man: Race, Anthropology, and Empire in France, 1850–1950*. Ithaca, NY: Cornell University Press, 2013.
Connelly, Matthew. *A Diplomatic Revolution: Algeria's Fight for Independence and the Origin of the Post-Cold War Era*. New York: Oxford University Press, 2002.
Cooper, Frederick. *Decolonization and African Society: The Labor Question in French and British Africa*. Cambridge: Cambridge University Press, 1996.
Cooper, Frederick. *Colonialism in Question: Theory, Knowledge, History*. Berkeley: University of California Press, 2005.
Cooper, Frederick and Ann Laura Stoler, ed. *Tensions of Empire: Colonial Cultures in a Bourgeois World*. Durham, NC: Duke University Press, 1997.
Copans, Jean. "L'Afrique noire comme paradigme fondateur des sciences sociales françaises et francophones du développement," *Ethnologie française* 41, 3 (2011): 405–414.
Coquery-Vidrovitch, Catherine and Odile Goerg, ed. *L'Afrique occidentale au temps des français: Colonisateurs et colonisés, c. 1860–1960*. Paris: La Découverte, 1992.
Coquery-Vidrovitch, Catherine and Henri Moniot. *L'Afrique noire de 1800 à nos jours*, 3rd ed. Paris: Presses Universitaires de France, 1992.
Corcuff, Philippe. *Bourdieu autrement: fragilités d'un sociologue de combat*. Paris: Textuel, 2003.
Crews, Robert D. *For Prophet and Tsar: Islam and Empire in Russian and Central Asia*. Cambridge, MA: Harvard University Press, 2006.
Crossley, Ceri. *French Historians and Romanticism: Thierry, Guizot, the Saint-Simonians, Quinet, Michelet*. New York: Routledge, 1993.
Cruise-O'Brien, Donal, Momar Coumba Diop, and Mamadou Diouf, ed. *La construction de l'état en Sénégal*. Paris: Karthala, 2003.
Curtin, Philip. *Cross-Cultural Trade in World History*. Cambridge: University of Cambridge Press, 1984.
Datta, Venita. *Birth of a National Icon: The Literary Avant-Garde and the Birth of the Intellectual in France*. Albany: State University of New York Press, 1999.
David, Paul A. "Clio and the Economics of QWERTY," *American Economic Review* 75, 2 (May 1985): 332–337.

Dean, William T., III, "Strategic Dilemmas of Colonization: France and Morocco during the Great War," *The Historian* 73, 4 (December 2011): 730-746.
Debaene, Vincent. *L'adieu au voyage: L'ethnologie française entre science et littérature*. Paris: Gallimard, 2010.
de Durand-Forest, Jacqueline. "Georgette Soustelle (1909-1999)," *Journal de la société des Américanistes* 85 (1999): 428-432.
de Ganay, Solange; Annie Lebeuf and Jean-Paul Lebeuf, and Dominique Zahan, ed. *Ethnologiques: Hommages à Marcel Griaule*. Paris: Hermann, 1987.
de Jong, Louis. *The Collapse of a Colonial Society: The Dutch in Indonesia during the Second World War*, trans. Jennifer Kilian, Cornelia Kist, and John Rudge. Leiden: KITLV Press, 2002 [1984-1986].
Delafosse, Louise. *Maurice Delafosse: le Berrichon conquis par l'Afrique*. Abbeville: F. Paillart, 1976.
de l'Estoile, Benoît, Federico Neiburg, and Lygia Sigaud, ed. *Empires, Nations, and Natives: Anthropology and State-Making*. Durham, NC: Duke University Press, 2005.
Deleuze, Gilles and Félix Guattari. *Capitalism and Schizophrenia, Volume II: A Thousand Plateaus*, trans. Brian Massumi. Minneapolis: University of Minnesota Press, 1987 [1980].
Delsaut, Yvette and Marie-Christine Rivière. *Bibliographie des travaux de Pierre Bourdieu*. Pantin: Le Temps des Cerises, 2002.
Desai, Gaurav. *Subject to Colonialism: African Self-Fashioning and the Colonial Library*. Durham, NC: Duke University Press, 2001.
Desbordes, Christian. "Jacques Soustelle et la défense de l'Occident." PhD Dissertation, University of Auvergne, 2000.
de Tarde, Guillaume. "La pensée politique de Lyautey," *Revue des Deux Mondes* 132, 3 (February 1960): 385-397.
Diouf, Mamadou. "The Senegalese Murid Trade Diaspora and the Making of a Vernacular Cosmopolitanism," *Public Culture* 12, 3 (2000): 679-702.
Dirks, Nicholas B. "Castes of Mind," *Representations* 37 (Winter 1991): 56-78.
Dirks, Nicholas B., ed. *Colonialism and Culture*. Ann Arbor: The University of Michigan Press, 1992.
Dirks, Nicholas B. *Castes of Mind*. Princeton: Princeton University Press, 2001.
Doury, Paul. *Lyautey: un saharien atypique*. Paris: L'Harmattan, 2002.
Drake, David. *Sartre*. London: Haus, 2005.
Drayton, Richard H. *Nature's Government: Science, Imperial Britain, and the "Improvement" of the World*. New Haven: Yale University Press, 2000.
Duchet, Michèle. *Anthropologie et Histoire au siècle des Lumières: Buffon, Voltaire, Rousseau, Helvétius, Diderot*, 2nd ed. Paris: Flammarion, 1977.
Durosoy, Maurice. *Avec Lyautey: homme de guerre, homme de paix*. Paris: Nouvelles Editions Latines, 1976.
Ellis, Stephen. "The Political Elite of Imerina and the Revolt of the Menalamba: The Creation of a Colonial Myth in Madagascar, 1895-1898," *Journal of African History* 21, 2 (1980): 219-234.
Emerit, Marcel. *Les Saint-Simoniens en Algérie*. Paris: Les Belles Lettres, 1941.
d'Esmé, Jean. *Gallieni: destin hors série*. Paris: Plon, 1965.
Evans, Martin. *Algeria: France's Undeclared War*. Oxford: Oxford University Press, 2012.
Fabian, Johannes. *Time and the Other: How Anthropology Makes Its Object*. New York: Columbia University Press, 1983.
Faivre, Maurice. "Le Colonel Paul Schoen du SLNA au Comité Parodi," *Guerres mondiales et conflits contemporains* 208 (October-December 2002): 69-89.

Faligot, Roger. *La piscine: The French secret service since 1944*, trans. W.D. Halls. New York: Blackwell, 1989.
Farias, P.F. de Moraes. *Arabic Medieval Inscriptions from the Republic of Mali: Epigraphy, Chronicles, and Songhay-Tuareg History*. Oxford: Published for the British Academy by Oxford University Press, 2003.
Feierman, Steven. *Peasant Intellectuals: Anthropology and History in Tanzania*. Madison: University of Wisconsin Press, 1990.
Ferry, Luc and Alain Renaut. *French Philosophy of the Sixties: An Essay on Antihumanism*, trans. Mary H.S. Cattani. Amherst: University of Massachusetts Press, 1990 [1985].
Fletcher, Angus, ed. *Literature of Fact: Selected Papers from the English Institute*. New York: Columbia University Press, 1975.
Foos, Paul W. *A Short, Offhand Killing Affair: Soldiers and Social Conflict during the Mexican-American War*. Chapel Hill: University of North Carolina Press, 2002.
Forget, Nelly. "Le service des centres sociaux en Algérie," *Matériaux pour l'histoire de notre temps* 26 (1992): 37–47.
Forth, Christopher E. *The Dreyfus Affair and the Crisis of French Manhood*. Baltimore: Johns Hopkins University Press, 2004.
Foucault, Michel. *The Order of Things: An Archaeology of the Human Sciences*. New York: Random House, 1970 [1966].
Foucault, Michel. "La vie: L'expérience et la science," *Revue de métaphysique et de morale* 90, 1 (January–March 1985): 3–14.
Foucault, Michel. *Dits et Ecrits: 1954–1988*, 4 vol. Paris: Gallimard, 1998.
Fournier, Marcel. "Pierre Bourdieu: la sociologie est un sport de haut niveau," *Awal* 27/28 (2003): 55–67.
Fournier, Marcel. *Marcel Mauss: A Biography*, trans. Jane Marie Todd. Princeton: Princeton University Press, 2006.
Galland, Jean. *L'indépendance, un combat qui continue*. Paris: Tirésias, 2007.
Gann, L.H. and Peter Duignan, ed. *African Proconsuls: European Governors in Africa*. New York: Free Press, 1978.
Geertz, Clifford. *Works and Lives: The Anthropologist as Author*. Stanford: Stanford University Press, 1988.
Gerassi, John. *Jean-Paul Sartre: Hated Conscience of his Century*. Chicago: University of Chicago Press, 1989.
Girardet, Raoul. *L'idée coloniale en France de 1871 à 1962*. Paris: La Table Ronde, 1972.
Glassman, Jonathon. "Slower than a Massacre: The Multiple Sources of Racial Thought in Colonial Africa," *American Historical Review* 109, 3 (2004): 720–754.
Godlewska, Anne. "Traditions, Crisis, and New Paradigms in the Rise of the Modern French Discipline of Geography, 1760–1850," *Annals of the Association of American Geographers* 79, 2 (1989): 192–213.
Goodman, Jane and Paul A. Silverstein, ed. *Bourdieu in Algeria: Colonial Politics, Ethnographic Practices, Theoretical Developments*. Lincoln: University of Nebraska Press, 2009.
Goody, Jack, ed. *Literacy in Traditional Societies*. Cambridge: Cambridge University Press, 1968.
Gosnell, Jonathan K. *The Politics of Frenchness in Colonial Algeria, 1930–1954*. Rochester, NY: The University of Rochester Press, 2002.
Greene, Norman H. *Jean-Paul Sartre: The Existentialist Ethic*. Ann Arbor: The University of Michigan Press, 1960.

Grémont, Charles. *Les Touaregs Iwellemmedan, 1647–1896: Un ensemble politique de la boucle du Niger*. Paris: Karthala, 2010.
Grenfell, Michael. *Pierre Bourdieu, Agent Provocateur*. New York: Continuum, 2004.
Grimal, Henri. *Decolonization, the British, French, Dutch, and Belgian Empires, 1919–1963*, trans. Stephan De Vos. Boulder, CO: Westview Press, 1978 [1965].
Gringeri, Anthony R., Jr. "Twilight of the Sun Kings: French Anthropology from Modernism to Postmodernism, 1925–50." PhD Dissertation, University of California, Berkeley, 1990.
Société française d'histoire d'outre-mer. *La guerre d'Algérie: Au miroir des décolonisations françaises, Actes du colloque International*. Paris: Société française d'histoire d'outre-mer, 2000.
Hall, Bruce S. "The Question of 'Race' in the Pre-Colonial Southern Sahara," *Journal of North African Studies* 10, 3 (2005): 339–367.
Hall, Bruce S. "Bellah Histories of Decolonization, Iklan Paths to Freedom: The Meanings of Race and Slavery in the Late-Colonial Niger Bend (Mali), 1944–1960," *International Journal of African Historical Studies* 44, 1 (2011): 61–87.
Hall, Bruce S. *A History of Race in Muslim West Africa, 1600–1960*. Cambridge: Cambridge University Press, 2011.
Hammoudi, Abdellah. *Master and Disciple: The Cultural Foundations of Moroccan Authoritarianism*. Chicago: The University of Chicago Press, 1997.
Hanretta, Sean. *Islam and Social Change in French West Africa: History of an Emancipatory Community*. New York: Cambridge University Press, 2009.
Harbi, Mohammed. *Le F.L.N.: Mirage et réalité*. Paris: Editions J.A., 1980.
Harris, Ruth. *Dreyfus: Politics, Emotion, and the Scandal of the Century*. New York: Henry Holt, 2010.
Harrison, Christopher. *France and Islam in West Africa, 1860–1960*. Cambridge: Cambridge University Press, 1988.
Hecht, Jennifer Michael. "The Solvency of Metaphysics: The Debate over Racial Science and Moral Philosophy in France, 1890–1914," *Isis* 90, 1 (1999): 1–24.
Heffernan, Michael J. "The Limits of Utopia: Henri Duveyrier and the Exploration of the Sahara in the Nineteenth Century," *The Geographical Journal* 155, 3 (1989): 342–352.
Heffernan, Michael J. "A State Scholarship: The Political Geography of French International Science during the Nineteenth Century," *Transactions of the Institute of British Geographers*, New Series 19, 1 (1994): 21–45.
Heidseick, Patrick. "Lyautey et les rapports franco-musulmans," *Etudes* 87, 283 (October 1954): 62–69.
Hill, J.N.C. *Identity in Algerian Politics: The Legacy of Colonial Rule*. Boulder: Lynne Rienner Publishers, 2009.
Hoisington, William A., Jr. *Lyautey and the French Conquest of Morocco*. New York: St. Martin's Press, 1995.
Hoisington, William A., Jr. "Designing Morocco's Future: France and the Native Policy Council, 1921–1925," *Journal of North African Studies* 5, 1 (2000): 63–108.
Horne, Alistair. *A Savage War of Peace: Algeria 1954–1962*, 4th ed. New York: New York Review of Books, 2006 [1977].
Hughes, H. Stuart. *Consciousness and Society: The Reorientation of European Social Thought, 1890–1930*. New York: Knopf, 1958.
Hunwick, John O. *Timbuktu and the Songhay Empire: Al-Sa'di's Ta'rikh al-Sudan down to 1613 and other contemporary documents*. Boston: Brill, 1999.
Inden, Ronald. *Imagining India*. New York: Basil Blackwell, 1990.

Jackson, Henry F. *The FLN in Algeria: Party Development in a Revolutionary Society*. Westport, CT: Greenwood Press, 1977.
James, Wendy. "The Treatment of African Ethnography in 'L'Année sociologique,'" *Année Sociologique* Série 3, 48, 1 (1998): 193–207.
James, Wendy and N.J. Allen, ed. *Marcel Mauss: A Centenary Tribute*. New York: Berghahn Books, 1998.
Johnson, Christopher. "Anthropology and the *Sciences Humaines*: The Voice of Lévi-Strauss," *History of the Human Sciences* 10, 3 (1997): 122–133.
Johnson, Christopher. *Claude Lévi-Strauss: The Formative Years*. Cambridge: Cambridge University Press, 2003.
Julien, Charles-André. *L'Afrique du nord en marche: Algérie-Tunisie-Maroc, 1880–1952*. Paris: Omnibus, 2002 [1952].
Kanya-Forstner, A.S. *The Conquest of the Western Sudan: A Study in French Military Imperialism*. London: Cambridge University Press, 1969.
Karady, Victor. "Le problème de légitimité dans l'organisation historique de l'ethnologie française," *Revue française de sociologie* 23, 1 (January–March 1982): 17–35.
Kent, John. *The Internationalization of Colonialism: Britain, France, and Black Africa, 1939–1956*. Oxford: Clarendon Press, 1992.
Khalidi, Tarif. *Arabic Historical Thought in the Classical Period*. Cambridge: Cambridge University Press, 1994.
Koditschek, Theodore. *Liberalism, Imperialism, and the Historical Imagination: Nineteenth-Century Visions of a Greater Britain*. Cambridge: Cambridge University Press, 2011.
Kramer, Paul. *The Blood of Government: Race, Empire, the United States, and the Philippines*. Chapel Hill: University of North Carolina Press, 2006.
Kratti, Graziano and Ghislaine Lydon, ed. *The Trans-Saharan Book Trade: Arabic Literacy, Manuscript Culture, and Intellectual History in Islamic History*. Leiden: Brill, 2011.
Kuhn, Thomas S. *The Structure of Scientific Revolutions*. Chicago: The University of Chicago Press, 1996 [1962].
Lacouture, Jean. *Le témoignage est un combat: une biographie de Germaine Tillion*. Paris: Seuil, 2000.
Laurière, Christine. *Paul Rivet: Le savant et le politique*. Paris: Publications Scientifiques du Muséum national d'histoire naturelle, 2008.
Latour, Bruno. *Science in Action: How to Follow Scientists and Engineers through Society*. Cambridge, MA: Harvard University Press, 1987.
Lawrance, Benjamin N., Emily Lynn Osborn, and Richard L. Roberts, ed. *Intermediaries, Interpreters, and Clerks: African Employees in the Making of Colonial Africa*. Madison: University of Wisconsin Press, 2006.
Lawrence, Bruce B., ed. *Ibn Khaldun and Islamic Ideology*. London: Brill, 1984.
Lazreg, Marnia. "The Reproduction of Colonial Ideology: The Case of the Kabyle Berbers," *Arab Studies Quarterly* 5, 4 (1983): 380–395.
Lebovics, Herman. *True France: The Wars over Cultural Identity, 1900–1945*. Ithaca: Cornell University Press, 1992.
Lecocq, Baz. *Disputed Desert: Decolonisation, Competing Nationalisms and Tuareg Rebellions in Northern Mali*. Leiden: Brill, 2010.
Lefebvre, Camille. "We Have Tailored Africa: French Colonialism and the 'Artificiality' of Africa's Borders in the Interwar Period." *Journal of Historical Geography* 37 (2011): 191–202.
Lefebvre, Camille. "Le temps des lettres: Échanges diplomatiques entre sultans, émirs, et officiers français, Niger 1899–1903." *Monde(s)* 5 (May 2014): 57–80.

Le Révérend, André. "Lyautey écrivain: 1854–1934." PhD Dissertation, University of Montpellier III, 1974.
Le Révérend, André. *Lyautey*. Paris: Fayard, 1983.
Leroux, Robert. *Histoire et sociologie en France: De l'histoire-science à la sociologie durkheimienne*. Paris: Presses Universitaires de France, 1998.
Le Sueur, James D. *Uncivil War: Intellectuals and Identity Politics during the Decolonization of Algeria*. 2nd ed. Lincoln: University of Nebraska Press, 2005 [2001].
Levtzion, Nehemia. "A Seventeenth-Century Chronicle by Ibn al-Mukhtar: A Critical Study of 'Ta'rikh al-fattash,'" *Bulletin of the School of Oriental and African Studies, University of London* 34, 3 (1971): 571–593.
Lorcin, Patricia M.E. *Imperial Identities: Stereotyping, Prejudice and Race in Colonial Algeria*. New York: St. Martin's, 1995.
Lorcin, Patricia M.E. "Imperialism, Colonial Identity, and Race in Algeria, 1830–1870: The Role of the French Medical Corps," *Isis* 90, 4 (1999): 653–679.
Lorcin, Patricia M.E, ed. *Algeria and France, 1800–2000: Identity, Memory, Nostalgia*. Syracuse, NY: Syracuse University Press, 2006.
Lyautey, Pierre. *Gallieni*, 3rd ed. Paris: Gallimard, 1959.
MacMaster, Neil. *Burning the Veil: The Algerian War and the "emancipation" of Muslim Women, 1954–62*. Manchester: Manchester University Press, 2009.
Mahdi, Muhsin. *Ibn Khaldun's Philosophy of History: A Study in the Philosophic Foundation of the Science of Culture*. London: G. Allen and Unwin, 1957.
Manchuelle, François. "Assimilés ou patriotes africains? Naissance du nationalisme culturel en Afrique française (1853–1931)," *Cahiers d'études africaines* 35, Cahiers 138/139 (1995): 333–368.
Mandouze, André, ed. *La révolution algérienne par les textes*. Paris: Maspero, 1961.
Mann, Gregory. "Fetishizing Religion: Allah Koura and French 'Islamic Policy' in Late Colonial French Soudan (Mali)," *Journal of African History* 44, 2 (2003): 263–282.
Martin-Criado, Enrique. *Les deux Algéries de Pierre Bourdieu*, trans. Hélène Bretin. Bellecombe-en-Bauges: Editions de Croquant, 2008.
Mathias, Grégor. *Les sections administratives spécialisées en Algérie: Entre idéal et réalité*. Paris: Harmattan, 1998.
Mbacké Majalis, Abdoul Aziz. "Bamba et Marty," www.sudonline.sn, accessed January 12, 2011.
M'bayo, Tamba Eadric. "African Interpreters, Mediation, and the Production of Knowledge in Colonial Senegal: The Lower and Middle Senegal Valley, ca. 1850s to ca. 1920s." PhD Dissertation, Michigan State University, 2009.
McDougall, James. *History and the Culture of Nationalism in Algeria*. Cambridge: Cambridge University Press, 2006.
McDowell, William. "From Entente Cordiale to Algeciras Conference: The Interplay of German Foreign and Domestic Policy during the First Moroccan Crisis." PhD Dissertation, University of Edinburgh, 1984.
McLaughlin, Glen. "Sufi, Saint, Sharif: Muhammad Fadil Wuld Mamin, His Spiritual Legacy and the Political Economy of the Sacred in Nineteenth Century Mauritania." PhD Dissertation, Northwestern University, 1997.
Megherbi, Abdelghani. *La pensée sociologique d'Ibn Khaldoun*. Algiers: Casbah Editions, 2010.
M'halla, Moncef. *Lire la Muqqadima d'Ibn Khaldun: deux concepts-clés de la théorie Khaldunienne, asabiya et taghallub (force et domination)*. Tunis: Centre de Publication Universitaire, 2007.

Michel, Marc. "Un programme réformiste en 1919: Maurice Delafosse et la 'politique indigène' en AOF," *Cahiers d'Etudes Africaines* 15, 58 (1975): 313–327.
Michel, Marc. *Gallieni*. Paris: Fayard, 1989.
Miquel, Pierre. *Les polytechniciens*. Paris: Plon, 1994.
Mitchell, Allan. *Victors and Vanquished: The German Influence on Army and Church in France after 1870*. Chapel Hill: University of North Carolina Press, 1984.
Morsy, Magali, ed. *Les Saint-Simoniens et l'Orient: Vers la modernité*. Aix-en-Provence: Edisud, 1989.
Moussa, Sarga, ed. *L'idée de "race" dans les sciences humaines et la littérature (XVIIIe–XIXe siècles)*. Paris: L'Harmattan, 2003.
Mucchielli, Laurent. "Aux origines de la nouvelle histoire en France: L'évolution intellectuelle et la formation du champ des sciences sociales (1880–1930)," *Revue de synthèse* 4, 1 (January–March 1995): 55–98.
Mucchielli, Laurent. "Aux origines de la psychologie universitaire en France (1870–1900): Enjeux intellectuels, contexte politique, réseaux et stratégies d'alliance autour de la *Revue Philosophique* de Théodule Ribot," *Annals of Science* 55 (1998): 263–289
Mucchielli, Laurent. *Mythes et histoire des sciences humaines*. Paris: La Découverte, 2004.
Murphrey, Elizabeth H. "Jacques Soustelle and the Passing of French Algeria." PhD Dissertation, Duke University, 1976.
Neale, Caroline. *Writing "Independent" History: African Historiography, 1960–1980*. Westport, CT: Greenwood Press, 1985.
Norris, H.T. *Saharan Myth and Saga*. Oxford: Clarendon Press, 1972.
Norris, H.T. *The Arab Conquest of the Western Sahara*. Harlow, Essex: Longman, 1986.
Nouschi, André. "Autour de *Sociologie de l'Algérie*," *Awal* 27/28 (2003): 29–35.
Nouvel, Maguelone. *Frédéric Le Play: Une réforme sociale sous le second empire*. Paris: Economica, 2009.
Nye, Robert A. *Masculinity and Male Codes of Honor in Modern France*. Oxford: Oxford University Press, 1993.
Oostindie, Gert and Inge Klinkers. *Decolonising the Caribbean: Dutch Policies in a Comparative Perspective*. Amsterdam: Amsterdam University Press, 2003.
Ortner, Sherry. *Anthropology and Social Theory: Culture, Power, and the Acting Subject*. Durham, NC: Duke University Press, 2006.
Osborne, Michael A. *Nature, the Exotic, and the Science of French Colonialism*. Bloomington: Indiana University Press, 1994.
Ould Cheikh, Abdel Wedoud. "Nomadisme, Islam et pouvoir politique dans la société maure précoloniale (XIème-XIXème siècle): Essai sur quelques aspects du tribalisme," 3 vol. PhD Dissertation, University of Paris V, 1985.
Ould Cheikh, Abdel Wedoud. *Eléments d'histoire de la Mauritanie*. Nouakchott: Institut Mauritanien de Recherche Scientifique, 1991.
Pagden, Anthony. *The Fall of Natural Man: The American Indian and the Origins of Comparative Ethnology*. New York: Cambridge University Press, 1982.
Paligot, Carole Reynaud. *La République Raciale: Paradigme racial et idéologie républicaine (1860–1930)*. Paris: Presses Universitaires de France, 2006.
Paligot, Carole Reynaud. *De l'identité nationale: Science, race, et politique en Europe et aux Etats-Unis, XIXe-XXe siècle*. Paris: Presses Universitaires de France, 2011.
Peabody, Sue and Tyler Stovall, ed. *The Color of Liberty: Histories of Race in France*. Durham, NC: Duke University Press, 2003.
Pellegrin, Arthur and Louis Massignon. *Un Africain: le Lt-Colonel Paul Marty, sa vie et son oeuvre*. Tunis: Editions de la Kahena, 1939.

Pinto, Louis; Gisèle Shapiro and Patrick Champagne, ed. *Pierre Bourdieu, sociologue*. Paris: Fayard, 2004.
Piriou, Anne and Emmanuelle Sibeud, ed. *L'Africanisme en questions*. Paris: Centre d'Etudes Africaines, Ecole des Hautes Etudes en Sciences Sociales, 1997.
Pitts, Jennifer. *A Turn to Empire: The Rise of Imperial Liberalism in Britain and France*. Princeton: Princeton University Press, 2005.
Poirier, Jean. "Marcel Mauss et l'élaboration de la science ethnologique," *Journal de la Société des Océanistes* 6 (1950): 212–219.
Porch, Douglas. *The Conquest of Morocco*. New York: Alfred A. Knopf, 1983.
Porch, Douglas. *The Conquest of the Sahara*, 2nd ed. New York: Farrar, Straus and Giroux, 2005 [1984].
Pyenson, Lewis. *Civilizing Mission: Exact Sciences and French Overseas Expansion, 1830–1940*. Baltimore: Johns Hopkins University Press, 1993.
Rabinow, Paul. *Reflections on Fieldwork in Morocco*. Berkeley: University of California Press, 1977.
Rabinow, Paul. *French Modern: Norms and Forms of the Social Environment*. Chicago: University of Chicago Press, 1995 [1989].
Reed-Danahay, Deborah. "'Tristes Paysans': Bourdieu's Early Ethnography in Béarn and Kabylia," *Anthropological Quarterly* 77, 1 (2004): 87–106.
Reed-Danahay, Deborah. *Locating Bourdieu*. Bloomington: Indiana University Press, 2005.
Regnier, Philippe. "Du côté de chez Saint-Simon: Question raciale, question sociale et question religieuse," *Romantisme* 4, 130 (2005): 23–37.
Renda, Mary A. *Taking Haiti: Military Occupation and the Culture of US Imperialism, 1915–1940*. Chapel Hill: University of North Carolina Press, 2001.
Rey-Goldzeiguer, Annie. *Le royaume arabe: La politique algérienne de Napoléon III, 1861–1870*. Algiers: Société Nationale d'Edition et de Diffusion, 1977.
Rice, Alison. "Déchiffrer le silence: A Conversation with Germaine Tillion," *Research in African Literatures* 35, 1 (Spring 2004): 162–179.
Rivet, Daniel. *Lyautey et l'institution du protectorat français au Maroc*, 3 vol. Paris: L'Harmattan, 1988.
Robinson, David. "Un historien et anthropologue sénégalais: Sheikh Musa Kamara," *Cahiers d'études africaines* 28, Cahier 109 (1988): 89–116.
Robinson, David. "France as a Muslim Power in West Africa," *Africa Today* 46, 3/4 (Summer 1999): 105–127.
Robinson, David. *Paths of Accommodation: Muslim Societies and French Colonial Authorities in Senegal and Mauritania, 1880–1920*. Athens, OH: Ohio University Press, 2000.
Robinson, David and Jean-Louis Triaud, ed. *Le Temps des marabouts: itinéraires et stratégies islamiques en Afrique occidentale française, v. 1880–1960*. Paris: Karthala, 1997.
Rolland, Denis. "Jacques Soustelle, de l'ethnologie à la politique," *Revue d'histoire moderne et contemporaine* 43, 1 (January–March 1996): 137–150.
Roudinesco, Elisabeth. *Philosophy in Turbulent Times: Canguilhem, Sartre, Foucault, Althusser, Deleuze, Derrida*, trans. William McCuaig. New York: Columbia University Press, 2008 [2005].
Sacriste, Fabien. *Germaine Tillion, Jacques Berque, Jean Servier et Pierre Bourdieu: Des ethnologues dans la guerre d'indépendance algérienne*. Paris: L'Harmattan, 2011.
Saint-Martin, Yves-Jean. *Le Sénégal sous le Second Empire: Naissance d'un empire colonial (1850–1871)*. Paris: Karthala, 1989.

Salama, Mohammad. *Islam, Orientalism, and Intellectual History: Modernity and the Politics of Exclusion since Ibn Khaldun*. New York: I.B. Tauris, 2011.
Sanson, Henri. "C'était un esprit curieux," *Awal* 27/28 (2003): 279–286.
Scham, Alan. *Lyautey in Morocco: Protectorate Administration, 1912–1925*. Berkeley: University of California Press, 1970.
Schreier, Joshua. *Arabs of the Jewish Faith: The Civilizing Mission in Colonial Algeria*. New Brunswick, NJ: Rutgers University Press, 2010.
Schrift, Alan D. *Twentieth-Century French Philosophy: Key Themes and Thinkers*. Oxford: Blackwell, 2006.
Searing, James. *"God Alone Is King": Islam and Emancipation in Senegal, the Wolof Kingdoms of Kajour and Bawal, 1859–1914*. Portsmouth, NH: Heinemann, 2002.
Seck, Ibrahima. *La Stratégie culturelle de la France en Afrique: l'enseignement colonial, 1817–1960*. Paris: L'Harmattan, 1993.
Segalla, Spencer D. "Georges Hardy and Educational Ethnology in French Morocco, 1920–26," *French Colonial History* 4 (2003): 171–190.
Segalla, Spencer D. *The Moroccan Soul: French Education, Colonial Ethnology, and Muslim Resistance, 1912–1956*. Lincoln, NE: University of Nebraska Press, 2009.
Le Seuil, ed. "Pierre Bourdieu et l'anthropologie," *Actes de la Recherche en Sciences Sociales* 150 (2003): 4–8.
Shapin, Steven. *A Social History of Truth: Civility and Science in Seventeenth-Century England*. Chicago: The University of Chicago Press, 1994.
Shepard, Todd. *The Invention of Decolonization: The Algerian War and the Remaking of France*. Ithaca, NY: Cornell University Press, 2008.
Sherman, Daniel J. "'Peoples Ethnographic': Objects, Museums, and the Colonial Inheritance of French Ethnology," *French Historical Studies* 27, 3 (Summer 2004): 669–703.
Shryock, Andrew. *Nationalism and the Genealogical Imagination: Oral History and Textual Authority in Tribal Jordan*. Berkeley: University of California Press, 1997.
Sibeud, Emmanuelle. *Une science impériale pour l'Afrique? La construction des savoirs africanistes en France, 1878–1930*. Paris: Editions de l'Ecole des Hautes Etudes en Sciences Sociales, 2002.
Silverstein, Paul. "Of Rooting and Uprooting: Kabyle Habitus, Domesticity, and Structural Nostalgia," *Ethnography* 5, 4 (2004): 553–578.
Singer, Barnett and John Langdon. *Cultured Force: Makers and Defenders of the French Colonial Empire*. Madison: University of Wisconsin Press, 2004.
Sirinelli, Jean-François. "Le temps des intellectuels?" *French Cultural Studies* 7, 125 (1996): 125–129.
Spillmann, Georges. *Napoléon III et le royaume arabe d'Algérie*. Paris: Académie des Sciences d'Outre-Mer, 1975.
Staum, Martin. "Nature and Nurture in French Ethnography and Anthropology, 1859–1914," *Journal of the History of Ideas* 65, 3 (2004): 475–495.
Stewart, Charles C. "A New Source on the Book Market in Morocco in 1830 and Islamic Scholarship in West Africa," *Hespéris Tamuda* XI (1970): 209–246.
Stocking, George W., Jr. *Delimiting Anthropology: Occasional Essays and Reflections*. Madison: The University of Wisconsin Press, 2001.
Stoler, Ann Laura. *Race and the Education of Desire: Foucault's History of Sexuality and the Colonial Order of Things*. Durham, NC: Duke University Press, 1995.
Stoler, Ann Laura. *Carnal Knowledge and Imperial Power: Race and the Intimate in Colonial Rule*. Berkeley: University of California Press, 2002.

Stora, Benjamin. *Les trois exils: Les juifs d'Algérie*. Paris: Stock, 2006.
Sullivan, Antony Thrall. *Thomas-Robert Bugeaud: France and Algeria, 1784–1849—Politics, Power, and the Good Society*. Hamden, CT: Archon Books, 1983.
Swartz, David L. "In Memoriam: Pierre Bourdieu, 1930–2002," *Theory and Society* 31, 4 (August 2002): 547–553.
Swartz, David L. "Drawing Inspiration from Bourdieu's Sociology of Symbolic Power," *Theory and Society* 32 (2003): 519–528.
Tamari, Tal. "The Development of Caste Systems in West Africa," *Journal of African History* 32, 2 (1991): 221–250.
Thomas, Martin. *The French Empire between the Wars: Imperialism, Politics and Society*. Manchester: Manchester University Press, 2005.
Thomas, Martin. *Empires of Intelligence: Security Services and Colonial Disorder after 1914*. Berkeley: University of California Press, 2008.
Thornton, John. *Africa and Africans in the Making of the Atlantic World, 1400–1680*. Cambridge: University of Cambridge Press, 1992.
Tilley, Helen. *Africa as a Living Laboratory: Empire, Development, and the Problem of Scientific Knowledge, 1870–1950*. Chicago: University of Chicago Press, 2011.
Tilley, Helen and Robert J. Gordon, ed. *Ordering Africa: Anthropology, European Imperialism, and the Politics of Knowledge*. New York: Manchester University Press, 2007.
Todorov, Tzvetan, ed. *Le siècle de Germaine Tillion*. Paris: Seuil, 2007.
Tournoux, Raymond. *La Tragédie du Général*. Paris: Plon, 1967.
Trumbull, George. *An Empire of Facts: Colonial Power, Cultural Knowledge, and Islam in Algeria, 1870–1914*. New York: Cambridge University Press, 2009.
Tyre, Stephen. "From Algérie Française to France Musulmane: Jacques Soustelle and the Myths and Realities of 'Integration,' 1955–1962," *French History* 20, 3 (2006): 276–296.
Ullmann, Bernard. *Jacques Soustelle: le mal aimé*. Paris: Plon, 1995.
Valensi, Lucette. *Le Maghreb avant la prise d'Alger (1790–1830)*. Paris: Flammarion, 1969.
Valette, Jacques. "Guerre Mondiale et Decolonisation: Le cas du Maroc en 1945," *Revue française d'histoire d'outre-mer* 70, 260–261 (1983): 133–150.
Van Gennep, Ketty. *Bibliographie des Oeuvres d'Arnold van Gennep*. Paris: A & J Picard, 1964.
Van Hoven, Ed. "Representing Social Hierarchy. Administrators-Ethnographers in the French Soudan: Delafosse, Monteil, and Labouret," *Cahiers d'études africaines* 30, 118 (1990): 179–198.
Vansina, Jan. *Living with Africa*. Madison: University of Wisconsin Press, 1994.
Vatin, Jean Claude, ed. *Connaissances du Maghreb*. Paris: Editions du centre national de la recherche scientifique, 1984.
Venier, Pascal. *Lyautey avant Lyautey*. Paris: L'Harmattan, 1997.
Vogt, W. Paul. "Un durkheimien ambivalent: Célestin Bouglé, 1870–1940," *Revue française de sociologie* XX, 1 (1979): 123–139.
Wacquant, Loic. "Following Bourdieu into the Field," *Ethnography* 5, 4 (2004): 387–414.
Webb, James L.A., Jr. *Desert Frontier: Ecological and Economic Change along the Western Sahel, 1600–1850*. Madison: University of Wisconsin Press, 1995.
Weisz, George. "Education and the Civil Utility of Social Science," *Minerva* 16, 3 (1978): 452–460.
Weisz, George. *The Emergence of Modern Universities in France, 1863–1914*. Princeton: Princeton University Press, 1983.
White, Melanie. "The Liberal Character of Ethnological Governance," *Economy and Society* 34, 3 (2005): 474–494

White, Owen. "The Decivilizing Mission: Auguste Dupuis-Yakouba and French Timbuktu," *French Historical Studies* 27, 3 (2004): 541–568.
White, Richard. *The Middle Ground: Indians, Empires, and Republics in the GreatLakes Region, 1650–1815*. Cambridge: Cambridge University Press, 1991.
Wilcken, Patrick. *Claude Lévi-Strauss: The Poet in the Laboratory*. New York: Penguin Press, 2010.
Wilder, Gary. "Colonial Ethnology and Political Rationality in French West Africa," *History and Anthropology* 14, 3 (2002): 219–252.
Wilder, Gary. *The French Imperial Nation-State: Negritude and Colonial Humanism between the Two World Wars*. Chicago: University of Chicago Press, 2005.
Williams, Elizabeth A. "Anthropological Institutions in Nineteenth Century France," *Isis* 76, 3 (1985): 331–348.
Wilson, K. "The Making and Putative Implementation of a British Foreign Policy of Gesture, December 1905 to August 1914: The Anglo-French Entente Revisited," *Canadian Journal of History* 31, 2 (1996): 227–255.
Wooten, Stephen R. "Colonial Administration and the Ethnography of the Family in French Soudan," *Cahiers d'études africaines* 33, 131 (1993): 419–446.
Wylie, Neville, ed. *The Politics and Strategy of Clandestine War: Special Operations Executive, 1940–1946*. New York: Routledge, 2007.
Wyrtzen, Jonathan. *Making Morocco: Colonial Intervention and the Politics of Identity*. Ithaca, NY: Cornell University Press, 2015.
Yacine, Tassadit., ed. *Amour, phantasmes et société en Afrique du Nord*. Paris: L'Harmattan, 2002.
Yacine, Tassadit. "Pierre Bourdieu in Algeria at War: Notes on the Birth of an Engaged Ethnosociology," *Ethnography* 5, 4 (2004): 487–509.
Yacine, Tassadit. "Rapports de genres et littératures postcoloniales chez Mouloud Feraoun et Mouloud Mammeri," *Awal: Cahiers d'études berbères* 38 (2008): 15–16.
Yacono, Xavier. *Les Bureaux arabes et l'évolution des genres de vie indigènes dans l'ouest du Tell algérois (Dahra, Chélif, Oursenis, Sersou)*. Paris: Larose, 1953.
Zumwalt, Rosemary. "Arnold Van Gennep: The Hermit of Bourg-la-Reine," *American Anthropologist* 84 (1982): 299–313.
Zumwalt, Rosemary. *The Enigma of Arnold Van Gennep (1873–1957): Master of French Folklore and Hermit of Bourg-la-Reine*. Helsinki: Suomalainen Tiedeakatemia, 1988.

Index

Abbas, Ferhat 98, 106, 109, 118–19
Afrique Equatoriale Française (AEF)105
Afrique Occidentale Française (AOF)41–2, 47–8, 51–6, 66, 69–73, 105
Algeria 2, 26, 40–2, 54, 73, 84, 103
    Bourdieu in 95–6, 123–5, 129–37, 139–40, 142, 145–6
    as central to study 6–8, 62, 97, 148
    Delafosse in 50
    Faidherbe in 9–20, 22–4, 88
    Lyautey in 27, 31–3, 35–9, 85
    peasantry 98
Année Sociologique 79, 81–5, 94, 128
anthropology 108, 134. *See also* ethnology
    functional 74, 93, 143
    physical 6, 9–10, 18, 22–3, 136
    structural 127–8, 132, 136–45
Arab groups 12, 53
    invasions 20, 38, 55–64
    kinship 20, 53, 55, 58–61, 108, 121
    nationalism 7, 100, 119, 121
    pan-Arabism 7, 115, 117, 120
Arabic language 2, 11, 13–14, 18, 25–7, 31, 41–3, 45, 50, 54–57, 68, 110, 113–16, 118, 130, 134, 148
Arabic philosophy 15, 52, 54–63, 110, 148
archaeology 24, 31, 56, 88
assimilation policy 1, 3, 91, 94, 99, 104
    Marty and Delafosse on 48–9, 51–2, 71–2
association policy 1–4, 6, 11, 79, 94
    academic journals and 72–3
    civilizational theory 102–3
    Faidherbe and 9, 12, 16–19, 22, 24
    failure 112–13, 123, 132, 139
    integration 96, 99–101, 104, 111
    Lyautey and 27–9, 33, 35, 37–46
    Marty and Delafosse on 47–8, 60, 63–4, 66, 71–3

Bâ, Amadou Hampaté 73, 148
Balandier, Georges 80, 98–9, 124, 131
Berber Vulgate 13, 21–2, 24, 31, 37, 40, 43, 62–4, 108, 113, 131–2, 145
Bourdieu, Pierre 2, 123–47
    anticolonialism 123, 130, 132, 134–5, 145, 147–8
    Lévi-Strauss and 127–8, 136–44
    margins 124–6, 130, 139–40, 146
    Mauss influence 81–2, 95–6, 121, 126–8, 141, 145
    phenomenology 126–8
    reflexivity 124, 131, 133, 136–8
    reproduction 132–3, 139, 142–4
    social capital 139, 142
    Sociologie de l'Algérie 131–3, 135
    sources 7, 118, 123–5, 129–31, 133–4, 139–40
Brazzaville conference 105–6
Broca, Paul 22–4, 136
Bugeaud, General Thomas-Robert 11–13, 30, 98, 114
Buh, Saad 52–3, 59–60, 65, 147
Bureaux Arabes. See also SAS
    Faidherbe and 10, 16, 26
    Lyautey and 31, 43
    Soustelle and 98, 114–15

Centres sociaux 107, 189 n.89, 116
class 31, 37, 49–58, 60, 62–4, 69, 107, 110, 125, 130–1, 139, 142, 145
    caste 15, 20
    intellectuals 21, 30, 33, 35, 40, 43–5, 49–52, 55, 58, 68, 113, 116, 133–4
Clozel, François-Joseph 70–1
Collège de France 71, 87, 101–2, 128
comité de l'Afrique française 32
Comte, Auguste 3, 11, 79, 84, 90, 94, 126
Conseil national de recherche scientifique (CNRS)87, 110, 145
Côte d'Ivoire 41, 47, 50, 61, 65, 67, 70, 74

Delafosse, Maurice 3, 6–7, 20–6, 45, 47–77, 105, 140
  archaeology and 56–7
  development policy 48, 61, 67–8, 71–2, 77, 100, 148
  elites 50–2, 57–9
  Houdas and 50, 55–6, 70
  on Islam 42, 48, 64–5, 67–9, 111, 113
  Mauss and 75, 77, 79–80, 82, 85–91, 93–5
  race 61–4, 72, 130
development theory and policy 3–4, 14–15, 20, 23, 28, 30–1, 35, 38, 44, 47–9, 52, 57, 61, 62–3, 65–8, 72, 75–7, 90–2, 94, 99–107, 111, 114–17, 120–1, 123–4, 131, 134–5, 141, 144–5
Diagne, Blaise 48–9
Diao, Yaro 19–20
divide and rule 6, 22, 29, 53, 65
Doutté, Edmond 85, 89
Dreyfus affair 25, 29, 34, 81, 83
Drif, Zohra 111–12
Durkheim, Emile 2, 7, 74, 77, 79, 81–2, 90, 92–5, 101, 126–8

école coloniale 72, 87, 94, 102
école des otages 18–19, 25
école normale supérieure 82, 84, 101, 125–6
école pratique des hautes études 82–4, 87, 94, 101, 120, 128
education policy
  Algeria 18, 43, 107, 109, 114, 116, 118
  Islam 18, 21, 37–8, 51, 53, 64–6, 68–9, 113
  literacy 82, 97–8, 107, 114, 116, 134
  Morocco 39, 42–5
  Senegal 18–19
  women 108, 116–17
Elites
  anti-colonial 7, 45, 112, 118–19
  as ethnological contacts 18, 34, 37, 43–4, 48, 57, 86–7, 100–1, 148
  intellectuals 25, 31, 49, 51, 58, 65, 70, 73, 128, 130–1, 133, 149
  as political rulers 18–19, 21, 40, 49, 51–2, 59–60, 63, 69, 114, 116–17

  traditions of scholarship 49–50, 55–6
ethnography 10, 23, 42, 44, 63, 70, 74–5, 80–4, 86, 88–9, 101, 108, 130–1, 137
ethnology 2–5, 23–4, 76–7, 92–4, 101–4, 134, 137–9
  effect of environment 82, 86–7, 136–7, 140
  oral sources 20, 42, 44–5, 79, 88–9, 91, 95, 133–4
  as political structure 9–10, 28–30, 33, 40–1, 46, 49, 70–2, 79–80, 85, 97–8, 100, 105–19, 129–30, 132–3, 141, 145, 148
  textual sources 47–8, 51–2, 56–8, 73, 88–9, 147

Faidherbe, General Louis-Léon-César 2, 9–27, 41, 53, 84
  in Algeria 12–16, 98, 112
  influence on Gallieni 6, 19, 25–6, 28–9, 33
  in Senegal 11, 16–22
  ties to Parisian anthropology 9–10, 22–5, 88
Feraoun, Mouloud 112, 116–17
fieldwork 7, 85–90, 101, 109, 118, 120, 125–30
First World War 126
  AOF and 47–9, 76–7
  Mauss and 73, 85–6
  Morocco and 40, 45–6
Franco-Prussian War 25, 30, 32–3, 81
French language 11, 16–19, 34, 41–5, 49–51, 53–4, 63, 73, 83, 113–17, 148
Front de libération nationale 105, 109–12, 130, 133
  political platform 99–100, 106, 114–15, 117–19
  response to SAS 117–19
  violence 97–8, 107, 115, 119
Funding
  educational 18
  ethnographic 7, 24, 26, 34, 87–8, 107, 110, 115, 118, 129
  Mauss and 82–4, 87–8
  university system and 82, 85

Gallieni, General Joseph Simon 48
    Faidherbe and 6, 19, 25–6, 28–9, 33
    Lyautey and 6, 26, 28–9, 33–5, 37
    Politique des races 35, 48, 65
    West African career 25–6, 29, 53
de Gaulle, General Charles 46, 103–6, 120
genealogy 58–64, 120–1
    as ethnological source 15, 20, 48, 51–5, 58–9, 63, 89, 108–9, 116–17, 148
    importance for Islamic elites 51, 55, 59–60, 64, 148
Griaule, Marcel 88–9, 94–5
griots 51

habitus 7, 95, 123 n.4, 124, 129, 133, 139–44
Hamet, Ismael 26, 45, 49–50, 54–8, 68–70
Hardy, Georges 72
    AOF and 42, 73
    education policy 43–4
    Morocco and 42–4
Houdas, Octave 49–50, 55–6, 69–70
humanism 4, 46, 75, 95, 126–9, 137, 153–5
    colonial policy and 12, 14–15, 19, 54, 61–2, 64, 92–3, 102–3, 109, 111, 120
    reform and 13, 48, 52, 76, 99, 123, 138–9, 158–9

Ibn Khaldun 3, 27, 44, 109
    civilizational model 15, 20, 38, 62
    class and 15, 61
    environment and 20, 61–2
    influence on Delafosse/Marty 49, 58–9, 61–3
    influence on Faidherbe 15–16, 20
    kinship and 15, 20, 58–9, 63
    state construction 38, 62, 77, 110
Indochina 6, 9, 28–9, 32–5, 37, 88, 99
Institut d'ethnologie
    Delafosse and 74, 85, 88
    fieldwork 80, 87–90, 91, 97, 101–3
    founding 74, 84–5
    Lévy-Bruhl and 74
    Mauss and 80, 85, 88–9, 97, 101
International Institute of African Languages and Cultures 72, 88, 94, 110

Islam
    animism and 21, 59, 64, 67, 93
    as Arab phenomenon 7, 21, 38, 56–7, 59, 62–3, 67, 76, 132
    education and 18, 42, 51, 53, 55, 66, 68–9, 113
    feudalism and 38, 64
    genealogy and 20, 52, 54–5, 57, 59–60, 120
    as illness 21, 67
    kinship and 20, 60–1
    as modernizing force 20, 22, 37, 39, 44, 65–6, 68, 85–6, 94, 110–11, 142
    nationalism and 7, 73, 98, 100, 103, 115, 117, 120
    Sufism 16, 51, 66–7

Juillet, Jacques 108–9, 118–19

Kabylia 33, 112, 120–1, 147
    importance for Bourdieu 124, 131–4, 137–40
    importance for Faidherbe 13, 25
Kamara, Shaykh Musa 51
kinship
    Delafosse and 58–62, 75–6
    Ibn Khaldun and 59, 62
    Islam and 59–61, 64
    Marty and 59–61
    political value 7, 49, 60–1, 89, 108–9
    refashioning 55, 63
    slavery and 59–60
    totemic concepts and 76, 93
al-Kunti, Shaykh Bay 52

Lévi-Strauss, Claude 2, 80, 89–90, 136, 145
    binaries 95, 138, 140, 142–4
    bricoleur 95, 143
    myth 95, 127, 143
    structuralism 7, 91–2, 121, 124, 126, 128–9, 140–3
    Tristes Tropiques 137–8
Lévy-Bruhl, Lucien 74, 83, 85–7, 101, 127, 136
linguistics 2, 10, 14, 21, 34–5, 48, 50, 59, 63, 75, 81–2, 91, 99, 113–14, 136
Lugard, Lord Frederick 72, 88
Lyautey, Hubert 27–46
    Gallieni and 6, 26, 28–9, 33–5, 37

Indochina and 33
influence on Soustelle 7, 98, 105, 107, 112, 114–16
intellectual classes and 30, 32–4, 40, 43–5
Madagascar and 34–5
Marty and 7, 42, 49–50, 65
Morocco 11, 26, 28–9, 36–46
progressive method 28–9, 35–6
publishing 35, 43–5

madrasa 68–9, 113
Mammeri, Mouloud 131, 134–5, 147
Marty, Paul 47–77
    Hardy and 42, 44
    "historical reconstruction" 45, 58
    intellectual elites 49–53, 58, 60, 65–6, 68–9, 111
    Lyautey and 7, 42, 49–50, 65
    textual Emphasis 50, 52, 54–6, 58–9, 70, 116
    translation 6, 47–8, 50, 59, 148
Mauritania 26, 41, 53–5, 59, 65–6, 76
Mauss, Marcel 79–96
    field investigation 77, 79–80, 82, 85–90, 94, 145
    gift giving 80, 92, 140
    Griaule and 88–9, 94
    history 82–3, 90–2
    individual vs group 79, 81, 92, 124
    Lévi-Strauss and 80, 89, 92, 95, 127–9, 141
    relativism 79, 90, 94, 105
    Soustelle and 7, 85, 87, 96–7, 100–1, 105, 112, 121
    state support 74, 83–5, 87–8
    Tillion and 89
    total social fact 80, 90–4
modernity 3, 76, 92, 141
    modernist reform 18, 27–8, 37, 43–4, 48, 69, 98, 100–2, 105–13, 117, 123–5, 128–33, 135–6, 138
Monteil, Vincent 105, 108–10, 118–19
Morocco 6–8, 19, 24, 50, 62, 67, 85–7, 103, 111
    Hardy in 42–4
    Lyautey in 11, 26, 28–9, 36–46
de Mun, Captain Count Albert 30–1

Musée de l'homme (Trocadero) 101–3, 106, 110, 120
Muséum national d'histoire naturelle 64, 87

networks 2–7, 9–11, 17–19, 22–4, 29, 46–7, 50, 66, 70, 73, 80, 83, 86–7, 97, 107, 111–12, 117–18
    dialogue 10, 17, 19, 26, 33–4, 44, 48–9, 58, 94, 100–1, 103–4, 131
    rhizome 5–6, 49, 70, 77, 80, 97, 100, 149

Peul (Fulbé)
    Delafosse and 57–8, 75
    Faidherbe and 11, 21
    Musa Kamara and 51
    origin stories 21, 58, 67
Pieds noir 8, 11, 135
    academic influence 130
    Bourdieu and 130, 136
    Soustelle and 105–6, 112–13, 117, 120
Ponty, William 48
primitivity 14, 20, 25, 27, 51, 67–8, 74–7, 83, 90–3, 101–2, 127, 136, 143–4

race 2–3, 7
    as caste 63
    as civilization 23, 26, 55, 62, 64, 75, 83, 89–90, 101–2
    as language 58, 76, 113
    politique des races 35, 48, 65
Radcliffe-Brown, Arthur 74, 88–9, 93, 143
Rivet, Paul 85–9, 101, 106–7

Sahara 14, 19–21, 31, 46, 53–70, 94, 148
Sahel 20–1, 26, 44, 51–73
Saint-Simon, Henri 3, 11, 30
Sartre, Jean-Paul 125–8, 131, 138
Sayed, Abdelmalek 131, 135
Schoen, Colonel Paul 105, 111–15
Second World War 73, 94, 100, 103–4, 110, 126–8, 134
    Free France 100–1, 103, 105–6
Sections administratives spécialisées (SAS) 114–18
Senegal 6, 9, 13–14, 16–22, 25–6, 28, 33–4, 39, 41–2, 53, 55–7, 65–7, 75, 77, 98, 123
    Four Communes 42, 48–9
Senghor, Léopold Sédar 77, 95, 97

Sidibé, Diokounda 17
Sidibé, Mamby 73
slavery 37, 59–60, 102
social engineering 85, 100, 108, 116–17
social evolution 3, 22–3, 35, 42–3, 47–8,
    60–6, 68–9, 75–6, 83, 90–4, 99–101,
    112, 127–9, 140–4
socialism 12–13, 83, 106–7
social structure. *See* anthropology; social
    evolution
Société d'anthropologie de Paris 10, 22, 24
sociology
    Bourdieu and 7, 123–39, 144–6
    Delafosse/Marty and 49
    Durkheim and 79, 81–2, 84, 90, 93, 126
    ethnography 42, 87–9, 91, 130–3, 140
    Mauss and 79–86, 90–4, 126–7
Songhay 55–7, 63
Soudan (Mali) 6, 29, 33–4, 51–8, 63, 68–9, 91
Soustelle, Georgette 101, 108–9
Soustelle, Jacques 97–121
    as governor-general 2, 7, 97–101, 103,
        105–21
    Lyautey influence 7, 98, 105, 107, 112,
        114–16
    Mauss and 7, 85, 87, 96–7, 100–1, 105,
        112, 121
    Plan Soustelle 113–16
    right-wing settlers 106–7, 112–13, 117,
        120
    Tillion and 107–11, 116–18
synchronic analysis 42, 90–2, 103, 130–2,
    140–1, 143–4, 148

Tarikh el-Fattach 56–7
Tarikh es-Soudan 54–7
Tillion, Germaine 103, 134
    in Algeria 89, 97, 107, 109–11, 117–18,
        129–30
    Mauss and 89
    Soustelle and 107–11, 116–18
totemism 76, 93
translation 13, 15–16, 26
    Delafosse and 50, 53, 55, 69, 72–3, 75
    effect on colonial policy 1–4, 7–8, 19,
        35, 48, 54–6, 77, 87, 147
    Hamet and 54
    history and 6, 54, 148
    Marty and 6, 47–8, 50, 59, 148
tribe 13, 15, 24, 36–7, 55, 59–61, 76, 82,
    91–3
truth 6, 10, 24, 58–63, 81–2, 90, 101–2,
    121, 124–7, 131, 133–4, 139–40,
    144, 147–8
Tuareg 21, 51–3, 73

Vaillant, Jean 13, 17
van Gennep, Arnold 20, 72, 74, 82–4, 93
de Vogüé, Viscount Eugène Melchior 32

women
    education 108, 116
    as ethnographic sources 26, 89, 97–8,
        108–9, 111–12, 115
    marker of civilization 27, 97–8, 111
    patriarchal analysis 14–15, 109, 132
    Soustelle and 97–8, 105, 108–9

www.ingramcontent.com/pod-product-compliance
Lightning Source LLC
Chambersburg PA
CBHW072147290426
44111CB00012B/2001